T0244130

THE WHY IS EVERYTHING

THE WHY IS EVERYTHING

A Story of Football, Rivalry, and Revolution

MICHAEL SILVER

W. W. NORTON & COMPANY

Independent Publishers Since 1923

Frontispiece: Kyle Shanahan and Sean McVay exchange a postgame handshake at SoFi Stadium in September 2023 following the 49ers' ninth consecutive regular season victory over the Rams.

"Deal," words by Robert Hunter, music by Jerry Garcia. © 1971 (renewed) Ice Nine Publishing Co., Inc. All rights reserved. Used by permission of Alfred Music.

For information about permission to reproduce selections from this book, write to Permissions, W. W. Norton & Company, Inc., 500 Fifth Avenue, New York, NY 10110

For information about special discounts for bulk purchases, please contact W. W. Norton Special Sales at specialsales@wwnorton.com or 800-233-4830

Manufacturing by Lakeside Book Company
Book design by Daniel Lagin
Production manager: Julia Druskin

ISBN 978-1-324-09360-2

W. W. Norton & Company, Inc., 500 Fifth Avenue, New York, N.Y. 10110
www.wwnorton.com

W. W. Norton & Company Ltd., 15 Carlisle Street, London W1D 3BS

1 0 9 8 7 6 5 4 3 2 1

Since it costs a lot to win
And even more to lose
You and me bound to spend some time
Wondering what to choose

—ROBERT HUNTER

For Greg and Robbie, who deconstruct the game and infuse it with hilarity and clarity.

And for Leslie and Natalie, who help me navigate the hubris and hysteria.

Contents

THE WHY IS EVERYTHING

Introduction

Three Mantras

I.

Players over plays.

It was a mantra, conceived amid conflict—an oft-uttered reminder from quarterback to coach that, at the highest level of football, his precious Xs and Os were beholden to the athletes charged with executing them.

When Kyle Shanahan arrived as the Atlanta Falcons' newly hired offensive coordinator in January of 2015, he had a reputation for clashing with talented players who dared deviate from his intricately crafted blueprints. He immediately encountered a formidable adversary. Matt Ryan, the Falcons' franchise quarterback since they'd made him the third-overall pick of the 2008 draft, had his way of doing things, and it didn't always conform to Shanahan's. Each also had a temper.

Just do what I coach you to do, and it will work, Shanahan implored the quarterback known as Matty Ice for his composure in critical moments. *There's a reason behind everything we do, but you have to do it the way we coach it for it to work.*

Ryan pushed back—it was one thing to draw up play cards and dissect defensive alignments and stay up until the wee hours workshopping new ways of manipulating 11 men around a 100-by-53⅓-yard patch of turf, or whatever it was Shanahan and his cadre of young, driven, and idiosyncratic assistants did. Actually executing those plays, with violence barreling in from every direction, was an entirely different endeavor. Amid the chaos of a play, those theoretical tenets only went so far.

Think players over plays, Ryan used to blurt out boldly, both as a dig at Shanahan's system and a reminder that this player couldn't be so easily controlled.

Now, two years into his Falcons tenure, Shanahan was a few minutes away from putting the finishing touches on his greatest professional achievement, and a day away from realizing his dream of becoming a National Football League head coach. It was February 5, 2017, in a loud and tension-filled stadium, with hundreds of millions of viewers waiting to see if the Falcons would shock the world and win their first-ever Super Bowl or complete the most embarrassing choke job in the history of the sport. And all Shanahan could hear was that annoying phrase in his head: *players over plays*.

At this particular moment, he wasn't mad at Matty Ice. How could he be? A few months after their first, challenging season together, Shanahan and Ryan had been sent to what many in the NFL community referred to as "marriage counseling." In truth, the two men had a clear-the-air session, over beers, at the Southern California home of Tom House, a former major league pitcher turned esteemed throwing coach. By night's end, Shanahan and Ryan understood one another better than they had before, realizing they each had perfectionistic tendencies and a penchant for locking into the task at hand and blocking out any dissent. They talked about what worked for each of them in the most charged moments, as well as in more mundane settings, and got a better sense of how they could collaborate and both feel heard. Each man showed up for training camp in a positive mood, and then the games began—and, *holy shit!*, something clicked. Shanahan constructed opponent-specific game plans that had defenders' heads spinning, and Ryan unleashed hell.

Already, they'd been rewarded. In mid-January, Shanahan struck a verbal deal to become the next coach of the San Francisco 49ers, the franchise for which he'd once served as a training camp ball boy, when his dad was the team's cutting-edge offensive coordinator. The night before Super Bowl LI, at the NFL Honors awards show in Houston, Ryan had been named the league's Most Valuable Player. Then, on Super Bowl Sunday, it got even better. Shanahan unveiled a new-age game plan that stretched the field, showcased the Falcons' superior speed, and completely baffled Bill Belichick, the greatest defensive strategist the game had ever known. Wide receivers blocked edge rushers, offensive tackles swept outside like wideouts, and the favored New England Patriots looked utterly lost. By the middle of the third quarter, the score was Falcons 28, Patriots 3, and Belichick was reduced to taking high-risk fourth-down gambles in his own territory and trying to adjust his defensive scheme on the fly.

It was over—except, it wasn't. Tom Brady, given an opening, kept prodding his teammates to do something audacious, and the Falcons' defenders got tired, and doubt began to creep in. Shanahan, in a coaching box high up in the stadium, stayed aggressive, dialing up a pass play intended to kill the comeback, once and for all. With the Falcons up 28–12 with 8:31 to go and facing a third and one from their own 36, Ryan had wide receiver Aldrick Robinson open for what would have been an easy touchdown. It was a great call, but the execution was horrible. Halfback Devonta Freeman blew his blocking assignment, and Patriots linebacker Dont'a Hightower charged in, clobbered Ryan, and dislodged the ball.

Soon enough, it was 28–20 with 4:38 to go. Ryan had just delivered a deep pass to the right sideline that Julio Jones, the league's best wide receiver, had somehow managed to catch inbounds while leaping over cornerback Eric Rowe. After Freeman was stuffed for a one-yard loss, it was second and 11 from the New England 23—easily in range for a game-clinching field goal. Conventional wisdom called for Shanahan to be conservative; his defensive-minded head coach, Dan Quinn, was passive, letting his coordinator decide. As Shanahan prepared to send in the next call, he couldn't shake that voice: *Think players over plays.*

It was a defining moment for the 37-year-old son of an NFL coaching great trying to reconcile his most basic belief—that the answers to football's greatest mysteries could all be uncovered and mastered via film study and schematic innovation and abstract thought—with his immediate circumstances. Shanahan could conceive of Xs and Os with rare skill. He'd taken the highly successful system popularized by his father, Mike, who had put a critical twist on Bill Walsh's renowned West Coast offense while coaching the Denver Broncos to back-to-back Super Bowl triumphs in the 1990s, and advanced it in a manner that had changed the game. Kyle and his Brat Pack of disciples—Falcons assistants Matt LaFleur, Mike McDaniel, and Raheem Morris, and wunderkind Sean McVay, a former Shanahan protégé from their days in Washington, whom the Los Angeles Rams had just made the youngest head coach in modern NFL history—could solve any strategic puzzle with energy drinks, creativity, and chutzpah. And yet . . .

Maybe, Shanahan thought, Ryan was right. Was it so crazy to trust the highly skilled laborers in front of him to use their superhuman talent and do what scrappy but athletically average players like him could only have dreamed of doing? In the biggest game he'd ever called, with the whole world watching, with his and so many others' legacies on the line, who was he to doubt the pinpoint passer who'd been bringing his Xs and Os to life?

Fuck it, Shanahan thought. *I'm going to Julio.*

He expected Belichick to play Tampa 2, a coverage Shanahan had learned inside and out as a young quality control coach on Jon Gruden's Buccaneers staff. He chose a high-risk, high-reward play designed to beat that coverage, a play that called for Ryan to take a seven-step drop. Jones, Shanahan believed, would be open on an out route. And if he wasn't? Ryan could surely get it to Freeman, the second read, who'd be running a flat out of the backfield.

Shanahan gave Ryan the call over the headset. It was a high-stress moment, but the coach was at peace. If going to Julio Jones with the season on the line turned out to be the wrong move, he could live with that.

Ryan took the snap and dropped back, surveying a coverage that was a bit different than what he and Shanahan had expected. Before he could adjust, the Patriots' Trey Flowers, who had blasted past Pro Bowl center Alex Mack and his broken left leg, engulfed Ryan and sacked him for a 12-yard loss. On the next play, Shanahan called a quick pass to receiver Mohamed Sanu, who sprinted ahead and got the Falcons back into sure-fire field goal range—but left tackle Jake Matthews was called for holding. Disaster. The Falcons punted the ball back to Brady, who engineered a dramatic touchdown drive and threw a two-point conversion to tie the game. Then the Patriots won the overtime coin toss, and Brady ended things with another touchdown drive, and the Falcons were forevermore the poster children for blowing a game that couldn't possibly be blown, and Quinn essentially threw up his hands and told the world, *It wasn't me*, and Kyle Shanahan was now the reckless idiot who should have run the ball and let his kicker win the game.

——

FOUR DAYS LATER, THE 49ERS FORMALLY INTRODUCED SHANAHAN AT A press conference at Levi's Stadium. Half the questions concerned the Super Bowl meltdown. Shanahan did his best to give honest answers, acknowledging the disappointment while insisting he'd gotten this far by being aggressive and had no intention of backing off. *Why didn't you just run the ball?* There were nuanced replies to be given that could have explained the thought process and the context, but at that point, as he stood there with his wife, Mandy, and their three young children, Shanahan figured, *Why bother?*

The man was used to having his process misunderstood, his accomplishments diminished. The words *nepotism* and *entitled* had followed Mike Shanahan's only son from the start, thrown around by fans, media members, players, and even other coaches after the Houston Texans made him the league's youngest offensive coordinator in 2008. The whispers grew louder when Mike Shanahan was hired by the Washington Redskins in 2010, picked his son as the offensive coordinator, and involved Kyle in a hiring process that resulted in a cabinet of similarly young and unproven position coaches.

They took heat right away. Kyle clashed with star quarterback Donovan McNabb, whose casual grasp of his system and poor attention to detail enraged the coach, and got crushed in the media when things fell apart. After two miserable seasons, Washington finally broke through in 2012, winning the NFC East thanks largely to rookie quarterback Robert Griffin III, for whom Kyle had created an entirely revamped scheme that mystified the rest of the league. The next season, however, the RG3 experiment imploded. Griffin's insecurity and insistence on being a dropback passer without mastering the intricacies of the position led to a breakdown in trust between him and his offensive coordinator. Organizational toxicity reigned, and by mid-December of 2013, it was clear that Mike Shanahan was a dead coach walking. His son, as usual, absorbed a hearty share of the public blame—and this time, his protégés took a beating as well. In an infamous article published by Jason La Canfora, Kyle Shanahan was decried by anonymous members of the organization as a product of privilege, a coach "empowered and enabled by his father . . . given a wide swath of power, and rubbing many people—players, fellow coaches and members of football operations—the wrong way." It went on: "The composition of this staff has fallen under criticism, as has the work of the Shanahans in particular, with the lack of experience and pedigree on the offensive side of the ball seen as a particular problem both within the organization and outside it."

The article included the following anonymous quote from one of Shanahan's coworkers: "This is the NFL. It's not supposed to be a training ground for coaches . . . Kyle's not that confident, so they set him up with a bunch of yes men rather than have some experienced coaches to push him. It's like Kyle is the pied piper and these kids just follow him around . . . How does that happen? How does [Mike Shanahan] end up hiring all of his son's buddies?"

Matt LaFleur, Mike McDaniel, and Sean McVay were specifically named as underqualified members of the staff; after reading the article, McDaniel thought, *Let's file this one away and revisit it in ten years.*

———

IT DIDN'T TAKE A FULL DECADE FOR A VERDICT TO BE RENDERED. BY 2022, "the pied piper and these kids" were head coaches at the forefront of a revolution in the sport. Looking back, it's clear that they weren't merely savants, although each one was and is, in his own way. At the same time, they were hyperdriven truth seekers striving desperately to find a novel path to dominating their opponents, their craft—and, ultimately, one another.

Those long days and nights in Ashburn, Virginia, were the start of a radical and disruptive process. Shanahan, LaFleur, McDaniel, McVay, Morris, and a few others cranked up the coffee pot on the second floor of the team facility before the sun rose and often closed down the bars at Reston Town Center. The offensive position coaches and lower-level assistants devoured game film and weren't shy about incorporating the latest concepts they came across—in the NFL or otherwise. Anything they could borrow, tweak, or conjure was fair game. They were coaches, and thus more inclined to think in such terms, but back then their ethos might well have been *plays over players.*

Not everyone knew what to make of them. Tight end Chris Cooley nicknamed them "The Fun Bunch," and it stuck. They were friends and fellow grinders, with each assistant striving to make his mark—and rushing to be the first to pitch Kyle Shanahan on an idea. Some, he would include. Others, he would fine-tune and improve upon. And some he would callously reject. Yet, in each case, there was one overriding theme: everything should be questioned. Nothing was off the table. None of the old rules applied.

II.

It just works.

Try dealing with *that* coaching point, Matt Ryan. This mantra, or some variation of it, has been pounded into the heads of football players for generations, even those at the highest level of the sport. Those three words provide comfort to coaches intent on evading theoretical discussions about their battle plans. It's the officer commanding the enlisted man to follow orders and trust the mission; it's the bandleader insisting upon the double-bass solo in the middle of a ballad because "that's how Jimmy Blanton did it for Duke Ellington."

Football has always been a militaristic sport, from the violence on the field to the pageantry surrounding it. So "it just works" might seem fitting. Yet, in recent years, players being told to study, memorize, and bring to life the Xs and Os of their taskmasters have increasingly wanted to know *why*. Some of the brightest and most engaging people in the profession have been able to offer vivid and clarifying explanations of their game plans, specific play calls, and overall schematic philosophies.

Yet the "it just works" crowd remains powerful and undaunted.

Sometimes, a coach who utters these words simply doesn't want to be bothered, or possibly is put off by the mere notion of players who think for themselves. Often, however, there's a more troubling dynamic in play. While uttered with conviction, the mantra may serve to mask the reality that, in his heart of hearts, the coach himself doesn't actually know why the play in question works, other than the fact that it has worked in the past and is part of an established tradition.

Systems are passed down. And some are more prevalent than others. The playbook containing Bill Walsh's seminal West Coast offense is akin to the Bible—an analogy I heard often while talking with many of the sport's premier players, coaches, and talent evaluators. But, especially today, in the "player empowerment" era, an order like "Trust us, this is a good play that has always been a good play" breeds skepticism, even if those asking for total devotion don't realize it.

———

COOLEY, A TWO-TIME PRO BOWL TIGHT END WHO SPENT NINE YEARS WITH the Redskins before retiring in 2013, used the phrase "faith-based bull-shit." Five years into his career, he'd grown weary of being spoon-fed instructions he either couldn't see the value in or had concluded were full of flaws. Then, in 2010, Mike Shanahan and his disciples arrived. In the presence of so many young, intellectually curious, and defiant strategists who resoundingly rejected the paradigm, including Cooley's offensive coordinator (Kyle Shanahan) and position coach (McVay), he could ask *why* and actually get illuminating answers in response. Often, he didn't even have to ask, which was eye-opening in and of itself.

One former Mike Shanahan pupil now running a major college program, University of Washington coach Jedd Fisch, described the transformation. In the past, he said, "offense was two things—you either threw the ball or ran the ball. There was no true correlation or difficult-to-defend type of scheme. You either dropped back or you handed it off." Two different play sheets, with no connection to one another. Said Fisch, who also worked under McVay in L.A., "The old school of 'run the play, execute the play, block them better than they can rush, run the route better than they can defend it, and throw the ball better than they can cover' is not what they're saying in that Shanahan world." For his part, as he began to assimilate the Shanahan scheme, Cooley latched on to "something that, for the first time in my career, made sense. It didn't need to be explained. You didn't need to say, 'Well, Bill Walsh did it this way, so we're going to continue to do it this way.' It was defined as something that made sense. Like, when people talk about religion now, you can go online and look things up and you're like, 'Yeah, I know, but even though you're saying it's biblical, it's proving to be not true.'"

Cooley went on. "I've seen coordinators on the offensive and defensive—and especially defensive—side of the ball just call fucking plays. It's fascinating. This was different. There's always a reason. Like, their offense made sense, and the way they call plays or the way they designed calls for our players to see defense—everything tied together. Everything was wrapped into a nice little bundle. It was 'This is why and this is how, and this is how we're going to kill them.'"

To be sure, there were—and still are—foundational elements to the Shanahan system. The outside zone running scheme, which threatens the defense from snap to sideline, one gap at a time; the naked-bootleg counter that can exploit defensive overplays; and the indissoluble marriage between the run and the pass apparent in every distinguishing nuance. At the same time, there is a constant push to innovate, along with a pliability stemming from the conviction that the system can be transmuted to maximize the skill sets (and conceal the limitations of) the actual players on the team, rather than existing as an unchanging aesthetic requiring specific personnel—or simply the best players around—to make it thrive.

Kyle Shanahan and his coaches didn't merely unveil a playbook and tell players where to line up and what to do. They treated each opponent as a start-from-scratch conundrum, deciphering the defense's rules, and then turning those rules against the defenders by putting them in untenable—or downright impossible—positions. And then, if and when the opposing defensive coordinators adjusted, the Shanahan system seamlessly shifted to built-in solutions that "broke" the new rules.

"They're not just coaching and calling plays," said Brandon Staley, McVay's former defensive coordinator with the Rams and, later, the head coach of the Los Angeles Chargers from 2021 to 2023. "They're trying to attack you. They're trying to beat you."

It didn't always work. Yet the exposure to the system turned cynical players into borderline evangelists. Left tackle Joe Thomas, a first-ballot Hall of Fame inductee in 2023, was seven years into his perpetually frustrating Cleveland Browns career when Kyle Shanahan arrived as the team's offensive coordinator in 2014. Thomas would spend only a single season playing in Shanahan's scheme—and a notoriously dysfunctional one, at that—but it nevertheless transformed him.

"Since I was in the league in 2007 until now, it's the biggest single change, schematically, and evolution of the sport that I saw," Thomas said. "I know you had the outside zone when Mike Shanahan was coaching in the '90s and 2000s. Kyle really opened it up and truly made people defend every blade of grass. It really changed the game because it put the offense back at the advantage where you could ask all 11 guys to do something that wasn't that hard, and it gave them an advantage as long as they were able to pay attention to the detail."

Thomas had played for a succession of coaches and offensive coordinators in his long career, and this was eye-opening. "I remember my first year in the NFL and we were running some of these older offenses; we had to be perfect and we had to have somebody win a one-on-one battle to have a successful play. With Kyle, the reason they've had so much success everywhere that scheme has gone is because it's like, 'Hey, just listen to what I'm laying out there, and if you pay attention to this detail, there's a mismatch because they just can't have enough people for the gaps that we have.' It was much less about individual wins than it was about 'Hey, if everybody's on the same page doing their job, it works, and this is why.'"

As with many revolutions, this one wasn't always smooth or linear, and there was plenty of resistance along with the way. Kyle Shanahan and his protégés felt as though they were coaching for their jobs, if not their careers, for seven consecutive seasons beginning in 2010, before he and McVay were hired as head coaches of the 49ers and Rams, respectively. Since taking over those longtime NFC West rivals they, along with La-Fleur (hired as the Packers' head coach in 2019) and McDaniel (the Dolphins' head coach since 2022) and many of the coaches they've helped groom, have fundamentally altered the sport. Their influence can be felt in so many ways, from the proliferation of outside zone–based attacks, to the tightening of traditional wide receiver splits, to the way coaches position themselves on the sidelines, to the expanding group of coaches who've decided to blow off the league's annual scouting combine.

Most important and telling is that their teams have largely flourished:

heading into the 2024 campaign, over the previous six seasons, Shanahan, McVay, LaFleur, and McDaniel had combined to appear in three Super Bowls (including one victory) and eight conference championship games, with 15 trips to the postseason. Then there is Raheem Morris, another integral member of the Fun Bunch. Morris, who in his early 30s spent three years as the Tampa Bay Buccaneers' head coach, specialized on defense, until Shanahan, as the Falcons' offensive coordinator, made him a receivers coach before the team's 2016 Super Bowl season. Morris, like Shanahan and Belichick, possesses a comprehensive knowledge of the sport that translates to either side of the ball. After serving three years as the Rams' defensive coordinator, and helping McVay capture a championship in the process, Morris was hired as the Falcons' head coach in January of 2024.

This Shanahan tree has been defined by rivalry, especially when it comes to Shanahan and McVay, whom Morris characterizes as "Enemy Friends." There have been blowups and blowouts. There has been pettiness and paranoia. There have been high-stakes gambles and egregious overreactions. The relationships among the coaches are complicated. So are their relationships with the men charged with implementing their plans while playing the most challenging position in team sports.

During a 2020 game, McVay, seconds before a pivotal play, said over the headset of a quarterback he once revered, "This'll work if Jared doesn't fuck it up." Months later, Shanahan traded three first-round picks to position himself to draft the passer of his dreams, then went against his instincts and talked himself into taking a different quarterback. LaFleur spent three years catering to a headstrong future first-ballot Hall of Famer. McDaniel transformed an embattled QB into a breakout star before triggering a controversy surrounding player safety and head trauma. When McVay grew detached and despondent after losing his starting quarterback and watching the Rams' operation crater in the wake of a championship run, Morris helped snap him out of it.

The stakes are high and the stress is pervasive in a profession that is basically impossible. More often than not, these coaches have answers, but that alone guarantees nothing. They are hyperdriven, sleep-deprived sages attempting to impose order amid the inherent chaos of the sport; like so many coaches, they are control freaks attempting to control the uncontrollable. Even in the most pressure-packed moments, Shanahan, McVay, and company are playing three-dimensional chess. Yet nothing is promised, even to the most deserving. As a coach, you can come up with the most inventive game plan imaginable, only to have it derailed by a bad call or tipped ball or untimely injury.

The obsessive quest continues. Kyle's father coached the Denver Broncos to back-to-back championships in the 1990s, but ended his career ingloriously amid dysfunction in D.C., leaving Kyle to fight for his own fledgling career. Mike had sought to be the greatest ever in his profession, but didn't quite get there. The scars and knowledge his son inherited have propelled a similar pursuit. Kyle's flaws—a brusque and sometimes bratty presentation style, a tendency to treat interactions as transactional and people in his midst as disposable, a general perfectionism that truly holds him back at times—may not be fatal in a football sense, but unless he wins a championship, they'll be used against him by the tens of millions of people who follow the sport, and by some of those who coach and play it.

"They've definitely made the league better, especially when it comes to a fan's perspective," said 49ers left tackle Trent Williams, an 11-time Pro Bowl selection and future first-ballot Hall of Famer, referring to Kyle and his tree. "From an offensive perspective, they've introduced so many schemes and so many blocking techniques and nuances to running the football. And I think it does make everybody better, because it's a copycat league. You see all these fly motions, shifts, wide zone–predicated offenses, bootlegs, getting quarterbacks on the perimeter and throwing behind the linebackers with play-action . . . that all started with Mike Shanahan, and obviously Kyle has carried it to a different level. The secret is out."

III.

Tell me the *why*.

I first heard McVay say this soon after the Rams hired the then 30-year-old in 2017. He was referring to the rules that applied while working for Kyle Shanahan in Washington: if you wanted to suggest a play or debate a nuance with the exacting offensive coordinator, you had to be able to justify your position by providing sound reasoning behind it, or you'd better get out of his office. Really, however, it applied to everything McVay was trying to establish in L.A. He insisted that his assistants and others in the organization "know your *why*" at all times—and, most important, that they be able to explain the purpose behind anything and everything they asked the Rams players to do. "Otherwise," McVay said, "what are we even here for?"

Over the ensuing years, I started hearing others enunciate some version of this phrase—players like Cooley, Thomas, and Williams, and coaches who'd worked with Shanahan and McVay—as a guiding principle. It was almost an intentional rebuke of the certainty behind "it just works." It was basically asking, *How can we expect our players to execute our plan if they can't feel our excitement when we lay it all out?* The *why* stuck in my mind. It captures the spirit of the revolution Shanahan and his cohorts have launched. It suggests the triumph of brains over brawn; provides insight into why some offenses around the league seem to be nearly unstoppable; explains how someone like Mike McDaniel, surely the skinniest NFL coach ever, and probably the funniest, too, was given the keys to a team; and much more.

The story of the *why* revolution hasn't yet been told. This book is the first to attempt to account for how it all happened. And it begins where it must: not with the son, but with the father, whose own search for enlightenment set the stage for everything that would follow.

PART I

THE PURSUIT OF
PERFECTION

Sean McVay, who joined Mike Shanahan's Washington staff as a 24-year-old quality control coach in 2010 and soon became a trusted confidant, expresses support for rookie quarterback sensation Robert Griffin III.

Chapter 1

The Scars That Bind

A rising senior at Eastern Illinois University named Mike Shanahan was standing in a ballroom at the Hyatt Rosemont, not far from the suburb west of Chicago where he'd grown up, when he was first forced to come to terms with how far he was from realizing his dream.

Actually, it was his *replacement* dream. A few months shy of his 21st birthday, Shanahan had already confronted his football mortality, and nearly more than that. During the spring game heading into his senior season, the undersized and ultracompetitive quarterback had been tackled hard while running an option play and winced from the pain that followed. Shanahan toughed it out, staying on the field for the completion of the scrimmage. He wasn't soft, and he was no quitter.

Afterward, in the locker room, Shanahan peed blood. Unaware of the potential danger, he went back to his apartment and began vomiting profusely. He insisted he'd be fine, but one of his roommates finally called an ambulance. At the hospital, doctors evaluated the patient and couldn't determine what was wrong.

Soon, Shanahan lost consciousness and was rushed into emergency surgery. The surgeons discovered that one of his kidneys had been split open and removed it. From that point on, things were touch and go. At one point, Shanahan's heart stopped beating for more than 30 seconds. A priest was summoned to read his last rites. As Shanahan's father, Edward, raced through the hospital's front entrance, he passed the priest heading out.

The younger Shanahan spent five days in the intensive care unit. Before he was discharged, he was told to avoid strenuous activity, something he came to view more as a suggestion than an edict. "A few days later, he was lifting weights," another of his roommates at the time, Mike Heimerdinger, recalled in 1997. "Then he was playing handball. About two weeks after the surgery, we took him river rafting."

Playing quarterback, however, was over for Shanahan. Coaching seemed like the logical pivot.

Now, here he was in the summer of 1973, one of hundreds at a coaching clinic, listening to the white-haired keynote speaker tell him just how difficult that path would be. Bill Walsh had full command of the room. The chief offensive assistant and presumed successor to Paul Brown, the Cincinnati Bengals' Hall of Fame coach, Walsh posed a question to the audience: "How many in here want to be head coaches?"

Every single attendee, including Shanahan, raised his hand.

"If you really want to be a head coach," Walsh said, "you'd better know how to coach every position on the field."

Staff turnover, Walsh explained, was inevitable at every level. Head coaches must constantly bring in new assistants, many of them unfamiliar with the existing system. To make sure the new coaches would be effective, the head coach would have to train each one of them to see the game like he did.

"You're going to lose coaches," Walsh said. "You've got to be able to coach the offensive line, the running backs, the defensive backs, the pass rushers—everyone. You can't just focus on your area of expertise; you have to be able to teach everywhere."

Shanahan did a quick self-audit: he knew quarterbacking, and that was about it. He thought about Walsh's words, and what they signified, and a terrifying thought arose.

Right now, I have no fucking chance.

LOSING A KIDNEY LED SHANAHAN TO REASSESS EVERYTHING. BUT IN some ways, Walsh's remarks were just as troubling. What was his path to becoming a head coach, let alone in the pros? Should he pursue high school jobs? Should he try to become a college assistant? If he specialized in one area, be it quarterback play or the offense overall, how would he develop the breadth necessary to become fluent in every position?

It was a lot to fathom. One thing he knew for sure: Walsh was an authority. In a profession full of risk-averse rule followers and copycats, Walsh was the rare innovator, a man whose schematic principles—a timing-based passing attack that featured short, high-percentage throws as a substitute for running plays—had already moved the sport forward.

Two and a half years later, Walsh would leave Cincinnati after being passed over by the retiring Brown, who chose another Bengals assistant to replace him. By decade's end, Walsh had parlayed a two-year stint as Stanford's head coach into his first opportunity to lead an NFL team, taking over a struggling San Francisco 49ers franchise. In his third season, Walsh led San Francisco to its first-ever championship, guiding an underdog 49ers team to one of the unlikeliest Super Bowl triumphs in history, over the Brown-owned Bengals. It got better and better. Walsh, also the team's de facto general manager, had created an NFL dynasty and left an indelible imprint on his profession.

When Walsh stepped away from coaching in January of 1989, having once again defeated the Bengals on the sport's biggest stage, the Niners had captured three Lombardi Trophies, with two more championships on the horizon. By then, Walsh had seeded a coaching tree that would live for decades. He'd made the West Coast offense the gold standard. And, most significant of all, he had established the blueprint for how to run a professional football franchise, from practice framework to game-plan installation to travel logistics. In the words of Steve Young, Walsh's second of two first-ballot Hall of Fame quarterbacks in San Francisco, "Bill is the one who put it all together. He executed all of it, from how we're going to practice, how we're going to travel, how we're going to watch film—all of it. It was 'We're not gonna do stupid stuff. We're gonna make it simple, useful.' So, yes, there are a lot of pieces to it. He actually brought it all together."

In a sport where even the top strategists shamelessly stole from one another, Walsh—who didn't exactly go to great lengths to reject his nickname, "The Genius"—was hardly the first great football mind. His direct exposure to Paul Brown, Al Davis, and Sid Gillman clearly shaped his sensibilities, just as Walsh's principles would one day influence Shanahan and so many other successful coaches.

Walsh got his first pro coaching job in 1966, hired as the Oakland Raiders' running backs coach. Davis had just stepped down as Oakland's head coach to become the commissioner of the American Football League—a job he would hold for only three and a half months, losing it after others secured a merger agreement with the NFL behind his back. He returned to the franchise as its chief executive and part owner, remaining in those roles until his death in 2011. The Davis-installed Raiders offense had been greatly influenced by Gillman, who, as head coach of the AFL's Los Angeles Chargers, had employed Davis as his receivers coach from 1960 to 1962. The Raiders' vertical passing game was mostly known for its deep strikes, but the brilliance of Gillman, known as the father of the modern passing game, was far more nuanced than just chucking it down the field.

Gillman brought geometric precision to the passing game and entrusted receivers to make route adjustments while working in tandem with one another. He motioned running backs to the slot to confuse defenses and motioned receivers before the snap as a way of helping quarterbacks discern the opposing defense's alignment. For all the talk about the Raiders' vertical attack, Gillman was the strategist who first unlocked the *horizontal* potential of the passing game. His offenses used the entire width of the field, relying on timing routes and the contributions of running backs and tight ends. Slot receivers running deep seam routes; protection adjustments by running backs; tight ends lined up wide of the tackles—all of these practices started with Gillman. He also created the three-digit system—later passed on to Don Coryell, Ernie Zampese, Joe Gibbs, and Mike Martz—that proved to be as enduring as Walsh's West Coast framework.

Walsh built on Gillman's concepts after joining the Bengals in 1968. The Bengals were an AFL expansion team. Already a living legend, Paul Brown had guided the Cleveland Browns (named in his honor) to four consecutive All-American Football Conference championships from 1946 to 1949 before the franchise joined the NFL, along with the 49ers and Baltimore Colts. Under Brown's guidance, Cleveland won the NFL championship in its first season, and, after three consecutive losses in the title game, captured additional championships in 1954 and '55.

Brown and Walsh would part on terrible terms, with Walsh not only getting passed over as his successor but also convinced that Brown had actively sabotaged other potential opportunities for him. Even if one doesn't consider Walsh himself to be part of Brown's legacy, that legacy rivaled, if not surpassed, Gillman's. Brown instituted film study of opponents. He created the framework for the modern playbook. He was the first coach to hire a staff of full-time assistants. He pioneered dropback pass blocking and invented the draw play, the modern face mask, and the practice squad. And Brown played a major part in breaking pro football's color barrier, signing the first Black player of the modern era, middle guard—as the nose tackle position was then called—Bill Willis.

Walsh, despite a challenging first season in Cincinnati, had big plans for the Bengals' offense. He was excited by the selection of quarterback Greg Cook, a former University of Cincinnati star, with the fifth-overall pick in the 1969 AFL draft, a year before the merger took effect. Blessed with a strong arm, Cook looked like a budding superstar in the first three games of his rookie season, but suffered a torn rotator cuff in his throwing shoulder. The severity of the injury went undiagnosed, and Cook—who ultimately took cortisone shots and played through it—was never the same. The Bengals turned to noodle-armed Virgil Carter, who could deliver short passes with accuracy but lacked Cook's downfield prowess. Out of necessity, Walsh developed the embryonic version of the West Coast offense, replete with horizontal timing routes, short throws, and the use of running backs as primary receivers. Carter led the NFL in completion percentage in 1971 and was the league's third-rated passer. Midway through the next season, he lost his job to the more talented Ken Anderson. By then, Walsh had advanced his system. A decade later, in Northern California, Joe Montana would take Walsh's schematic brilliance to a level never before witnessed on the football field.

Walsh, a few months before he died of cancer in 2007, told me how deeply he came to regret his decision to resign in the aftermath of the Niners' third Super Bowl championship eighteen years earlier. "I should have continued to coach," Walsh said as we sat in a country club dining room in Menlo Park, not far from the Niners' training facility in Santa Clara. "If I could've taken a month off, or something, to get away . . . but I had all the other jobs. I couldn't leave. The draft was coming, and I was the general manager. So, I didn't see any place to go. I should've turned it over to other guys and taken off. It would've been alright. Of course it would have. But I didn't do it."

His handpicked successor, George Seifert, who'd been Walsh's defensive coordinator, guided the Niners to another championship in his first season. Two years later, offensive coordinator Mike Holmgren, a Walsh protégé, left to become the head coach of the Green Bay Packers. Seifert, under pressure after missing the playoffs in 1991, needed someone to run the scheme that Walsh had built and Holmgren had sustained. For the first time, the Niners turned to an outsider.

———

THE CHOICE, SHANAHAN, WASN'T A PARTICULARLY POPULAR ONE. SEIfert's new offensive coordinator had just been fired by Denver Broncos head coach Dan Reeves, who accused him of insubordination. Reeves felt Shanahan and his future first-ballot Hall of Fame quarterback, John Elway, had gone behind his back to plot strategy. Shanahan strenuously disputed that claim, but publicly, he laid low. He was reeling. This was his second high-profile firing in a two-and-a-half-year span.

Shanahan had been a rising star in the coaching profession, beginning with nine years in the collegiate ranks and continuing in Denver under Reeves, who'd promoted the 32-year-old to offensive coordinator in 1985. Three years later, Davis hired Shanahan to coach the Raiders. It was the first time the Raiders (then based in Los Angeles) had enlisted a head coach from outside the organization since Davis himself took the job 23 years earlier, and Shanahan was hailed as a whiz kid who would restore the Silver and Black to the sustained excellence of the '60s, '70s, and early '80s.

It did not go well. Shanahan clashed with Davis from the outset, went 7–9 in his first season, and was fired after a 1–3 start the following year. Davis, claiming he fired Shanahan for cause, stiffed him out of the remaining money owing on the coach's contract, leading to a drawn-out dispute ultimately resolved by NFL commissioner Paul Tagliabue. In the end, Shanahan would get at least some of the money due to him.

Repairing his reputation would prove to be a more daunting challenge. In January of 1992, he needed a landing spot—or, more accurately, a lifeline. It happened when 34-year-old Bill Cowher, who'd just taken over as Steelers coach from four-time Super Bowl winner Chuck Noll, offered Shanahan a job as Pittsburgh's offensive coordinator. Since Cowher was a defensive coach, Shanahan would have free rein.

The deal was basically done, until Seifert called. Davis, Shanahan's former boss with the Raiders, had warned the 49ers against reaching out to him, but Seifert did it anyway. Shanahan's head started spinning. The 49ers had Jerry Rice, already considered the greatest receiver in NFL history. Their other starting wideout, John Taylor, was perhaps the NFL's most underrated player at his position. Tight end Brent Jones was a prolific pass catcher, too. Two-time league MVP Montana, having missed the entire 1991 season after surgery to his throwing elbow, was back to try to reclaim his job from Steve Young, who'd won the NFL passing title in his absence. "I've gotta go take a look at it," Shanahan told Cowher. Midway through his interview with Seifert, he knew this was the job he needed. *Man, I have to take this*, he told himself.

It was a seismic decision, the impact of which would reverberate throughout Northern California, and later Colorado—and, ultimately, across the football landscape.

BOTH SHANAHAN AND SEIFERT BENEFITED FROM THEIR THREE-YEAR coaching marriage. The biggest beneficiary, however, was Jon Steven Young.

Sitting in his Palo Alto office on a spring afternoon nearly three decades after Shanahan's arrival in the Bay Area, Young got emotional while discussing their collaboration. "We had a symbiotic relationship. You always want somebody who can give you a sense of 'You go as far as you can. I'm going to call plays and I'm going to prepare this team, and I'm going to show you that nothing's in your way.' And I think that's an amazing thing for any human, to have someone around them that allows you to do that. And that's why I would tear up if I didn't want to be embarrassed with you [while talking] about how I feel about him."

To say that Young, at the time of Shanahan's hiring, was having trouble escaping Montana's Transamerica Tower–sized shadow in San Francisco was an understatement. Supremely talented, amazingly athletic, tough, and intelligent, Young's skill set was the envy of fan bases across America. Among the 49er Faithful, though, his name might as well have been "Not Joe." Young didn't patiently hang in the pocket and read defenses like Montana. He didn't exude calm or cool. Young's vibe was frenetic and unpredictable; he was an improv artist who kept opposing defenses *and* his own offensive teammates off guard.

The main issue was that Young didn't win. Montana had turned the perpetually unsatisfying Niners into a dynasty. Before Super Bowl XVI, no professional sports team based in San Francisco had ever captured a championship. That all changed in January of 1982, and the Niners became a symphony on grass in an otherwise brutal sport, with a magical quarterback as the conductor.

For four years, Young had served as Montana's restless and pushy backup. Their shared existence wasn't anything resembling harmonious, and yet the Niners managed to win through it, with Super Bowl victories following the '88 and '89 seasons. Then, in the summer of '91, Montana tore an elbow tendon, had surgery, and went on injured reserve for the entire season.

Now, the Niners' hopes rested on Not Joe.

During a tumultuous first season as starter, Young, in the eyes of a fretful fan base, could do no right. One morning during the season, he went to his front door and saw the *San Francisco Chronicle* at his feet. On the front page was the headline "The Gulf War: It's Steve Young's Fault." Though it was obviously in jest, Young took it hard.

It wasn't as though Young lacked great teachers. He'd come to San Francisco at the behest of Walsh, who swung a trade with the Buccaneers because he worried that Montana, having undergone a major back surgery during the 1986 season, might be breaking down. Before he went to Tampa Bay, Young's first professional experience had been under the tutelage of none other than Sid Gillman, who'd been a consultant for the United States Football League's Los Angeles Express when that franchise signed the former Brigham Young University star to a record-breaking $42 million contract.

Shanahan's first move upon taking the 49ers job was to immerse himself in all things Walsh. This was relatively easy because Walsh—a pioneer in this regard, too—had left behind an extensive video library, one that included not just old games and practices, but also meetings and installations. Shanahan holed up in his new office, watching everything he could find, which helped him learn the West Coast offense and understand Walsh's methodology. Eventually, Shanahan spent a day with Walsh, who two weeks earlier had come out of retirement to coach Stanford for the second time, walking away from a deal to return to the 49ers as a consultant.

Soon after, Shanahan met with Montana. They watched some film together, and Shanahan noticed a trend. Walsh's offense was based on timing and progressions, with the quarterback making up to five reads on a single play to find the open receiver. "On some of these plays," Shanahan told Montana, "[reads] 1 and 2 are just not even viable. They're never gonna happen against those defenses. It looks like you know that—and that you're just going straight to 3, 4, and 5." Montana laughed. "Yeah," he said, "I was hoping you wouldn't catch on to that." It was something Montana hadn't advertised, because he had no intention of giving Young any extra help.

When Shanahan met Young, he met himself: an aggrieved football obsessive on a quest for redemption. They had a lot in common. Both men had been fast-tracked for massive success, only to suffer high-profile setbacks. Each was now at a pivotal point in his football life. Each had to change the narrative, or forever be burdened by what might have been. "We both had scars," Young recalled. "Al Davis had kind of embarrassed him. He'd been beat up. It was set up perfectly for both of us to heal."

In early August of 1992, Montana jogged off the field early during a training camp practice at Sierra College in hot, dusty Rocklin, California, unable to throw even medium-range passes without pain. His time as the 49ers' starting quarterback was finished. He went on injured reserve for a second consecutive season and had another elbow surgery in September, but he continued to experience numbness in two fingers of his throwing hand because of pressure on the ulnar nerve. By the time he was ready to return, Young, fueled by Shanahan's unyielding support, had become the best player in football.

SHORTLY BEFORE THE START OF THE '92 REGULAR SEASON, YOUNG EXPE-
rienced what he called a "seminal moment," one that still gives him chills.
It happened one afternoon on the practice field at the team's Santa Clara
training facility. By then, all of Young's teammates had gone back into the
locker room. He and Shanahan were the only ones still outside.

Recalled Young, "He said, 'Steve, I love to attack. And you allow me a
chance to do that. And so, I'm not going to worry about you; I want you to
worry about me. You protect me. I'm going to call plays; I'm going to let it
rip. And then *you* figure out how to make sure that I'm protected.' And I
said, 'Great—let's just let it rip.'

"I remember feeling, like, 'This is an incredible opportunity. I don't
want to let him down.' He was all in. I'd been around [the 49ers] for five
years, and the narratives had been built, and I needed someone new and
fresh to go, 'No! That's not right!' He is a truth seeker. Like, 'That's not *true*!
Steve Young is not what you think. I'm going to *show* you who he is.' The
whole thing changed. It changed how I felt about myself. And it gave me
space to create a new narrative."

The Shanahan–Young partnership would reinvigorate the Niners'
attack and, in the process, obliterate the stigmas attached to each of them.

During Seifert's first three seasons as head coach, with Holmgren calling the offense, the Niners had mostly stuck to the basics of Walsh's scheme.
Walsh had hired Holmgren, who'd been Young's quarterbacks coach at
BYU, to fill the same role in San Francisco in 1986. Promoted to offensive
coordinator after Walsh's retirement, Holmgren's premise was *Our players
are great, our system is great, and our plays are great. We'll run what we run,
and if we execute, it doesn't matter what you do on defense—we'll succeed.*

"We were kind of imperial about it," Young said. "We had all our plays,
and we were really good at them, and that's how we rolled. And I think
Mike showed up and said, 'OK, that's cool. I love what you're doing. I've
always felt kinship with it. But let's lean in.' There was a new iteration that
he was willing to do. And so, in that way, he found an accelerator."

Young saw something different, and exceptional, in Shanahan. "What
we'd been doing here for ten-plus years, Mike came in and actually added
an incredible amount of surety. Mike was *sure*. I think he'd been roaming
around knowing that, 'I know.' And then he goes to Oakland and he gets

a wackadoodle [boss] and all of a sudden he's on his heels while knowing that he's right. He's like, 'I'm right! But I can't prove it right now.'" That would change in San Francisco. As Young put it, "It was like he couldn't be his full self until he had a platform like this. It was 'Let's make it as easy on the quarterback as we can, and as complex for the defense as possible.'"

Many offensive coordinators studied opposing defenses and tried to figure out the best ways to attack them. Shanahan took that approach several steps further. He dissected the schemes that awaited the Niners, in all their permutations, and constructed an opponent-specific game plan designed to humiliate defenders. Each week's plan was stand-alone, largely built from scratch. Sure, there was carryover from week to week, but only if those familiar plays could be delivered unpredictably and with purpose. At his best, Shanahan could devise ways—via formation, pre-snap motion, tempo—to isolate an opponent's tendencies and make its collective behavior predictive. And then he would attack, relentlessly. As Young recalled, "Mike wouldn't just say it; he wouldn't just put it in; he would *call* it. Like, a lot of guys say it, talk about it, and then on game day, it's like, 'Well, you know, we've got some good plays, and we're going to rest on those and stick with our go-to plays.' Mike wanted it over at halftime, and I did, too!"

Shanahan's coaching style was about as subtle as Metallica, the Bay Area band that rose to prominence shortly before his arrival in San Francisco. It wasn't merely about beating that week's opponent; he was trying to dismantle the psyche of the defensive coordinator (and/or head coach) responsible for the game plan, and the confidence of the players charged with executing it. "He would make it very personal," Young said. "He'd personalize offense and defense, making sure that players knew that we were not playing some amorphous team. He loved dreaming up ways to just throttle a defense. He'd come in on Wednesday morning, and the first thing he'd say is like, 'OK, we've got the Falcons this week—we're going to CRUSH them.' And then he'd tell you how! And by the end of the meeting, you'd be like, 'He's right!'"

Shanahan, Young remembered, would say of his opposing coaching counterpart, "He thinks he can get away with this. Look at this! People have been letting him get away with this! This is a joke. We're going to embarrass him." It was the same with opposing players. "There were guys that we felt were not worthy, and we were going to expose that. 'This safety, he actually thinks he's a good player, but he is so out of position. We're gonna expose him.' It was like he was a truth seeker, determined to force out the truth."

Young was a revelation in 1992, throwing for 3,465 yards and a league-leading 25 touchdowns, with an NFL-best passer rating of 107.0. He ran for another 537 yards, but there were far fewer complaints from media and fans about his impatience and unwillingness to hang in the pocket. Much smoother than in past years, and consistently lethal, Young was voted the league's Most Valuable Player.

Shanahan's reputation was turned on its head. The Niners had the league's top-ranked offense, in both points and yards, with exquisite balance: San Francisco ranked third in both rushing (powered by the emergence of dual-threat running back Ricky Watters) and passing.

As Shanahan and Young grew closer, Seifert had reason to feel threatened. Once, during practice, Shanahan and Young were engaged in a private conversation. That annoyed Seifert, who interrupted and gathered the entire team around him. Seifert asked Young a question, and Shanahan jumped in to respond. Seifert went ballistic. "Fuck, when I'm talking, I want everybody to shut up, and that includes you!" Seifert yelled, pointing at his offensive coordinator. It was so quiet, you could hear 53 jaws drop.

Shanahan shook it off, realizing he'd messed up. *Fuck, I deserve it*, he thought to himself. He walked off the field after practice and was about to go through the locker room door when Seifert intercepted him and pulled him aside. "Mike," he said, "I knew you could handle it. Let me tell you what happened when Bill Walsh did the same thing to me. [Bill] said, 'You'll find out within the next couple hours that everybody on the team hates me right now for what I did, because they really like you.' Within two hours, I had everybody on the team come up to me and say, 'Fuck him.'" Sure enough, Shanahan would have a similar experience—in the wake of Seifert's upbraiding, he'd never been so popular.

⸻

FOR SHANAHAN AND YOUNG, THE ACCOLADES KEPT COMING. SHANA- han had the league's best offense in 1993, and the Niners finished a close second the following season. Young was first-team All-Pro in '93, and the next year was voted league MVP for the second time while owning the highest passer rating for the fourth consecutive season.

Yet, as 1994 turned to 1995 and the top-seeded 49ers prepared for the postseason, the mood was decidedly tense. In each of the previous two years, they'd suffered wrenching defeats in the NFC Championship Game to the Dallas Cowboys, who'd gone on to win the Super Bowl. Young hadn't played well in either game—amplifying the complaints of the "Not Joe" chorus. With the Niners and Cowboys on a collision course for a third consecutive showdown, the prospect of a similar outcome haunted even the proudest competitors in the 49ers' training facility.

After winning four Super Bowls in nine seasons, the Niners were now five years removed from a championship, and it felt like 50. Young once told me, his tone almost one of embarrassment, how wrenching and disruptive any defeat was during that era. "When we lose a game, it just *rips* people up around here. It's weird to even say this, but it truly feels like someone died. That's how brutal it is."

Postseason losses were exponentially worse. In 1987, after the top-seeded 49ers suffered a shocking divisional-round defeat to the Minnesota Vikings, owner Eddie DeBartolo reportedly refused to speak to Walsh for six weeks. He let Walsh stay on as coach, but stripped him of his team president title, replacing him with . . . Eddie DeBartolo.

It wasn't a stretch to say that a third consecutive setback to the Cowboys would have caused an existential crisis for the 49ers. They'd loaded up with free agents before that season, signing future Hall of Famers Deion Sanders, Rickey Jackson, and Richard Dent. They'd beaten the Cowboys in a regular-season game at Candlestick Park in mid-November. Salvation was there for the taking—Young and his teammates had to take it, or else.

The win-or-perish mentality resonated with Shanahan, who'd been on the wrong end of three Super Bowl blowouts as a Broncos assistant. Like Reese Bobby in *Talladega Nights*, "If you ain't first, you're last" was his guiding principle, one he'd soon carry back to the Rockies. That almost impossibly severe standard seeped into Shanahan's son's psyche, too. Kyle Shanahan, who'd just turned 13 when his father joined the Niners, spent enough time around the team—as a training camp ball boy and frequent in-season visitor—that the maniacal drive he encountered became the new normal. Even in his college years, Kyle took his dad's playoff losses *hard*, mourning outwardly in the immediate aftermath in a way that even Mike Shanahan did not.

There was another level to this, too. As he prepared for the '94 postseason, Mike Shanahan wasn't desperately focused on winning three games; rather, his mission was to *obliterate* the opponents standing between the 49ers and a championship. He had the blueprint. He had the weapons. He had the quarterback. Young, he felt, was ready. Now it was Shanahan's job to convince him.

Chapter 2

The Mastermind

et's go over it again.

It was an hour and a half before the start of Super Bowl XXIX in Miami, the game that would change Steve Young's life forever. The heavily favored 49ers were a confident bunch going into this matchup with the San Diego Chargers. Young had immersed himself in every element of Mike Shanahan's game plan, and the quarterback couldn't wait to try to bring it to fruition.

What Young did *not* want to do during this anxious moment was review the plan for what seemed like the 700th time during the two-week period before the big game. Shanahan was undeterred; Young could practically picture the blood in the coordinator's crimson cheeks at full boil. Over the course of his career, Shanahan would inspire many nicknames— most notably, as the Broncos' controlling head coach, he'd be referred to by some players as "The Little General." Young's own pet name for his coordinator, however, would remain Mike "Let's Go Over It Again" Shanahan.

When Shanahan sidled up to Young's locker, the quarterback shook his head.

"Mike, I can't do it again."

"You don't need to," Shanahan replied. "We're going to throw eight touchdowns."

Now Young was truly perturbed.

"Don't say stupid stuff," the quarterback said. The NFL record for most touchdown passes in a game was seven, set by the Bears' Sid Luckman in

1943. Montana held the Super Bowl record with five, a feat accomplished in the Niners' 55–10 blowout of the Broncos (for whom Shanahan was the quarterbacks coach) five years earlier.

Shanahan just stared at him. It took a few seconds before Young realized his coach wasn't joking.

"No—that's what we're doing," Shanahan declared, as though it were absurd to suggest otherwise.

When Shanahan got like this, fighting him was futile. That's something Young's backup, Elvis Grbac, certainly knew. As Grbac warmed up before that season's opening game against the Raiders at Candlestick Park, Shanahan pulled the young quarterback aside and pointed across the field.

"See that guy in the white sweatsuit?" Shanahan asked, referring to Al Davis, the man who'd fired him after just 20 games and tried to avoid paying him the rest of the money due on his contract. "I want you to take this football and throw it right at him."

For a few seconds, Grbac thought Shanahan was kidding. He smiled. Shanahan stared back coldly.

"I'm fuckin' serious," the coach said. "Throw the ball at him."

Said Grbac, "If I hit him, do you know what he could do to me?"

Shanahan's glare persisted. "Throw the fucking ball."

Grbac unleashed a spiral aimed right at Davis's head, some 30 yards away. The owner saw it at the last second and ducked, barely avoiding it. Stunned, Davis looked up to see Shanahan waving. The Raiders boss flipped him off.

So, yeah, Shanahan was serious about the eight touchdowns—or, at least, he sure seemed to be. Either way, it was tough to argue with a coordinator who'd just helped Young scale the greatest obstacle of his playing career: defeating the dreaded Dallas Cowboys, who'd ended the 49ers' season in each of the previous two conference championship games while on the way to Super Bowl triumphs. When Shanahan began game-planning for their NFC Championship Game clash, he felt he needed a new wrinkle to keep the daunting Dallas defense off balance. Finding a way to unleash Jerry Rice, who'd been held to 83 receiving yards and no touchdowns in the previous year's conference title game, was paramount. Shanahan's other issue: figuring out how to slow star pass rusher Charles Haley, whose trade from San Francisco to Dallas before the '92 season had helped swing the balance of power in the NFC.

Shanahan began toying with the I formation and some other running looks from his past, with Rice lined up in the backfield. Twenty-seven years before Shanahan's son, Kyle, would turn around his team's season—and nearly reach the Super Bowl—by using star wideout Deebo Samuel as a running back, he planned to take the sport's greatest receiving threat and deploy him in a manner the Cowboys could never have expected.

Seifert, however, hated the idea. He called Shanahan into his office and said, "Hey, what are you putting Jerry Rice in the backfield for?" Shanahan explained that he wanted to create favorable matchups for Rice and catch the Cowboys off guard, and that it could help slow Haley's rabid pursuit of Young in the pocket.

"Well, Mike, I don't want him there," Seifert said.

"George," Shanahan pleaded, "if we don't put him in there, I'm not sure we can beat 'em."

Seifert held firm, and Shanahan relented. The next day, Seifert approached the coordinator and revisited the topic.

"Do you still feel very strongly about that?" he asked Shanahan.

"Yes. I think it would be the difference between us winning and losing the game."

Seifert looked hard into Shanahan's eyes. "Go for it," he said. Shanahan did, and the 49ers jumped all over the unnerved Cowboys, going up 21–0 and taking a 31–14 halftime lead on Young's 28-yard touchdown pass to Rice with eight seconds remaining, en route to a 38–28 victory.

Two weeks later, Super Bowl XXIX played out almost exactly how Shanahan had envisioned it. Young threw two touchdowns in the first 3:02 of the game, staking the Niners to a 14–0 lead. And they kept on rolling into the fourth quarter. With 13:49 remaining, Young threw his third touchdown pass to Rice—and sixth of the game—to make it 49–18. He'd broken both Montana's record and the spell that had rendered him a second-class citizen to so many Northern California sports fans.

The next time the Niners got the ball, Young was wearing a baseball cap as Grbac jogged onto the field at Seifert's behest. Excited by his triumph, Young, soon to be the Super Bowl MVP, picked up the sideline telephone that connected him to Shanahan in the upstairs coaching box.

"Mike—congratulations! Awesome!" Young exclaimed.

"Get back in there!" Shanahan ordered Young. "You've got two more to throw."

It wasn't going to happen, but Young, to this day, appreciates the sentiment. "I always tell people, if you want to throw six touchdowns in the Super Bowl, go for eight. *That's* how you do it. That's Mike."

AT THE VICTORY PARTY, IT OCCURRED TO YOUNG HOW MUCH MORE HE and Shanahan could accomplish together in the coming years, as the strategist flexed his creative muscles and pushed the limits of the craft. The best was surely yet to come. Looking back, Young could see that he was naive—Shanahan, once consigned to the damaged-goods section, was now in high demand. In fact, he was about to become the head coach of the Broncos, a deal that got finalized while the rest of the 49ers players and coaches partied at their Miami hotel. Young didn't know it, but Shanahan was upstairs in his room with Broncos owner Pat Bowlen, nailing down the details.

At the start of the meeting, it wasn't a given that they'd get the deal done, especially with the 49ers floating a succession scenario in which Shanahan, with a hefty raise, would stay on for two more seasons as Seifert's coordinator, with a contractual claim to the head coaching job after that. Two years earlier, in January of 1993, Bowlen had tried and failed to make Shanahan Denver's head coach. A season into his Niners tenure and only a year removed from his ignominious firing by then Broncos coach Dan Reeves, Shanahan turned down the job. He had his reasons. The short answer was that Shanahan didn't like the look of replacing Reeves after the coach's hurtful accusations that he and quarterback John Elway had, in effect, undermined his leadership and conspired against him. As Shanahan told me in 1997, "Things had gotten so bad with me and Dan the previous year, and everyone thought I was after his job. I didn't want to be the asshole who took Dan's job. It just didn't feel right."

It also didn't feel as though Bowlen was manically driven to capture Lombardi Trophies in the same way as his 49ers counterpart, Eddie DeBartolo. It was easy to make direct comparisons. Beginning in 1984, on both sides of that ill-fated 20-game interlude as the Raiders' head coach, Shanahan had spent seven seasons as a Broncos assistant. Three times, all with Elway at quarterback, Denver had gone to the Super Bowl. On all three occasions—within a four-season span—the Broncos had been blown out, including that record-setting, 55–10 molly-whopping by the 49ers in January of 1990.

During their conversations in early 1993, Shanahan had presented Bowlen with three requests designed to ensure that the Broncos could close the gap: that they'd rank in the top half of the league when it came to paying players (as measured by the salary cap), that his assistant coaches' salaries would rank in the NFL's top ten, and that the owner would pay for meals and hotel rooms for players participating in the offseason program. In other words, the type of perks for which DeBartolo was famous. When Bowlen refused to put any of those requests in writing, Shanahan, mindful that if his second shot at being an NFL head coach didn't go well, he almost certainly wouldn't get a third, knew it wasn't the right job for him.

Two years later, after firing Wade Phillips and watching Young throw those six TDs on Super Sunday, Bowlen *really* wanted Shanahan to be his head coach. Shanahan asked for the same three things, and Bowlen agreed to put the first two in the contract, but not the third.

"Fine," Shanahan said. "I'll pay for the meals and hotels."

It was an unusual move that, like most things about Shanahan's Broncos tenure, worked out well.

"A few weeks into it," Shanahan remembered, "Pat called me into his office and said, 'Fuck you.' He said, 'You don't know how many people have come in here and thanked me for the meals.'"

Embarrassed, Bowlen told Shanahan he wanted to pick up the cost of the players' meals—and all meals moving forward—and asked the coach not to share their conversation with anyone, including Shanahan's wife.

"Pat," Shanahan said, "you think I'm crazy? I *never* told Peggy a word of this. She'd have killed me."

Bowlen laughed, said he could relate, and shook his head. A few weeks later, the owner decided to pick up the tab for the offseason hotel rooms, too.

IT WASN'T JUST BOWLEN THAT SHANAHAN NEEDED TO WIN OVER. ELWAY, his confidant during his days as an assistant, would also be asked to sacrifice.

Having been immersed in the West Coast offense—and having spent the previous three years coordinating what at that point were some of the most prolific attacks in NFL history—Shanahan was intent on importing timing-based route principles. Elway, however, was resistant to the idea of operating primarily under center, which had been the Walsh way. As Shanahan remarked of his time in San Francisco, "We had no shotgun. They fumbled the snaps before they'd go into shotgun, because the quarterbacks didn't like it."

What Shanahan envisioned in Denver was a hybrid system that featured many of Walsh's principles in the passing game—albeit with a shotgun-heavy point of attack, to appease Elway—and a juiced-up running game that would provide balance. The idea was to take pressure off Elway, one of the greatest playmaking quarterbacks in history, and set up low-risk, high-percentage throws against defenses designed to stop the run. Elway, of course, would have to buy in.

"The first thing we're going to have to do is, we're going to have to run the ball," Shanahan told Elway. "You can't take the shots you've been taking. The only chance we've got to win the Super Bowl is to give you a good run game. They're not going to talk about you a lot, and you're not gonna throw as many touchdown passes, but we've got a chance to win."

Elway's response was simple: "Hey, I don't give a shit about that. I want to win."

"OK," Shanahan said, "just understand that when you want to get together with me after the game and [complain that] you haven't been throwing it, that we've talked about this."

The Niners had been highly successful on the ground during Shanahan's three seasons in San Francisco, with Ricky Watters emerging as a nightmare for opposing defenses. Shanahan, however, now conceived a radical change in his approach to running the ball. Longtime 49ers offensive line coach Bobb McKittrick favored smaller, agile offensive linemen who employed "man" blocking techniques against specific defenders, sometimes going to the ground (the infamous "cut block" and its asso-ciated techniques, some of which are now banned) to neutralize the size advantage of opponents. As much as Shanahan admired McKittrick, with whom he'd roomed at training camp in Sierra College, he had a different vision. Shanahan was ready to put his faith in a concept—outside zone—that would upend the sport.

THE BRONCOS' FUTURE—AND THE LEAGUE'S, AND HIS SON'S—COULD BE traced to Shanahan's past. In 1975, as a 23-year-old offensive assistant on Barry Switzer's Oklahoma staff, he spent his first-ever coaching stint watch-ing the Sooners dominate college football with the wishbone. Oklahoma's wishbone, which featured a loaded backfield (including a fleet-footed quar-terback) employing a triple-option attack behind a lead blocker, had con-founded defenses for the first part of the decade. In 1971, as the Sooners' offensive coordinator, Switzer had presided over a unit that averaged an obscene 472.4 rushing yards per game, still an NCAA record. Now, as a head coach, he was in the process of winning a second consecutive national championship, and Shanahan was taking notes.

What stood out to Shanahan was how the wishbone stressed defenses from sideline to sideline, forcing opponents to make decisions about which players to attack and which gaps to fill, with any false move or dubious decision easily exploited. That's the way he wanted the Broncos' rushing attack to go after defenses. He had another motive, too: exhausting the Broncos' opponents. To implement the outside zone, Shanahan brought back Alex Gibbs, who'd been the Broncos' offensive line coach from 1984 to 1987, in a similar capacity. Since the early 1980s, Gibbs had been study-ing plays that featured elements of "wide zone"—which would later become a euphemism for outside zone—blocking techniques. He watched Bengals offensive line coach Jim McNally run such plays for hefty running back Ickey Woods toward the end of that decade; he also saw Iowa offensive line coach (and future Hawkeyes head coach) Kirk Ferentz employ similar tactics at the collegiate level during the '80s. In 1990 and '91, Gibbs, as the San Diego Chargers' line coach, had success with wide zone plays featur-ing running backs Marion Butts and Rod Bernstine. In the latter season, the Chargers averaged an NFL-best 4.8 yards per carry. Gibbs relished the idea of building an entire system around the outside zone, but he needed a head coach to embrace that notion and go all in. Shanahan was the first NFL head coach to see it the way Gibbs did.

Shanahan also saw something else: a way to combine the outside zone with Walsh's principles in the dropback passing game, a timing-based attack which tied the quarterback's reads to his footwork. That prompted him to declare, "We're gonna call this the East Coast offense."

Together, Gibbs and Shanahan placed an emphasis on acquiring smart and agile linemen, though linemen who were bigger than the ones McKittrick preferred—blockers to hold up against the likes of mammoth Green Bay Packers defensive linemen Reggie White and Gilbert Brown, who in the middle of that decade routinely swallowed up San Francisco's relative lightweights. Shanahan ended up finding the players he coveted at great value, building a nearly unstoppable force that featured a starting center drafted in the seventh round (Tom Nalen), two starting guards picked in the tenth (Mark Schlereth and Brian Habib), and an undrafted starting right tackle (Tony Jones).

The outside zone was based on stretching runs to the sideline and testing the defense's collective gap integrity, with the ballcarrier a threat to put his foot in the ground and make a quick cutback at any time. Any defender who flowed just a bit wide of his assigned gap, on either side, was susceptible to the back's sudden burst. It unnerved some opponents to the point that typically aggressive fronts became far more passive, as players became prone to flowing outside reactively and waiting for the back to make his decision.

"What the outside zone did is that it made defensive players run from sideline to sideline," Shanahan said. "Penetrating teams would play soft; they just didn't know how to play the [outside] zone. Regardless, the defense is getting tired. Our objective was that if we could run the ball like that, we could tire them out and then have our big plays come in the second half."

That is exactly what happened in January of 1998, when Shanahan's Broncos upset the Packers to win the first of back-to-back Super Bowls (and break the NFC's 13-year winning streak over the AFC). Denver's winning points came on Super Bowl MVP Terrell Davis's third rushing touchdown of the day; the sixth-round pick from the previous year's draft carried 30 times for 157 yards despite sitting out the entire second quarter with blurred vision—there was no concussion protocol back then—after getting kicked in the helmet during a first-quarter run.

"Our game plan was to tire them out," Shanahan recalls. "Green Bay was *soooo* tired."

For the record, Shanahan's plan was a bit more sophisticated than that. His superpower—isolating an opponent's tendency and exploiting it—was on full display in front of one of the largest television audiences in history. Packers defensive coordinator Fritz Shurmur loved to blitz, relying in particular on future Hall of Fame safety LeRoy Butler, who had a knack for derailing running plays in the backfield. Through film study, Shanahan discovered that by lining up in the "slot" formation, which featured two receivers to one side of the line of scrimmage and the tight end on the other, he could predict Butler's assignment based on how the safety was positioned. He was correct, and the Broncos took full advantage. Denver had spent its entire season running primarily out of its base alignment (one receiver on each side of the line, with two running backs and a tight end) and throwing out of the slot; on Super Sunday, all Broncos runs came from the slot.

"The Packers were outcoached, pure and simple," Broncos star tight end Shannon Sharpe told me after the game. "LeRoy Butler and Reggie White are their two best defensive players. Where were they today?" Butler had nine tackles, most of them downfield, but no big plays; White, perhaps the greatest defensive lineman in NFL history, had only one tackle.

"Where I think Mike was a genius was formations," said Jedd Fisch, who would serve as Shanahan's receivers coach a decade later. "Forget the zone running game; forget keepers and bootlegs; he was so far ahead [when it came to] formations. He was willing to be in 'empty' when no one was willing to be in 'empty.' He was willing to be in condensed splits when nobody was willing to be in condensed splits. He was willing to motion guys at a certain tempo when no one was motioning guys. That is the real conflict you put on a defense. That's where everybody wanted to learn from Mike."

That explains another Shanahan nickname, sometimes used sarcastically by critics: "The Mastermind," lifted from my 1997 *Sports Illustrated* profile of him.

Some of Shanahan's chess moves from those days are still talked about reverentially in coaching circles. Current Broncos coach Sean Payton, an esteemed offensive strategist who coached the New Orleans Saints to victory in Super Bowl XLIV, recalled a classic Shanahan moment from Denver's victory over Reeves and the Falcons in Super Bowl XXXIII in 1999. "Where Elway runs the deep boot and [Rod] Smith runs the comeback past—we've never seen that route before. It was like, 'Ah!' We were all putting that in. 'Tupelo'—we gave it a name. Mike invented that. He was a part of that. And then to hear it was, like, a sideline adjustment was [incredible]. Man, there's just so many things that he's done from an innovative standpoint."

In another interview, Payton remembered a Shanahan wrinkle from a 1998 Broncos–Cowboys game. Shanahan split Sharpe wide, beyond the receivers, forcing the defense to declare its coverage. If a cornerback lined up on Sharpe, that meant zone. If a safety or linebacker did, it meant man. The move, copied by virtually everyone, altered football, prompting coaches like Bill Belichick to counter by making safeties and corners interchangeable. "Mike split the atom," Payton said of his fellow Eastern Illinois alum.

As the years passed, defenses became more familiar with the outside zone approach and developed containment strategies that were sometimes effective, but Shanahan continued to innovate. The outside zone would serve as a base, with obvious countermoves, such as the naked bootleg, that proved to be highly productive. Since most of Shanahan's plays, by design, looked identical at the start, defenses were kept off balance. The threat of the wide run set up easy completions for Elway, an aging player who still possessed enough of his once-freakish athleticism to run naked bootlegs and keepers to the backside and throw on the move to targets who were often wide open. It could be a tight end, like future Hall of Famer Sharpe, who instead of holding his block, released to the virtually abandoned backside. Or perhaps the tight end held his block and a receiver came across the formation to fill the empty space.

Once teams adjusted, Shanahan had additional countermoves. The

Broncos ran several plays out of the same formations, such as the three-man bunch (three receivers lined up in a cluster) and two-man stack (one receiver deployed directly behind the other), tweaking them with each week's game plan. The Broncos also became well versed in the *inside* zone approach—a quicker-hitting rushing attack that exploited the expectation of interior defenders that they'd be forced to flow outside. Offensive linemen would go through the early steps they would take on an outside zone run, but the back would be instructed either to cut back right away or plow straight ahead, often catching defenders off guard. In short: *We're going to make you think this is outside zone, and once you react accordingly, we're charging straight ahead and blasting you off the ball.*

Shanahan was pummeling his peers. Davis, also a future Hall of Famer, had his brilliant career derailed by a knee injury early in the 1999 season, when the two-time defending champs were adjusting to life without the retired Elway—and yet, the ground game stayed strong. Olandis Gary, a rookie fourth-round draft pick, rushed for 1,159 yards that season after taking over as the starter in week five. The next year, Mike Anderson, a sixth-round rookie, ran for 1,487 yards and 15 touchdowns. Two seasons later, rookie second-rounder Clinton Portis gained 1,508 yards and ran for 15 TDs. Shanahan had built a machine, and the parts appeared to be more interchangeable than anyone could have predicted.

For 14 years, Shanahan stayed ahead of the game, until Bowlen fired him after an 8–8 season in 2008. It was an abrupt and surprising move that prompted Kyle Shanahan—by then the Texans' offensive coordinator—to alter his perspective on the question of whether he should work for his father. Nothing was promised; any opportunity to join forces needed to be seized. After a year off, Mike returned in 2010 as the head coach in Washington and entrusted the bulk of his offensive responsibilities to the young coordinator who would become that decade's most original football mind. Without realizing it, Mike Shanahan had set up his son to fulfill the promise of the outside zone's potential, and much, much more.

Chapter 3

Hold On to Your Nuts

"Hey Mike," Deion Sanders said to the 49ers' offensive coordinator one day at practice in 1994, his tone and facial expression conveying disapproval. "You've got to talk to your son."

Shanahan braced himself. Sanders, the flamboyant, two-sport star known as "Prime Time," had signed with San Francisco in mid-September, part of an all-out push to overcome the rival Cowboys and win the franchise's fifth Super Bowl. The previous night, 13-year-old Kyle Shanahan had gone to a team function with Sanders and some of his new teammates. Clearly, the kid had done something to leave a poor impression.

"What about?" Shanahan asked the All-Pro cornerback.

Sanders explained that young Kyle had come to him with a confession: While in possession of a No. 21 jersey that Sanders had autographed for him, he'd been offered $150 by a collector to part with it. Kyle had refused, believing it would be a betrayal of the player's trust.

When Sanders found out—a couple of months before his rap song, "Must Be the Money," hit the charts—he was aghast. "Are you a fricking idiot?" he asked the stunned teenager. "Hey, we can get that jersey for 20 bucks! We can go into business, you and me. Never leave money on the table like that!"

The younger Shanahan's response wasn't surprising. Football, to him, was serious business—"life or death," as he'd later describe it. Like most coaches' kids, he and younger sister Krystal understood the volatility of the profession firsthand. Kyle had already moved five times in his young life as his father progressed from college jobs (Minnesota and Florida) to NFL opportunities (Broncos, Raiders, Broncos again, and now 49ers), enduring abrupt and messy firings in L.A. and Denver. To Kyle, games weren't just games—and defeats were potentially cataclysmic. He hated being uprooted, saying goodbye to his friends and switching schools.

"I always looked at the football as a job, 'cause I always looked at it as 'Man, that's where we're gonna live the next year,'" Kyle recalled later on. "What happens on Sunday . . . I'd be so worried going to school on a Monday, the two articles that were gonna come out in the paper that everyone was gonna read, and it was gonna say whether my dad sucked or whether he was good, and it would be, like, kids saying, 'Are you gonna move? Are you not?' . . . I can't imagine how it would be like now with the phones and stuff . . . But you just deal with that mindset always."

As much as he detested the prospect of displacement, Kyle loved the sport. He'd spend Sundays with his mother, Peggy, watching games in person or on television, immersed in the drama. When John Elway famously led the Broncos on "The Drive" in the 1986 AFC Championship Game at Cleveland Municipal Stadium, with Mike Shanahan calling the plays for Denver, Kyle, who'd just turned seven, was back home in Colorado, screaming at the TV for all 15 plays and 98 yards. It made sense that he was drawn to football as a possible vocation—he wanted to play, not coach—though his parents had other ideas. "From a young age, we always thought he'd be a lawyer," Peggy Shanahan said, "because he could argue so well, and he loved to argue so much."

One source of contention was Kyle's schoolwork. He wasn't that into it. Despite his quick mind and obvious intelligence, Shanahan was a B-minus kind of kid. When his parents warned that he'd never get into college without improving his grades, Kyle's ready-made retort was that he'd earn a football scholarship. He'd habitually lose his homework—not to mention, as he got older, his wallet, keys, and cell phone. He'd wait until the night before the test to start studying. He *did* meticulously prepare when it came to his wardrobe. As Peggy recalled, "I mean, he was so picky. I couldn't even dry his shirts. Because they had to just fit in a certain way and if I dried them, then they might fit a little bit different. I had to hang them up. I mean, it was just weird. And he's still that way."

As he entered his teenage years, Kyle had an edge to him that was noticed at 49ers training camp, where he spent three summers as a ballboy. During those five-week stays at hot and dusty Sierra College in Rocklin, California, the offensive coordinator's son got caught up in the prank wars that broke up the two-practices-a-day drudgery. Players and coaches often used rented bicycles to get around campus, and it wasn't uncommon for those bikes to end up in tall trees, hanging above the cafeteria or meeting room—often put there by the same golden right arm that had quarter-backed the 49ers to four Super Bowls in the previous decade. "Well, he was scrappy," recalled the Niners' *other* future first-ballot Hall of Fame quarterback of that era, Steve Young. "We teased a lot; we made fun of everybody. We did practical jokes. It was a pretty tough environment. And I remember Kyle as a little kid, kind of like a little bull—like, he was not afraid. You were like, 'Bro, you do not want to get involved in this stuff.' He had that chippy kind of attitude."

Bunking in a dorm room with his father and Bobb McKittrick, the 49ers' notoriously blunt offensive line coach, Kyle was in football heaven. "Players would take him out," Mike Shanahan recalled. "He could read them as people. He'd tell me about Harris Barton and 'Tom [Rathman], your fullback.' He'd notice things like how they would treat the ballboys. After two years, I realized he was right about all of them."

———

BY MIKE SHANAHAN'S SECOND SEASON WITH THE NINERS, KYLE WASN'T merely reading players as people. As an eighth grader on his middle school football team in affluent Saratoga, situated in the heart of the Silicon Valley, the younger Shanahan began studying how Jerry Rice, John Taylor, and the 49ers' other receivers perfected their craft. Though he started the season as a quarterback, Kyle was hampered by lingering elbow soreness, prompting his father to suggest a position switch. Recalled Mike, "I told him, 'Your elbow bothers you, and with your quickness and your ability, I think you're gonna be a wide receiver.' Back in eighth grade, he'd come into my office, and [by season's end] he had broken down every route Jerry Rice and John Taylor had run, on film."

The next year, Kyle was a standout receiver on Saratoga High's junior varsity team, though he filled in as the starting quarterback in one game and threw a game-winning touchdown on the final play. Meanwhile, the 49ers continued their relentless championship pursuit, with Sanders and fellow future Hall of Famers Rickey Jackson and Richard Dent among those enlisted for the cause. After the 49ers blew out the Chargers in Super Bowl XXIX and the Broncos hired Mike Shanahan as head coach, Kyle moved back to Denver for a third time, enrolling at Cherry Creek High School. He was a 145-pound receiver. He compensated for the lack of size by mastering the intricacies of his position, studying Denver receivers Ed McCaffrey, Rod Smith, and Anthony Miller and mimicking their moves. Sometimes, at the team's training facility, he'd sit in on his dad's team meetings but would tune out while "trying not to fall asleep." On Sundays when the Broncos were at home, Kyle had the best view in the house: he stood next to his father, ensuring that the head coach's communication cords didn't get tangled.

There were additional perks in the offseason. Kyle and his friends would crash spring and summer workouts, both formal and informal, sharpening their routes and catching passes from actual NFL quarterbacks. He got tips from receivers and defensive backs, learning how to create space, recognize leverage, and set up defenders. He loved the game within the game, but not because he had designs on following in his father's footsteps. Kyle's obsession was *playing*, and he looked for any opportunity to give himself an edge, especially given his thin frame and lack of explosiveness.

It was pretty sweet being Mike Shanahan's son during those high school years, as the Broncos rose to prominence, captured their first Super Bowl victory, and repeated the following year. Kyle was a popular kid, though there were always resentful accusations of favoritism. Asked before the Niners' Super Bowl LIV appearance about having grown up with a famous father, Kyle put it this way: "I would never say it's difficult. It gave me a real good life. But yeah . . . When I made the basketball team in high school, it was because of my dad, if you ask the people who didn't make it."

When Kyle suffered a broken collarbone before his senior football season, it looked like he might not play on the next level, after all. Salvation came the following spring when a Duke assistant coach visited the Broncos' facility and noticed Shanahan running routes against Denver's defensive backs. "They go, 'Who's that guy?'" Mike Shanahan recalled. "Well, that's Kyle, he got hurt in camp last year and missed the first few games of the season. He said, 'Can I see all of his routes?' And he saw how Kyle could set people up and offered a scholarship on the spot."

On paper, Kyle's dream had been realized. In practice, however, he was unfulfilled. Duke was a basketball school with strong academics; the football program was almost an afterthought. The 1999 Blue Devils went 3–8 and Shanahan couldn't get on the field in what turned out to be a red-shirt season. Texas coach Mack Brown, who'd recruited Shanahan before the collarbone injury, now expressed interest in bringing him to Austin— though as a walk-on, not as a scholarship receiver. Still, this was a chance to play big-time college football, and he seized it.

When Kyle told his parents he was planning to transfer from Duke to Texas, it was not especially well received. Despite his subpar academic credentials, football had allowed him to get into an esteemed university, and now he was throwing that away.

"What?" Mike Shanahan said, incredulously. "You got a *full scholarship at Duke.* Do you realize what that opportunity is, a full scholarship at Duke? It could set you up for life."

"Dad," Kyle shot back at the Eastern Illinois grad, "you went to a *directional* school. You did OK."

BO SCAIFE WAS HAVING A HIGH SCHOOL GRADUATION PARTY AT DEN-ver's Observatory Park in June of 1999—a bunch of friends, a few kegs, nothing that elaborate. Scaife, a *Parade* All-American tight end at Mullen High who was headed to Texas in another month or so, had a buddy from a rival high school, Cherry Creek, who knew Shanahan, a 1998 graduate.

"Kyle's having a party, too," the friend told Scaife. "He said we should bring everybody over there."

Scaife, surprised, considered the idea.

"Why not?" he said, and soon he and his people were descending upon Mike and Peggy's Cherry Hills home. Kyle hosted some legendary parties in that house, and this was one of them. "It was like *Project X* before *Project X*," Scaife recalled, referring to the 2012 comedy in which three high school friends, in an effort to gain popularity, throw a party that quickly spirals out of control. "It wasn't destructive like that, though. It was a well-organized machine. You're always going to get stragglers and people from other schools and stuff like that, but Kyle was never beefing with people."

Scaife, like most people in the Denver area, had heard descriptors like "entitled" and "spoiled" thrown around in relation to Shanahan. "When you have Shanahan attached to you, everybody's looking at you sideways and sizing you up," Scaife said. "But, once you meet him, it's like, 'You're being an asshole. Like, you do *not* know Kyle. Cause Kyle is cool as shit.' "

Soon, Scaife and Shanahan were part of a close-knit circle of teammates at Texas. Once again, there was skepticism about the skinny white kid with the renowned dad, but Shanahan overcame it. "Kyle's biggest strength was always showing how hard of a worker he was," said Scaife, who is Black. "Running, conditioning, lifting, and stuff like that—that's how he really gained the respect from everybody. Then, once you start hanging out with this dude, it's just like, 'This is a cool-ass white boy.' Down at Texas, a lot of kids grew up in predominantly Black neighborhoods, and they didn't even know how to deal with white people on that level, really. Some didn't have a lot of white teammates; just maybe their teachers. They were standoffish with him, but [eventually] you could see how everyone put their walls down when they got around Kyle. Then they were like, 'This white dude's crazy.' "

Shanahan made it his mission to crack a lineup full of ultratalented skill players, some of whom, like future All-American receiver Roy Williams, were clearly headed for NFL careers. Precise route running was his only hope of standing out, and he got better and better, learning how to make every pattern look the same, until it wasn't.

One spring, Shanahan returned to Colorado at semester's end and reclaimed his spot in Broncos offseason workouts. He was no longer the awkward high school kid living out a scene from a football fantasy camp; now he was a slightly less skinny receiver from a major college program, eager to strut his stuff. In drills without pads and helmets, Shanahan continually got open against Broncos defensive backs, causing a bit of a stir at practice. One by one, professionals played off the line of scrimmage and got burned by the college kid—and would hear all about it from the

Broncos' wide receivers. Most of the DBs either knew Kyle from his high school days and didn't take the ribbing seriously or at least understood that his dad was their boss, and thus the power dynamic was not in their favor. One player, a more recent acquisition named Billy Jenkins, became increasingly unamused.

"Billy says, 'Fuck this shit,'" Mike Shanahan recalled. "He jammed him at the line of scrimmage. They didn't have helmets on or anything, and in fact he jammed him so good . . . Kyle's face was so fucked up, so swollen."

Bloodied, stunned, and embarrassed, Kyle started to leave the field and head toward the training room. His father stopped him. "No," Mike told him. "You go in there, you have no chance. You'll lose all respect."

"Dad," Kyle said, "I can't see."

"You don't have to see. Just give yourself a few minutes and get in the back of the line and do it again."

He did, and earned some credibility among the Broncos players. It was a frequent topic of discussion that night as many of them attended a party in Cherry Hills to celebrate Krystal Shanahan's high school graduation. "He was walking around with his face so messed up," Mike said of his son, "you couldn't even tell it was Kyle."

Recalled Scaife, "His lip was huge—like, it was *huge*. A few drinks in, he wasn't even worried about it. He didn't even care."

In Austin, Shanahan attracted attention because of his maniacal focus on his craft. He hung with a crew that included Scaife and another team-mate who had a famous football father—Chris Simms, son of the Giants' Super Bowl–winning quarterback. Simms, a left-handed passer, and Shanahan fueled one another's obsession with the sport and became very close in the process. How close? Egged on by Scaife and others, Simms and Shanahan had one another's initials tattooed on their ankles. "It was a team thing," Shanahan later insisted. Shanahan, Simms, Scaife, and teammates Montrell Flowers and Rod Babers referred to their close-knit crew as "The Wood," in reference to the 1999 romantic comedy starring Omar Epps, Taye Diggs, and Richard T. Jones. Simms marveled at his friend's energy and passion; he and others gave Shanahan, known to his teammates as "Shan-O," the alternate nickname "Stressball." The quest for improvement was constant. Case in point: Shanahan even sought training tips from the Longhorns track and field coaches in an effort to improve his speed.

"He just saw the game differently," Scaife recalled. "He was very detail-oriented, able to explain stuff. He was coaching and teaching in college—just how to run routes, how to drop your hips, how to get in and out of your breaks, how to use your hands."

It was clear where Shanahan's priorities lay—and where they didn't. As he recalled in 2023, "I went to college to play football." During his first season at Texas, when he was ineligible to play as an incoming transfer, Shanahan, like some of his teammates, had finals scheduled that conflicted with the Longhorns' Holiday Bowl practices. Players were supposed to miss practice to take the exams. Shanahan, unwilling to waste the opportunity to demonstrate his commitment, showed up at practice anyway, even after some of his friends tried to talk him out of doing so. "I know I'll fail the class," Shanahan recalled explaining, "but that's a decision *I'm* making." Sure enough, his C grade dropped to an F. "It shows how one-track my mind was," he said.

Shanahan was intent on earning a scholarship by any means necessary. Fellow receivers, like Williams, who'd go seventh overall in the 2004 draft, and B. J. Johnson, intimidated him with their speed and athleticism. As did the Longhorns' defensive backs. Yet Shanahan, through his route running and ability to manipulate cornerbacks and safeties, got open a *lot* in practice. In one-on-one drills, he was known to make cornerbacks—even Quentin Jammer, the fifth-overall pick in the 2002 draft—look silly, sometimes causing them to flip around awkwardly or even fall to the ground. Brown noticed, giving Shanahan some run during the 2001 season, during which the walk-on caught seven passes.

His personal life also experienced a sudden and unexpected change of direction. On his first summer home from Duke, Shanahan had dated Mandy O'Donnell, who'd been a year behind him at Cherry Creek High School. Now, with Mandy in her junior year at the University of Colorado, they reconnected amid some traumatic circumstances: during a routine outpatient procedure, doctors discovered that Mandy's mother, Nancy, had Stage 4 gallbladder cancer. Kyle served as Mandy's emotional rock, often flying home on weekends. He accompanied Nancy on walks and wrote her letters from Austin. She died at 57 in January of 2002, fewer than three months after her diagnosis.

"He completely stunned me," Mandy later said. "Kyle, hands down, got me through that. After going through that with him, I couldn't imagine being with anyone else. What was so alarming to me, being that young and going through something that devastating, I realized it's not going to be the last sad thing that I go through."

Under happier circumstances, Mandy's acerbic sense of humor became legendary among Shanahan's circle of friends. She knew all about his ravenous social appetite, one that raged on after his younger sister, Krystal, followed him to Texas. During her freshman year, she roomed with Jenna Bush, daughter of the sitting U.S. president, and the two of them often accompanied her big brother and his friends out—along with some serious-looking escorts. "You always had the Secret Service," Scaife recalled. "They would be outside the little bars and clubs we were at. No one even really cared. We were just having a good-ass time." When Mandy and Kyle got serious, she proudly proclaimed to his friends, "Yeah, I shut that shit down."

AFTER A STRONG SERIES OF SPRING PRACTICES IN 2002, SHANAHAN was awarded the much-coveted scholarship. He had arrived, and he wanted more. Now 6-foot-3 and 185 pounds, Shanahan was slated to the be the third receiver for a loaded team, which he hoped would set him up for an NFL career. Back home in Colorado that summer, he went to retrieve a ball one night for the family's black Lab, Magic. As he casually hopped the fence surrounding the property, his hand slipped and disaster struck. He was suspended in midair, the fence's decorative metal tip impaled in his left thigh, too deep to extract. He called out to his friend, Zach Zucker, who was inside the house. As Zucker reached him, Shanahan was pushing off on the fence and freeing his leg. Said Scaife, "He had to push himself off the stake. That was a pretty beast move."

Following two hours of surgery and three layers of stitches, Shanahan cursed his recklessness and started coming to terms with the accident's impact on his football career. He was told it would take a full season to recover; he pushed through the pain, got back onto the field in 18 days, and played in a game seven weeks later. As one teammate recalled, "He worked his ass off; he did everything, around the clock. He was a psycho . . . taking, like, 70 vitamins a day." Said Scaife, "I just remember how bummed he was, but he was a rehab machine."

The missed practice time caused Shanahan to slip down the depth chart, and he never fully regained his speed, such as it was. After finishing the season once again with seven catches, Shanahan received a coveted invitation to the NFL scouting combine. He thought long and hard about his future—and decided to turn it down. "I remember them saying I had a chance to go to the combine," he said on Chris Simms's podcast, *Unbuttoned*, in 2020. "I could pursue this, and that's when I just thought really hard about it and I felt so exhausted with trying to turn myself into something I wasn't. Like, I thought I could maybe go compete and be a last guy [on the roster] and maybe earn a practice squad [spot] one day, but I was never gonna be physical enough to do special teams or anything like that. So, that's when I was like, 'Alright, I want to coach.'"

Once Shanahan made the decision to enter his father's profession, it felt as if the fog had cleared. After years and years of trying to will himself into becoming a high-level player, this felt attainable, if not natural. As he said to Simms in 2020, "I realized within a couple of weeks, like, how much easier this was than playing. I actually felt talented. I felt like, whether it was genes or my life circumstances from growing up, I just felt I had an advantage over most people. And then, when I got around other coaches, I thought everybody was gonna be like my dad. All I knew was my dad. And my dad is still, to this day, the biggest grinder I've ever seen. He just works so hard and is so detailed in everything he does, and I didn't know if I could be like that. [I thought], *Man, I don't know if I can grind as hard as he did. I like to have a little bit more fun.* Then, when I decided to do it and I got into it, I was like, 'Oh my God, not everyone *is* like my dad. That's why he was so good. Oh my gosh, I can be like this, too.'"

Shanahan, determined not to be dismissed as a pure product of nepotism, was opposed to working for his father—but not for his father's friends. He started off at UCLA in 2003 as a graduate assistant on the staff of Karl Dorrell, who'd worked for Mike Shanahan as the Broncos' receivers coach the previous three seasons. That December, he got a call from Jeremy Bates, who was the Tampa Bay Buccaneers' offensive quality control coach. Bates told Shanahan that head coach Jon Gruden was about to promote him to assistant quarterbacks coach, creating a QC opening—which was not yet known to anyone outside the building. Mike Shanahan called Gruden, who agreed to interview Kyle and ultimately gave him the job. It was almost too good to be true: Simms was one of the Bucs' quarterbacks.

As entry-level NFL gigs go for a prospective play caller, it was pretty close to perfect. Gruden had football's highest-volume playbook—"offense on steroids," in Kyle's words—sometimes putting 200 plays into a given week's game plan. "I was able to get so much knowledge there," Shanahan said. "Jon doesn't do anything like [my father]; he does stuff totally different. I had to draw all his plays, and Jon did more plays than anybody in football. So, I actually got to draw and have experience on every play that was being run in the NFL . . . it just put a lot of stuff in my head that I needed to learn."

And that wasn't even the best part. Mike Shanahan, mindful of the advice Bill Walsh had offered at that coaching clinic long ago, understood that the optimal way for Kyle to mold himself into a future head coach was to learn defense. Gruden happened to have one of the most respected defensive strategists in the world, Monte Kiffin, as his coordinator—a position Kiffin had held since 1996, when Tony Dungy began his highly successful run as Tampa Bay's head coach. Kiffin's Tampa 2 scheme, featuring a four-man line, two deep safeties and corners playing a Cover 2 zone, and a rangy, deeply deployed middle linebacker, had helped transform the NFL. The Bucs' top-ranked defense had fueled a Super Bowl–winning performance in January of 2003 and annually ranked among the league's best. Kiffin's staff included one respected veteran position coach in Rod Marinelli (defensive line) and a quartet of younger strategists eager to make a mark: Joe Barry (linebackers), Mike Tomlin (defensive backs), Raheem Morris (assistant defensive backs), and Joe Woods (defensive quality control).

"Hey, you don't know this, but they may have the best defensive staff that you're ever gonna have," Mike Shanahan recalled telling Kyle. "You've got a chance to learn from these guys. You don't realize what an opportunity this is. It's like a who's who at your age. And you're not actually a full-time guy, so they're gonna share things with you that they wouldn't normally share."

After practice each day, Gruden would give Shanahan a long list of plays, and the young QC would go into his office and draw them. At first, that process took eight hours. Soon, Shanahan got faster. That left him time, late in the day, to sit in on defensive meetings, which Kiffin welcomed. Eventually, Shanahan was tasked with compiling the "tip sheets" the coaches used before beginning their week of game-planning. At the time, the Bucs had a bare-bones training facility near the Tampa airport, and those defensive meetings were conducted in a small trailer. Shanahan would sit on the floor in the back of the room, soaking up everything.

The experience was transformative. Eventually, as he'd consume Gruden's offensive playbook, Shanahan would begin to consider those plays from a defensive perspective: *This would be hard on the defense if they're playing this front. What's the linebacker's responsibility here? Because if he's two-gapping, it will be hard for him to stop, but if he's spilling, man, this play sucks.* He was starting to think differently about the game. It wasn't about calling cool plays and seeing them come to life. Instead, it was about knowing a defense's rules and using those rules against it; it was about understanding how defensive players were being coached and exploiting them based on that knowledge.

Sitting there on the trailer floor, Shanahan was mostly an awestruck observer. However, as he became comfortable with his offensive responsibilities, his confidence grew, and his personality began to emerge. This was especially true on the practice field. About five or six months after being hired, Shanahan was gutsy enough to speak his mind. He thought, *Damn, I wish I'd known all this as a player. I could have been so much better. I was focused on the wrong things.* In retrospect, he came on a bit too strong. "It's hard, especially as a young coach, you can't just speak up and give your opinions all the time," Shanahan told me in 2008. "I used to do that and get stares. People would look and think, *Is this guy showing off?* No matter how good I thought the idea might have been, I learned it was better to catch [another coach] on the way out of the meeting and suggest it gently."

Back then, Shanahan's frustration overrode any semblance of tact. Still possessing a receiver's mentality, he grew perplexed by the lack of detail and consistency in the Bucs' approach. It felt like Gruden had overloaded his players with verbiage and route assignments at the expense of precision and clarity. "There's too much gray area," Shanahan might protest during practice. Or, "This rule's not right." Recalled one former Bucs player, "Gruden would just say, 'Run a slant.' And we'd go out there for practice and the ten guys would run the slant ten different ways. And Kyle would be like, 'I don't know how they expect the quarterback to complete any. You've got ten different routes from ten different guys. How do they think [the quarterback's] gonna know where they come out of the break?'" Shanahan's suggestion to Gruden: "It's got to be a three-step slant to marry with the three-step drop of the quarterback. And then we'll find different ways of how we vary it, according to how we're being played."

———

IT WASN'T JUST THE MARRIAGE OF THE QUARTERBACK AND RECEIVER'S footwork, or of the run and the pass, that occupied Shanahan's attention. He and Mandy wed in the summer of 2005, giving him stability at home. Soon, after his second season in Tampa, he and Mandy were on the move, the way his parents had been so many times before. Gary Kubiak, a former Broncos quarterback and offensive coordinator, was hired to coach the Houston Texans in January of 2006 and offered Shanahan a job as his receivers coach. Shanahan accepted, becoming, at 26, the NFL's youngest position coach.

Now, for the first time, Kyle immersed himself in his father's famed offensive system. It was an abrupt transition. His initial reaction: "It was the most boring thing in the world." The Texans had nowhere near the number of plays that Gruden's Bucs did, and the concepts were much simpler. "So, I'm calling my dad and I'm talking to Gary—'How can we do this? We're gonna get killed! We've got to do a lot more.'"

Still, he loved the detail and clarity. "It was very similar to the defense in Tampa with how their run fits were," he recalled. "It was very anal and exact and not a bunch of stuff, but it all fit." As that first season played out, he felt a sense of relief: some of the nuances he'd obsessed over in Tampa weren't a big deal in Kubiak's offense, and it still operated efficiently. And yet, he also felt that there were elements of Gruden's scheme that could spice up his father's attack. *Man,* Kyle would think to himself, *you know how much better we could do if we did it this way, like we did in Tampa?* He began to devise what would become his own offensive philosophy: a mixture of the Gruden-inspired creativity and the beautifully self-contained craftsmanship of his dad's system, always predicated upon the opposing defense's rules and tendencies. Every play, formation, and variation had to have a reason; there had to be a *why.*

There was plenty of skepticism in the building when Kubiak brought in his former boss's son, but that dissipated quickly. "Cynically, you look at him and you're like, '[He's] the skinny dude that got his job because his dad,'" recalled Robert Saleh, then a Texans defensive quality control coach. "But it took about a week to realize, 'Wow, this dude's pretty frickin' good.'" To Sage Rosenfels, the Texans' backup quarterback at the time, the hire felt like "classic NFL nepotism; the guy probably doesn't know his stuff. It didn't take very long to be like, 'Damn, this guy's really good.' And that's unusual."

After a year in his new job, Shanahan was elevated to be the Texans' quarterbacks coach. Now he worked even more closely with Kubiak's offensive coordinator, Mike Sherman, a former Packers head coach with an extensive background in play-action principles. Kubiak's scheme was largely devoid of fakes to the running back, other than its bread-and-butter, change-of-pace call: the natural counterplay to an outside zone run was the naked bootleg, with the quarterback faking the handoff and then rolling back without blockers to the other side of the field, with options to throw to receivers on that side or to pick up yards on the ground by taking advantage of overpursuing defenders. As Shanahan began conjuring play-action possibilities for the Texans attack, he'd sometimes call his father—still the Broncos' head coach—and ask why certain plays weren't in Denver's offense. Naturally, that would spark an argument.

Following the 2007 season, Sherman left to become Texas A&M's head coach, and Kubiak promoted Shanahan again. At 28, he was the NFL's youngest offensive coordinator. Again, many people in the coaching community and beyond believed he'd been handed the opportunity for obvious reasons. "I know it's out there," Shanahan told me shortly before the start of the season. "You get a job this young, people are going to say, 'It's 'cause of your dad' or 'It's 'cause of your name.'" Determined to prove he belonged, Shanahan expanded Kubiak's playbook. When Shanahan put in a couple of play-action calls that had been taught to him in Tampa by former Walsh assistant Paul Hackett, the Bucs' quarterbacks coach in 2005, they worked beautifully. Now the Texans had bootlegs *and* another way to keep defenders honest, and it showed. Houston finished third in total offense in 2008, averaging 382.1 yards per game, and fourth in passing offense. The next year, the Texans were fourth in total offense (383.1 yards per game) and had the league's best passing attack.

This despite the reality that the Texans weren't perceived as a team loaded with offensive talent. The quarterback, Matt Schaub, was a 2004 third-round pick who'd backed up Falcons star Michael Vick for his first three seasons. He wasn't fast or blessed with an amazing arm, but he faithfully followed Shanahan's teachings, went through his reads, and generally got the ball to the place his coordinator wanted it to go. He was mobile enough to throw on the run, typically off of bootlegs, and accurate enough to complete roughly two-thirds of his passes. Then again, there were a *lot* of very open receivers in those years. The Texans had a superstar wideout in Andre Johnson and, in 2009, found an undrafted steal in running back Arian Foster, who eventually developed into a Pro Bowl player. Wide receiver Kevin Walter and tight end Owen Daniels were considered ordinary at best, but with Shanahan scheming them into space, they were potent and prolific.

There was something else going on, too. Shanahan, despite his age and relative inexperience, didn't coach scared. He operated during games with an *I'm good and I know it* cockiness that aligned more with a gangsta rapper's persona than a professorial play caller's. This was not a coincidence. Shanahan idolized Lil Wayne, aka Weezy, the New Orleans rapper (born Dwayne Michael Carter Jr.) who'd burst onto the scene at the turn of the century, when Shanahan was in his formative years at Texas. Lil Wayne's swagger and bombast were legendary, even by hip-hop standards. Shanahan's regard for him was such that, when he and Mandy had their second child in 2008 (daughter Stella had been born the previous year), he persuaded her to name the boy Carter in the rapper's honor. (Eventually, after learning of Shanahan's fandom, the rapper sent signed posters and CDs to father and son—Carter got the non-explicit version—via then 49ers receiver Pierre Garçon, who had a connection to Lil Wayne's manager.)

It didn't take long for Shanahan to establish his personality as an offensive coordinator. In the fifth game of the 2008 season, the Texans, who were 0–4, hosted the Miami Dolphins. Trailing 28–23 in the final minute and facing fourth and ten from their own 36, Houston stayed alive when Schaub threw toward a tightly covered Johnson, who somehow managed to pull the ball away from safety Yeremiah Bell for a spectacular 23-yard catch. Matt LaFleur, an offensive assistant at the time, remembered it as "one of the greatest catches I've ever seen. Schaub just threw it up for him, and Andre went over the top of the defender's head and ripped it away from him. Unbelievable."

With seven seconds to go, Houston faced fourth and two at the Miami 3. It would all come down to one play. Shanahan had an idea. On the previous play, he'd motioned the back to the line of scrimmage, creating an "empty" set, with only Schaub in the backfield. A Dolphins linebacker had vacated the middle of the field to cover the back. By going empty again, Shanahan felt he could bait the Dolphins into playing a similar defensive alignment. That, and the element of surprise, could create an opening for the speed-challenged Schaub—who hadn't broken five seconds in the 40-yard dash during the predraft process—to score on a quarterback draw.

"Hold on to your nuts, guys, quarterback draw!" offensive assistant Mike McDaniel announced in the upstairs coaches' box.

"Oh my God," Saleh said, his heart pounding.

A few seconds later, everyone was celebrating as Schaub lumbered over the goal line. "Kyle, he had some fucking brass balls," LaFleur said. "He didn't give a shit. He just went for it."

Now Shanahan had people's attention. The Texans had just gained a franchise-record 485 yards, with Schaub having thrown for 379—178 to Johnson, who also set a franchise mark. The Texans rallied to finish 8–8, and Shanahan stayed aggressive. Kubiak, Rosenfels said, was "a little more traditional—like, he sort of has his plays he likes, with a few new nuances. NFL coaches have this thing that's like, 'We didn't practice it or even walk through it during the week; we're not going to run it in the game.' Kyle was like, 'Why wait?' He'd spot something and say, 'We'll just change that one route, and we'll just know that guy's gonna run that route instead—this is the coverage they're playing, let's just go and do that.' Very proactive, and a little more of a risk-taker.'"

IN TIME, SHANAHAN AND HIS DISCIPLES WOULD TURN THE FOOTBALL world on its head. The analogy becomes especially appropriate when one considers the bizarre pregame routine that Shanahan adopted when he took over as Houston's offensive coordinator. Four hours before kickoff, he would find a quiet, solitary place—a vacant storage room, a shower stall, or even a janitor's closet—to examine his game plan, section by section. (Becoming a head coach in 2017, with his own private dressing area, made things easier.) He'd begin visualizing the plays, sometimes calling in other coaches to clarify or justify specific routes, protections, or blocking schemes. He'd insist upon having four red pens and coffee that was just the right temperature. Shortly before taking the field, he'd hold a good luck charm given to him during the week by Carter and look at a picture of his kids (daughter Lexi arrived in 2013). Finally, in an effort to clear his mind and reduce stress, Shanahan, a yoga practitioner, would stand on his head for 45 seconds before heading to the tunnel.

For Shanahan, the challenge was to slow down the thoughts racing through his head and hyperfocus on the task at hand, one play at a time. He tried to fight against his darker impulses: a quick temper, a tendency to unload on those around him when the plan executed properly, a penchant for recklessness when caution was the smarter course of action. The plays he called were generally well designed; the detail with which he coached set up his players for success. He had built-in adjustments for a defense's countermoves, and a clarity of purpose. In a sport that could feel chaotic and arbitrary, he often felt in control.

He wasn't just running a knockoff of the Mike Shanahan offense. He strove to master the essential elements of his father's existing system while continuing to evolve whenever possible. One of his first and most pivotal innovations was to tighten the splits of receivers in many formations, expanding upon a practice unveiled, on a limited basis, by his dad in Denver. In the West Coast offense, wide receiver was a literal term, with the X and Z receivers lined up reasonably close to the left and right side-lines, respectively. Kyle moved them in, closer to the tight ends and tackles, giving him a multitude of new ways to manipulate defenders and create openings in both the running and passing games.

Originally, the idea was that condensing the splits could dictate lever-age on the back end of the defense. Because there was now so much room between the receiver and the sideline, the cornerback lined up against him would no longer be able to play "head up" (directly opposite the receiver) or "inside leverage" (lining up on the receiver's inside shoulder and working him toward the boundary) techniques, with time to make up the difference on balls thrown to the outside. Instead, corners would inevitably deploy in an "outside leverage" alignment designed to funnel everything inside. Tightened splits also dissuaded cornerbacks from playing "press" coverage and jamming receivers on the line, because there was now so much ground to cover on both sides once the receivers broke free. For the most part, in response to the tightened split, the corners would align well behind the line of scrimmage and give the receivers cushions—all of which played into Shanahan's hands.

Being able to predict a cornerback's leverage and deployment opened up all sorts of possibilities. Shanahan began installing "widened" versions of existing routes to take advantage of the favorable angles and extra room. It made it harder to stop "stack" and "bunch" formations designed to create confusion off the ball and tangle up defensive backs. The beauty was that he also found that tightened splits created an edge on running plays as well.

Receivers had always been used as essential blockers in his father's scheme, especially on outside zone runs. Now, however, they were better able to take favorable angles and reach safeties, especially a safety that dropped down into the box, closer to the line of scrimmage, as an eighth run defender. That, in turn, often forced unblocked cornerbacks to tackle the ballcarrier—they were coached to replace the "cracked" safety and fill the hole—creating even more discomfort for those playing the sport's most vulnerable position. "There's nobody the offense wants making tack-les more than corners," Rosenfels said. "So, they force corners to make tackles a lot, and put a lot of pressure on them. But then when a corner gets too aggressive, now you go with some sort of play-action over the top of his head. And if they're going to play back a little bit because they're worried about the play-action, now you're going to have six- and seven-yard runs all day."

The philosophy also took pressure off the quarterback. Traditionally, the safety's presence in the box triggered an audible—or, in Shanahan's offense, a "can" (which meant "canning" the play and pivoting to the second of two predetermined options)—to a pass, or to a run to the weak side. With tightened splits, the receiver would theoretically still be able to reach the safety in time, so there was less danger of the play being blown up.

As Shanahan worked on his scheme, he made a change to the receivers' footwork that reflected the desire to have them take on safeties at the optimal angle. Explained T. C. McCartney, who later coached under Shanahan in Cleveland and San Francisco, "They're a step off compared to everyone else. [Other teams' receivers traditionally] put their inside foot up, whereas if you watch all Kyle's tape, when you get inside the numbers [in condensed splits], they put their outside foot up. They do it so they can block the safety and not false-step—so they can run to bounce reads and wide zones." Shanahan, in turn, timed up his receivers' routes to reflect the outside-foot-up stance. Said McCartney, "They built their two biggest routes—drift routes and scout routes—off footwork and being inside the numbers. They built all their routes off that, and it times up better." The NFL being a copycat league, other offensive coaches stole the footwork—without necessarily understanding the rationale behind it. As McCartney put it, "Some teams do it and some teams don't, but nobody really knows why. They just watch Kyle do it and count the steps."

Shanahan, from his experiences as a scrappy walk-on receiver at Texas, understood the importance of precision and technique. Defenders had to be threatened by every break, which meant that everything, be it a run or pass, had to look to the same. No play ever stood alone; it always existed as part of a larger plan. Sometimes, a two-yard run or routine screen pass was called simply for the purpose of showing it to the defense, a setup for a similar-looking play with a twist later in the game. His thought process wasn't *This play works.* Rather, it was *How do they take this play away? And then what do we do?*

It wasn't just *what* Shanahan was teaching, either; it was *how.* One of the reasons he didn't like school was because most of the instruction didn't align with his natural way of learning. To him, a lot of time and effort was wasted trying to absorb unessential information; he preferred clarity and cutting to the chase. As a result, for all the detail of his system, he came up with some all-encompassing rules that simplified many of his players' studying processes and ensured a better chance of collective success. It was strictly *need to know.* Most coaches taught run plays to wide receivers as though they were offensive linemen. Shanahan decided that was an unnecessary overload; the receivers didn't need to know the different combination blocks that were happening in the trenches. On an outside zone run coming to the receiver's side, the receiver simply needed a clear-cut rule that applied to all situations. The Texans' playbook might have had 40 variations on outside zone runs, with names such as 18 Weak, 18 Wanda, 18 Mike, 18 Quatro, 18 Force, 18 Arc, 18 Release, 18 Structure, 18 Support, and 18 Weezy. Shanahan decided, *No no no—everything's 18! Your rules are "18." You have the corner and the safety with push-track technique, no matter what.*

"That way of teaching was revolutionary in the game of football," said McDaniel. "Receivers only needed to know how eight or nine techniques should be blocked; you lump a ton of shit together. Well, that's all over our offense, from techniques, to play calls, to the way we learn—everything. Kyle's genius was creativity, but it was also how to manage information for players so that the sum of the parts would be less than the whole. And that's how we've all learned."

The kid who hated schoolwork was now becoming an accomplished instructor in the only field he'd ever loved. One thing hadn't changed from his childhood, however: success was a prerequisite—or Shanahan would have to move.

Chapter 4

Not That Type of Coach

I f Raheem Morris ever needed confirmation that Kyle Shanahan would have his back, he received it early one morning at the 2005 NFL scouting combine in Indianapolis. Morris, the Tampa Bay Buccaneers' assistant defensive backs coach, had just finished conducting informal interviews at the train station in downtown Indianapolis, a hectic scene in which lower-level coaches and draft prospects mingled in an effort to get acquainted. Now he, his friends Shanahan and Dan Quinn, and a group of other assistants from various teams were ready to hit the town. This was normal behavior at the combine, which is essentially a spring break for coaches and talent evaluators, many of whom party into the wee hours before getting up and resuming their evaluation process.

A little after 2 a.m., as Morris and his friends were attempting to enter the Have a Nice Day Café, he was abruptly tackled by a group of police officers, who handcuffed him after applying a chokehold while pinning down his face on the cement. Shanahan, perceiving the incident as racially motivated, lost his mind. Said Shanahan's longtime confidant Mike McDaniel, "Kyle didn't even realize that overt racism existed like that firsthand. So, he's asking for badge numbers and shit."

The cops didn't take it well.

"Literally two minutes later," Morris recalled, "he's laying down right next to me. We didn't know what was going on. They put us both in the wagon and took us in."

It was not an ideal situation for the son of a well-known NFL head coach, but it *was* a sign of Shanahan's ride-or-die mentality when it came to Morris, who'd already become one of his closest friends. On paper, they had little in common. Morris had grown up in the shadow of Newark International Airport in New Jersey before playing college football at Hofstra. He wasn't the son of a two-time Super Bowl–winning coach; Morris's father held three jobs at one point, working 20 hours a day, six days a week, to help the family make ends meet. Yet he and Shanahan had bonded over their shared thirst for football knowledge, underscored by the young offensive quality control coach's constant presence in the Bucs' defensive meetings. Morris and Shanahan each had a no-bullshit mentality. The difference was that Shanahan could sometimes come off as entitled, abrasive, or condescending, whereas Morris possessed natural charm and a sense of humor.

That didn't help at the Have a Nice Day Café. A few hours later, Morris left the police precinct with no wallet and no explanation. Years on, he'd receive an apology from the Indianapolis Metropolitan Police Department, saying the officers had mistaken Morris for a suspect in another incident. At the time, however, Morris had to deal with the potential fallout from his arrest.

Shanahan, charged with misdemeanor intoxication, would take the much bigger hit. Because of his famous father, he was ridiculed by several prominent media members, portrayed as a poster child for what was wrong with the profession.

"Kyle had to fly back to Tampa, do a press conference, go through a whole bunch of stuff," Morris said. "He was a name; his dad was a head coach. Kyle was really pissed. It was bullshit. Then they pulled his picture up on *SportsCenter* of him being plastered at a Texas party when he was in college. He was like, 'That wasn't even [from] that night!'"

THREE YEARS AND TEN MONTHS LATER, MORRIS WOULD BE THE BUCCA-neers' head coach. Thrust into the job with zero warning at the age of 32, Morris needed an offensive coordinator. His first call was to Shanahan, who'd just finished his first season in that role for the Texans. Soon, Morris realized he needed a Plan B. "He made too much money," Morris recalled.

How Morris had ended up in a position to assemble a staff was one of the wilder stories of that era. No one had seen it coming—least of all Morris, whose life changed when he was chopping it up at the barbershop on a Friday afternoon in January of 2009, getting ready for a big weekend in Tampa. At the time, Morris, a member of Jon Gruden's staff, had been newly promoted to defensive coordinator. He had dinner plans with Rondé Barber, the team's star cornerback—a player who, at 33, was his elder.

Morris' cell phone rang, and he answered. It was Bruce Allen, the Bucs' general manager.

"Hey, can you come into the office? The Glazers want to see you," Allen said, referring to the team's owners.

"Uh-oh," Morris said. "Am I in trouble?"

"No," Allen assured him. "They just want to talk to you."

At that point, Allen didn't know why the Glazers (brothers Bryan, Joel, and Ed) wanted to talk to Morris—and Morris didn't know where to find his bosses. The Bucs had just opened a brand new training facility, and the young coach hadn't yet learned his way around the building. Instead, he went to Allen's office, and the GM walked him through the back door of the team's draft room and into the meeting.

Allen left. Then Morris's world shifted.

"What do you think about being a head coach?" one of the Glazers asked.

At first, Morris was confused. A week earlier, he'd interviewed for the Denver Broncos' head coaching job—one that had opened after the shocking dismissal of Mike Shanahan. The vacancy had since been filled by Patriots offensive coordinator Josh McDaniels. Morris assumed the question related to his recently completed interview, and he began to describe the experience.

"No," one of the brothers interrupted. "We mean now. Here."

Morris gulped. The Bucs had a high-profile head coach to whom he felt immense loyalty. Gruden had run the show in Tampa since 2002, when the Bucs spent two first-round picks, two second-round selections, and $8 million to pry him from the Oakland Raiders—only days after Morris had come aboard as a defensive quality control coach. Less than a year later, Gruden coached the Bucs to a Super Bowl XXXVII blowout of the Raiders to give the franchise its first championship. Tampa Bay had gone 9–7 in

2008. No one believed Gruden's job might be in jeopardy, and Morris definitely didn't want to be the reason his boss got fired.

So, Morris politely told the Glazers no. They shook their heads.

We're firing Jon, they assured Morris. *We're moving on. We want to move forward with you. You'd be the first choice, as opposed to us going through the whole process.*

Morris remained noncommittal. The whole thing seemed surreal. Two years earlier, his close friend Mike Tomlin had been hired as the Pittsburgh Steelers' head coach at the age of 34. In another 16 days, Tomlin would hoist a Lombardi Trophy in the Bucs' home stadium after the Steelers' dramatic Super Bowl XLIII victory over the Arizona Cardinals. The door finally seemed to be opening for young, Black assistants.

It wouldn't be the smoothest transition. The Glazers told Morris they planned to fire Allen, too, and usher in a new era by cutting costs—meaning they'd be getting rid of many of the veterans who'd helped Morris become a hot prospect in the first place. They were going young and cheap, in what amounted to a full rebuild. Morris, however, had been betting on himself for a long time, since his reluctant stint as a de facto assistant coach for his old Pop Warner team, the Irvington (New Jersey) Golden Knights, during his sophomore year of high school—after his parents decided his grades weren't good enough and forced him to sit out the season. Becoming an NFL head coach would be to realize a long-held dream, one that was coming true about a decade before he ever expected it to.

Later that evening, Morris—now en route from the facility to Bryan Glazer's house—texted Gruden, who'd already been given the news of his dismissal, and told him he'd accept the job only if the outgoing coach gave his blessing.

"Go for it," Gruden replied. "Take it and run with it."

So, Morris, who still hadn't finished filling out his defensive staff and was scheduled to interview one position coach candidate the next morning, accepted the job. So much for a relaxing weekend. "It was eerie," he'd later recall. "It was all happening so fast."

IN FAIRNESS, THE FAST-TRACKING OF RAHEEM MORRIS HAD BEEN IN
motion for a long time. He'd made it out of Irvington, rife with violent
crime and crack cocaine, thanks partly to the dedication of his parents. At
one point, Morris's father, Hilton Vaughn, held two full-time jobs and a
part-time job concurrently, meaning he spent those 20 hours a day, six days
a week fixing buses, working as a distributor for a pharmaceutical company, and driving a delivery truck. Raheem's ability to land a scholarship
to play college football was obviously a huge boon.

The recruiting pitch from Hofstra, a Long Island–based university
about 50 miles east, turned out to be prophetic. Head coach Joe Gardi, a
former Jets defensive coordinator during the Sack Exchange era, said to
Morris on his official visit, "Let me tell you about *nepotism*: Raheem, you're
going to play for me for years, and you're going to coach for me eventually."
Morris wasn't sure what to make of that, but Gardi sold him in other ways,
too. "I don't know if it was legal," Morris said, laughing, "but he took us to
dinners. 'Rah, you want to go eat? I got a great Italian spot.' And he'd throw
me the keys, and [the other recruits and I] would go to eat in restaurants."

Sure enough, Morris signed a letter of intent. The coaches saw him as
a natural leader. Playing alongside fellow safety Lance Schulters, who'd go
on to have a ten-year NFL career after being picked in the fourth round of
the 1998 draft by the 49ers, it was tough for Morris to stand out. He made
a major impression, though.

"He was a safety, and he was a great communicator," remembered
Washington Commanders coach Dan Quinn, who was Hofstra's defensive
line coach from 1996 until 1999 and defensive coordinator in 2000. "He
was already coaching; he was just [concurrently] playing, too. He had such
a good way to communicate to players. He could connect with anybody.
That's a pretty rare person—there aren't a lot of leaders that are like that.
But Raheem was like that as a player. Offensive player, defensive player,
anybody would have fought for him. Long story longer, his superpower is
his ability to connect with people, tell the truth, come at you. He can disagree with you and not be disagreeable or make you feel shitty about it."

Shortly after the completion of his senior season, Morris, who'd
majored in physical education, was fulfilling a student-teaching require-
ment and confronting his football mortality. "The NFL dream had just

been shot in the face," he remembered. "I was sad about that. I got some love [from lesser pro leagues], Canada, and stuff like that. But I was gonna finish college."

When discussing his future with a student-teaching advisor, Morris revealed that he hoped to become a coach.

"You can coach," she replied, "but your money's going to come from education, from being a teacher, so you should probably focus on that."

Thought Morris, *Not that type of coach.*

He wasn't trying to be a dude on a playground with a whistle; he wanted to coach in stadiums full of fans and TV cameras. Gardi hired him as a graduate assistant, making him responsible for tasks such as video breakdown, computer-input analysis, coaching the scout team, and developing scouting reports. After a year at Cornell as a defensive backs coach, Morris made a lateral move back to Hofstra, joining an impressive staff that included Quinn (a future NFL head coach) and Joe Woods (later an NFL defensive coordinator for three teams). It was, in Quinn's words, "a good time for a bunch of young coaches that were hungry to do good shit." Morris would make a strong impression upon a visitor in the spring of 2001, as Hofstra ran through a practice in the indoor bubble they shared with the Jets, whose training facility at the time abutted the campus in Hempstead, New York. Herman Edwards, a former NFL defensive back who'd just been hired as the Jets' head coach, walked over to check out the Pride's practice. While standing with Gardi, Edwards—who at the time was one of three Black head coaches in the NFL—noticed Morris putting the defensive backs through a spirited set of drills.

"Who's that?" Edwards asked Gardi, who proceeded to extol the virtues of a former player who viewed him as a surrogate father—or, in Morris's words, "my Football Dad."

When practice ended, Edwards approached Morris and introduced himself.

"What are you doing this summer?" asked Edwards, who then offered Morris a training camp gig as a defensive coach under the league's minority intern program. Morris parlayed that into an off-the-books arrangement in the fall; he worked on special projects for Dave Merritt, the Jets' linebackers coach. "I basically turned it into a year [with the

Jets]," Morris recalled. "I was literally across the street, working full time at Hofstra, and I was able to go over [and help]. It was awesome. Herm was unbelievable."

The following February, Edwards called Morris with an idea. The Bucs had just fired highly successful head coach Tony Dungy while pledging to retain his entire defensive staff. Dungy, quickly snapped up by the Colts, had poached defensive quality control coach Alan Williams, creating an opening. A couple days later, Morris got a call from someone purporting to be Monte Kiffin, the Bucs' idiosyncratic and much-admired defensive coordinator. "Heard a lot about you," the caller told Morris. "Just want to bring you down for a small interview." Morris was skeptical at first, believing one of his friends was pranking him by imitating Kiffin's high-pitched twang. He was finally convinced of the call's legitimacy when Gardi told Morris, "Well, I just got a call from Monte Kiffin. He wants to bring you down and interview you, buddy. Go down there. Be your best self."

Morris flew to Tampa, checked into the InterContinental Hotel, and went to bed. The next morning, he exited the lobby to find the car that would take him to the Bucs' facility. "I walk out, and I'm thinking some intern's going to grab me," Morris said. Instead, there was Kiffin—wearing gray sweats and raring to commence one of his "legendary" (in Morris's words) and very hands-on interviews.

Sure enough, Kiffin soon had Morris drawing plays and formations on a greaseboard in his office, teaching him concepts that he then asked the young coach to replicate. He later took Morris out to the practice field and had him simulate a series of defensive backs drills. Then it was time for each of Kiffin's position coaches to size up the candidate. Linebackers coach Joe Barry gave Morris a document detailing various defenses and asked him to re-create it within a fixed time period. When Barry returned, he looked at Morris's submission and said, "Man, this is great," before disappearing. Morris's next meeting, with defensive line coach Rod Marinelli, also seemed promising. Marinelli waxed poetic about some of the great coaches he'd worked with, handed Morris an article to read, and left without grilling the interviewee.

Morris had reason to be confident. He'd become familiar with Kiffin's signature Tampa 2 scheme during his time with the Jets, with safety

Damien Robinson—a former Bucs player the team had signed in free agency—providing insights as Edwards's staff adopted some of the same principles. He was feeling pretty good about things until Tomlin, the Bucs' newly hired defensive backs coach, entered the room.

"Dude," Tomlin said, fixing his gaze on Morris, "you're not going to scam me. Who taught you the fucking defense?"

Morris smiled and came clean, telling Tomlin about his experiences with the Jets.

"Good," Tomlin replied, "because you weren't scamming *me*. I knew you had something up your sleeve. But I like you."

A friendship was born, and soon Morris and Tomlin were workshopping ways to improve the secondary. Just hours after Morris's hiring as a quality control coach, the Bucs shook up the football world by swinging the blockbuster deal for Gruden, who, after reviving the Raiders, had grown dissatisfied in Oakland, having clashed with owner Al Davis over numerous issues, including his value. Morris rode the wave, earning a promotion to defensive assistant in 2003 and assistant defensive backs coach the following season, when he formed a close bond with the newly hired Kyle Shanahan.

———

MORRIS'S CLOSEST COACHING FRIENDS, SHANAHAN AND TOMLIN, would both leave the Bucs after the 2005 season. So would Morris, who, after some soul-searching (and despite lobbying by Allen, the Bucs' GM, to stick around), decided to accept a job as Kansas State's defensive coordinator. Morris, however, insisted on remaining with the Bucs for the remainder of the season, delaying his arrival on campus for more than a month. After the Bucs' first-round playoff defeat to Washington, two private planes sat waiting on the nearby airport tarmac: one, sent by the Minnesota Vikings, to pick up Tomlin, their new defensive coordinator; the other, sent by the Wildcats, to transport Morris to Manhattan, Kansas.

During his first season at Kansas State, Morris got a call from Allen, who offered him a chance to return as a position coach, in charge of the defensive backs. Two years later, Kiffin left to serve as defensive coordinator for his son, Lane, who'd just become the University of Tennessee's head coach. Morris, picked as Kiffin's replacement, was still interviewing prospective position coaches (including Barry, whom he'd told to stay in town following an interview, in anticipation of his return as linebackers coach) when he went to the barbershop that Friday afternoon and got the phone call summoning him.

Shortly after accepting the Glazers' offer to succeed Gruden, Morris got a call from Tomlin, who was preparing to coach the Steelers in the 2008 AFC Championship Game. In describing what awaited his friend, Tomlin chose a not-so-subtle metaphor.

"Dude," Tomlin said, "there's a tube over your desk, and shit's just gonna fall out of it, and you've got to handle it. That's exactly what [the job] is."

One of the first things Morris had to handle was a salary purge that would result in the abrupt release of many of his favorite players. The Bucs had already moved on from a pair of future Hall of Famers, safety John Lynch and defensive tackle Warren Sapp, who'd fueled their Super Bowl victory. A third, Barber, was spared during the housecleaning. A fourth, linebacker Derrick Brooks—an eventual first-ballot selection—wasn't so fortunate; he got the bad news via a call from Morris. So did three offensive veterans—running back Warrick Dunn and receivers Joey Galloway and Ike Hilliard—who were older than the new head coach. The franchise also moved on from quarterback Jeff Garcia, linebacker Cato June, defensive end Kevin Carter, and cornerback Phillip Buchanon, among others. The coach called them all.

"We basically had a team reset," he recalled, "and we're moving on from all these veteran players . . . [including] all the people that really kind of helped me become a head coach. I felt obligated to call."

At the time, only Lane Kiffin had become an NFL head coach at a younger age during the Super Bowl era than Morris had, and Kiffin's recently completed fiasco of a stint with the Raiders had lasted just 20 games. Eight years later, both would be eclipsed by an even younger coach: Sean McVay, who was 30 when the Rams hired him in 2017. At the time, though, even McVay got swept up in the Bucs' 2009 purge: after having spent the previous season as an offensive assistant under Gruden, McVay was not retained by Morris, something the two coaches would later joke about after becoming good friends and, eventually, head coach and defensive coordinator of a Super Bowl–winning Rams team.

Morris's first year in charge was a real struggle. Part of the Bucs' plan, enunciated to Morris before his hiring, was to install a pair of experienced coordinators. As so often happens when NFL coaches aren't afforded full control of their staffing decisions, the arranged marriages did not go well. After the third preseason game, Morris fired offensive coordinator Jeff Jagodzinski, the former head coach at Boston College, and replaced him with Greg Olson. Meanwhile, veteran defensive coordinator Jim Bates had insisted on a switch from the Tampa 2 scheme to a two-gap system, and the Bucs' defense seemed to lose its identity.

The Bucs lost their first seven games under Morris. The seventh of those defeats was particularly dismal: a 35–7 thrashing by the New England Patriots in London. Unlike normal road games, the Bucs didn't head straight from the stadium to the airport; instead, they returned to the team hotel and flew back to Tampa in the morning. The front office decided to set a curfew, which Morris didn't think was a great idea—players weren't used to having their behavior monitored after games, and the Bucs were heading into a bye week. Still, he went with the edict and told the players to abide by it. Upon returning to the hotel, Morris encountered a small party in the lobby—the brainchild of another team official, and another idea he didn't love—and stuck around and mingled. Long after the assigned curfew, a group of players walked through the front entrance. One of them, second-year cornerback Aqib Talib, had already been immersed in enough off-the-field drama that Morris had publicly labeled him a "wild child." Trying to head off trouble, Morris confronted him and told him to go to his room. Talib resisted, prompting former Bucs fullback Mike Alstott to say, "You should be in bed."

"Motherfucker, I don't know you!" Talib screamed, and things degenerated from there, with Morris loudly breaking up the interaction. There were a *lot* of witnesses, and when news of the incident leaked, it helped fuel the preexisting perception that Morris was blurring lines that most head coaches don't cross. As a single man in the same age range as many of his players—and someone who enjoyed hitting the town—Morris didn't think it was a big deal, even when he hung with some of the dudes on his roster. After all, that ability to connect with and relate to the people in uniform had been a big reason he'd gotten the job.

The headaches continued. After Tampa's tenth game, Morris took over defensive coordinator duties from Bates and brought back the Tampa 2. The Bucs finished 3–13. Josh Freeman, selected 17th overall in the 2009 draft out of Kansas State, had become the team's starting quarterback, reflective of a relentless push to get younger. Mistakes and indecision had ensued.

Looking back, Morris wishes he'd been better equipped to manage some of the shit falling out of Tomlin's metaphorical tube. "Things were coming out that you've got to handle," Morris said, "and I handled some well—I made some quick, fast, decisive decisions. But there were other things that you can't handle well because you don't know exactly how to do it. You wish you could do some of those things better. You always learn from those experiences."

In his second season, Morris suddenly seemed to have figured it out. The Bucs went 10–6, narrowly missing a playoff berth. Freeman looked like a rising star, throwing for 25 touchdowns and only six interceptions. Morris finished second to Bill Belichick in Coach of the Year voting. The Glazers rewarded him with a contract extension. The team was a trendy pick to make a playoff run heading into the following season.

Then it all came crashing down. Freeman backslid to an alarming degree. The Bucs, with the NFL's youngest roster, handled the heightened expectations poorly. There was drama in the locker room. Morris thought he could tamp it down. He was wrong.

"You take some unnecessary chances when you're young, because you feel like you can handle everything," he said later. "You can't handle everybody's problems, but when you're younger, you feel like you can."

After a 3–1 start in 2011, Tampa lost 11 of its final 12 games and had the league's worst scoring defense. At season's end, the Glazers fired Morris and replaced him with Rutgers coach Greg Schiano, a notorious taskmaster with close ties to Belichick. Morris was no longer a wunderkind; he was now a failed head coach who needed a new job.

One of the first people to call him following his dismissal was Kyle Shanahan.

FOR YEARS, SHANAHAN HAD BEEN TELLING PEOPLE HE TRUSTED THAT Morris was a star. Two weeks into his Bucs quality control tenure, Shanahan called his father and said, "Do whatever you can do to hire this Mike Tomlin guy. But if you can't get him, you have to get his assistant, Raheem Morris. They both will be head coaches eventually."

Morris's predicament post-firing resonated deeply with Mike Shanahan, who was still scarred by his rocky 20-game tenure with the Raiders two decades earlier. He hired Morris as his defensive backs coach, giving his staff yet another youthful voice heading into the 2012 season.

Recalled Morris, "That was one of the better moments, for me, as a young guy. I'd just come from being a head coach, and then to be around him, and to be around that kind of lineage of experience. I just feel like Mike made everything feel easy."

Morris fit right in with the crew, ultimately lending a defense-centric perspective as they scrambled to revamp their scheme for Robert Griffin III in 2012. And while he still liked to go out and have fun, he was growing up and calming down. A lot of that had to do with him falling in love. During the 2013 offseason, he bought an engagement ring and had it shipped to the house in Tampa he shared with Nicole Moulton. She signed for the package, which Raheem told her was a thumb drive containing some coaching-related files.

She was still in the dark—literally—when he decided to pop the question, as the two were lying in bed late one night. What happened next confounds her to this day. "Guess what he does after? Goes to sleep. He can fall asleep in two seconds, when he wants to. Unfazed by anything; most adaptable human in the world. I'm like, 'You're seriously going to go to bed? You just proposed to me! I have to tell my family and friends!' And then I just sat there, staring at the ceiling, wondering, 'How are we going to get from A to B?' He's snoring, already at B."

For Morris, it was a lot more relaxing than being in a paddy wagon with Shanahan—the ultimate *ride or die*.

Chapter 5

Psychopath Ballboy

Growing up in a single-parent household in Greeley, Colorado, Mike McDaniel didn't have much in the way of extravagant material possessions.

What *no one* could take away from him: his unflinching love for the Denver Broncos.

Each summer, the Broncos would head 75 miles north and spend a month or more getting ready for the upcoming season in Greeley, where McDaniel's mother, Donna, worked as a credit consultant at a beef company. Money was tight, and child care was expensive, so Donna came up with a creative solution to occupy her only child. From the time he was eight, Mike would ride his bike 20 minutes to the University of Northern Colorado campus and spend his late-July and August days watching the Broncos' training camp practices and soaking up the scene.

Training camp was a mecca for the hopeful and the devoted, and McDaniel was both. Shortly before his seventh birthday, having already enunciated his dream of one day suiting up for the team he loved, McDaniel watched the Broncos reach the Super Bowl for the third time in four seasons, only to experience the cruelest of outcomes: a whipping of epic proportions, even more severe than the two that had immediately preceded it. The Broncos still had John Elway, providing at least some optimism that the team could bring home the state's first major professional sports championship. But, by the summer of 1993, with the Broncos coming off an 8–8 season and having missed the playoffs for the second time in three years, only the true believers like McDaniel still thought the Lombardi Trophy was within reach.

It wasn't just Elway whom McDaniel idolized. The ten-year-old could rattle off the attributes of players up and down the roster. For example, newly signed combo back Robert Delpino, acquired in the NFL's first true class of unrestricted free agency, carried the promise of physical short-yardage running, sure-handed pass catching out of the backfield, and stout blocking. When McDaniel had a chance to get Delpino's autograph after an afternoon practice, he did everything he could to seize that opportunity—twice.

After pushing his way through the crowd outside Lawrenson Hall and waiting for Delpino to make his way through the somewhat anarchic receiving line, McDaniel secured the running back's signature on a football card from Delpino's days with the Rams. Now, the plan was to get him to sign a second card, but McDaniel—as usual—had thought it through and was already a couple of steps ahead. He was wearing a brand new fitted Charlotte Hornets hat, a gift from his mother to reward him for doing well in school. The hat, in all its bright-teal splendor, was not subtle. McDaniel worried that he'd be recognized as a double-dipper. He placed the hat on the stone wall, positioned himself accordingly, and surreptitiously scored the second autograph. When he went back to retrieve the hat, it was gone.

McDaniel panicked, cursing himself for his greed. Sure, he'd wanted that second autograph, but he valued that hat more. He looked around frantically; soon, tears streamed down his face. The boy eventually caught the attention of a man who asked him what had happened; McDaniel politely answered that his new fitted Charlotte Hornets hat had disappeared, describing it in scrupulous detail. The man, Broncos video operations assistant Gary McCune, went back to check the lost and found and came up empty. Struck by the child's sincerity, he asked McDaniel to repeat the description, right down to the size. After work, McCune went to the Greeley Mall, found a similar hat, and bought it. The next day, he recognized McDaniel, brought him into the Broncos' video room, and presented him with the new hat, complete with attached price tag.

"I-I can't take that," McDaniel stammered. "It's too nice."

The boy was a little unsettled. He had his reasons. Above all, he hadn't had much exposure to generosity from an adult male. He'd never known his father, who died in a car accident when Mike was four. His mother was estranged from many of her family members, who'd ostracized her because she'd married a Black man and who had, by extension, collectively forgone a relationship with her biracial child. Donna and Mike had pretty much gone it alone.

McCune, sensing the boy's trepidation, insisted that it would be OK. He pulled out a business card. "I'll tell you what," he said. "Show this to your parents. If they're wondering why some man is buying you a hat, tell them to call me."

Donna called. When the weekend came, she accompanied Mike to Broncos camp and they watched practice from inside the ropes, as McCune's guest. Soon after, she and McCune started dating. That led to some awkward moments. One day, as McCune rode by on a Gator with other Broncos staffers while heading to practice, the guileless McDaniel saw him and yelled out, "My mom will meet you at eight tonight!" McCune took endless grief from his colleagues for that one.

Three years later, McCune married Donna and became Mike's stepfather. They moved to the suburbs south of Denver, and the now-teenaged McDaniel's affection for the Broncos only intensified. He returned to Greeley for training camp in 1997—this time, thanks to McCune, as a Broncos ballboy. The franchise constituted a major part of his identity; that was an understatement.

In 1996, Mike Shanahan's second season as Denver's head coach, the Broncos emerged as the best team in the AFC, and possibly all of football. Winning the top seed in the conference after a 13–3 regular season, Denver hosted a divisional-round playoff game against the Jacksonville Jaguars and suffered one of the most stunning upsets in NFL postseason history. The Jaguars, in their second year of existence, had only qualified for the playoffs because future Hall of Fame kicker Morten Andersen shanked a 30-yard field goal that would have knocked them out on the final play of the regular season. The 14-point underdogs scored on six consecutive possessions, including a field goal early in the fourth quarter that should never have been: the Broncos had forced a punt earlier on the drive, but defensive tackle Michael Dean Perry didn't get to the sideline in time, a

12-men-on-the-field penalty that gave Jacksonville a first down. It was an infamous sequence in a 30–27 defeat known as the Ambush at Mile High, and it would be burned into the psyches of true Broncos fans—especially McDaniel, who felt he was finally in position to do something about it.

To say he stood out as a ballboy upon his return to Greeley was like saying Lauryn Hill stood out in the Fugees, or Joe Pesci in *Goodfellas*. "I was a fucking die-hard, obsessive-compulsive Broncos fan," McDaniel told me in 2019. "Because I was, like, a fan that married into the bottom, I was the hardest-working fucking psychopath ballboy ever."

Specifically, when McDaniel ran onto the field to spot the football between plays and then raced back to the sideline, he felt he was sending an institutional message. Perry's failure to get off the field, in his mind, had cost the Broncos a Lombardi Trophy. McDaniel was underscoring the urgency needed to be champions. Before long, his sprints spread to off-the-field endeavors: if someone needed to go back and fetch a kicking tee from the equipment shed, McDaniel did his best Carl Lewis impression.

"The other ballboys would laugh at me for being a kiss-ass or whatever, but I just said, 'Fuck it,'" McDaniel remembered. "So, everywhere I'd go, I'd run around."

McDaniel, short and skinny, was a decent athlete. Yet, around the time he started middle school, it began to dawn on him that playing for the Broncos might not be a reasonable dream. He would have to amend it to something more in line with his biological limitations. In Mike Shanahan, he saw a slender, 5-foot-9 former Eastern Illinois quarterback who'd never had a prayer of playing in the pros. Perhaps McDaniel could be *that*.

In the meantime, he had another dream: to be one of the "cool kids" at Laredo Middle School in unincorporated Arapahoe County, not far from the Broncos' training facility in Englewood. In seventh grade, McDaniel had become best friends with a boy named Dan Soder, and they proceeded with a shared ambition. "We were both kind of awkward, [with] oversized head-to-body ratio, but we wanted to get involved in the cool kids [scene]," McDaniel recalled. "We had aspirations of middle school popularity like everyone does, and we had a little sect of friends that, at that time, was like a skateboarding crew. But we weren't cool enough to be cool in middle school, 'cause to be cool in middle school, you had to be smoking Marlboro Reds, and girls had to be interested in us. And on days when we had a ton of unrest, with people poking at us, we'd be like, 'You know, one day, you're gonna be a standup comedian, and I'm gonna be a head coach, and *then* they'll laugh.'"

Eventually, Soder made it, both as a standup comedian and a comedic actor (playing Dudley Mafee, a recurring character on the popular Showtime drama *Billions*). McDaniel, whose quick mind, offbeat personality, and dry delivery also lent themselves to comedy, would have to settle for being known as the NFL's funniest head coach, which is kind of like being the most sculpted sumo wrestler. He viewed his dream as attainable mostly because his mother, for the entirety of his existence, had told him he was special and could accomplish anything he worked for. In kindergarten, Mike had a habit of simultaneously blurting out answers while raising his hand, something that contributed to his teacher advising Donna to hold her son back a year, because he wasn't socially ready. Donna ignored the advice, she said, "because I didn't want to ruin his hunger for knowledge."

———

MCDANIEL HAD LONG FELT HE DIDN'T FULLY FIT IN ANYWHERE. ONCE, IN his preschool years, he'd visited his paternal grandmother's house and noticed that, in all the family photos displayed, his and Donna's were the only light-skinned faces. Later on, distraught because certain friends' parents kept nixing sleepovers at his house, McDaniel demanded answers from Donna, who told him the parents had done so because he was biracial. His sense of fashion was as unique and idiosyncratic as his sense of humor—and he had a strong sense of self, thanks largely to Donna's emphatic support.

By the end of his time at Smoky Hill High School, where the 5-foot-9, 145-pound McDaniel played wide receiver on the football team and ran track in the spring, he had hoop earrings in each ear, thick glasses, and a red Mustang (a gift from Donna because of his good grades). He got admitted to Yale, earning a partial academic scholarship (though he'd end up taking out student loans he wouldn't fully repay until he was 32) and intent on making the football team as a non-recruited walk-on.

"How does a kid get into Yale on his own and be good enough to play college football?" asked Chandler Henley, who became close friends with McDaniel during their time as Bulldogs receivers and later went into coaching, ultimately joining McDaniel's Dolphins staff as assistant quarterbacks coach. "I'm telling you, because I've worked at Yale, I know what it's like to recruit there. If you get a walk-on that's any good, that is fucking the biggest gravy in the world. Yale doesn't have scholarships. The way you get in is based on you're smart enough and you're good at football. They treat it like first-round draft picks. I was a first-round draft pick for Yale because I was barely above the [academic] line, but I was really good where I was a borderline [Division I] scholarship player. Mike was that smart—without being on their radar at all, he got in."

How smart is McDaniel? In the cynical culture of most NFL locker rooms, players tend to mock coaches who carry themselves as though they have just split the atom while performing brain surgery. Yet McDaniel's intelligence was clearly exceptional. In the words of former Pro Bowl tight end Chris Cooley, who would spend the last two years of his Washington career interacting with McDaniel, then an offensive assistant on Mike Shanahan's staff, "McDaniel's just brilliant. He's like fucking Matt Damon in *Good Will Hunting*. And I don't mean that on a school level; I mean that on a social, like, 'I'm gonna fuck with you' level, ''cause I'm better than you.'

"He's a 'How do you like them apples?' kind of person."

Henley, a Denver-area kid who'd first become acquainted with McDaniel when they were rival high school senior wideouts tearing up the Centennial League, was an instant starter at Yale. McDaniel? Well, he found other callings. Specifically, he became an elite partier, even by collegiate standards. Before arriving in New Haven, McDaniel hadn't been much of a drinker. By his sophomore year, when he was engaging in wildly competitive beer pong games staged at the Zeta Psi Fraternity, McDaniel had a reputation. He and his friends, most of them football teammates, formed "BOT," a spoof of Yale's old money–drenched secret societies. BOT stood for "Black Out Thursday," and "meetings" took place at the New Haven establishment known as Bar, where there were dollar mixed-drink specials from 9 to 10 p.m. "I had a 'four-and-three' existence," McDaniel recalled. "Sunday through Wednesday nights, I'd be in the library till midnight or 1 a.m. Then came Blackout Thursdays. We'd triple-fist and stuff. We would black out and do crazy-ass shit." On Friday and Saturday nights—except during football season—they'd do the same.

McDaniel was prone to instigating outlandish acts, though he didn't always remember them clearly, if at all. Once, upon returning home at 4 a.m., McDaniel discovered a massive pile of thick New Haven phone books in the lobby of his apartment building, having yet to be distributed. McDaniel decided that it would be a grand idea to toss them, one by one, up into the adjacent second-floor apartment occupied by an ex-girlfriend (or, as he described it, someone with whom he'd hooked up frequently the previous school year).

Later on, McDaniel's binge drinking would become a career-threatening problem, costing him opportunities and allowing other talented coaches to leapfrog him. At one point, he'd be banished to the United Football League, working as a running backs coach for the Sacramento Mountain Lions, a team owned by Paul Pelosi (whose wife, Nancy, was a two-time Speaker of the House). Ultimately, McDaniel would seek help and find sobriety. In his college years, even at one of the world's most prestigious universities, he was able to survive and thrive academically despite himself.

What's more, McDaniel stretched his intellectual muscles, and those of his friends, by embracing the acquisition of knowledge, rather than just checking boxes in the name of achievement. He sometimes attended classes in which he wasn't enrolled, dragging along his roommates. "He was huge for my academic standing," Henley said. "I went to class a lot because of him, because he was like, 'This is an interesting class. We should go hear the professor.' Otherwise, I would have fucking slept in."

———

THE ONE THING McDANIEL COULDN'T PULL OFF WAS WHAT HE WANTED most: cracking the Bulldogs lineup. He played sparingly, for reasons Henley believes were somewhat unfair, despite his best efforts to force his way onto the field. Said Henley, "He wanted to play. That was always his driver. The knock on him was that he was small. He recognized that the only way he was going to do it was to transform his body. So, just like he does in anything else, he put his mind to it, and he's like, 'I'm gonna fucking get huge.' Lifted, [took] creatine, worked his ass off. You should have seen him."

As a senior, McDaniel won an award for being the strongest player on the team, pound for pound—a title he underscored by doing 39 consecutive pull-ups. During games, McDaniel would typically stand with punter Ryan Allen—one of his and Henley's roommates and close friends—and critique the coaches' play calls in real time. He'd impress Allen by telling him what was coming, whether it would work or not (and why), and what might have been a better way to attack the opponents' defensive alignment on that snap.

Early on in college, McDaniel had assumed he was headed into the business world. He'd done a summer internship at an investment banking firm and later looked into jobs with UBS and other financial institutions. He spent another summer interning in the front office of a car dealership, supplementing his income by working as a youth baseball umpire. Football, however, remained his true love—he wrote his senior thesis on the NFL–AFL merger. As graduation neared, McDaniel wrote letters to all 32 NFL teams, inquiring about internships or entry-level positions; he also reached out to every major college football program. Upon his return to Denver, he went to the Broncos' facility and met with Mike Shanahan, hoping he could get a letter of recommendation for a job as a low-level graduate assistant for any collegiate team that would have him.

Shanahan agreed, writing a glowing recommendation on Broncos stationery. However, when McDaniel sent it out to schools across the country, he got no response. The next time he saw Shanahan, the coach said, "I'll do you one better. You can be an intern here, for the summer."

McDaniel soon figured out that it would not be a traditional internship. "It was 'hang around, learn, and put it on your résumé.' The entire time I was there, while everyone thought it was a summer thing, I'm thinking, *There is no way this is gonna be it—this is gonna be my gig. I'm just going to figure out shit to do that people don't want to do, and I'm going to do it, and then they'll have to keep me.*"

Technically, he was an unpaid intern, performing tasks such as helping repair the scout team jerseys. Every so often, Gary Kubiak, the offensive coordinator, would float him some off-the-books money. It helped that McDaniel could live with his mother and stepfather, who had a place close to the facility. He could also get many of his meals at the Broncos' cafeteria, though he ended up skipping many of them.

McDaniel noticed early on that Shanahan, after practice, would go back and watch each play on the computer screen in his office. The coach needed to know specifically what he was looking at, but the technology at the time made such an endeavor problematic. McDaniel solved it. "Practice would happen, you'd come in, and the film would be downloaded," he recalled. "Now, we have it built so that every script we type out—for the hard copy for players to have—automatically inputs into the [visual] field. But not then, at that stage of technology. You had to type in the formation, personnel, and play manually after practice was downloaded, so that Coach Shanahan would see the play on the screen when he watched it. So, after a two-hour-long practice, you'd have to go in manually, play by play, and figure out a system so that you could type it fast. It was rudimentary. It took about half an hour, and no one wanted to do it. So, I would not eat. I would come in and do whatever it took to get it done, period. And to this day, I don't ever eat after practices."

The strategy worked. Shanahan viewed McDaniel as indispensable and kept him around for the 2005 season. The Broncos reached the AFC Championship Game, and shortly thereafter Kubiak was hired as the head coach of the Houston Texans. He asked Shanahan if he could bring McDaniel with him, and Shanahan gave his blessing. "I told Mike, 'Go with Kube. You've got to experience something else,'" Shanahan said. "And Mike, at that time, had to grow up a little bit."

WHEN McDANIEL ARRIVED IN HOUSTON, HE WAS INTRODUCED TO KYLE Shanahan, Kubiak's newly hired receivers coach. McDaniel quickly realized that Mike's son was the furthest thing from an incompetent nepotism hire. "I immediately knew he was on a different level," McDaniel remembered. "Offensive assistants, a lot of times, are at liberty to fit whatever position group needs it. About a week in, way before people are even thinking about what room I should go in, I wanted to go with Kyle. I asked Kube, and Kube agreed."

McDaniel became the assistant receivers coach, if not by title, then by practice, and soaked up knowledge from Shanahan for an entire season. He created a database of plays via two Microsoft software programs, Visio and Excel, on which he was self-taught. "I could tell how smart he was," recalled Sage Rosenfels, the Texans' backup quarterback at the time. "But I also could tell how sold he was on Kyle's style of offense and that that was the best way to go. I mean, he was very much sold on it."

As Shanahan transitioned to quarterbacks coach in 2007 and offensive coordinator the following year, McDaniel remained an offensive assistant, albeit an invaluable one. In 2008, Matt LaFleur joined McDaniel in that role; LaFleur had been recommended by his close friend (and former fellow Central Michigan graduate assistant) Robert Saleh, a Texans defensive assistant at the time. By then, McDaniel felt he should have been higher on the food chain; Kubiak, however, had his reasons.

In college, McDaniel had gotten away with his binge drinking, and he remained high-functioning in Houston—with some glaring exceptions. On a few occasions, typically in the early morning, Kubiak called McDaniel with questions and the phone went unanswered—an obvious indication that the young coach was not in his office, grinding along with the rest of his peers.

"He went hard," Saleh recalled. "We were all young. Shit, we had the NFL logo. It was frickin' party time. I don't blame him. We were all doing the same thing. Mikey had a way of talking—he had this confidence, that same awkward confidence. He would just have everyone flocking to him. He just had that electric and magnetic personality."

After the 2008 season, Kubiak quietly got rid of McDaniel, who landed in the UFL. In 2011, he'd get another chance to resume his NFL path—this time, as an offensive assistant in Washington, where Mike Shanahan was entering his second year as head coach, with Kyle as his offensive coordinator and LaFleur as quarterbacks coach. When McDaniel returned, his golden-boy status was long gone, and LaFleur wasn't the only young coach on the staff who'd seemingly surpassed him.

It was humbling, and for a couple of days, he was shaken. Then, once again, McDaniel identified an area of need and adapted accordingly. It was a shrewd move that would ultimately make him Kyle Shanahan's most indispensable aide, even as McDaniel remained a relative secret to most outsiders through the balance of the decade. Like the "psychopath ballboy" he once was, McDaniel charged ahead and kept chasing his dream.

Chapter 6

The Instigator

You're an idiot.

Matt LaFleur's first thought on a dark and chilly southwestern Arkansas morning in January of 2008 was one of self-flagellation—and, by all appearances, he wasn't being dramatic.

LaFleur, 28, a newly hired Houston Texans offensive assistant, was sitting in the driver's seat of his Chevy Trailblazer in a Walmart parking lot, and the predawn scene looked sketchier than some skid rows. He'd impulsively spent the night there because of his new financial reality. LaFleur, formerly the offensive coordinator at Ashland University, a Division II school in Ohio, had just accepted a job that would reduce his $45,000 annual salary by a third. His close friend Robert Saleh, a Texans defensive quality control coach since 2006, had convinced head coach Gary Kubiak to offer the low-level gig to LaFleur by phone, and he'd accepted on the spot. Within about an hour, LaFleur had loaded up the car with his clothes and basic belongings, said goodbye to his wife, BreAnne (who had a job of her own and couldn't bolt abruptly), and set off on the 16-hour drive, intent on going the distance.

Sometime after midnight, LaFleur became groggy. He thought it best to stop and get a few hours of sleep. He looked for a Comfort Inn or Motel 6 or some other cheap lodging. Then he saw a sign—*Welcome to Hope*—and called an audible.

LaFleur, like most Americans of that era, had heard of Hope, Arkansas, an unremarkable town of 10,000, except for one bit of important trivia:

it was the birthplace of President Bill Clinton, who'd famously ended his speech at the 1992 Democratic National Convention by telling millions of viewers, "I still believe in a place called Hope." LaFleur assumed that pulling over anywhere in Hope—a Walmart parking lot, for instance—would be a perfectly fine idea.

Wow, that's where Bill Clinton's from. It can't be that bad of a place, LaFleur figured.

Now, he was quickly reassessing. After opening his eyes and starting the engine, LaFleur drove to a nearby gas station and wondered if he were in danger of getting jacked.

"I was like, 'Holy shit, where am I?'" LaFleur would later say. "I kept thinking, *I can't believe I just did that.* But hey, I saved $100."

It was not LaFleur's only serious miscalculation that winter. After arriving in Houston—and crashing at Saleh's house—it was time to meet his new boss, Kyle Shanahan, who'd just been promoted from quarterbacks coach to offensive coordinator.

LaFleur was well aware of Shanahan's pedigree. And, like so many others, LaFleur was skeptical about the rapid ascent of Mike Shanahan's only son. If nothing else, LaFleur figured he and Kyle were peers: he was a month older and had just spent a year running an offense, albeit a lower-level one.

When LaFleur showed up at the office to attend his first-ever staff meeting, he was anxious to meet Shanahan. As 7 a.m. approached, however, there was no sign of the new boss. Kubiak convened the meeting and started going over various items, but . . . no Kyle Shanahan!

"He had overslept," LaFleur remembered. "First fucking day as offensive coordinator for the Houston Texans. It was just an anomaly; he just fucked up. I remember him getting his ass ripped [by Kubiak]. I'm like, 'What a slacker.'"

This fortified LaFleur's suspicion that Shanahan's standing might have been a product of his father's fame. If it gave LaFleur a false sense of security, it didn't last long.

Recalled LaFleur, "I just remember coming in and thinking, *Well, this guy's the same age as me. He can't know that much more than me.* And very soon after that, I was like, 'Holy shit—I don't know *anything.*' It was eye-opening, like, how much more detailed everything was, just the volume of football . . . it was completely different than what I'd been doing."

AS LAFLEUR BEGAN THE PROCESS OF WHAT HE'D LATER CALL "GETTING my PhD in football," it cemented a foundational belief in the overall mission. As with Kyle Shanahan—perhaps even *more* so—coaching was in LaFleur's blood and was embedded in his value system. Growing up in Mount Pleasant, Michigan, he watched his parents, Denny and Kristi, coach and teach as a way of life.

Denny had been a linebacker on Central Michigan University's 1974 team that won the NCAA Division II championship and was voted the Associated Press's "College Division national champion." There, he met Kristi, a Chippewas cheerleader, whose father was a high school football coach in Kalamazoo. Beginning in 1978, Denny would spend two decades as a defensive assistant at Central Michigan before becoming a high school coach, ultimately taking over as the head coach at Mount Pleasant High School, where fellow teacher Kristi had long since established herself as a competitive cheer and track coach.

Matt, the older of their two sons, was born on a Chippewas game day late in the 1979 season—Central Michigan tied 7–7 at Toledo, its only blemish in a 10–0–1 campaign. Denny missed that game to be there for the delivery. Thirty-four years later, Matt, in his fourth and final year as an assistant on Mike Shanahan's Washington staff, would experience his second son's unplanned delivery via C-section from afar while talking to Bre on a cell phone—and sitting next to his friend Sean McVay—on a bus ride from the Nashville airport to the team hotel, on the eve of a preseason game against the Titans.

Growing up, Matt spent a great deal of time at Chippewas games and practices and was heavily invested in their success. After all, winning and losing shaped the collective mood of his household. "We were poor losers," he remembered. "I feel like I handle losing a lot better now than I did then. I can remember when they lost games, my mom would be crying afterward."

Once, shortly before LaFleur's ninth birthday, he was on the sidelines for a game in which Central Michigan blew a 20–0 lead and lost to Ball State. Afterward, he was hungry and lobbied hard to go to McDonald's. Crammed into the middle row of his grandfather's old brown minivan, Matt pressed his case.

"My mom was *not* in the mood," he said. "I must have given her some lip, and she came across the frickin' seat and swatted me pretty good. My mom didn't really do that; it was the one time she smacked me."

Matt, at that age, didn't quite appreciate that a defensive coach could go from a blown lead to a lost season to a pink slip to a moving van. From a young age, he assumed he'd play as long as he could and then coach and teach and repeat the cycle. "I figured that's what I was going to do. I think a lot of us are a product of our environment, and you end up doing what your parents did. That's kind of all I really knew, and I grew up with it. And I got a teaching degree."

Denny finally got fired during Matt's senior year of high school, hastening a transition to the high school coaching ranks. By then, Matt was an undersized quarterback with dreams of playing Division I football, to the point that he was willing to switch positions. After walking on as a quarterback at Western Michigan, LaFleur—like future friends and colleagues Shanahan, McVay, and Mike McDaniel—ended up playing collegiate wide receiver. Well, kind of. "I wasn't very fast," he recalled. "It's funny, because we had a pretty good receiving corps—[future Packers star] Greg Jennings was coming in, and I knew he was really good. I was like, 'Man, I don't know if I'm going to play.' So, I transferred to Saginaw, not knowing if I was going to play quarterback or receiver."

Saginaw Valley State was a Division II school, meaning LaFleur was allowed to work out for coaches during his recruiting visit. They put him through quarterback and receiver drills and offered him a partial scholarship. He showed up unsure which position he'd be playing and finished spring practice as the No. 2 quarterback. The starter got hurt in the first game of the season, and LaFleur entered in the fourth quarter. "I went one-for-seven, and we ended up losing the game by two points," he said. "There were plays that were *so close*, but one-for-seven is one-for-seven, and we lost. The next week, I was the starter, and we're playing Grand Valley State. This is just before they started going to all those national championships.

We were down 21–7, and we came back and beat them 28–21, and I ended up starting there for three years."

The Cardinals reached the playoffs in each of those seasons, and LaFleur left as the school's all-time leader in passing yards and touchdowns. After brief stints in the National Indoor Football League as a backup quarterback with the Omaha Beef and Billings Outlaws, LaFleur faced reality and turned his attention to coaching. He spent a year as a graduate assistant at Saginaw Valley State before newly hired Central Michigan coach Brian Kelly, who'd coached that Grand Valley State team that LaFleur defeated in his first start, and who'd known Denny since attending CMU football camps in the '90s, gave him a shot.

INITIALLY, LaFLEUR WAS HIRED TO BE KELLY'S DEFENSIVE GRADUATE assistant. A few weeks later, the plan changed. Saleh, a defensive assistant at Michigan State, had completed a two-year GA stint with the Spartans and needed a new gig. Saleh called Kelly seeking a position coach job, but none existed.

"You can come be a GA," said Kelly, who promptly shifted LaFleur to the offensive side of the ball. The two GAs and future NFL head coaches quickly became close friends and roommates.

"We lived together for a year at some low-income housing [apartment] in Mount Pleasant," LaFleur said. "It was a good time. There were a lot of war stories, if you know what I mean."

The apartment famously had a kitchen table with no chairs. There was no cable TV, either, and the refrigerator was mostly empty. LaFleur's childhood home, however, was about a mile away. Denny and Kristi were at work much of the time, while Matt's younger brother, Mike (whom Saleh would hire as his offensive coordinator after becoming the New York Jets' head coach 17 years later), was a high school senior. That meant easy access during lunch and dinner breaks to a stocked fridge, TV with video game console, swimming pool, and other amenities.

LaFleur and Saleh were eager to escape second-class status by becoming full-fledged position coaches, and networking was a logical path toward that end. In January of 2005, the American Football Coaches Association

(AFCA) held its annual convention in Louisville. The two of them got in the car, drove to Kentucky, schmoozed with everyone they could, and slept in a cramped hotel room for a couple of nights with some other CMU assistants. After driving back to Mount Pleasant, the two bachelors were ready for a night on the town. First, however, LaFleur had to tend to some important business.

"When you're in your early 20s, you're into trying to look as good as you can," LaFleur remembered. "So I said, 'I'm going to go hit the tanning booth.'"

The young woman working there amid the unrelenting UV rays, Bre-Anne Maak, had interacted with LaFleur before—she was also a student trainer for the CMU football team. They struck up a conversation.

"So, what are you doing tonight?" LaFleur asked.

"Oh, nothing. I just broke up with my boyfriend."

"Oh, you should come out with me and Saleh tonight."

She said sure, but there was one complication: LaFleur had already planned to meet another woman at the bar. Bronzed and undaunted, he would eventually marry Maak, with Saleh in the wedding party, as LaFleur was for Saleh's.

SALEH LEFT SOON AFTER THAT AFCA CONVENTION, FIRST FOR THE UNI-versity of Georgia, and then, weeks later, for a defensive internship with the Texans. LaFleur's less glamorous path included stints at Northern Michigan and Ashland before Kubiak's call.

As a low-level assistant in Houston, LaFleur became one of the "Piss Boys," a group of grunts that included Saleh, McDaniel, Richard Hightower, and Perry Carter. Their duties, Saleh said, included having "to clean out the air ducts at the tight end coach's house, fix the copier . . . You get pissed on."

Once he knew how behind he was on the learning curve, relative to Shanahan and others, LaFleur dove into his new world with abandon. Along the way, he became known among his peers for two things. First, for someone in a cutthroat profession, he was stunningly guileless. Those who mistook his earnestness for phoniness eventually scolded themselves for their cynicism. Though he was a hypercompetitive grinder, he didn't seem to have a disingenuous bone in his body. In Mike McDaniel's words, "There's a LaFleurism that he's the furthest thing away from being calculated, that he's just kind of naive in a certain way."

The other LaFleurism, incongruous as it may have seemed, was that, in his own words, he's a shit disturber of epic proportions. He is frequently guilty of saying the *one thing* he knows will set someone off.

"He just crawls under your skin," Saleh said, "because Matt's going to say exactly what everyone else is thinking. And it's healthy. You need that guy in your life to always keep you in check and make sure you're checking the boxes. You may not like what you're hearing, but you're going to sit back after being mad and be like, 'Bitch was right.' It was good. It was productive. You need those people in your life, and that's what I love about him."

McVay, who hired LaFleur as his offensive coordinator after getting the Rams' head coaching job in 2017, felt similarly. "He said a lot of the things I needed to hear; I just didn't maybe want to hear it at the time. But, of course, it comes from such an authentic place. He would intentionally get me riled up in games because, you know, I'd be saying something like 'I see this [defensive wrinkle]—nobody bring this back up.' And Matt would bring it up, just like, 'Ooh, I like to get you fired up.' I'd say, 'Hey, we all know they're doing this; we don't have to say it again.' And he would intentionally go, 'Hey, you know that backside end is *really* closing flat.' And I'd go, 'I know, Matt!!!' He loved it. He was an instigator, whether he admits it or not."

He admits it. "I think Sean and I are so close that there are a lot of times he wouldn't want to hear it," LaFleur said. "I'm a glutton for punishment by nature, so I would throw it at him regardless. Sometimes, I'd know that he didn't want to hear it, and I'd still give it to him. And he'd fire back at me and get pissed off. But we're like brothers, too. Typically, the people that you really trust, the people that mean the most to you, you can kind of let your guard down a little bit, too, and be real, because you know that you can have a disagreement and they're still going to be right there and have your back. We were at each other's throats quite a bit. I was the same way with Kyle."

Ejiro Evero, the Rams' safeties coach in 2017, remembers McVay and

LaFleur yelling at one another on a daily basis. "Sean and Matt must be *really* good friends," he said.

LaFleur and Shanahan, after stints together in Houston and Washington, became so combative during their two seasons in Atlanta that they were intent on separating following the 2016 season, which ended with the Falcons' devastating Super Bowl LI defeat and Shanahan taking the 49ers' head coaching job. (Shanahan hired Mike LaFleur, who'd also been on the Falcons' staff, while Matt chose McVay and the Rams over staying on in Atlanta.) It was, said Matt, "a mutual parting. We were at each other's necks. I was always the guy that was going to tell him how I saw it, whether he agreed with me or not. I didn't care. I think you need people like that to tell you what you don't want to hear all the time. It doesn't mean I'm right. I'm just giving you my perspective. Sometimes it didn't align with his vision. That's good—you've got to make that decision—but I think he always respected that from me. We would always go back and forth quite a bit. I'm sure it wore on both of us. I got my ass ripped a lot."

Dan Quinn, the Falcons' head coach at the time, quickly recognized that LaFleur, his quarterbacks coach, was an instigator. "He has that side of him. Mike [LaFleur] does, too. It might be a LaFleur thing; you better call their father and find out, 'Hey, were you a shit disturber?'" The La-Fleur brothers' most celebrated clash occurred on a Lake Michigan beach in the summer of 2008, not long after Matt had taken the Texans job. Mike, heading into his senior season at Elmhurst College in Illinois, had been converted to safety after two seasons as a quarterback for the Division III Bluejays. Shorter and smaller in stature than his older brother—and more than seven years younger—Mike was feeling feisty as the family vacationed at a rented cottage in South Haven, Michigan. He'd been lifting weights and adopting a safety's headhunting mindset, and after the brothers got a few beers in them, one thing led to another.

"He thought he could take me," Matt recalled, "and I got him in a headlock. And I'm lying on top of him, and I'm taking sand and just pouring it in his face."

The scene was witnessed by Denny and Kristi, Bre, and Lauren Ball, Mike's girlfriend and future wife. In an apparent effort to motivate her vanquished man, Lauren exclaimed, "Stop lying there like a dead fish!"

"Shut the fuck up, Lauren!" Mike yelled.

Now he had bigger problems.

"Needless to say," Matt recalled, "that wrestling match was like a record scratching to a halt."

As hard as he was on his brother in that notorious moment, Matt LaFleur could relate to Mike's misery. In Washington, his penchant for worrying—and self-immolating—was somewhat legendary. Said Mike McDaniel, "You talk about overaccountability. You'd have to talk that guy off the ledge; like, if something was the wrong direction during a walk-through, Matt would be cursing himself, and you'd have to say, 'Matt, it's OK!' And he'd go, 'No, it's not!' It was just genuine humility and account-ability that has stood the test of time."

Chris Cooley, the former Redskins tight end, once tried to liven things up on a team flight by creating a "Least Popular Coach" poll among team-mates. Cooley walked to the section where the assistant coaches were seated and announced his intention, then passed out paper and pens to his fellow players and pretended to tabulate their votes. It was a prank designed to provoke sharp reactions, and it worked. Richmond Flowers, an offensive assistant who would go on to become a prominent coaching agent, was named the "winner." And LaFleur, perceived by Cooley as the most likely to get upset, was declared the second-least popular member of Mike Shanahan's staff.

Cooley insists that LaFleur, upon learning the "news," shed some tears. At the very least, his eyes welled up. "It was hurtful," LaFleur conceded. Years later, when Cooley described LaFleur to me as "so sensitive and sweet," it did not come across as an insult.

Over time, the profession would harden LaFleur—largely because of those similarly driven young coaches he worked with in Washington, and the rivalries that would form among them as they went their separate ways.

Chapter 7

The Mayor of Earth

Sean McVay stood at the whiteboard, black marker in hand, ready to seize the moment. Less than a year earlier, he'd been a college senior, pondering the disappointing end to his playing career and wondering what to do with the rest of his life. Now he'd found his calling—never mind that he was currently unemployed.

This was a different kind of school, and on this spring morning in 2009, McVay was determined to ace the test.

"School" had started early that morning, well before dawn. That's how it worked at the FFCA, short for the Fired Football Coaches Association. Despite its sarcastic christening by Jon Gruden in the wake of his abrupt dismissal as the Buccaneers' head coach a couple of months earlier, the FFCA was no joke. The office space he'd rented in Tampa was conceived as a haven for out-of-work coaches to watch film; it would later evolve into a sort of football think tank. Now Gruden, still keeping coach's hours, was grilling McVay, the 23-year-old who'd been his gopher the previous season, about the most basic of West Coast offense principles.

Gruden had just given McVay a rudimentary schematic lesson; now it was time for the kid to prove he could retain and explain the information.

"Sean," Gruden had said, "get up there and teach me the play."

McVay went to the board, doing his best to mimic Gruden's lecture. This wasn't going to be hard: the kid had an incredible memory, perhaps even photographic, though that wasn't something he liked to admit.

Something was terribly wrong, however.

"Stop," Gruden said, cutting off McVay in mid-sentence and staring at the diagram on the board. McVay looked at him quizzically.

"Those are the shittiest circles I've ever seen in my life," Gruden said.

That night, McVay found a store that sold whiteboards, bought one, and took it home to his Tampa condo. He stood alone at the board, practicing his circles and squares, fine-tuning his approach until they were perfect. McVay would stand there and do mock installations of plays and game plans, preparing himself for the next morning's session with Gruden.

"It was a great chance to almost be able to interview every day," McVay would later recall.

McVay had known Gruden forever, but he didn't take this opportunity lightly. Their football families were intertwined: Sean's grandfather, John, while coaching at Dayton, had hired Gruden's dad, Jim, as one of his assistants. Later, as an assistant coach at Indiana, Jim Gruden had recruited Sean's father, Tim, to play safety for the Hoosiers. As the 49ers' general manager in 1990, John McVay had brought Jon Gruden into the organization as an "offensive assistant" whose job duties included aggregating road-game ticket requests for players.

Nearly two decades later, it was Sean McVay's turn to do entry-level grunt work. While McVay was still in high school, Gruden brought him on as a Bucs training camp assistant. Upon McVay's graduation from Miami of Ohio—the same school his grandfather had attended—he landed the "offensive assistant" title in Tampa that vastly overstated his actual importance to the organization.

"I was basically a glorified secretary," McVay said. "I won't even say 'glorified.' I was his secretary."

If Gruden needed his dry cleaning picked up? McVay picked it up. If the coach was holed up in his office, feeling hungry? McVay would order takeout and deliver it to Gruden's desk.

The kid certainly wasn't complaining. Though McVay might have been a classic product of nepotism, he was determined to overcompensate. Grinding relentlessly wouldn't be an issue—he was wired that way, and he loved football. However, it wasn't just the work ethic that would allow McVay to overcome the stigma that he was coasting on his family name. Like Raheem Morris, the young man was ultrapersonable, charming, capable of winning a room without it seeming contrived or forced. He looked you in the eye, listened intently, remembered every detail of the conversation, and made you feel good about it.

WHEN McVAY WAS IN COLLEGE, MIAMI OF OHIO GRADUATE ASSISTANT Frank Smith—who, years later, would be the Dolphins' offensive coordinator for McVay's friend Mike McDaniel—summed up McVay's appeal: "I used to call him 'The Mayor' back then. I was always like, 'Fucking McVay, the Mayor.'"

Later, in Washington, McDaniel would christen McVay the "Mayor of Earth."

The people skills came largely from Tim, a loquacious man who enjoyed a successful career as a broadcast executive, spending 39 years with Cox Television, on the sales and marketing side of the business. Tim's outward ebullience masked a deep-seated commitment to his craft that wasn't easy to turn off, something the eldest of his two sons also inherited. McVay's mother, Cindy, an interior designer, centered him emotionally. In Sean's words, "The empathy, the emotional intelligence, but also the raw emotion of being real and being a human being—I think that is what I got from my mom. Both my parents, I couldn't ask for better influences."

Parenting McVay wasn't an easy task. His energy, enthusiasm, intensity, and quest for perfection seemed ingrained. "He was one of those bright-eyed, highly engaged, competitive little kids," Tim McVay said. "Even at the very youngest of ages, he wanted to win. He played soccer when he was little, and he would run up and down the field like a maniac. Same with basketball; he wasn't tough to spot. And when he got up in the morning, bright and early, he was fired up, and I'd be like, 'Get out of my room.'"

Sean's tendency to beat himself up after perceived failure was also apparent at an early age. Said Tim, "There were times I had to say, 'Don't be so hard on yourself. You did pretty good.' And there'd be times when he'd say, 'Hey, Dad, I know you love me, but I don't want to hear your pep talk. That was terrible. I'm embarrassed.'"

Conveniently, Sean, who spent most of his childhood in suburban Atlanta, had many more triumphant moments than terrible ones. He loved sports, and he was good at many of them. After starring in soccer during his middle school years, he switched to football, becoming a four-year starter at quarterback and defensive back at Marist School. As a senior in 2003, McVay led the War Eagles to a 14–1 record and the state championship. Along the way, he displayed the strategic savvy and bravado that would define the youngest head coach in modern NFL history.

In the state quarterfinal game, Marist trailed top-seeded Shaw by five points in the game's final minute and called time-out on third and goal. Shaw, the state's most physical team, had continually stuffed the War Eagles on a power formation called Wham. McVay, an option quarterback, had spent the previous week deep in film study of his opponent. While huddling with his coaches on the sideline, he offered a suggestion: he wanted to run a play they'd never before used, a naked bootleg off of Wham. McVay would fake a handoff, hide the ball, and roll out with no blockers in front of him. For it to work, the entire defense would have to be fooled.

"I'm just telling you, the naked boot's there," McVay said to head coach Alan Chadwick, Georgia's second-winningest coach.

"You better be right," Chadwick finally said.

"Coach," McVay answered, "I know I'm right."

He was. "He just had this crazy ability to feel out plays," McVay's high school friend and teammate Chris Ashkouti recalled. "He knew. I mean, I've never seen anything like it. He walked into the end zone."

It wasn't just prescience that fueled McVay's success. He was falling in love with the game. He gravitated toward the mind games that came with the quarterback position. The process established a blueprint for fine-tuning the zone read principles he would engage with as one of Mike Shanahan's assistants in Washington in 2012.

Running the triple-option version of the wishbone attack—the potent scheme to which Mike Shanahan had been exposed as a young assistant to Barry Switzer at Oklahoma—McVay spent his Friday nights playing out the angles and running lanes and getting pummeled in the process. "I used to do [the triple option] from underneath the center and just get killed," he recalled. "And if we were inside the five, man, I was pulling that thing [and trying to score], no matter what."

In the state championship game, the last of his high school career,

McVay rushed for 102 yards and a touchdown on 14 carries, attempting only three passes. He played the second half with a broken foot—and celebrated the school's first state title since 1989.

After the season, he was named the Georgia 4A Offensive Player of the Year, beating out a receiver from Sandy Creek named Calvin Johnson. Tim vividly remembered his son's reaction to winning out over the future first-ballot Pro Football Hall of Famer: "That's kind of a joke, isn't it, Dad?"

IT WAS A GIVEN THAT McVAY WOULD TRY TO PLAY IN COLLEGE. WHICH position was another question. Because he stood less than six feet and had played in an option-based offense in high school, his only shot to play quarterback at the Division I level was to find a college program that favored a similar attack. Rice, Air Force, and Navy showed interest. Georgia Tech got in late on the local product. In the end, McVay accepted a scholarship to attend Miami, which had recruited him as a slot receiver and "athlete" (the all-encompassing recruiting term for "we like him, we're just not sure yet where to put him"). The RedHawks were coming off a 2003 season that had ended with them ranked tenth in the country, and led to quarterback Ben Roethlisberger being picked in the first round by the Pittsburgh Steelers.

That Sean had chosen to attend his grandfather's alma mater wasn't coincidental. More than half a century earlier, John McVay had been a Miami center under collegiate coaching legends Woody Hayes and Ara Parseghian. Bo Schembechler, who would go on to become the most successful coach in Michigan's history, played tackle on the same offensive line, as did future New York Giants head coach Bill Arnsparger. Sean was not only close with his grandfather, but mindful of his stature in the sport and what it might mean for his future.

Whispers about Sean's game-changing athletic ability preceded his arrival on campus. As another member of McVay's recruiting class, linebacker Mickey Mann, said, "They recruited him as an athlete. He was a real hotshot recruit, so we were all anxious to see him. Then we were like, 'Wait a second . . . He's a 5-10 white kid? We recruited him as an *athlete*? What are we missing here?' But his sheer athletic ability was exceptional, and his work ethic was insane."

It didn't go as planned: a broken ankle suffered early in his redshirt freshman year kept him off the field and permanently robbed him of some of his athleticism. "What was really frustrating about my college career was just some of the unfortunate injuries that occurred where you just weren't able to stay available and be the player, the available teammate, that you wanted to be," McVay remembered. "There was a lot of frustration. There were a lot of things that you kind of learn at the time, but I always think I had a pretty good, realistic perspective."

McVay fought his way onto the field as a receiver, catching 38 combined passes over his sophomore and junior campaigns. He earned a reputation among his peers for being hyperintense, competitive, and, in Mann's words, having "no off switch."

Recalled Mann, "When we'd work out, he didn't just want to be the best receiver . . . He wanted to be the best, period. In the weight room, he'd come down and try to bench press with me and [Chris] Shula and the other linebackers. He was a specimen. He'd do agility drills with the defensive backs and sprints with the receivers. Everything he did, he wanted to compete against the best. And by no means did Sean ever have a sense of entitlement about anything."

Sean wasn't naive about his privilege. Because of his grandfather's connections, McVay figured he'd have a shot at getting an entry-level personnel or coaching opportunity after college. Shortly after graduation, McVay headed south to be Jon Gruden's de facto secretary, trying hard to prove he wasn't an entitled legacy. He'd bike to work from his condo at 3:30 a.m. in a vain effort to try to beat the head coach to the facility.

His gig with the Bucs didn't last long. Gruden's surprise firing in January of 2009, and the subsequent hiring of Raheem Morris to replace him, meant McVay no longer had a guardian angel in the building. Morris could have kept the kid around, but chose not to. Later, after they'd become close while serving on Shanahan's staff in Washington, and even closer when McVay hired Morris to be the Rams' defensive coordinator in 2021, this became a source of great amusement between them. "I love giving him shit about that," McVay said in 2023. "One of my best friends is the only guy to fire me."

McVay was bummed at the time, but he enjoyed his apprenticeship under Gruden at the FFCA while waiting for his next opportunity. He'd already determined that coaching, and not scouting, was his preferred path.

"As soon as I got going and realized the differences," McVay recalled, "I was like, 'Alright, what lights me up is being around these players and teaching and continuing to learn and understand the nuances in regard to the techniques and fundamentals within the framework of a call, on both sides of the football. What are those rules, and what are the different ways that you cause conflict and problems for the opposing side?' That was the kind of stuff that lights you up, and you just realize, 'Man, I thought I knew what was going on as a player. I didn't know shit.'"

McVay assimilated a ton of knowledge from Gruden, who would soon infiltrate America's living rooms as a prominent *Monday Night Football* analyst, while unconsciously adopting his speaking style and mannerisms. It was, McVay said, "like getting your doctorate in coaching"—under the tutelage of a blunt, salty professor. Of Gruden, McVay said, "Nobody's going to be more challenging to interview and present in front of that's going to give you real feedback."

SOON, McVAY GOT ANOTHER JOB FROM ANOTHER GRUDEN: FLORIDA Tuskers offensive coordinator Jay, Jon's younger brother, helped McVay land a gig as a quality control/wide receivers coach for the United Football League franchise. In reality, McVay got exposure to more facets of the coaching operation than his title suggested. He worked in tandem with the running backs and tight ends coaches and dabbled with the team's defensive scheme as well. Said McVay, "You get a chance to get real coaching experience. How do you present? What kind of dynamic do you have in front of the room with making it a dialogue? How are you making things digestible to the players and able to solve certain problems? That was the foundation of what I learned about football, and I'm forever in debt to Jon and Jay for that."

A year later, another family connection—former Bucs GM Bruce Allen, who'd since joined Washington as executive vice president/general manager (as part of a pairing with newly hired coach Mike Shanahan)—summoned McVay for a chance to interview with Shanahan as an "offensive assistant." Once again, McVay knew he was privileged, and—assuming he could land the job—was determined to dispel any whiff of entitlement by grinding like a maniac.

He wasn't merely driven, however. And he wasn't just lucky. By then, he was already good—or, at least, showing signs of it. His recall alone made him stand out. Mike Shanahan, who'd worked for the 49ers in the '90s when John McVay was the general manager, probably didn't need a ton of convincing when Sean—sporting a beard in an attempt to appear older than 24—entered the offensive staff room for the interview. Also sitting in was newly hired offensive coordinator Kyle Shanahan, the person with whom Sean would be working directly, essentially as his quality control coach. "I know Sean," Mike Shanahan had told his son. "I know his grandfather. His grandfather was the best, I promise. What a class guy." A few minutes into their conversation, Mike became convinced that Sean was enough like his grandpa that he'd be an ideal fit.

Matt LaFleur, already aboard as quarterbacks coach, didn't think much of it when McVay arrived for his interview, which took place in an adjacent room. "I was in Kyle's office," LaFleur recalled. "I was doing something for Kyle, like putting together cutups or something like that. Sean was projecting *very* loudly. I might as well have been sitting in the room. At beautiful Redskins Park, the walls were paper thin. You could hear everything."

Years later, McVay, LaFleur, and McDaniel would recall the moment with great levity. Said LaFleur to McDaniel, "I mean, he likes to project."

McVay: "Maybe that's why coach Kyle said, 'Stop yelling at me!'"

What LaFleur heard that day was revelatory; McVay not only had presence, but his knowledge of the game ran very deep. "I was like, 'Holy shit. This guy, he's really good,'" LaFleur said. "I remember the first time I met him. I was like, 'Well, he'll be a head coach. He's charismatic and knowledgeable and has a way with people that's just different. He's got that *it* factor.' He has a presence about him. He's funny. He can grab the attention of the entire room. And he's obviously extremely intelligent. So, it was pretty obvious to me early on that he was pretty special. I used to tell people, 'This dude will be a head coach. I guarantee it.'"

For now, McVay would become, in in former Washington tight end Chris Cooley's words, "like the best QC ever." His duties included binding playbooks, photocopying documents, writing out play sheets, and making cutups of opposing defenses. He could study another coach's play sheet for 20 minutes and then recite, by memory, upwards of 100 plays. He was so good at the job that Kyle Shanahan wanted to keep him in that role for at least a couple of seasons.

However, the plan was derailed late in the 2010 campaign by a coaching hire in Boulder, Colorado—setting off a chain of events that would eventually result in McVay becoming Shanahan's greatest rival.

PART II

BREAKTHROUGHS AND HEARTBREAK

Mike Shanahan shares a lighthearted moment with Washington defensive backs coach Raheem Morris during a 2012 game. Morris, rebounding from a trying three-year stint in charge of the Tampa Bay Buccaneers, would wait 13 years before his next head coaching opportunity.

Chapter 8

The Fun Bunch

Chris Foerster had a job, and he took it very seriously.

No, not his job as the Washington offensive line coach under Mike Shanahan, a position he'd driven thousands of miles—on faith—in the hopes of landing. That was Foerster's primary area of focus, and he grinded with the best of them.

This job, however, was more specific, something only a man with incredible tolerance and stamina could handle. Sometimes, after work in the offseason or a relatively quiet period, Shanahan would invite his assistants to Jackson's, or another spot at nearby Reston Town Center. The head coach would pull out his credit card, open a tab, and have a couple of drinks before shutting it down.

Most of his younger assistants would stay behind, including Kyle Shanahan. Foerster, despite being much closer in age to the head coach, would also stay behind. So, too, would Mike Shanahan's credit card. The coaches would talk Xs and Os, sometimes using salt and pepper shakers to help make their points. Foerster was responsible for closing out the tab at night's end, leaving a good tip, and giving the head coach his plastic back in the morning.

Usually, upon presenting the card to Shanahan, Foerster was dragging. After all, he'd had a lot of help running up the bill. Sean McVay would tell Foerster, "I always love drinking with you, because when the first sip of vodka hits your lips, it's like truth serum." Mike McDaniel, who joined the staff in 2011, was a drinker of epic proportions. It didn't help that there was a lockout that offseason that kept the players away from the facility for months and left the coaches with far more free time than usual.

Foerster wasn't officially a member of the "Fun Bunch," the nickname bestowed upon Kyle Shanahan and his young assistants by veteran tight end Chris Cooley during training camp in 2011. Nor, technically, was Shanahan's close friend Raheem Morris, brought on after that season as an assistant coaching defensive backs following his dismissal as the Buccaneers' head coach. The nickname—a callback to the Redskins' receiving crew from the early '80s and its signature end zone–leaping celebration—was intended as a statement about the group's collective intensity, energy, and "zero fucks" mentality.

Foerster was enjoying himself at the workplace, too. That hadn't been the case at his previous stop, San Francisco, where in 2009 he slogged through an 8–8 season under neophyte head coach Mike Singletary. Foerster was already a coaching lifer, having worked for three major college programs and six NFL teams.

After two years as the 49ers' offensive line coach, he wanted out. Foerster didn't want to coach anywhere, for anyone—with one exception.

He wanted to work for Mike Shanahan.

———

AT THE CORE OF FOERSTER'S CAREER CRISIS WAS A NAGGING THOUGHT: *Am I actually good at this?* Shanahan, along with Bill Belichick, was his contemporary coaching barometer. If he could work for Shanahan, he would know one of two things: *Either I'm a good coach, or I'm not a good coach and he can help me become one.*

So, Foerster, at the end of the 2009 season, packed up his office, putting his belongings into boxes. "It was kind of like burning the ships," he recalled. Still under contract with the 49ers, Foerster pulled the sliding doors of his office shut and left, with no intention of coming back. He had a plan, albeit a precarious one. He got in his car and started driving east, calling his friend and former Baltimore Ravens coaching colleague Jedd Fisch along the way. Fisch had worked for Mike Shanahan as the Broncos' wide receivers coach in 2008, a year after leaving Baltimore, and swore by him in all ways—his strategic genius, his discipline, his incredible attention to detail, and more. Foerster, who'd heard all about it, told Fisch what he was doing: driving across the country, preparing to hole up in a hotel room in Tysons Corner, Virginia, and hope that Shanahan would interview him to be his offensive line coach.

Fisch had been talking to Shanahan about coming to Washington before deciding to go to Seattle under newly hired coach Pete Carroll. The lines of communication were open, and Fisch placed another call.

"Coach," he said, "the best line coach I've ever been around is Chris Foerster. If I can give any recommendation for any one person in this whole profession when it comes to somebody that I think would be great for what you and Kyle want, it would be Chris."

Fisch believed it was good fit because Foerster, in a world of meathead offensive line coaches, was much more of a free thinker. Not that Foerster was all over the place—he had deep conviction in his beliefs. Simultaneously, he kept an open mind. Said Fisch, "Chris is a football junkie. Chris loves to talk football, watch football, study film. That's what Coach and Kyle get off on also. It's this ability to just thrive on football knowledge, but yet Chris isn't afraid to be like, 'I don't get that. I don't understand that. What are we asking them to do there?' [Once] they explain, he'll be like, 'I'll run through a wall for them.'"

Foerster landed an interview, much to the surprise of Singletary, who initially denied Shanahan permission. The meeting, which began at 8 a.m., went very well. Within two hours—"during the first pee break," Foerster recalled—Shanahan told him, "That's the best interview I've ever had. This is awesome. We're going to get this thing done."

FOERSTER WOULDN'T JUST BE WORKING FOR SHANAHAN, OF COURSE. Their salaries were both being paid by Dan Snyder, the impetuous and ill-tempered billionaire who ranked among the sports world's most reviled owners. To many, it made little sense that Shanahan, after a year in hibernation, would choose to work for Snyder upon his return. Surely, a two-time Super Bowl–winning coach didn't have to settle, especially since his Denver deal ran through the 2012 season, meaning he could stay unemployed and continue to get paid. But here he was, jumping into business with a notoriously meddlesome and abrasive boss for a reported $7 million a year.

Coming to Washington was partly about money, and this went beyond Shanahan's hefty salary. His glory years in Denver had come under Pat Bowlen, an owner who was willing to spend aggressively in pursuit of top-tier talent (via manipulation of the salary cap) and in the name of organizational excellence. Before that, as coach of the Raiders, Shanahan had been beholden to Al Davis, who carried the sensibilities of an earlier era when it came to such matters. Davis had made all his money from owning the team and didn't throw it around as cavalierly. Snyder, as the steward of his beloved hometown team, had many problems, but spending money wasn't one of them. "Mike had his choice," said McDaniel. "And with his scars and his experiences, he saw the competitive disadvantage he had if you didn't have a rich owner. That was his No. 1 concern."

Soon after accepting the job, Shanahan realized he had another concern: convincing established assistant coaches to come to a notoriously toxic workplace. Snyder, who on more than one occasion in the late '90s had different flavors of ice cream delivered to the desk of defensive coordinator Mike Nolan—to underscore his belief that Nolan's scheme was too "vanilla"—was the kind of overbearing owner coaches with options strove to avoid. "Nobody wanted to come to Washington," Mike Shanahan recalled. "So we had to get young guys."

It had already been decided that one of those young guys would be Mike's son, as offensive coordinator. A couple of months after his father's abrupt firing by the Broncos, Kyle Shanahan—then finishing his first year as the Texans' offensive coordinator—had completely shifted his perspective. "Whenever my dad comes back, I'm going with him," he told me. "I always said I wanted to forge my own path and not be tied to him and his success, but now that this happened, I feel completely different about that. I want to work with him whenever I can. This shit can go away so quickly. It might be my only chance."

Mike reasoned that if Kyle was going to have a bunch of young assistants, it was paramount that his son feel comfortable with such a crew. In came LaFleur, who'd been Shanahan's quality control coach in Houston, and Richmond Flowers, whom Kyle had befriended during their time as

Duke wide receivers. Keenan McCardell, who'd begun and ended a long, successful career with Washington (with a quick stop in Houston during his final season in 2007, overlapping with Kyle Shanahan) and was new to the profession, was hired to coach the wide receivers.

Foerster would join Bobby Turner, Mike Shanahan's longtime running backs coach, and tight ends coach Jon Embree as the few offensive assistants who bucked the youth-movement trend. Otherwise, it was a conspicuously inexperienced staff. "People made fun of us all the time," McDaniel recalled. "They'd make fun of 'all Kyle's little clones.' Kyle pushed the envelope of what a staff looks like. But his dad was so important—that wisdom. So often, people say, 'Well, we do it because we have to do it this way, because blah blah blah.' We were totally autonomous, with no constraints, 100 percent accountable for what we put on tape. We had no limitations."

IT TOOK FOERSTER SOME TIME TO ADJUST TO ALL OF IT, INCLUDING THE outside zone scheme he'd long admired. He wasn't the only one struggling to thrive amid trying circumstances. The previous year, Snyder's aggressive spending had included a notoriously bloated deal for motivationally ambivalent free-agent defensive tackle Albert Haynesworth, putting the team in a difficult salary cap position. For now, it wasn't an issue. With the owners having voided their collective bargaining agreement (CBA) with the NFL Players Association, setting up the lockout, 2010 became an uncapped year, meaning teams no longer had an enforceable ceiling or floor when signing players.

Washington needed a quarterback, and naturally, Snyder threw money at the problem. Shanahan wanted veteran Marc Bulger, who'd just been released by the Rams after nine seasons and could be acquired cheaply. Snyder insisted on trading for Donovan McNabb, a six-time Pro Bowl selection who'd led the rival Eagles to five NFC Championship Game appearances and a Super Bowl during his 11 seasons in Philly. Shanahan had been an admirer of McNabb's, but when he watched the quarterback's film from the previous season, he felt he saw a player whose heart wasn't in it anymore and whose physical skills were declining, possibly because of poor conditioning.

From the start, McNabb and Kyle Shanahan were a terrible match. McNabb, breezy and self-assured and accustomed to getting things done on the fly, was a larger-than-life presence who'd been the face of a franchise for more than a decade. By contrast, Kyle was a hyperconfident and exacting offensive coordinator whose dad was (other than Snyder) the most powerful person in the building. Kyle wanted a grinder who studied and saw the game the way he did and got the ball to the place the coordinator wanted it to go. McNabb, at 33, wasn't super receptive. Kyle prepared scouting tapes for McNabb, which he suspected the quarterback wasn't watching. To prove his point, the coordinator tried putting attention-grabbing clips at the ends of the videos—perhaps a woman in a thong bikini, or some of McNabb's highlights from Syracuse. Shanahan hoped McNabb would notice and that the two would later share a laugh. To his chagrin, McNabb never mentioned anything. Eventually, Shanahan called him out on it, and McNabb bristled.

Things fell apart quickly. McNabb got benched late in an October 31 game at Detroit, with Washington 4–3 at the time. He got his job back, but after his agent complained publicly, Snyder gave the quarterback a five-year, $78-million financial apology, with $40 million guaranteed. After the season, Washington dumped both McNabb and Haynesworth. Then the owners locked out the players. The Shanahans still needed a quarterback. There was a lot of work to do.

Mike Shanahan was focused on big-picture issues—in Foerster's words, "having to be the head coach of Washington, which was a handful"—and attempting to make decisions, in tandem with Allen, that weren't derailed by Snyder's impulsiveness. Kyle Shanahan, tasked with leading the offense, was still growing into the role. Unlike Morris and McVay, he was not a commanding, appealing presence. Early on, when leading a meeting, he didn't even stand up; he sat in his coaching station, in the corner, with his back to the group and spoke while looking at the video screen. When he had to address the players directly, he'd turn his head and talk while looking back at them. "It was kind of awkward," one witness recalled. "Kyle has come a long, long way as a speaker."

In 2010, when the Shanahans arrived, Trent Williams was a rookie, embarking upon a resplendent career that would see him rejoin Kyle in

San Francisco a decade later. Looking back, the future Hall of Fame left tackle remembered the young offensive coordinator's inauspicious beginning: "Sometimes, I sit there and look at Kyle and just kind of laugh—like, man, 13 years ago, walking into that first install meeting, him being a 30-year-old hotshot coordinator. Everybody questioned him at the time 'cause that was kind of unheard of. Those positions were sacred. You had to put in years and years. You never really saw a coordinator under the age of 50, let alone 30."

LATE IN THE 2010 SEASON, ANOTHER YOUNG COACH ON MIKE SHANAhan's staff was put on an accelerated track. On December 5, Colorado hired Embree as its head coach, and he left for Boulder shortly thereafter. With four games remaining, Shanahan tabbed McVay, then 24, to take over as the interim tight ends coach.

"He knew everything," Chris Cooley recalled. "He knew everything about everything. Sean's biggest problem through the first three years was how to relate what he knew to the players without being a condescending prick. And he was, initially. But I was the perfect person for him to be around, 'cause you can be a condescending prick to me and I'm just going to challenge you more. And he will never quit on what he knows. He wasn't always right. But how many times have you told someone how right you are, and then affirmed it, and they just agree with you? When you seem like you feel like you're right, everyone will just say, 'Yeah, I think so.'"

Right or not, Cooley figured McVay's stay in the tight ends room would be temporary. And it would have been—the Shanahans planned to find a new tight ends coach at season's end and have McVay revert back to his former role—if it weren't for the intervention of Jon Gruden's younger brother. Hired as the Cincinnati Bengals' offensive coordinator, Jay Gruden offered McVay a job as his receivers coach. Kyle Shanahan urged his father to block the move, which led to McVay receiving an offer to be Embree's permanent replacement.

"The lifelong debate in coaching is 'When do I let a guy go?'" Cooley said. "Kyle's problem was that Sean was, like, the best QC ever. He was the good wife. He did everything the way Kyle wanted it."

Shortly thereafter, McDaniel arrived, returning from coaching exile. He had not spent his time in the UFL idly. While working for former Minnesota Vikings head coach Denny Green (a former Walsh protégé), for a franchise that morphed from the California Redwoods to the Sacramento Mountain Lions during that period, McDaniel familiarized himself with the basics of the West Coast offense and plotted his comeback.

"When I got to Washington, I had been out of the league for two years," McDaniel said. "And in that time, I had made this manual for our offense that was head and shoulders—it's one of the coolest things ever, thousands of hours, that basically took all of our data, three different things we'd make and put them into one. It would go to a play, like Drift, and it would be historically our stats since 2006, when I became a QC. And then it would have the detailed, written-out quarterback progression, which is never given to other players outside of the quarterback. That's the one piece of information that the Shanahans don't [disseminate], right? And then it had all the different formation pictures underneath that. This is all on one page. I made this whole thing of our [entire] offense, and brought it when I got to Washington. This was not needed. This is something that I just came up with—I was trying to take advantage of the fact that I had too much time. And something that didn't have any practical application to anything that we were doing. Matt and Sean saw it, and by the next year, they had done one like that as their own position manuals."

McDaniel got something else out of his time in Sacramento: an eventual life partner. One night, while players and coaches celebrated a Mountain Lions victory at Social Nightclub in downtown Sacramento, running back Steve Baylark began dancing with a woman named Katie Hemstalk. McDaniel, his position coach, half-jokingly pulled rank, telling Baylark, "Sorry—she's dancing with *me*, or you're not on the team next year." Baylark laughed as his coach supplanted him on the dance floor. Hemstalk thought it was funny and played along, and the two soon became a couple. In 2014, she and Mike got married.

———

WHEN McDANIEL MADE IT BACK TO THE NFL, HE WAS DETERMINED TO stay. Consider that, in 2022, after finally realizing his dream of becoming a head coach, McDaniel *still* kept an index card in his office with the number 865 inscribed—noting the days between NFL coaching gigs. After arriving in Ashburn, Virginia, it didn't take him long to read the room. If he was insecure about having been surpassed by other young Shanahan disciples, those fears were confirmed when he reacquainted himself with LaFleur and encountered McVay.

Early on, while sitting in a staff meeting, watching cutups of the previous season's plays and brushing up on Shanahan's offense, McDaniel had some questions about the passing game. "And Matt LaFleur and Sean McVay are chiming in in an annoying fashion," he recalled, "because they're very young at the time. I was like, 'These guys know a lot.'"

McDaniel didn't want to be the third fiddle—and he didn't want to enter what he viewed as a frantic contest to become Kyle Shanahan's favorite.

What is no one talking about? he asked himself.

He got his answer when, in the same meeting, the focus shifted to the running game. Suddenly, McVay and LaFleur were less involved. Shanahan spoke mostly to Foerster about blocking schemes and gaps and the running back's rules for a given play.

That guy, McDaniel thought. *I want to go with him. I want to know what he knows.*

Shanahan soon granted McDaniel's request to work directly with Foerster, who, McDaniel said, "became my window" into the ground attack. This was before the advent of titles like "run game coordinator," but that's essentially what Foerster was, with McDaniel as his assistant. Assistant offensive line coach Chris Morgan, another new hire, focused on protections, mostly centered around the passing game.

"There was really no place for him to go," Foerster said of McDaniel. "I don't know how he decided, but from the minute he got there, [Kyle] was like, 'You're going to be the run drawer; you're going to work with the run game with Chris.'"

A year into what he viewed as his career-defining endeavor, Foerster knew something was missing. His impression had been that, in working for Mike Shanahan, he'd be mimicking the teachings of Alex Gibbs, the Broncos' legendary line coach from 1995 through 2003. He thought he knew what the Shanahans wanted. He soon realized, however, that there was a disconnect. Foerster concluded that, for all those years, Gibbs had been coaching his linemen to block a certain style that differed from what the backs were being taught. Gibbs based his teachings on the premise that, on outside zone plays, the back was on a three-step read. By his third step outside, the ballcarrier had to read his blockers and make a decision—either bounce the run further outside, or plant his foot and cut back inside. That was not, however, the way Mike and Kyle Shanahan were coaching their backs. Said Foerster, "You're running at your landmark. It was a one-gap-at-a-time read. Never once did they ever talk about a three-step read. I watched people coach the back one way, and the line the other. I'm like, 'This is not congruent.' So, we made a change."

Offensive line coaches typically aren't known for their flexibility, but Foerster was an outlier. He and Kyle Shanahan would trade ideas and work out the intricacies of each week's ground attack—with McDaniel as the go-between, beginning a decade-long run as a de facto translator between Shanahan and his other assistants. "Mike was the ping-pong ball between me and Kyle the rest of the time," Foerster said. "We'd be game-planning, and Kyle would have questions of 'Why isn't this in?' He'd go yell at Mike. Mike would come into my office and say, 'Hey, Kyle wants this, this, and this. Why isn't it in?' I would go back and [explain]. Mike went between us for the rest of our time in Washington. Our relationship was much better because of Mike."

Suffice it to say that McDaniel, skinny and quirky, didn't fit the stereotype of the classic offensive line coach. "Mike was shoulder to shoulder my rookie year as a quality control guy in the offensive line room," recalled Williams. "I remember looking at him like, 'What is he even doing here?' His stature doesn't look like he ever played offensive line. It's crazy, man. It teaches you to [nurture] your relationships and really put effort into them."

———

THE FUN BUNCH NICKNAME MAY HAVE BEEN SEMI-IRONIC WHEN COOLEY conjured it, but the coaches in question did their best to bring it to life. There were drinks and laughs and bonding moments and high-fives and more drinks during their time together, as a group of (mostly) young, hungry, hypercompetitive dudes trying to make a mark in an extremely challenging profession brought it every single day—working hard, playing hard.

Driven, sometimes delirious, and prone to busting balls, the coaches were extremely competitive with one another—mostly competing for Kyle Shanahan's attention, and the unofficial designation of "Best Young Guy"—amid the dysfunction of Snyder's operation.

"Just a bunch of overambitious, average athletes," McDaniel said. "We're all Napoleon complex dudes. And we're competing against people that are the exact opposite dichotomy—they're all 'What are the rules? What did Bill [Belichick] say to do?' It was Steve Jobs—that aesthetic. We weren't outside the box; we didn't have one."

Staff meetings were notoriously long because of all the back-and-forth, as those who spoke up were implored to justify their *why*. Said McDaniel, "We'd just talk through it or have opinions 'cause we're all invested in it, and we're all also trying to make a name for ourselves with Kyle. And it was encouraged—it was kind of demanded—to speak up if you have a different thought."

There was plenty of yelling—Kyle Shanahan tended to run hot, especially on game day, and some of his assistants (especially McDaniel, LaFleur, and Flowers) were more prone to getting an earful than others. Most of these coaches came off as cocky to the players, which could have been off-putting; the system being taught, however, made so much sense that they tended to get away with it.

"Good ball is good ball," Cooley reasoned. "They have a good system, and there's no one that knows football that's going to dispute it. I don't care about the politics or the bullshit behind it or who is what or who does what. Kyle had a good system, and it made me love football more than I've ever loved it, and understand it, and see it. And he had a lot of young coaches that also were competitive and felt the same way."

Yet, as much as Cooley loved the scheme—well, he believed the schemers loved it even more. In his words, "The one thing that all of these guys did in Washington was tell themselves that the scheme was more important than the player. And so, they all had to evolve away from that. Now, that's my opinion, let me be very clear . . . With all of these guys, they're all given so much credit for being so good with the people skills. They're mostly shitty with the people skills."

When Cooley said that to me in December of 2019, we were sitting on his couch in rural Northern Virginia watching *Monday Night Football*. I put my beer down and asked, "Even McVay?"

"He's less bad," Cooley said, "but he's not as good as people give him credit for."

In what sense? "His awareness of how people actually see him that are close to him. Like, all of these guys are brilliant, but you need to know how people view you."

In learning to see football the way Kyle Shanahan saw it, the Fun Bunch was getting a collective education that would help change the sport. To say they were obsessed with their craft—talking about it, thinking about it, fighting about it—would be an understatement. "I'm a big believer in you become the company you keep, and I do think there was a positive peer pressure amongst each other that was healthy," McVay said. "That knowledge was something that we were always trying to figure out—where can you find those edges and those margins? How can you understand what are the rules of all 22, and then how can we utilize that to our advantage? It was a positive peer pressure, is the best way that I can describe it. When you have people that push the envelope—whether it be coaches on offense, coaches on defense, other younger peers—I think those were instrumental in shaping a lot of the core philosophies and the core beliefs."

The young assistants also competed with one another to come up with creative plays, formations, and other nuances that could be brought to life on Sunday, should Kyle Shanahan deem them worthy. (McDaniel tried to get Shanahan to name the plays he suggested, believing it would make the coordinator more invested.) LaFleur described the dynamic as an "organic competitiveness." LaFleur, said Foerster, "knew everything Kyle needed and wanted before Kyle even asked for it." LaFleur stood out for his attention to detail and penchant for pointing out flaws to even the best-designed plays. McVay spiced up workout sessions by creating competitions such as "Who can name all the red zone plays in the game plan?" and inevitably won them.

Through it all, LaFleur, McVay, and McDaniel—three wunderkinds vying for attention and supremacy—forged lifelong friendships that belied their charged circumstances. Things got even livelier, and more innovative, when Raheem Morris came on as the defensive backs coach following the 2011 season.

Morris, still just 35, fit right in with the Fun Bunch, and brought a defensive-minded perspective to their discussions. "It was awesome," LaFleur recalled. "Rah lived right down the street from me, so we were always hanging out. Just the energy he brought every day was crazy; it was next-level. He's got a wealth of knowledge, and he's got a lot of confidence, too. We'd always go back and forth. It was a great learning experience. He was the first guy that I met that, within five minutes of meeting him, he was bagging on me about my eyebrows. That was the first time someone called me out like that—just commenting on how nice my eyebrows were—and I was like, 'Holy shit—who is this guy?' "

They were managing to have a good time even as the team was losing. The Skins had gone 6–10 and 5–11 in Mike Shanahan's first two years and didn't have an answer at the quarterback position. Snyder, famously impatient, wouldn't tolerate the status quo much longer. The tenuousness of the situation was underscored after the 2011 season, when Snyder, the team's three minority-share owners, and Allen, the GM, sat down with Shanahan for what the coach believed was a debriefing.

Instead, it quickly devolved into an inquisition.

"They said, 'Kyle doesn't know how to run the football. You're gonna have to take over the play calling,' " Shanahan recalled. "And I said, 'Do you guys have any idea of what it takes to run the ball? Let's take a look at our offensive line. Let's take a look at our wide receivers . . . We've got a chance to be better next year. We've got $40 million [in salary cap space] coming back.' Not knowing . . ."

Mike Shanahan couldn't have known how much drama the next few months would hold, and how much he'd have to adjust. In the moment, he successfully staved off his son's demotion—Kyle, the group agreed, could continue as the team's primary play caller. What no one in the room realized was that, eight months later, the plays he'd be calling would be wildly different than anything the league had seen before.

Chapter 9

Full-Blown
Australian Toilet

The epiphany came at golden hour. Sitting on the back deck of his Northern Virginia home on a muggy mid-June early evening, Kyle Shanahan and Mike McDaniel were discussing the monumental challenge that awaited them: how to adapt their intricate offensive system to maximize the skill set of rookie quarterback Robert Griffin III, a breathtaking talent whose short stint as a collegiate superstar had given him only a rudimentary exposure to the requirements of the professional sports world's most challenging position.

Desperate for a star quarterback, Washington owner Dan Snyder had gone all in for the Heisman Trophy winner known as RG3, making a blockbuster trade with the St. Louis Rams for the second-overall pick in the 2012 draft. The move mortgaged the franchise's future, derailed Mike and Kyle Shanahan's courtship of Peyton Manning, and created a seemingly daunting problem. How could Griffin, a player who'd never been asked to take a snap from under center or go through traditional passing progressions during his time at Baylor, have a prayer in hell of executing a complicated, highly detailed, timing-based attack that required its quarterback to be an extension of his coach's brain?

For the past four months, the Shanahans and their offensive assistants had scrupulously studied the zone read–based attacks employed at Baylor and other college programs to try to determine the best way to roll out Griffin against NFL defenses, and to attempt to incorporate some of those principles into their well-established system.

After two seasons in Washington, Kyle was a scapegoat for the failed Donovan McNabb experiment and the 21 defeats in 32 games during those miserable campaigns. Now, handed a raw rookie who seemed content to fall back on his physical gifts rather than grind his way through a comprehensive quarterback education—in some ways, the worst possible person to pair with him—the younger Shanahan knew he had to figure out how to make it work. If he wanted to save his reputation and cling to his dreams of becoming an NFL head coach, this unsolicited experiment could not blow up.

As he and Shanahan sat on the deck drinking Red Bull and vodkas, McDaniel noted that rookie running back Alfred Morris, an anonymous sixth-round draft pick out of Florida Atlantic, had shown a lot more pop than expected in the final practice of offseason workouts. Morris's late burst of brilliance had been something of a fluke: the Redskins had practiced on split fields throughout the offseason because they'd drafted two rookie quarterbacks—Griffin and fourth-rounder Kirk Cousins, the latter a hedge handpicked by Kyle—and the coaches wanted to get each young passer as many reps as possible. That meant they needed two fullbacks, and Morris, a 222-pound sixth-round pick from Florida Atlantic, had spent OTAs (organized training activities) and minicamp working as one of them. On the last practice of the last day of the offseason program, they tried putting Morris at halfback, and the result was revelatory. "He'd be so good in our [regular] offense," McDaniel said. "One cut and go." Shanahan agreed, saying, "We've gotta get him some reps with the ones and twos [during training camp]." The trick, both men understood, was how to fuse the plays and blocking schemes that showcased Morris's ability with a system that Griffin could digest and operate from the get-go.

That's when Shanahan came out and said it.

"Why don't we just run everything out of the pistol?"

McDaniel cocked his head and stared at Shanahan. He took a sip of his drink and furrowed his brows. He was thinking.

Everything?

"The whole fucking thing," Shanahan said, answering a question that McDaniel hadn't verbalized. "Zone read. Inside zone. Outside zone. All the plays. Let's go for it."

Shanahan's idea—to import the intricacies of his existing scheme into the pistol, a wholly unfamiliar alignment in which the quarterback lined up four yards behind the center (three yards closer than in a traditional "shotgun" formation), with a single running back three yards directly behind the quarterback—was simple on its face. Yet it was also radical, presenting a complex set of challenges that would have infuriated a traditionalist. Integrating a souped-up version of the zone read—a scheme popular in college in which the quarterback decides whether to hand the ball to a running back, or pull it back and keep it, based on the response of the nearest defensive end—wasn't a natural fit for the Shanahan system. It would require inverting their blocking concepts on one side of the formation while remaining true to their existing ones on the other. It would be hard to visualize, even for abstract thinkers like Shanahan and McDaniel, and challenging to convey to the players. It would turn a whole lot of seemingly sacred rules and principles, such as running toward the tight end and threatening the defense one gap at a time, on their heads. It would make for a disjointed and uncomfortable training camp.

And Shanahan, having danced around the issue for months, having jokingly threatened to install a pistol-exclusive attack a few times during offseason workouts and meetings, had finally embraced the endeavor, said, "Fuck it," and gone all in. Coming up with the theoretical blueprint was one thing; other coaches might have done that. Having the balls to do a complete overhaul, on the fly, in practice? That was rare and unusual, a credit to both father (Mike Shanahan's credibility having made it all possible) and son. "An abstract's dream," McDaniel would later describe it.

"When we come back," Kyle Shanahan said, "we're gonna fully operate out of the pistol. Until we decide otherwise."

As soon as Shanahan shared the epiphany, as they sat there on the deck, McDaniel thought, *I'm in the presence of a visionary.* The question, to him, no longer was "Should we do stuff out of the pistol?" It had become "Why doesn't *everyone* do it out of the pistol?"

Then McDaniel started laughing. "Yep," he said, "that's the way to get good at it. Of course we run it out of the pistol. It makes total sense. And in some way, shape, or form, it's gonna freak everybody out."

The young coaches were living on the edge, and it was invigorating.

Their plan had to work, or jobs would surely be on the line, and careers possibly derailed. And yet, their purpose was pure. Typically, relatively inexperienced coaches like McDaniel, Matt LaFleur, Sean McVay, and even Kyle Shanahan were brought into an existing system and expected to keep the pistons pumping and gears turning. Whether the West Coast offense or a different scheme, the mentality was similar, and it traced back to Bill Walsh: This is what we do. We run these plays because they worked then, and if we run them correctly, they'll work now. We know which players thrive in our system, and we will find them and acquire them, and you will coach them up to follow our long-standing rules.

This was totally different. It was subversive, sanctioned by a decorated leader who wasn't scared of the fallout. Said McDaniel, "Mike Shanahan was fearless. He would just do whatever made sense, at all costs. Everything was open to being questioned. When you're young, everyone is in awe of the veil of 'The Shield.' It's 'Hey, there's a way that things are done,' and you're a product of your environment, to a degree, until you know better. And our environment was full-blown Australian toilet. Opposite."

MIKE SHANAHAN'S MINDSET MAY HAVE SET THE TONE, BUT IN THIS CASE the circumstances were dictated by a higher power: Snyder. After the season, Shanahan had flown to the Bahamas, where the owner owned an estate, to meet with him on his luxury yacht and plot a course for an abrupt reversal of the franchise's fortunes. The obvious way to do that was to get a superstar at quarterback. In this case, for the first time in NFL history, one was available in free agency. Manning, after 13 prolific seasons as the Colts' starting quarterback, was on the open market after being released; Indy planned to draft Stanford's Andrew Luck with the No. 1–overall pick. The catch was that Manning, who was about to turn 36, was coming off four neck surgeries.

While in the Bahamas, Shanahan learned that Manning had scheduled a visit with the Broncos, who were eager to move on from the inexplicably successful (and accuracy-challenged) folk hero Tim Tebow. Shanahan, who still owned his house in Cherry Creek, reached out to Manning's agent and set up a visit there with the quarterback for the morning after the conclusion of his Broncos visit. As Kyle Shanahan recalled in the spring of 2023, "I was told 24 hours before [the meeting] that I'd have three hours with Peyton Manning. I was in my office, preparing for the biggest meeting of my life." Both Shanahans later flew to Denver—Mike from the Bahamas, Kyle from Dulles. While they were in the air, news broke that general manager Bruce Allen, at Snyder's behest, had traded three first-round picks and a second-round selection to acquire the second-overall pick in that year's draft, with RG3 as the obvious target.

Kyle Shanahan was flat-out crushed. He figured the meeting with Manning would be canceled, but his father indicated otherwise, insisting they could still sign him—"probably trying to let me down easy," Kyle Shanahan said in retrospect. At the meeting, Manning and Kyle hit it off immediately, spending several hours watching film and talking offensive theory and strategy. When Manning left, Kyle was hyped. "Oh, he's not coming here," Mike Shanahan said, now shooting his son straight. "There's no way—we just traded all those picks for Robert."

The aftermath of that disappointment led Kyle to the pistol. It was a monumental decision with major ramifications. The 2012 season would define the Fun Bunch, and set its members off on their respective trajectories. As McDaniel put it, "When I tell the story to people about that year, they'll be like, 'OK, who came in and clinic-ed you on zone read?' Well, no one. We were an independent venture, taking an offense that we knew and adapting it to this quarterback and adding stuff that wasn't very prevalent at the time. Tim Tebow had, like, 30 zone read plays that [previous] year in Denver; that was the only NFL football we could watch at that time that was zone read. We would watch all the college stuff, but they were just doing no-huddle, which was really fast—you couldn't even figure out what they were doing.

"But the bottom line is, in our formative years, we were doing NFL football uncharted, and that doesn't happen. Everything's grandfathered in. You run stuff because it worked. Since Bill Walsh. Bill Walsh had a system and then found his guys to [bring it to life]. We were coming up with a system to fit a particular set of talent."

It started, as most things involving Mike Shanahan did, with film study. "After we did draft Robert, we had this long-ass cutup, like, 200 plays or something," LaFleur recalled. "It was the stuff they did at Baylor. It was some of the stuff that was going around the league with Tebow in Denver and Cam Newton in Carolina. It took us a couple hours to get through it. We're all kind of tired, all the assistant coaches and Kyle. Mike's like, 'Alright—let's run that back and watch it again.'

"We're like, 'What? Are you fucking kidding me?'"

Oh my god—this guy is on a different level, LaFleur thought.

Somewhere, Steve Young was laughing: *Let's go over it again.*

"Mike must have watched it six times," Raheem Morris recalled. "He made a pilgrimage to Baylor and talked to their coaches. Watching them go through the process and figure it out was one of the cooler things."

Said LaFleur, "That's just how [Mike Shanahan] was. That's a big reason why we all are the way we are now, because we learned from him and his detail. It's like nobody I've ever been around. This dude had an attention span, a laser focus, like I've never seen before."

———

KYLE SHANAHAN CAME UP WITH THE MACRO SOLUTION IN MID-JUNE, enunciating it to McDaniel as they sat on his deck. Previously, NFL teams had stopped zone read plays by keying on an offset back and overloading, because they essentially knew the play could only go in one direction. By running the entire offense out of the pistol, and thus not declaring their intentions, the Redskins could preserve the threat of zone read on every play and keep defenses from tilting their formations to one side.

It was so blissfully simple; it made so much sense. "It wasn't as complicated as everybody thought it was," LaFleur said. "The genius behind the pistol was we could run everything that we did under center, and everybody thought we had two different offenses. There were some parts of it that were a little bit different, but the concepts were all the same."

From that point on, Kyle Shanahan and his assistants furiously turned their attention to solving the micro, a process that presented a steady series of challenges. For the offense to make sense, many things had to be reconciled. The pillar of the new attack, the zone read, would require Griffin to base many of his decisions off the behavior of the weakside defensive end. On most designed running plays, Griffin, after receiving the center's airborne snap in the pistol four yards deep, would tuck the ball into Morris's gut—with the option to pull it out. If the defensive end (typically to his left) stayed outside to protect the sideline, Griffin would hand the ball to his halfback, who'd flow to his right in search of a vulnerable gap and cutback opportunity in what was a modified outside zone concept. If the defensive end crashed inside to try to stop Morris, Griffin would pull the ball out and race to the vacated area toward the sideline.

This presented some inconsistencies. For one thing, Morris was being taught to start in one direction, receive the handoff, and then flush back toward the opposite end of the line. It also meant that the blockers on the weak side of the formation would be asked to set up for an outside keeper in that direction while those on the strong side (where the tight end lined up) would be threatening gaps toward the other sideline, à la the classic outside zone alignment. It was confusing, at first, even to the coaches; conveying the proper responsibilities to the players presented another level of stress.

That led to newly christened terminology such as the 50 Series, which accounted for the dual-direction blocking assignments on zone read runs. McVay came up with that one, partly because those digits were available. In the 50 Series, an odd number call such as "53"—universally used to denote a run to the left—meant "block right" to half of the people on the line of scrimmage.

As they descended down the rabbit hole, Kyle Shanahan and his assistants created so many new wrinkles and so much new terminology that the head coach finally said, "Enough!" In an effort to limit the verbosity, Mike Shanahan decreed that a single word—in this case, "Bear"—would be used to inform players whether they were reading the right or left defensive end on the zone read run in question. "We tried to put it all in one box, and we couldn't even do it," LaFleur recalled. "We had all these different terms for all these different variations of it."

McDaniel, Kyle Shanahan, Foerster, and the others felt that the Bear designation was overly broad and failed to account for specific deviations, some of which were not yet built into the newly installed system. And they worried that it could leave the defensive end in question totally unblocked and in position to pummel Griffin if the play went awry. Explained McDaniel, "That's where Kyle's brain is so good at understanding how to build things from the ground up, from a verbiage [standpoint], system-wise. We didn't want to limit things." For example, the assistants wanted to play off the Bear call with offshoots like Grizz that sent the tight end to the second level from across the ball.

"There are just different variations," LaFleur explained. "A Bear block was: envision a pistol, and the fullback would be offset to the left. If it was 50 Bear, he would arc release to the side of the action and block the second-level defender, depending on who showed up. Let's say we wanted to move a guy on the right side. Well, you couldn't call it 50 Bear. Then we'd call it a 'Grizz' block, like grizzly bear. Now it was 50 Grizz. Then we'd have, if the action's going to the open side, Wanda Grizz. We'd have all these different tags."

LaFleur—always partial to making concepts easier for players to assimilate—pushed for shortened calls. Wanda Grizz became Wag, for example. "It all had to do a lot of it with formations and what you're asking these guys to do," LaFleur said. "Is it to an open side? Is it to a closed side? Is the fullback strong? Is he weak? The position of that guy."

The head coach still thought it was too much. "You don't need all these words," Mike Shanahan insisted, but his assistants were convinced that they did, even if they couldn't adequately explain why. At one point, Kyle Shanahan told Foerster, "You've got to stand up to my dad and tell him he's fucking wrong." Responded Foerster, "You're the offensive coordinator. You tell him!" As it turned out, in the middle of the regular-season opener, Mike Shanahan had a rush of realization. "You guys are right," he conceded over the headset. "I totally get it. This thing can grow."

IT WAS ONE THING TO WORK OUT THE THEORETICAL MACHINATIONS OF the scheme change. Putting it into practice was the real test. The coaches, predictably, concealed their plans throughout the preseason, keeping things as vanilla as possible in training camp practices that were open to the public and in their preseason games. The unveiling came in the regular-season opener against the New Orleans Saints, and it was not subtle.

On September 8, 2012, the night before the game, Kyle Shanahan lay in his bed at the team's New Orleans hotel, feeling amped-up and anxious.

A few hours later, in the middle of the night, he awoke suddenly—while blurting out an entire play call. He tossed and turned for a couple more hours and headed to the notoriously loud Superdome, where he paced around nervously, waiting for the unveiling.

When he walked to the visitors' sideline at the Superdome and put on his headset, Shanahan was locked in and ready. At least, he thought he was. Notorious for memorizing intricate calls and spitting them out flawlessly early in the play clock, giving his quarterback ample time to align the offense and receive the snap, the young offensive coordinator was supercharged, as if he'd mainlined espresso. After three Drew Brees incompletions and a Saints punt, Washington took over at its own 32-yard line. And then Shanahan, to the shock of McDaniel and his fellow assistants, rattled off the zone read play he'd been waiting to call for weeks and weeks—and transposed the digits, causing the tight end to cross the formation and go around the defender whose actions would dictate the quarterback's decision, and essentially rolling out a play that didn't actually exist.

Confused, Griffin threw a short pass to wide receiver Pierre Garçon that went for no gain. Shanahan felt sick. But he got the next call in without incident, and Griffin read the defensive end and kept the ball around the right side for a 12-yard gain. Then RG3 hit Garçon on a short pass that the receiver turned into another 12-yard gain, and they hooked up for nine more on the next play. The drive ended with a Billy Cundiff field goal, and the Saints responded with a go-ahead touchdown drive, with Brees finding tight end Jimmy Graham down the middle of the field.

The Superdome was swirling with energy. The hometown Saints, nine-point betting favorites, were taking over the game. A holding penalty on the ensuing kickoff backed the Skins to their own 12 yard line. The crowd got even louder. Shanahan exhaled and sent in a call . . . and Griffin, having frozen several defenders with a play fake to Morris, zipped a pass downfield to Garçon, who beat single coverage, raced up the seam, and continued for an 88-yard touchdown.

Across the football world, as the highlight flashed on scoreboards and television screens, pulse rates quickened. RG3, a run-first quarterback, was seven-for-seven for 121 yards—and he was just getting started. At game's end, Griffin had thrown for 320 yards to lead the Skins to a shocking 40–32 victory, and he and Morris had combined to run for another 138 yards. Even though Washington would lose its next two games, and six of its next eight, it was clear to opposing defensive coordinators that the Shanahans had done something truly new. The emblematic play of the season came in a week six game against the Vikings, when Kyle called a quarterback draw on third and six—and Griffin cut to the left sideline, raced 76 yards for a game-clinching touchdown, and got mobbed by delirious fans behind the end zone.

Starting in mid-November, Washington rattled off seven consecutive victories to capture the NFC East title. The revolution was real. Griffin—rather than Luck, and rather than revelatory third-round pick and future star and Super Bowl champion Russell Wilson—would be named the NFL's Offensive Rookie of the Year.

For numerous reasons, his rookie season would turn out to be RG3's peak. Yet, for the young offensive coaches, it was a foundational experience. It taught them that they could construct plays, concepts, and entire systems that fit their players, even if they were operating completely outside their comfort zone. It fortified their conviction that anything and everything could be questioned, and that it was acceptable to try to improve on a seemingly finished product. It made them fear stagnation and obstinance more than failure.

"That was really cool to experience," LaFleur said, "and honestly, it shaped a lot of my beliefs to this day about how you get the most out of players and the willingness to be flexible and study other things—not just do what we've always done, because everybody's a little bit different. It's about trying to put these guys in the best position possible. It just kind of stirred the pot of just the creativity that you can have, that you need to have, and your willingness to evolve and not worry about if you don't know a certain scheme and you just study the shit out of it. Hopefully, you got enough smart people in the room that you guys can figure it out. It was probably one of the better coaching performances I've ever been around."

There were other benefits to the scheme shift, too. Because the 2012 Redskins were the only ones doing what they were doing, unsettled defensive coordinators across the league tried to come up with untraditional ways of defending them on the fly.

"Another residual was that we all got live experience on how to do NFL football and get used to the idea of defenses being different on game day than they are for other opponents," McDaniel said. "Every time you'd play a team, you'd get different things that weren't on tape. All of a sudden, from an Xs and Os standpoint, there's an extra gap that defenses have to defend when the quarterback is a threat to run. So, you'd show up on game day and they would have a different defensive structure than they'd play all season."

That was particularly unusual at the time, with one notable exception. As McDaniel put it: "It used to be just Bill Belichick that would be random as hell and all of a sudden show up and play different shit. Now, that is kind of commonplace. And we as offensive coaches got to experience that almost weekly, instead of just when you play the Patriots. It gave us all a window into how to innovate, not for the sake of innovation, but for the sake of problem-solving."

In 2012, the countermoves by opposing defensive coordinators largely failed. Even the coaches who had come up with the Skins' blueprint were shocked by their success. After the season, some of the Washington coaches crunched the numbers and determined that, of Griffin's 3,200 passing yards, more than a third had come via a single concept known as Drift. It was a simple endeavor that didn't require RG3 to go through progressions or read defenses at an advanced level—he'd fake a handoff and, with his back to the defense, turn, put his foot in the ground, and make a 12-yard throw to a wide receiver who had slipped behind a run-suspecting linebacker. The play exploited the fear opposing defenders had of Griffin's running ability and of Morris's productivity in the adjusted inside zone/outside zone attack, and it worked over and over and over again.

As the season dragged on, even as Drift became increasingly familiar to opposing defensive coordinators, they remained seemingly powerless to adjust. The same was true for the other basic passing concepts that Washington was running, all in an effort to keep things as simple as possible for their raw rookie. The key to it all was a Shanahan staple: the marriage of the run and the pass—with the run, in this case, being especially threatening and easily disguised.

To Mike Shanahan, the season evoked memories of his first job as an assistant on Barry Switzer's 1975 Oklahoma staff. "The zone read, basically, was the wishbone. I ran that at Oklahoma, and we were national champions. It is the same as the wishbone, except you do it out of [the pistol]. The concept is the same—you're doing different things to spread the defense out, and you'd do some [basic] things in the passing game, and defenses didn't know how to stop it. We only ran three or four pass plays the whole year [in 2012]. And if they did try to take away the running game, he had enough speed to make plays. Robert wasn't very nifty. He couldn't make anybody miss, and he wouldn't slide. He didn't even know how. But he could get to the edge."

The zone read triggered memories for McVay, too—it was a reminder of his roots as a high school option quarterback. "That's Marist football, man. The triple option—you're running the wishbone. I used to do that underneath the center and just get killed."

EVENTUALLY, OPPOSING COACHES WOULD ADJUST BY PLAYING "QUARters" (a zone coverage with four defensive backs spread across the secondary) and bringing a safety down to the side where the quarterback might run. That was after spending an offseason studying the Washington scheme. During the course of the 2012 campaign, the attempted fixes were more of the duct tape variety. This was not to say that Skins were unbeatable. Griffin was still a rookie learning as he went, and they still lacked talent in other areas. The offensive line, outside of Pro Bowl left tackle Trent Williams, was unremarkable. Garçon missed six games with an injury and still led the team in catches, a reflection of a mediocre receiving corps. The defense ranked 28th out of 32 NFL teams.

And the season ended in wrenching fashion, with a home playoff defeat to the Seahawks in which Griffin suffered a severe knee injury and Washington blew a big lead.

Snyder, who'd given up so much to get RG3, viewed the rookie as a transformative player and couldn't fathom that he had legitimate flaws. Griffin, who considered himself a game-changing icon, fed into that narrative. Both owner and quarterback were convinced that the perception of RG3 as a run-first quarterback was skewed and that he was, in reality, a true dropback passer who happened to be exceptionally fast. That irked

Mike Shanahan because Griffin, despite his intelligence, didn't seem to be driven to grasp the intricacies of the position. Throw in the hovering presence of Griffin's starry-eyed father, Robert Jr., who wasn't shy about voicing his opinions—to Snyder, to Shanahan, and to journalists—and it created a highly combustible situation. After the season, Griffin Jr. would tell *GQ*, "You name one quarterback out there that would rather run the football than throw the football and I'll show you a loser."

Even during the winning streak, there was drama. Late in a December 9 clash against the Ravens, Griffin was knocked out of the game with a right knee injury. In came fellow rookie Cousins, the overlooked fourth-rounder who had been a Kyle Shanahan favorite from the start. Cousins threw a game-tying touchdown pass and two-point conversion to force overtime, and Washington pulled out a 31–28 victory. To say Griffin was insecure about the presence of Cousins was an understatement. As Cooley told me in 2018, "Robert would never call Kirk by his name when he talked about him publicly. He was dismissive in interviews. I felt like he never liked that Kirk was there."

The next week, Cousins started a road game against the Cleveland Browns, who were riding a three-game winning streak. The Shanahans scrapped the zone read and put Cousins on the move, conceiving a game plan heavy on bootlegs. "Kyle played to Kirk's strengths," recalled Vikings guard Tom Compton, a rookie for Washington that season. "I think they might have run ten rollouts that game, and Kirk executed." After an early interception, Cousins settled down and stepped up, completing 26 of 37 passes for 329 yards and two touchdowns in a 38–21 victory. Then things got awkward. According to more than half a dozen witnesses, Snyder entered the locker room and made a beeline for Griffin, stepping right past Cousins in the process. Then, with Cousins at an adjacent locker, the owner proceeded to reassure his injured quarterback that he was still the unquestioned starter. Recalled Mike Shanahan, "[Snyder] sat right next to Robert in the locker room, and all he talked about was how good he was, that he was a franchise guy—and he was sitting right next to Kirk when he did it."

Adding to the chaos, Griffin's father, who had seethed while watching the game from the sideline, confronted Mike Shanahan in the locker room. "His dad got so mad," Shanahan remembered. "He goes, 'You guys didn't run one running play for the quarterback.' I don't know how he got in the locker room; he was standing behind [RG3]. I said, 'Do you realize that Kirk Cousins is not a runner? He can't run the ball. He did have the option to roll out, but he threw the ball on the run.'" Said Matt LaFleur, "I really think that game gave certain people a lot of insecurities, and it hurt us . . . because there were a lot of questions going on that led to all the bullshit."

Said Cooley, "I know that Robert was irate after that [Cleveland] game, because Kirk got all the bootleg stuff he thought he should have been running. The next week, he was in team meetings, doing physical therapy the entire meeting, in the back of the room, doing leg-strengthening exercises and stuff with the medicine ball. He brought the training room into the meeting room. It was insane. Then I watched the kid play the next week when he shouldn't have been playing."

Several coaches and players believe Griffin's uneasiness about Cousins also factored into his decision to remain in the game during that 24–14 playoff defeat to the Seahawks, despite having reinjured his knee in the first quarter. He was knocked out midway through the fourth quarter and diagnosed with a torn ACL, LCL, and meniscus, which required reconstructive surgery and launched his career on a downward trajectory.

At halftime, after consulting with the team physician, Dr. James Andrews, Shanahan told Griffin he could stay in the game because he had "earned that right." Kyle agreed, telling his father, "If we pull him now, we might lose him forever"—meaning Griffin would no longer trust them. It was a move that all parties would come to regret, for different reasons. Griffin's was obvious: he was never the same player. "We left him in. I regret it now," Shanahan told me more than a decade later. "We would have won the game if we put Kirk in. I'm the head coach. I should have made that call."

After the season, disturbed by the growing disconnect between him and Griffin, Mike Shanahan went to Snyder with a proposition.

"We should trade Robert," Shanahan said.

Predictably, the owner was not enthused. The coach pressed his case.

"It's the perfect time," he said. "His value is the highest it'll ever be. We've gotten the most we can out of him. Nobody else knows that. Let's trade him before people figure it out."

Shanahan felt that Cousins was good enough to become a franchise quarterback. Unlike Griffin, he was a pocket passer who obsessed over the details of the Shanahan offense and typically delivered the ball where Kyle wanted it to go. Less than a year after giving up a boatload of premium draft picks to get RG3, Shanahan was sure Washington could deal him and secure a similar package from another team, if not more. "It was the perfect scenario," Shanahan would later recall.

Snyder resoundingly rejected the idea, allowing an increasingly toxic situation to fester. Then things got worse.

———

BEFORE TAKING THE WASHINGTON JOB, SHANAHAN—ENVISIONING THE train wreck that could occur upon a new CBA being reached—conferred with NFL commissioner Roger Goodell, a longtime friend. Goodell was enthusiastic about Shanahan taking over a storied franchise in the nation's capital, and strongly encouraged him to do it. Shanahan explained that he foresaw having to cut a lot of high-priced players as part of a rebuild, something that normally would accelerate money into the salary cap. With the uncapped year, that wouldn't be a worry, but such moves could be viewed by other owners as attempting to game the system. Shanahan wanted assurances that Washington wouldn't face recriminations down the road. Goodell told Shanahan that as long as they didn't sign new players and load up the contracts to take advantage of the situation, they'd be fine.

They weren't. In March of 2022, Goodell levied a $36 million salary cap penalty, spread over two league years, for violating a rule that (as per the terms of the CBA) couldn't technically exist. The timing was terrible; Washington got the news three days *after* trading away all those picks, with RG3 as the target. Now, they'd have to release several high-priced veterans, some of whom theoretically could have been replaced with newly drafted rookies.

Shanahan was furious when he got the news. Soon thereafter, he went to league headquarters in New York City and met with Goodell in his office.

"What did we do wrong?" Shanahan asked. "I asked you about every contract. You said every one of them was OK."

"Mike," Shanahan remembers Goodell answering, "you didn't do anything wrong."

"Then how in the fuck do we have a $36 million penalty?"

Things degenerated from there. Shanahan was livid, questioning Goodell's manhood and screaming, "This is my fucking career!"

In the weeks that followed the 2012 season, there had been some conversations between Washington executives and high-level people at the NFL office about the possibility of softening the penalty—perhaps even giving the team back the $18 million of cap space for 2013 in advance of free agency. The conversations had gone well enough that Shanahan was hopeful. Morris had ties to two free agents from his time in Tampa Bay—cornerback Aqib Talib and defensive lineman Michael Bennett—who could have greatly improved the Skins' defense. Allen, Washington's GM, had a history with future Hall of Fame defensive back Charles Woodson, who was also about to hit free agency. Shanahan believed that, with the $18 million forgiven, he'd be able to land all three players, and that all three players intended to come to Washington.

And, once again, no dice. Just before the start of free agency, the team received word that no relief would be forthcoming. Shanahan and his assistants, as usual, would have to try to scheme their way out of this predicament. And this time, it would be even more difficult.

FOR KYLE SHANAHAN, ESPECIALLY, ADAPTATION AND INNOVATION WERE part of the premise of coaching. Even during that special season, as the RG3-led attack dismantled the rest of the league, Shanahan knew in his heart it couldn't last. The Redskins had embarrassed too many defenses in 2012. There was no way they could sustain it. As always, he would have to evolve.

Throughout the 2012 season, mystified defensive coordinators mostly defended Griffin out of the pistol by playing a Cover 3 alignment, with the strong safety walked down as an eighth run defender (also able to cover underneath routes), and two cornerbacks and the free safety each responsible for a third of the field on the back end. "Which is exactly what we wanted," LaFleur said, "because it defined our targets."

Given an offseason to adjust, defensive coordinators would surely come up with a better plan. The Shanahans needed another wrinkle. Their countermove to the expected counter: a sped-up no-huddle attack designed to catch opposing defenders off guard, tire them out, and make it difficult to substitute. Another NFC East rival, the Philadelphia Eagles, had hired Oregon's Chip Kelly as head coach that January with a plan to install such a scheme. Kyle Shanahan, too, was intrigued.

"Because everyone was going to catch up to us, that next offseason was no-huddle," recalled McDaniel, who was promoted to receivers coach following the 2012 campaign. "We were benefiting from people not knowing how to defend us. We had to stay ahead, so we were going to figure out how to do Chip Kelly's tempo offense in two-back and [we] started the framework for the no-huddle process. When we came back from the break [in late July] and went to Richmond for training camp, Kyle had a whole system of no-huddle."

Switching things up was hardly a cure-all. As Shanahan and his assistants had predicted, defenses in 2013 were ready for them in a way they hadn't been the previous year. Said LaFleur, "What happened the second year is we got a shit ton of quarters. That was actually a better way of stopping it."

The shift would pay dividends down the road. Looking back, McDaniel believes that the emphasis on a sped-up attack in 2013 led McVay down a schematic path that ultimately changed the game. Four years later, when McVay became the youngest head in modern NFL history and transformed the Rams' offense, he was using many of the same foundational concepts.

"What we built in 2013 is what Sean uses today, 90 percent of the time," McDaniel said in 2020. "That is a system that he's evolved, because that's the expectation from the tutor—that you're always evolving. That was the starting point. Sean added a bunch of elements to it and took it to another level that we all kind of use schematically."

WASHINGTON WAS 3-5 AT THE MIDPOINT OF THE 2013 SEASON. THEN, recalled LaFleur, "it all went to shit." The Skins dropped their final eight games, and their dysfunction became the talk of the football world.

By December, the bombshell reports started dropping. One, citing an anonymous source, said Mike Shanahan had become so disillusioned with Snyder that he'd cleaned out his office in advance of the previous season's playoff game against the Seahawks, later changing his mind about quitting in the wake of RG3's knee injury because of optics. The day of that report, the Redskins lost to the Chiefs, 45–10, at FedEx Field. LaFleur told his wife, "Well, Bre, I think I'm going to be looking for a new job here."

A week later, Jason La Canfora's story came out, with anonymous current and former staff members portraying Kyle as an entitled brat surrounded by unqualified buddies who were little more than yes men. If Shanahan hated that depiction, he was even more stung by the concurrent assault on his father's reputation—and, ultimately, on his dad's legacy. It would be the final season of Mike Shanahan's coaching career, and it left a bitter taste, clouding his son's view of the sport and profession he loved. "That killed me when I worked for him—like, killed me," Kyle told the *Athletic*'s Jourdan Rodrigue in 2023. "I had such pride in my dad's legacy. It [seemed] like he [was] losing that. And I went for a while where it made me hate football."

Though he'd interview for head coaching jobs with the Raiders and 49ers the following year, Mike would never return to the sidelines. However, in McVay's eyes, Shanahan's inglorious ending had residual value for his young assistants. "I actually think the things that we went through in Washington had us better equipped for any scenario that could take place moving forward. We experienced all different types of adversity. We had successes, but the ball was always the main thing and it was always at the forefront of just trying to push the envelope and doing it with the right kind of people. He was teaching us lessons that I don't think you appreciated until you have the reflection of a handful of years in hindsight with some of the experiences that we've all accumulated and accrued."

The end of Shanahan's tenure was such a rancid and rancorous mess that, in theory, each of the young coaches could have been irrevocably sullied. Yet the combination of Snyder's well-earned stigma and the lingering admiration in NFL circles for the previous year's scheme shift served as equalizers. In McDaniel's words, "That [2012 season] was a successful venture—successful enough to sustain credibility within the NFL. But it was the Redskins, so it blew up. Because of that, we've all bounced around."

McDaniel would join Kyle Shanahan on the firing line—and, eventually, in Cleveland, with Shanahan as the Browns' new offensive coordinator and McDaniel as receivers coach. LaFleur rejoined Brian Kelly, for whom he'd once been a graduate assistant, as Notre Dame's quarterbacks coach. It wasn't a total blowout, though. McVay not only stayed with the Skins, but he also got a promotion—to offensive coordinator. That was only possible because Washington hired, of all people, Jay Gruden to replace Mike Shanahan. Their preexisting connection and longtime family ties made it logical for McVay to stay; it didn't hurt, either, that Allen, the GM, had been in Tampa when McVay began his career as Jon Gruden's de facto secretary.

"It was really a weird feeling, because you're a part of the reason things didn't go well, just as much as anybody else," McVay recalled. "But yet, as a result of Jay getting hired, it actually worked to my advantage to where you get a promotion out of it. That was very weird. It's why I don't ever take for granted how lucky and blessed I've been, because of the legacy that my grandfather established. It's a joke how lucky I've really been." There was another unlikely survivor: Foerster, the veteran offensive line coach who'd come to Washington desperate to work for Mike Shanahan, was also retained.

AS MIKE SHANAHAN CLEANED OUT HIS OFFICE—THIS TIME, FOR GOOD— he tried to leave what he believed was a sincere parting gift for his successor, and for the owner he reviled. In an exit meeting with FedEx founder and CEO Fred Smith and the team's other minority owners, Shanahan offered some stark advice: he told them to trade the quarterback. This time, however, he wasn't talking about RG3. "Look," he said, "whoever you hire as head coach, you've gotta get rid of Kirk Cousins. Because no coach in his right mind would play Robert over Kirk."

In Shanahan's recollection, Smith and the others "kind of snickered."

They likely weren't laughing the following November, when successor Jay Gruden benched Griffin for Colt McCoy, or in August of 2015, when Gruden named Cousins his starter. A year later, Cousins was selected to the Pro Bowl while Griffin, now with the Cleveland Browns, would experience his final weeks as a starting quarterback.

The Shanahans' success in Washington was fleeting. The imprint on the football world, however, was lasting.

"That was an incredible, underappreciated thing that happened in the NFL," Raheem Morris said. "You think of the greatest teams in NFL history, and they usually have these championships and epic wins. With us, it wasn't like that. This team didn't win anything, because of various circumstances. But there was greatness happening. The rest of the league was blown away, and nobody figured out a way to stop what we were doing all season. And the impact is still being felt."

A few months after being hired as the Dolphins' head coach in 2022, McDaniel turned to the world of professional basketball for an analogy about his time with the Redskins (the team had since changed its name to Commanders): "I would equate it to Golden State, with Steph Curry and those dudes. Like, the game is so much different now. When they had the skill players to do it, they all of a sudden start launching a million threes. The whole game is different now, 'cause of that. At that level, it's a big difference when it's tried and successful. Everyone sees that it can be done and adapts accordingly."

For Kyle Shanahan and his young disciples, it was time to adapt and survive. They had pulled off the unthinkable: they had broken the game. And they had uncovered some guiding principles that would shape their careers.

Chapter 10

The First Life Raft

I *can't believe it's happening again.*

Mike McDaniel threw his backpack over one shoulder and headed to the underground parking lot outside the Georgia Dome, stung by the defeat he'd just experienced as a member of the Atlanta Falcons' coaching staff and his now-murky future.

As usual, Kyle Shanahan and his closest coaching disciples—McDaniel, Matt LaFleur, and now relative newcomers like Rich Scangarello and Mike LaFleur—had installed a promising offensive system, only to face an off-season of uncertainty. In this case, with Shanahan as the Falcons' first-year offensive coordinator in 2015, a 5–0 start had turned to 6–1, to 6–7, and now, after a season-ending defeat to the New Orleans Saints, a highly unsatisfying 8–8.

Shanahan and star quarterback Matt Ryan were disconnected and combative. Things were even worse between the coordinator and four-time Pro Bowl receiver Roddy White, who'd encouraged the perception in some league circles that Shanahan was an entitled nepo baby who couldn't get along with players.

"We weren't on solid footing for, like, the eighth year in a row, it felt like," McDaniel would recall years later. "We'd only gone to one playoff game in all our time together. So, there was the narrative of 'They have a successful offense that doesn't win.'"

McDaniel had an even bigger issue: busted once again for drinking on the job, he would soon go to a rehab in an effort to save his career and turn around his life.

Certainly, the stress of the workplace, particularly in the 36 months between Washington's tumultuous 2012 playoff defeat to the Seahawks and this underwhelming Falcons season finale, had contributed to his situation. Each season, for Shanahan and McDaniel, it felt like they were coaching for their careers—and that wasn't a total exaggeration.

After things imploded in Washington in 2013, Shanahan was hired as the Cleveland Browns' offensive coordinator, taking McDaniel with him as his receivers coach. Yet the 2014 Browns proved to be as deeply dysfunctional as the franchise they'd departed, prompting Shanahan, with McDaniel's help, to force his way out the following January.

Dan Quinn, the Falcons' newly hired coach, gave Shanahan safe harbor in Atlanta—largely on the strength of Raheem Morris's recommendation. Morris, who'd known Quinn since his days as a Hofstra safety, had been hired as the Falcons' assistant head coach and defensive backs assistant. Shanahan got Matt LaFleur, who'd spent the previous season as Notre Dame's quarterbacks coach, to join his staff in that role. Mike LaFleur, Matt's younger brother, followed Shanahan from Cleveland (where he'd been an offensive intern) to Atlanta (as an offensive assistant).

So, other than Chris Foerster (who'd returned to San Francisco as offensive line coach) and McVay (still Washington's offensive coordinator), the band was essentially back together.

And that first season with the Falcons, and its aftermath, played out like a series of scenes from *This Is Spinal Tap*—with about as many fits and starts as the fictional rockers' attempts to take the stage in the "Hello Cleveland!" debacle.

SHANAHAN ARRIVED IN CLEVELAND IN THE WAKE OF HIS FATHER'S FIRING in Washington, and with his own reputation damaged. The Browns, a franchise constantly churning through head coaches, had hired Mike Pettine, a Rex Ryan disciple coming off stints as a defensive coordinator for the Jets (2009–12) and Bills (2013). Pettine and Shanahan saw the game from different perspectives. To Pettine, the purpose of the offense was to control the clock with a strong running attack, avoid turnovers, and keep the game close, allowing his aggressive defense to make decisive plays. Shanahan operated as though he wanted to score a touchdown on every play; the more points the offense could score, the better.

It didn't help that, because Pettine already had some other staff members in place, Shanahan wouldn't be able to interview and select most of his position coaches. Most significant, offensive line coach Andy Moeller had already been hired, meaning Shanahan would have to guide him through basic outside zone principles.

There was also the matter of personnel. Cleveland's general manager, Ray Farmer, was new to the job, having been promoted from assistant GM after yet another organizational shakeup following the 2013 season. There seemed to be little alignment between him and Shanahan, especially when it came to the all-important quarterback position. Shanahan wanted to trade for Kirk Cousins, who'd been with him the previous four years in Washington. It probably wouldn't have cost Cleveland much—possibly, as little as a fifth-rounder. Yet Farmer—and, more to the point, owner Jimmy Haslam—had other plans.

The Browns, to be charitable, were a mess. The previous season had ended in surreal fashion, with Cleveland suffering a 20–7 defeat to the Steelers in Pittsburgh to fall to 4–12. About an hour after the game, reports surfaced that first-year coach Rob Chudzinski would be fired. It was a shock, given that Haslam and his top front-office executives, Joe Banner and Mike Lombardi, had preached patience, stability, and continuity after hiring Chudzinski. It also made for an exceptionally awkward bus ride back to Cleveland.

"I'm on the wrong bus and I'm very happy I don't have to sit on Bus 1 [with Chudzinski] in awkwardness," one player texted me after the game.

"This organization is a joke," another Cleveland veteran texted. "I'm completely in the dark about this. Please [rip them]."

Said a third Browns player, "We are so dysfunctional. These billionaires need to pick somebody and stay with them. These aren't girlfriends. You can't dump them if they [fail to please you] one time. Too many dominoes fall and [screw stuff] up when that happens. This is highly upsetting."

A MONTH AND A HALF LATER, HASLAM FIRED BANNER AND LOMBARDI.
The owner wasn't done, however. Embroiled in a federal investigation
into allegations that his truck stop chain, Pilot Flying J, had deliberately
defrauded customers out of rebates, Haslam didn't have much credibility
in league circles. Ultimately, while 17 of his former employees pled guilty
or were convicted for their roles in the fraud scheme, Haslam was able to
cut a deal to avoid criminal prosecution, paying $92 million in fines while
reimbursing customers another $56 million. That deal was announced just
before the start of training camp in July of 2014.

By then, Haslam had already embraced another budding scandal.

With the 22nd-overall pick in the draft, the Browns selected Johnny
Manziel, who in 2012 had become the first freshman ever to win the
Heisman. The brash, polarizing Texas A&M quarterback known as
"Johnny Football" had scared off most NFL talent evaluators and coaches
after a series of off-the-field acts, some of which became public. Manziel
had been sent home early from the Manning Passing Academy for missing
a session and being late to another, and had been escorted out of a frat party
at the University of Texas. There were legitimate worries about his party
habits, aversion to studying, and aura of entitlement. To suggest that he was
not the ideal quarterback to match with the Browns' newly hired offensive
coordinator was putting it mildly.

Naturally, Haslam was all for it. Better yet, he explained his decision
by saying a homeless man in Cleveland had told him to do so. "Here in
Cleveland, everywhere I go, people know me," ESPN reported, quoting
Haslam. "And I was out to dinner recently and a homeless person was out
on the street, looked up at me, and said, 'Draft Manziel.'"

It felt like a disaster waiting to happen, but Shanahan was able to help
forestall it. Pettine, with Shanahan's support, gave the starting job to Brian
Hoyer, a Cleveland native who'd flashed the previous season after replacing
injured starter Brandon Weeden, leading his hometown team to consecutive victories before tearing his ACL in a nationally televised Thursday
night game. Hoyer didn't have exceptional talent, but the former backup to
Tom Brady in New England was a hard worker and highly engaged, prodding teammates and coaches as though he were a player of Brady's pedigree.

Shanahan, with McDaniel's help, made Hoyer's job easier by installing the outside zone scheme and getting production from three running backs: Terrance West, Isaiah Crowell, and Ben Tate. The offensive line was an area of strength for the Browns, with future first-ballot Hall of Famer Joe Thomas at left tackle, standout veterans Alex Mack (center) and Mitchell Schwartz (right tackle), and rising rookie guard Joel Bitonio. A fractured fibula in week five would end Mack's season; the Browns' line, however, remained a force.

For Thomas, Shanahan's arrival felt like a godsend. "I had some friends that played for him in Washington," Thomas recalled, "and everyone said, 'Oh my gosh, you're going to love this guy. He's a gangster.' As an offensive lineman, you're always jealous of that system. Going back to before the NFL draft, I was interested in having Denver draft me because the system they ran makes it easy on the O-line. All I have to do is run as fast as I can, and it doesn't matter how big or strong I am? I like that system. And you don't have to do a lot of dropback passes. The fact that those [linemen] were constantly having great seasons—nobody ever gives up a sack, they're running for all this yardage, they're running the ball a bunch—we were really jealous. I was really excited about playing in the system. You heard whispers that occasionally [Shanahan] didn't get along with certain guys. I kind of brushed that aside because I knew guys had played for him in Washington that were like, 'Oh my gosh, you're going to love this dude.'"

Mack, who'd already been to a pair of Pro Bowls, was similarly excited by Shanahan's arrival. For one thing, they were a great intellectual match. Mack, who as a Cal junior had won the Draddy Trophy—also known as the "academic Heisman"—was a notorious worrier who was constantly envisioning scenarios that could derail a play or scheme and planning for contingencies. He wanted to have answers. He wanted to know the *why*.

Shanahan, of course, had answers. "I asked a lot of questions in the Cleveland days," Mack said. "They were always well received."

For example, Moeller, the offensive line coach, had been harping on a specific coaching point: the need for Mack (and other linemen) to gain ground on the first step. It made sense—that would allow Mack, after snapping the ball, to be the aggressor as the Browns set up a wide run—yet it was treated as doctrine. Mack couldn't understand why it was an absolute. Eventually, he went to Shanahan and asked, "Why are we doing this?"

"You can get there quicker," Shanahan answered, referring to the spot the center was supposed to reach as the run developed.

Mack persisted. "As a center, my feet are even. I don't have a stagger to my stance. If I put a stagger in, maybe that'll work, but if we change directions [before the snap], I will not be able to go the other way."

Many coaches would have blown him off, essentially saying, "Just do it the way we coach it." Shanahan was open to workshopping ideas. Mack came up with one: "What if I just try to gain lateral ground, lose a little depth on my step? Would that work?'"

The coordinator's answer surprised him.

"Yeah, that makes sense," Shanahan said. "Yeah, do that."

Another thing that excited the linemen was that Shanahan, unlike their previous coordinators, held the wide receivers to a high standard as blockers.

Said Thomas, "It was the first time I've ever had an offensive coordinator who could coach, in detail, every one of the 11 positions. That was sort of a wakeup call. Typically, throughout the NFL, at least up until that point, you got an offensive coordinator whose background is quarterback, passing-game stuff, which is fine. Kyle was a receiver in college, so it seemed like he was no different. The difference was, typically your offensive line coach is your run game coordinator, and he's also the guy that's in charge of the blitz protections. He's also the only one that knows the technique that's required to be able to get all those guys in the right spots to be able to make the holes where they need to be. You sit in there with the offense, and the offensive coordinator is coaching the receivers, the skill guys, the quarterbacks. Then, if there's a problem in the run game, he looks at the offensive line coach, who then yells at you for screwing something up.

"Kyle was totally different because he would sit in there and just go down the line and coach everybody up like he was their position coach. It was really a wild moment, because I think it brought everybody together and you got a different level of buy-in, especially among the offensive line. We were like, 'Holy shit, this dude's holding the receivers accountable for *blocking*? He actually knows how I'm supposed to get my job done?' He knows, not just how it's supposed to look—'OK, hat on a hat, here's the cut.' He knows, 'This is where you're supposed to step. This is why you have to step there. This is where your hands have to go. This is where your eyes need to be. This is what I want the uncovered man to do. This is how I want him to do it.'

"The beauty is, he said, 'This is *why* you have to do it.' Then he'd show you clip after clip of the coaching that he was giving, working with Trent Williams and those [Washington linemen]. You could see what we were trying to get done."

It was revelatory to Thomas, who was used to the old model. Most offensive coordinators, he believed, were pass-first and "run when they have to, when the head coach calls in and goes, 'What the fuck? Why haven't we called a run? We need to smash these guys.' Then he's like, 'Alright, coach of the offensive line, Donny, what do you like in the run game?' He says, '96 Power.' It gets two yards. 'OK, great, now I can throw again.' "

Now, suddenly, the run and pass were intertwined. "It was just a different mindset of how everything fit together and how Kyle actually wanted to run the ball," Thomas said. "He coached people, and he demanded perfection—from how the receivers blocked and how the quarterbacks carried out their fakes to how the offensive linemen tied together. He demanded perfection from every position."

It worked better than anyone could have reasonably expected. By Thanksgiving, the Browns—the Browns!—were 7–4 and in playoff contention. For veterans like Thomas and Mack, it was a totally foreign experience. "We were, like, 3–2 when I broke my leg," Mack recalled, "and I'd never had a winning record. Never happened. It was the most success I'd ever seen. Then, 7–4 . . . That was my best season as a Brown, and I was injured for it."

And then, abruptly, the franchise's dysfunction engulfed them all.

Behind the scenes, things had been simmering. The organizational push to get Manziel onto the field was strong, and Farmer, the team's general manager, had broken NFL rules (for which he'd ultimately receive a four-game suspension at the start of the 2015 season) to try to hasten it. In more than one game, he sent text messages to quarterbacks coach Dowell

Loggains, who was in the upstairs coaching box, that questioned Shanahan's play calling and use of personnel. Farmer also pointedly told Loggains he wanted Manziel to play instead of Hoyer.

On November 30, Farmer finally got his wish. Down big in a road game to the Buffalo Bills, Pettine pulled Hoyer and inserted Manziel, who promptly completed three of four passes for 54 yards and ran for a ten-yard touchdown. Hoyer started the following week's game, a 25–24 defeat to the Indianapolis Colts. Two days later, Pettine announced that Manziel would start the following Sunday's home game against the Cincinnati Bengals.

"It was a weird moment," Thomas remembered. "Brian had not played well in that game. We kind of knew all season long that the Browns' management, whoever that was, wanted to play Johnny. He was your first-round pick. They kind of knew that Hoyer was not the future. However, anybody that watched practice—which would be coaches, players, scouts, GM—they knew that Brian gave us the best chance to win. I remember when Pettine called me in and basically told me about the decision. He was like, 'It's kind of out of our hands.'

"I think everybody knew that Johnny wasn't ready, including Kyle. It really dejected Kyle. I remember watching him the Friday before Johnny's start, and we honestly had a hard time completing a pass. A Friday practice is supposed to look like a Pro Day workout where you complete every ball and the guy looks like the next John Elway. I think we were like two out of 30."

It carried over to Sunday. The rookie could not have been less prepared for the moment—years later, in the documentary *Untold: Johnny Manziel*, he admitted that he didn't watch a single minute of tape during his time with the Browns. Johnny Football's first start happened to be on Shanahan's 35th birthday, but Manziel's lack of readiness spoiled the party. The Bengals rolled to a 30–0 victory, intercepting him three times.

All of Shanahan's instincts told him that his current situation was unsustainable. After another subpar December start, and a defeat that eliminated the Browns from playoff contention, Manziel went on injured reserve with a hamstring injury. He wasn't done making noise, though. On Friday, December 26, two nights before the Browns' season finale against the Baltimore Ravens, Manziel threw a raging party at his Cleveland apartment that was attended by numerous teammates. The following morning, Manziel, who was required to report to the team facility for treatment on the hamstring, and star receiver Josh Gordon, who was on the active roster, were absent when the walkthrough began. The Browns were so concerned about Manziel that they sent their security staff to his apartment—"to make sure he was alive," in one player's words. Shortly after the season, Gordon, sidelined by the Browns for the season finale in the wake of the incident, would receive a minimum one-year suspension for violating the NFL's substance abuse policy. Manziel, meanwhile, would check himself into a rehab facility for substance abuse.

SHANAHAN, STILL UNDER CONTRACT, WANTED OUT. THE STAKES WERE immense. Once Mike Shanahan heard about Farmer's texts mandating that Manziel be put into the game, he told his son, "You're gonna have to get out of there." He repeated the advice at season's end, telling Kyle, "You've got to get out of there, or it could be your career. If you stay, it's a disaster and they're gonna end up firing you. They may hate you for it, but you've got to try to get out."

As Shanahan was formulating a plan, he was assessing potential escape routes. There was a chance to go to Baltimore as John Harbaugh's quarterbacks coach, with Marc Trestman as offensive coordinator. Dan Quinn, closing in on landing the Falcons job, was also interested in hiring him; Quinn's goal was to run the outside zone–based system. Recalled Quinn, "When he was under contract, I said, 'Hey, man, this is a no-brainer, but this is not going to be easy to do.' He said, 'Give me a shot, to see if I can.' I said, 'Well, if you can, then we got a deal.' That part made a big impact on me to [know], 'This guy would really be committed to it because he would have to fight his way to get out, so there's not an option B.'"

Shanahan called McDaniel and briefed him on the situation. He told McDaniel to make a list of reasons why he should be allowed to leave— issues they'd encountered, examples of the lack of organizational and staff alignment, signs that things were not likely to improve. Two days later, McDaniel showed up at Shanahan's house with his list; it was skewed toward specifics involving the team's receivers, the position group he coached. Shanahan expanded upon the list, and together the two coaches typed it up. There were 32 reasons.

Later, Shanahan went to Pettine's house and presented it. The head coach was sympathetic; if his coordinator wanted out, he did not intend to try to stop him. Pettine's bosses, however, weren't so receptive.

"They said they weren't gonna do it," McDaniel remembered. "And then they drafted up a statement that [Shanahan] had to make so they could save face. And then Kyle and Sashi [Brown, then the team's executive vice president] went back and forth on that statement. 'Cause they wanted him to say some crazy shit, like . . . how he's sorry that he's letting the players in the organization down, all this shit."

According to one person close to Shanahan, Farmer tried to get Shanahan to sign a document saying he'd tried to hurt the organization. Shanahan ultimately called the GM's bluff, threatening to go public with his grievances. Ultimately, the team relented and allowed him to resign; he did so, with the following statement: "I appreciate the opportunity Mike Pettine, Ray Farmer, and Jimmy Haslam gave me to lead the Browns' offense in 2014. The Browns organization is committed to improvement and winning. I regret how the inner workings of the organization were represented publicly over the last few days. Ray and Mike both have the work ethic, experience, and talent to work together to turn this organization into a winner. In light of the circumstances, I have decided to resign. I'm grateful for my time with the Browns and wish them great success going forward."

In the NFL coaching world, it was viewed, to borrow Thomas's word, as a gangster move. Teams tended not to let valuable coaches break their contracts for lateral moves out of the goodness of their hearts. Even some of the coaches Shanahan left behind in Cleveland applauded his gumption. "He was on the first life raft off the Titanic!" said Anthony Weaver, the Browns' defensive line coach in 2014 and 2015. "Can't fault a guy for knowing what he needs to win."

THE FIRST THING QUINN NOTICED ABOUT SHANAHAN WAS THAT HE WAS special. Like many offensive coordinators, Shanahan had a clear grasp of the system he wanted to run, the plays he wanted to install, and what he was looking for in a quarterback. His talents went well beyond that, however.

Quinn later recalled that "he was probably one of the very first people I'd ever seen that could talk about every position like he was the coach of that position. In the old days, [Bill] Walsh had done that. Kyle could have been the position coach at any position. For most people, you focus on one thing and climb the coaching ranks. It's like Apple. You make the fucking chip, and you ride the train up. This was different, and it was just eye-opening to see—he could just talk about every part of the offense with great detail. I said, 'Man, he has full command of all these positions.' I remember [assistant general manager] Scott Pioli coming out of there saying, 'That was fucking awesome!' I said, 'Yeah it was.'"

The issue was that Quinn and Shanahan weren't building a new operation from scratch. Rather, they were trying to revive a strong team that had faltered. In 2008, newly hired general manager Thomas Dimitroff and coach Mike Smith had the energized the Falcons and, with first-round draft pick Matt Ryan at quarterback, made a surprising run to the postseason. Ryan, the Offensive Rookie of the Year that season, kept getting better, and Dimitroff built around him. After a 9–7 season in 2009, the Falcons made the playoffs in each of the next three years, going 13–3 in 2010 and 2012—and suffering a close defeat to the 49ers in the NFC Championship Game in the latter season. Dimitroff had taken a big swing in 2011, making a draft-day trade to move up and select Alabama wide receiver Julio Jones with the sixth-overall pick. Pairing Jones with veteran Roddy White, a first-team All-Pro in 2010, had given Atlanta one of the top receiving duos in recent memory.

Consecutive losing seasons had spelled the end for Smith, but Dimitroff still believed he had, in Ryan, a quarterback capable of carrying the Falcons to their second-ever Super Bowl—and first championship. Jones had blossomed into a superstar; White, now 33, had caught 80 passes for 921 yards and seven touchdowns in 2014.

Shanahan arrived with some very specific ideas about how to install his offense and how it should be executed. He met with resistance from the start. Ryan, a true alpha, didn't want wholesale change. "We've been pretty good on offense here for a while," Ryan would tell Shanahan, whose mind immediately went to *Yeah, but what have you guys won?*

White was an even trickier matter. He was close with the owner, Arthur Blank, and exceptionally comfortable with his position coach, Terry Robiskie, a holdover from the previous regime. Shanahan felt White was casual, at best, about his practice habits, something that could influence Jones and the team's other younger receivers. And, with his 34th birthday on the horizon in November, White appeared to his new coordinator to be a descending player.

From White's perspective, Shanahan—who hadn't gotten along with Donovan McNabb or RG3, who'd been run out of Washington and bailed out of Cleveland and seemed to be drafting in his father's wake—was coming into *his* house and failing to show him the proper respect. White saw his practice reps decline, with Leonard Hankerson—who'd been with Shanahan in Washington—getting more run. Second-year running back Devonta Freeman and tight end Jacob Tamme became bigger parts of the passing game. And that first season, 2015, Jones was more of a focal point than ever before, catching a franchise-record 136 passes for 1,871 yards, just 93 shy of Calvin Johnson's all-time single-season mark. White would catch a mere 43 passes for 506 yards and one touchdown.

White wanted more passes thrown to him and would loudly make his feelings clear to the man delivering the football. This put pressure on Ryan—and sometimes kept him from going through his progressions the way Shanahan demanded him to. With the Falcons starting 4–0, but with White sitting at only eight receptions in total, the receiver told ESPN.com's Vaughn McClure, "For me, at the end of the day, I want to catch passes. I'm not out here just fucking around just to sit around to just block fucking people all day. It's not what I want to do."

A disgruntled star wideout was one thing. Shanahan's clashes with the franchise quarterback were more significant. Ryan was used to having more control at the line of scrimmage, where he could diagnose the defense before the snap, make adjustments, call out the protections, and, if desired, throw out the play and call an audible. Shanahan wanted the play run his way, sometimes with a second, preselected option (a "can," in his terminology).

"It was not all rosy," said McDaniel, whose title in Atlanta was offensive assistant. "It was an adjustment for Matt Ryan, and he'd been very successful. He and Kyle had both been successful in their own way."

The man in the middle was Matt LaFleur, the quarterbacks coach, who often literally stood between Shanahan and Ryan on the sidelines in games and in practice. Four years later, as the Packers' first-year head coach, LaFleur would face some of the same challenges while attempting to get Aaron Rodgers to adjust to the same scheme. In Atlanta, he mostly got yelled at, especially by Shanahan.

After getting to 6–1, the team lost six games in a row to fall from contention. As Shanahan said, "Being in this league long enough, if you lose two games in a row, it's Armageddon. We lost six."

The quarterback and coordinator tried to make adjustments as they learned about each other. Ryan wanted the game plan finalized as early as possible—ideally, by Thursday night. Shanahan's process was to keep probing and tweaking, sometimes adding plays the night before the game. "Matt didn't like that," LaFleur recalled. "It took us a minute to realize, 'Hey, if we find a nugget the night before, just don't tell anybody about it, and we'll put it in the next day, in-game, and make [it look] like an in-game adjustment.' There were just some communication things that first year."

On Sundays, Quinn worried that Ryan was sometimes *too* prepared. His intensive study sessions on Fridays and Saturdays had left him mentally exhausted by the time kickoff rolled around. Said Quinn, "Matt's very process-driven. Going into the end of the week, going through his checks, I think there were times when he went into a game mentally tired, which is common for a lot of overprepared people."

———

QUINN FELT FORTUNATE TO HAVE SHANAHAN AS HIS COORDINATOR, BUT theirs wasn't the smoothest relationship. Just as Ryan struggled to align with the new play caller, Quinn, too, had a tough time adjusting to Shanahan. They had completely different office demeanors: Quinn would roam the halls, ebulliently looping in everyone he could, making it all feel collaborative. Shanahan typically watched film and crafted plays behind a closed door, communicating primarily with McDaniel (who was helping to design the run game) for much of the week.

"It was hard on me, too, because we were different in that way," Quinn told me later. "It wasn't all-access. I think he functioned in that [closed-off] environment really well. I like including people—'What do you think about this?' I like the ideas. Then I can sort them. Whereas he would use Mike McDaniel as the bridge and say to the line coaches, 'Hey, we need this formation. It doesn't matter the run that's going to come out of it, but we need to have it because it's going to be up for another play.' I thought Mike McDaniel was this really important bridge that helped the run game and the pass game connect."

McDaniel's role as a connector was vitally important. He was cut out for it. When he left the organization, following Shanahan to San Francisco after the 2016 campaign, Quinn tried to write down McDaniel's job description—and struggled mightily. "It was such an important role, but how are you the person that sees around the corners? Creative thinkers are sometimes hard to pin down [when you] say, 'Tell me what you do on a regular basis.'"

Yet, while Quinn might have understood his value—and Shanahan quite obviously relied upon his skill set—McDaniel was in a bad place. Driven by personal ambition and competitiveness, upset that he'd been seemingly surpassed by McVay and LaFleur, possibly threatened by the presence of Mike LaFleur (who now had the same title as McDaniel: offensive assistant), he managed his strong feelings the way he had since college: by drinking heavily at times. In his words, "I was a party boy." He thought he could handle it; he was high-functioning, for the most part, and a very convincing actor when under the influence. "No one would ever know. There are so many times people have been like, 'You were there, don't you remember?' I'm like, 'No, dude, I was blackout.' And they were stunned."

Even after his firing in Houston and his two-year United Football League exile, McDaniel had now managed to keep drinking for five consecutive NFL seasons without paying a public price. Late in that 2015 season, his run of clandestine excess without consequence abruptly ended. On the Saturday morning before the season finale, while chasing a hangover, he drank in his office at the Falcons' facility. Mike LaFleur noticed the alcohol on his breath and told Shanahan. And then Shanahan—who, in McDaniel's words, "had been cosigning me forever [and] felt obligated to tell Dan"—took it to the head coach.

On January 4, 2016, the day after the season, McDaniel was summoned to Quinn's office. He walked in not knowing if he'd still have a job, or an NFL future, when he exited. He feared the worst, but he had one of the sport's most empathic head coaches in Quinn, who reassured him: "We're gonna stand by you. You're not losing your job right now. I'm going to take that off the table. What we now need to do is help Mike the dude, not Mike the coach. There's not anybody that needs to know about this. There's not anything that needs to be said about this. We've got your back."

McDaniel felt comforted by Quinn's support, but his head was spinning. He was angry—at LaFleur, for ratting him out ("Go to my wife, not my *boss!*" he reasoned); at the situation (all he'd done, in his mind, was chase a hangover); and, of course, at himself.

"It was a 'What the fuck?' moment," McDaniel said. "I knew the risks that I was taking. I was pushing the envelope too much. I was trying to connect the dots: why I'd make myself vulnerable to this and how I became dependent on alcohol like that. Then it's like, 'Well, you're not becoming a receiver coach' . . . and I miss out on the opportunity to be Julio Jones's position coach. And I'm freaking out."

Finally, McDaniel concluded, *Fuck all this. There's something wrong.*

He needed to stop drinking. He was going to rehab.

The damage to his career? He'd deal with that later.

———

IN McDANIEL'S MIND, BECOMING A POSITION COACH ONCE MORE—AND specifically a receivers coach, with the NFL's best receiver in his meeting room—was the obvious goal. When Mike Mularkey, newly hired as the Tennessee Titans' coach, tabbed Robiskie as his offensive coordinator, Quinn had a sudden and unexpected opening. Yet, even if McDaniel's issue with alcohol hadn't sidetracked his promotion, Quinn viewed it differently.

Based on his manifest ability and familiarity with the scheme, McDaniel would have been the obvious candidate to replace Robiskie. Yet Quinn wanted Shanahan to mesh with the rest of the offensive staff more than he already had. For that to happen, he needed McDaniel to stay where he was—not in an even more encompassing role. As Quinn pondered the opening, he called Morris, his longtime confidant, and they spitballed. The two came up with a working list of four candidates, and Quinn asked Morris to vet them.

Morris made some calls. One candidate, he felt, was exceptionally strong. Two others, he believed, would also be good choices. Morris—at a mall with his wife, Nicole—gave Quinn the lowdown. Then he added, "Realistically, we need somebody that Kyle can trust and bounce ideas off of. It doesn't have to be the best receiver coach, because Kyle *is* sort of a receiver coach. That's his passion. He understands it so well. So, it really could be someone who coaches any position, as long as Kyle trusts him."

Quinn was intrigued. "I never thought about it like that," he told Morris before ending the conversation.

A while later, Morris—still at the mall—answered a call from Quinn.

"What about you?" Quinn asked. "I need two of you, and I can't have two of you. This would be the next best thing."

Morris, who'd never coached offense, pondered the question. "I'll do anything you need for the team," he said. "Just make sure Kyle's cool with it."

Shanahan was. Soon, he called Morris, fired up about the possibility. "Sweet," Morris said. "Sign me up."

That night, in bed with Nicole, Morris fielded another call from Quinn that made it semiofficial.

"What was that all about?" Nicole asked. "What just happened?"

"I guess I'm gonna go over to offense," he answered. "I don't know; I'll see in the morning."

And then, in keeping with the recurring theme in their relationship, Morris closed his eyes and fell asleep.

To Quinn, the move solved a problem that had been gnawing at him: how to make Shanahan less walled-off in his process.

"I thought Raheem was the right person," Quinn recalled. "He's the most charismatic coach that I've ever been around and probably ever known, next to Pete [Carroll]. How would that not make an impact on somebody when they already had a good friendship and working relationship? I thought, *What a cool challenge for [Morris] to bring to it.* It took me a year to know the best way to support Kyle. I also wanted certain things communicated to the staff, knowing that I want other people included. I didn't want it to just be the Kyle and Mike McDaniel and Mike LaFleur show, and then everybody else just waiting for their stuff. I wanted Raheem to be a connector in that."

The connections among Shanahan, Morris, Matt and Mike LaFleur, and, once he got out of rehab, McDaniel—and between those coaches and Ryan, the team's quarterback—would be crucial to the Falcons' immediate future. And the success on the horizon, in turn, would alter the futures of each of those coaches (and of McVay, who was taking notes from afar). The Falcons' 2016 season would also remake the sport.

Chapter 11

Airing It Out

Matt LaFleur called it "our kumbaya sessions"—his term for the clear-the-air sessions in March of 2016 that some in the NFL community would snidely come to call "marriage counseling."

Shanahan, in his laconic style, portrayed it as "having beers."

Whatever it was, the day and night that Shanahan, LaFleur, Dan Quinn, and Matt Ryan spent in Orange County, California, a couple of months after the Falcons' disappointing 2015 season, became the foundation for a special 2016 campaign.

Hosted by Tom House, a former major league pitcher who'd crafted a second career as a throwing guru for quarterbacks, and his partner, Adam Dedeaux, the summit was designed to establish each of the participants' preferred processes and put everything on the table. As with the Costanzas and Festivus in the classic *Seinfeld* episode, there was an airing of the grievances that would achieve semiapocryphal status in coaching circles.

First, however, there was an assignment. Each of the four men took a personality assessment test and met separately with House. That night, at House's home in Seal Beach, everyone met in a group, shared the results, and, over their drinks, began voicing their perspectives and feelings.

Recalled Quinn, "We took a personality assessment. I think it was more just to see where our imbalances are. I think, like most things, when you're in a relationship, you come to appreciate somebody's strengths and [avoid] putting them in a space that they're not comfortable with."

Quinn—and, by extension, Shanahan and LaFleur—were willing to expose themselves to potential discomfort because they understood the stakes. As Quinn put it, "I thought, *This is important enough for Matt [Ryan], let's all go out there. He's wanting to go dig in to make a difference.* Matt was really committed to it. I said, 'Hey, this is an easy one for us to do the same.' We all went out to L.A. and spent the day there doing that. It was definitely a worthwhile trip, just to find a connection, find a space to meet on common ground."

LaFleur got it from all sides. At one point, House took a pass at describing LaFleur's position—caught in the middle between Shanahan and Ryan, a pair of headstrong competitors who weren't shy about venting.

"Matt," House said, "you're the taint. You're between the dick and the balls."

In the end, however, LaFleur thought it was a positive experience, saying later, "You talk about being vulnerable—when you're doing those assessments and they're telling you everything that's kind of wrong with you, in front of everybody. That helps build the trust, too, when you leave yourself open to some criticism or whatever it might be. I think we all approached it the right way."

At one point, Ryan told LaFleur he wasn't assertive enough. How, exactly, the quarterback phrased the comment is a mystery that has taken on a life of its own. Some claim, at second hand, that the quarterback said, "I respect you as a coach, but I don't respect you as a man." There's another version in which Ryan used the word *pussy*.

Whether his actual words were that severe, the message definitely got through.

"It was probably saying, 'Go ahead and coach me hard,'" Quinn said. "Matt was a real competitor, and Kyle would coach him hard. 'No, you're fucking wrong. That's not how we're gonna go.' Matt [LaFleur] might be like, 'Well, you could do it that way or this way.' I think [Ryan] was basically telling him, 'Get off the fence. If you think it's wrong, say it's wrong. If you think it's right, say it's right.' I think [Ryan] was probably saying, 'Either have my back or don't, but don't play both of us. *Oh, I can see your point too . . .* Don't do that.' I doubt, knowing Matt Ryan, that it came from a shitty place like that. I would say that he would want to say, 'Just shoot it to me straight.' He doesn't always like the answer, but he wants to be shot straight. He's got the Philly side of him that's like, 'Just fucking give me the bad medicine.'"

The kumbaya sessions, in retrospect, had the intended effect. The following January, after the Falcons defeated the Seahawks in their playoff opener, Ryan told me, "We just worked it out over a couple of beers . . . we basically sat there and figured out some things. [Shanahan] learned what works for me, and I learned what works for him, and it was that simple. And we're in a really, really good place now."

A few minutes later, I got Shanahan's version: "Look, this all sounds totally overdramatized, but we've definitely grown over the past year. One thing I've learned about Matt is that he and I are extremely similar. We're both intense, we're locked in, we give it everything we can, and we take our jobs very, very seriously. We're both perfectionists, too. Because of all that, it's a perfect combination. But it takes time."

The meeting was also a potential rules violation, per the terms of the collective bargaining agreement between the NFL and the players union. When recalling the meeting in 2023, Quinn, asked to pinpoint the time it had taken place, said, "It was during the offseason prior to us getting together [for the offseason program]. I'm sure it was totally fucking illegal to do that. Retro-fine me. There's got to be some statute of limitations."

THERE WAS MUCH WORK TO BE DONE—AND MIKE McDANIEL, FRESH OUT of a three-week stay in rehab and still undergoing outpatient treatment, was right in the middle of it all, even if he hadn't been present at the Seal Beach summit. It is a truism for all coaches, but his personal challenges intersected with his vocational ones. He'd done a ton of self-assessing in rehab, and bared his soul in therapy sessions. He had a new outlook on his ambition, his goals, and his closest professional relationships.

The first thing McDaniel had to do was understand the *why*. In this case, why he abused alcohol. He would later say, "My best rehab was reading. Because I found books that kind of tailored learning to what I was going through—because there was this turmoil about being sad. And I ended up finding out that I was using alcohol for depression. And I was depressed. But I had to figure all that shit out."

McDaniel concluded that, on some occasions, his mind was spinning so fast that it made things uncomfortable. Drinking, for him, was a way of leveling that off. In his words, "It's miserable at times. You want to check out."

Quitting, for some, is a lifelong struggle. McDaniel was lucky. He came out of rehab committed to sobriety and never looked back.

"He has literally the strongest will I've ever seen," said McDaniel's close friend Chandler Henley. "Anybody that stops drinking cold turkey . . ."

All of it was tied into his career survival. McDaniel's most triggering thoughts—that he'd been overtaken by McVay and Matt LaFleur, with Mike LaFleur now on a similar trajectory, all while failing to reach Shanahan's level—needed to be reordered. He now learned to block out those worries and focus only on the job at hand, trusting that the rest would eventually take care of itself.

When it came down to it, McDaniel framed his circumstances as a defining test of his leadership skills, even if he didn't share that with any of his colleagues.

"It was like, 'OK, you're not becoming a receiver coach,'" he remembered. "And then I was faced with this choice."

Specifically, it would be McDaniel's job to train Raheem Morris, who'd spent his entire career playing and coaching on the defensive side of the ball, to be Shanahan's new receivers coach, the job McDaniel had so desperately craved. Even more challenging was the fact that Mike LaFleur—his fellow "offensive assistant" and the person who'd reported him to Shanahan for drinking on the job—was going to be Morris's de facto assistant. That meant McDaniel, who'd been Shanahan's receivers coach in 2013 (with Washington) and 2014 (with the Browns), would have to train LaFleur, too.

"So, I was faced with my first decision," McDaniel said. "How am I going to do this? What type of man am I? Can I really give them the keys? And that's where I went back to 'If I'm really worth a shit, if I am special or different, then what would be the hardest thing, the path of most resistance, the great thing that most people would struggle to do?' I decided, 'I'm going to go all in.'"

In doing so, McDaniel needed to fight against the impulse to view LaFleur's decision to report him as a calculated move to surpass him on the coaching depth chart, rather than as a well-meaning attempt to help a colleague and friend. His mind went to "devilish" places: *If he was trying to take me out, that sucks for him, because it needed to be a death.* Now, the power dynamic had changed. During arguments—mainly with his wife, Katie, or his boss, Shanahan—McDaniel exercised restraint. For him, "it was the ultimate test for me to do that with Mike without any reservation."

On some level, McDaniel understood that he might be overdramatizing LaFleur's decision to tell Shanahan about the workplace drinking, which had likely come from a place of concern. That's the way LaFleur later portrayed it to me, saying, "It was hard because you just didn't know how many more opportunities he was going to get. You just don't want to waste such a good brain, and a good person. He's genuinely a good person."

In the end, McDaniel repelled whatever dark thoughts plagued him about LaFleur's behavior and found a new perspective that ultimately set him up for greater successes.

"I got over it," he said in 2019, when he was the 49ers' run game coordinator and LaFleur their passing-game coordinator. "I have him to thank for angling me to push myself to places I never knew [I could go]. It was a cool thing to happen when all eyes were on me. So that, moving forward in my career, I'll know how to lead in certain—and I'm not sure if that makes sense. But there's a different type of leadership when you stop personalizing other people's outputs. When you really wrap your head around the fact that everyone has so much shit going on, and you're a very small fixture. And just being able to lead people emotionally in the game of football . . . It was a big climax where I got to put my theories to test. And I felt fucking outstanding."

THE GAMBIT OF MOVING MORRIS TO OFFENSE, MEANWHILE, PAID OFF— for the Falcons' receivers, who benefited from his communication and strategic skills; for Morris's fellow coaches, including Shanahan; and for Morris himself, who would spend four seasons in the role before returning to the defensive side of the ball, in a bigger job.

"What he did for us on offense in 2016," Shanahan said, "was something very few people could have pulled off."

Morris jumped into his new role, working with McDaniel and Mike and Matt LaFleur to help freshen up Shanahan's system. His knowledge of defense—what the rules were of various defensive schemes, how defensive coaches and players thought about the game—proved invaluable.

"He used to make comments all the time," Matt LaFleur recalled, "like, 'Oh my god, you guys are so fucked up.' . . . Just how drastically different the shit we worry about is, as opposed to the shit [defensive coaches] worry about. We'd voice our concerns and he'd say, 'A defensive guy wouldn't even think about that.'"

It changed LaFleur's perspective to the point where, once he became a head coach, he sought out similar arrangements: "I always want somebody with a defensive background on offense, and vice versa—just to give you a fresh take."

In part owing to Morris's presence, Shanahan seemed much looser in 2016, adapting to the ethos of the close-knit "brotherhood" that Quinn espoused throughout the facility. As Quinn said, "I really saw another side of Kyle's personality come out in 2016, which I thought was really needed. We had a lot of competitions, always in front of the players. We had a big basketball hoop in the corner of our meeting room—the old team room, where the press conferences were. I remember one time, it was Kyle up against somebody else. We were playing HORSE. There was a three-foot stage that sat up a little high. All of a sudden, he leaps from the stage and dunks it, just throws it down. Everybody was going crazy. It was cool to see him talking shit and having fun and knowing that you can be this competitive dog of a coach that you are, and also really enjoy it and have a good time, too."

Ryan also felt more at ease—partly because of his newly acquired backup. Initially a Falcons second-stringer during the Michael Vick era, Matt Schaub had been Shanahan's starting quarterback during his three years as the Texans' offensive coordinator. Now, he was back as a veteran free agent. Schaub helped Ryan see the beauty of the Shanahan scheme. In Houston, he had been Shanahan's ideal QB—following his rules, adhering to his reads, and distributing the ball to the coach's desired spot. Schaub showed up and knew all the answers to the test, which activated Ryan's competitive instincts and made him a more strenuous student.

Schaub also turned out to be a helpful buffer between the coach and quarterback. Mike LaFleur cited Schaub as "an unsung hero, just being a sounding board for Matt Ryan."

There was another, higher-profile free-agent signee who made a major impact: Alex Mack, the perennial Pro Bowl center who'd learned Shanahan's scheme in Cleveland two years earlier. Mack, who always wanted to know the *why*, who constantly worried about unseen flaws that could sidetrack a play, helped Ryan get comfortable in the Shanahan system. In giving Mack a top-of-the-market, five-year deal, the Falcons seemed to be overvaluing the center position. In this case, they got their money's worth.

As the offseason played out, Quinn continued to monitor the Shanahan–Ryan relationship. Things had improved since the meeting with House and Dedeaux, but the expectation remained that Ryan had to adjust to the scheme in ways that he hadn't the previous season.

Quinn wanted Shanahan to adjust as well. "We've got to give Matt a win," Quinn told him. He had a specific idea: Ryan, under previous coordinator Dirk Koetter, had favored a streamlined play-calling system during two-minute, hurry-up situations: Koetter came up with preset plays, numbered 1 through 12, with which the entire offense was familiar, enabling Ryan to call them at the line quickly and without hesitation. That had changed under Shanahan, who favored far more variety—and control—with the game on the line.

Shanahan didn't see the need to adapt to Ryan. Quinn persisted. "Matt's doing a lot. This makes his life easier. Hey man, give him one win. Fuck it."

In the end, Shanahan acquiesced—and found that he liked the streamlined approach. As the year progressed, Shanahan relied more and more on no-huddle, hurry-up plays during the course of the game.

Another post–Seal Beach tweak that helped Shanahan and Ryan's relationship had to do with simple geography. Shanahan, at Quinn's behest, moved from the sideline to the upstairs coaches' box, leaving Matt LaFleur to serve as the battering ram and buffer. LaFleur, on the field, might hear Shanahan scream into the headset, "What the fuck was Matt thinking on that throw?" LaFleur would then ask Ryan, "Uh, Kyle wants to know what you saw . . ."

"Tell him I fucking saw the safety cheating inside and I threw it to the guy that was open!" Ryan would snap back.

Good talk . . .

As a result, there was far less direct conflict between coordinator and quarterback, which Quinn believed was a positive.

"Kyle is obviously demanding, and he expects things a certain way," Matt LaFleur said. "That's not a knock on him. I think that's one of his strengths, to be honest with you. But also, when things aren't going right, you can feel his frustration, and you can feel his anger. That's not always the best, on game day, for the guys. If the quarterback can feel that, it's not good. What you don't want to do is steal people's confidence. They need to be confident and have that belief. They've got to know that you believe in them. Just because you get frustrated doesn't mean you don't believe in them, but if you come off that way . . ."

There was another reason Quinn wanted Shanahan up high: he'd learned the value of seeing the game from an overhead perspective from Pete Carroll, his former boss in Seattle. Carroll, in turn, had gleaned that insight as George Seifert's defensive coordinator with the 49ers in 1995— just after Mike Shanahan had departed as offensive coordinator.

Everything clicked. The 2016 Falcons scored 540 points—71 more than the next best team, and tied for the seventh-highest total in NFL history. "Being able to sit behind Kyle was like watching someone paint a masterpiece," Mike LaFleur said. "It was awesome watching that."

Said Ryan of the Falcons' offensive coaching staff: "You could sense the brainpower in that room. That pushed all of us in ways we hadn't been pushed before."

———

IN WEEK SIX, THE FALCONS TRAVELED TO SEATTLE TO FACE THE SEA-hawks, Quinn's former team. Shanahan, now in his second year of practicing against Quinn's defense and its Seattle 3 scheme—with the strong safety deployed closer to the line of scrimmage, and the free safety and cornerbacks each covering a third of the field on the back end—was extremely familiar with that defense's rules. He had figured out how to crack the code.

As explained by former Seahawks cornerback Richard Sherman, Shanahan discerned the defense's rules for dealing with "displaced" receivers: any wideout or tight end who lined up outside the tackle box, and not in a three-point stance. He knew that displaced receivers who ran short slants would be the responsibility of the corners, who'd have to come up close to the line of scrimmage to defend them. So, Shanahan had both outside receivers run one-step slants while deploying two tight ends on the line of scrimmage, in three-point stances, as (non-displaced) presumptive blockers. He sent both tight ends on seam routes up the middle, exposing the holes left by the corners. When Shanahan unveiled this play late in the third quarter, Ryan found tight end Levine Toilolo wide open for a 46-yard touchdown, giving Atlanta a 24–17 lead and creating a crisis on the Seattle sideline.

"It broke the defense," Sherman said. "It literally was against every rule that we had, so we had to change the rules of the defense in order to combat that situation. But nobody had ever done it." Recalled one Atlanta coach, "Richard Sherman was so pissed, he was screaming at [defensive coordinator] Kris Richard on the sideline. Kyle took great pleasure in that, because he caused that."

Yet the Seahawks came back and won that game, dropping Atlanta to 4–2. Going into their bye week in mid-November, the Falcons were only 6–4. Still, their confidence was high. After a 38–19 victory over the Cardinals coming out of the bye, Atlanta had a chance to beat the Chiefs at home. Down by five, the Falcons scored a touchdown to go up by one with 4:32 remaining and attempted a two-point conversion, the logical move. Ryan's pass over the middle to rookie tight end Austin Hooper was intercepted by K.C. safety Eric Berry, who took it all the way back to the opposite end zone for a two-point play, giving the Chiefs a 29–28 lead they wouldn't relinquish.

"That was a hard moment," Quinn recalled. "After that, we came up with a term: 'safe two.' In a situation like that, we'd call a back-pylon throw where only Julio could get it, or nobody else. I think probably through the first season and a half, there was a lot of 'OK—we're not gonna make that mistake again.' But when we got going, we were really hard to deal with towards the end of the year."

AFTER THAT DEFEAT TO THE CHIEFS, THE FALCONS ELEVATED. THEY closed out the regular season with four consecutive victories, scoring 42, 41, 33, and 38 points in those games. Ryan's eye-popping regular-season numbers would earn him MVP honors. He completed 69.9 percent of his passes for 4,944 yards, 38 touchdowns, and seven interceptions. His passer rating was a league-best 117.1, and he set an NFL record by completing touchdown passes to 13 different receivers.

And then, in the playoffs, it got even better. The Falcons, as the NFC's No. 2 seed, earned a first-round bye, and Quinn prepared his players for a lengthy run, laying out a schedule that extended all the way through the Super Bowl. He was trying to drive home a point. It worked.

The first playoff opponent: the Seahawks, again. Shanahan, having "broken" Seattle's defense during the regular season, came up with a masterful plan for the divisional-round rematch. During practice that week, Quinn noticed that his players seemed nervous. He finally snapped, stopping practice and bringing the entire team to the center of the field.

"I could feel people were tight," Quinn remembered. "Someone dropped [a pass]; we jumped offsides. Some stuff like that happened. I just brought the whole team up and said, 'Fuck this. This is not who we are. We ain't tight. I'm not gonna be tight. I don't want you to be tight.' I think that helped going into the playoffs to know: 'We're gonna do what we do. We're aggressive. We're disciplined. But we ain't tight.' I think that day helped loosen everybody up a little bit."

The Falcons rolled to a 36–20 victory over the Seahawks. Both coordinator and quarterback were locked in, and it was too much for their overmatched opponents.

"He played his ass off, man," Shanahan told me afterward. "There were a few times when I called throws against that defense that you can't block, at least for as long as the routes take, and he just let it go early with touch and trusted our guys to go get it. And it was especially cool because it wasn't always the guys we planned on—Julio went out for a while, and we had to change our personnel, but the guys that were out there came through."

A few days later, Shanahan, who'd interviewed for the 49ers' head coaching job, was told he would be the team's choice—something that couldn't be made official until after Atlanta's season ended. Quinn announced the news in a coaches' meeting, leading them in a celebratory ovation for Shanahan. He understood the stress of being a hot coordinator who interviews for head coaching jobs while his team is still in the postseason, having gone through it two years earlier during a Seahawks Super Bowl run.

The following Sunday, nobody accused Shanahan of having been distracted. The Packers' upset victory over the top-seeded Dallas Cowboys in the prior round meant the Falcons got to host Green Bay in the NFC Championship Game, setting up a duel between Ryan and Aaron Rodgers. It wasn't much of a contest: Atlanta jumped out to a 31–0 lead and rolled to a 44–21 victory.

Before the game, I spent some time on the field with a highly interested observer: McVay, who, earlier that month, had been hired by the Los Angeles Rams—becoming, at 30, the youngest head coach in modern NFL history. McVay, an Atlanta-area native, was technically a guest of his friends Matt LaFleur and Mike McDaniel. Yet he was also scouting Shanahan, in anticipation of the rivalry that was about to escalate between the former colleagues and soon-to-be stewards of California-based NFL teams with a long history of intense competition.

Watching the Falcons' offense that day, McVay was struck by the speed, certitude, and precision. When they went no-huddle, Ryan and company were impossible to contain. His mind was racing; he was formulating the early stages of a schematic shift that would feature a hefty dose of what Shanahan called "Turbo," a tweak that would help the Rams' maligned second-year quarterback, Jared Goff, completely turn around his career.

THE FALCONS WERE THE HOTTEST TEAM IN FOOTBALL, AND MATTY ICE was at the top of the sport—but the Super Bowl presented a daunting challenge. The New England Patriots, in the Bill Belichick/Tom Brady era, had been to six Super Bowls and won four, including a stunning victory over the Seahawks two years earlier. That game—which ended with Pete Carroll infamously deciding not to give the ball to star running back Marshawn Lynch on the New England one-yard line, only to watch Russell Wilson throw a ruinous interception—was one that Quinn, the team's defensive coordinator at the time, would never get over. Against Belichick and Brady and the Patriots, he would take nothing for granted.

The Falcons showed up in Houston feeling relaxed and expectant. Shanahan, with McDaniel's help, had put in a game plan the coaches felt mitigated their biggest weakness—offensive line play—and created opportunities to get the ball out quickly to their skill players, on the perimeter and in space.

McDaniel had crafted another plan, too, this one without Shanahan's input or blessing. He was going to come clean, publicly, about his alcohol issues and subsequent recovery, and he was going to do it at Super Bowl Opening Night, the spectacle formerly known as Media Day.

McDaniel's former coaching colleague in Washington, Richmond Flowers, was now his agent, and the two men schemed it up. While the head coach and best-known players had their own podiums at the Monday night event (which, in this case, was held at Minute Maid Park, home of the baseball Astros), assistant coaches generally posted up in a less crowded area, accessible to whichever reporters might seek them out. For a lower-level assistant like McDaniel, there wasn't likely to be much of an audience, if any. Flowers alerted a reporter he knew well, Tom Pelissero, then of *USA Today*, that McDaniel was ready to open up about his struggles with alcohol. The two found a place to talk "in the shadows," according to McDaniel, who then "went Eminem in *8 Mile*"—a reference to the climactic rap battle in which the protagonist disarms his opponent by first addressing his own shortcomings and eviscerating himself.

"I'd been a student of the NFL for so long," McDaniel said, "and I knew that the Super Bowl was my best opportunity."

McDaniel had told Matt LaFleur and a couple of other colleagues of his plan, and they'd expressed skepticism. He hadn't told Shanahan, assuming that it would not have been well received. He was right. "He's still pissed at me to this day for that," McDaniel said in the summer of 2019.

Yet McDaniel had no regrets, because it answered the central question about his career, asked mostly by people inside the coaching profession: If he was as good as advertised, why did he keep getting lapped by his peers?

"I decided, 'I'm going to call my fucking shit out,'" he recalled. "Because you know what the biggest problem was? I had all these other guys that were ascending and everyone was saying that I'm so good, but then why did Sean and Matt LaFleur pass me up? And I knew deep down the real story was actually better than the imagination for my career."

So, McDaniel spilled to Pelissero, revealing that Browns coach Mike Pettine had discovered bottles of cheap vodka under his desk during the 2014 season, among other embarrassing moments. He praised Quinn and the Falcons for helping him address his problem, saying he'd been subsequently diagnosed with depression, which had led to a psychological dependence on alcohol so that he could "check out" of reality. "Everyone's always said the same thing about me: how talented I am, how smart I am—*but*," McDaniel told Pelissero. "And I wanted to figure out why I kept sabotaging myself and what I was missing."

The story didn't make a massive splash amid the pre–Super Bowl hype, but it made its way through coaching circles, which was McDaniel's intent. He wanted everyone to know that he had defeated his demons.

"Because once I did that, I was like, 'Fuck it, I'm bulletproof,'" he said. "And their only [dirt on] me is that I'm a party drunk? OK. Now, what can people say about me, if I don't drink anymore? People get all scared about revealing shit to the public. Over time, you learn that everyone's pretending, and the one thing everyone can relate to is failure. Ironically, everyone's so scared to have that failure happen. But really, that's the story that everyone wants told."

THE STORY THAT PLAYED OUT ON SUPER SUNDAY WAS ONE OF THE MOST compelling in the game's history. Actually, it was two stories. At first, it appeared to be a death-of-a-dynasty moment in which Belichick was subjected to an embarrassment he'd never before experienced. Using the full width and depth of the field and calling the perfect plays for every situation, Shanahan had the Patriots reeling.

He had correctly anticipated that Belichick would employ double coverage to stop Jones in certain situations and predicted which fronts Belichick was likely to use to stop the run and the play-action pass. Shanahan believed his 21 package (the first digit standing for the number of running backs in the formation, the second denoting the number of tight ends) would bait Belichick into playing his base defense. Though Belichick changed it up by primarily playing nickel in those situations, Shanahan was ready for that, too. He used spread formations that exploited New England's speed disadvantage and found creative ways to get the ball to the outside. Conversely, Shanahan also employed tight formations—"condensed splits," a staple since his Texans days—that meant new options for blocking players on the edge and kept defenders off balance. And Shanahan had Ryan throwing quick, play-action backside slants, preventing Patriots pass rushers from all-out pressuring the quarterback in the pocket.

Recalled McDaniel, "That was cool because we had two weeks to prepare and we were totally outmatched up front. So, we were under pressure. We [realized]: We have huge receivers, right? And we have fast backs. But we couldn't block their defensive linemen. So, we used receivers as downblock edge players and pulled tackles and did a bunch of what we call 'transportation,' which was kind of my [brainchild]."

Quinn's defensive wrinkle—leaning on the Falcons' speed by playing more man-to-man than usual—was similarly successful. Very quickly, the game was a blowout in the making. Brady threw a pick-six to Robert Alford, who raced 82 yards the other way. When Ryan flipped a swing pass to running back Tevin Coleman, who effortlessly skipped into the right corner of the end zone with 8:31 left in the third quarter, the Falcons held a 28–3 lead, and it was time to start pondering potential parade routes up Peachtree Street.

And then, somehow, it all fell apart. "The script flipped," Matt LaFleur recalled. "Then it's a nightmare, and you can feel it. I don't know another way to describe it other than you can just feel that momentum shift."

For Mack, who played despite having suffered a broken left fibula in the NFC Championship Game, it was a painful experience on more than one level. "That's such a blur of what went down and how it happened, a very unenjoyable memory—I'm daily trying to forget. Ten things had to go the wrong way, and all ten things went the wrong way. I'm sure everyone would have regrets, but shit happens. Football's dumb. It's such a thing of luck. Some crazy things happen, the ball bounces weird, and shit happens. No one internal was like, 'So-and-so let us down.' It was, in general, 'What the fuck just happened?'"

As Brady began rallying the Patriots, Quinn's schematic wrinkle caught up with the Falcons: chasing quick receivers like Julian Edelman, Danny Amendola, and Chris Hogan, as well as running back James White, all over the field took its toll on the defenders who'd been deployed in man coverage.

"Eventually, when you're into the 90th play, you start running out of gas," Quinn said. "It was hard. I'm not one of those persons that would be like, 'I wouldn't change a thing.' Fuck that, I'd change a lot."

There were moments that will be forever burned into the psyches of Quinn, Shanahan, and the entire coaching staff. "Trust me," Morris said, "a *lot* of things happened. Not all of it is known, but I know. There was a lot of blame to go around."

After the Patriots had completed their incredible comeback, winning 34–28 in overtime, Shanahan got the bulk of the blame. He was criticized for being overly aggressive, the very quality that had characterized the Falcons' approach all season. Never mind that Quinn bore the ultimate responsibility for the decisions that fell under the scrutiny of hundreds of millions of viewers. Shanahan, long viewed with skepticism and operating from behind a plexiglass barrier in the upstairs coaches' box, was the more convenient scapegoat.

There was the deep drop Ryan took on a third-and-one play from the Atlanta 36, with the Falcons up 28–12 and 8:35 remaining. Coleman had been hurt on the previous play, meaning running back Devonta Freeman, who was not as adept at pass protection, would be on the field. On the play, Freeman let blitzing linebacker Dont'a Hightower blow right by him and pummel Ryan, forcing a fumble. Had Freeman put up any resistance, Ryan would likely have hit receiver Aldrick Robinson, who was open deep downfield, for a game-clinching touchdown.

"It's the perfect play call," McDaniel recalled. "Aldrick Robinson would've been [a hero]. Like, it was a wide-open touchdown. Perfect play call, perfect play design. Perfect time to call it. And he busted protection."

The Patriots turned that turnover into eight more points. Then, with a 28–20 lead, the Falcons—after an amazing catch by Jones on the right sideline for 27 yards—had the ball at the New England 22 with 4:40 remaining. Freeman lost a yard on a first-down run. Atlanta could have played it safe, tried two more runs, and then sent hyperreliable kicker Matt Bryant out for a very makeable field goal try. Quinn, the head coach, certainly could have mandated as much.

He didn't, and Shanahan decided to get after it. "When shit's on the line, do you want to go with the risky thing or do you want to go with the conservative thing? Well, my personality is [to go with] the risky thing, there's no doubt about that," Shanahan said in 2023. "As I get older and mature more in life, I learn, like, maybe you shouldn't jump off that cliff, maybe you shouldn't drive that fast, just like we all do as we get older. But you learn that through life experiences."

Think players over plays. Shanahan could hear Ryan's chiding voice in his head as he made the high-risk call, with Jones as the primary target and Freeman as the secondary one. Standing on the sideline next to Schaub, the backup quarterback, Matt LaFleur swallowed hard when he heard Shanahan's voice in his headset.

"I was standing right next to Schaub and we kind of looked at each other," LaFleur recalled. "It was a situation where we ran the ball on first down [and] we lost yardage on a toss play. A lot of times on our call sheets, we have our 'get back on track section.' You go to that section and you're like, 'boom,' and you call the play—instead of just thinking about the overall situation: 'OK, if we just run the ball three times, try to kick a field goal, game's over.'

"I wish I would have spoken up, if I would do it over again, or encourage them to do a time-out or do something. I just remember hearing it; I was like, 'Holy shit. Seven-step route *right now*?' It wasn't a bad call; it just didn't work out. When it doesn't work out, then it becomes a bad call."

It turned out to be disastrous: the Patriots' Trey Flowers blasted off the line, pushing past Mack and his broken leg, and dropped Ryan for a 12-yard sack, putting Atlanta on the fringe of field goal range. On third and 23, Shanahan called another pass, and Ryan hit Mohamed Sanu on a nine-yard sideline completion that would have set up a 44-yard kick, which Bryant would have been highly likely to convert. However, left tackle Jake Matthews was called for holding edge rusher Chris Long, who had made a desperate lunge at Ryan, and the Falcons moved back another ten yards. When Ryan's third-and-33 pass fell incomplete, Atlanta punted—and Brady proceeded to tie the game with a touchdown drive and two-point conversion.

The Falcons had one more possession, which began at their own 11 with 52 seconds remaining in regulation. It went nowhere. New England won the overtime coin toss. Brady led a 75-yard touchdown drive, adding to his legend. Confetti fell. Tears were shed. And Shanahan was blamed for the biggest choke job in Super Bowl history.

Was it fair? Many people—including some Falcons players—didn't think so. They questioned whether Quinn, who had ultimate green-light authority, should have accepted more of the blame. "I wasn't surprised [people blamed Shanahan]," Quinn said. "I was the one that was responsible, not him, but he was such a good competitor that he felt part of it, too."

"I don't fault him," LaFleur said of Shanahan. "He was being aggressive. That's how he called games that year. If he didn't call it that way, we wouldn't have been in that situation anyway. He did what had got us there."

———

SHANAHAN TOOK IT HARD. THAT NIGHT, HE AND MANDY RETREATED TO their Houston hotel room and, his wife recalled, "We just sat in a dark room for an hour. You're speechless. [Kyle] was broken." He flew back to Atlanta with the team the next day and was still in that state when he greeted the couple's three children. "It was the first time that our kids have seen their dad crumble when he walked through the door," Mandy said in 2017. "That's hard to watch."

Later that week, Shanahan got on a plane to Northern California and formally became the 49ers' head coach, taking McDaniel and Mike LaFleur as assistants in charge of the run and passing games, respectively. He also hired Rich Scangarello, who'd been on his 2015 Falcons staff, as quarterbacks coach. Shanahan wanted Morris as his defensive coordinator, but Quinn blocked the interview request, promoting Morris to assistant head coach/passing-game coordinator/wide receivers coach.

Matt LaFleur, after two years as the taint, had already decided that his time with Shanahan had run its course. He would either stay in Atlanta, as newly hired offensive coordinator Steve Sarkisian's quarterbacks coach, or go with McVay to L.A.

"I was torn because I loved Atlanta," LaFleur recalled. "I loved working for D.Q. I wasn't gonna go. It was one of those things where you get passed up for the coordinator spot, and they're bringing somebody from the outside in. I was like, 'Fuck it. I have to go.' But I almost didn't go."

One more thing happened in the immediate aftermath of Super Bowl LI: Shanahan got an out-of-the-blue voicemail from Belichick, who, like everyone else, had been blown away by the Falcons' offensive plan. He told Shanahan he'd gone into the game thinking there was no way Atlanta could block the Patriots' front seven and that the Falcons had the worst offensive line he'd seen all year.

In McDaniel's version, "Bill called Kyle and said, 'Uh, unbelievable game plan—but fuck you. Because I'm gonna have to work on that down-block tackle play and figure it out, 'cause the whole league's gonna run it against us next year.' "

It didn't make Shanahan feel OK about the biggest disappointment of his career, or even close to OK. But it helped a little.

Chapter 12

Enemy Friends

Jared Goff was down in Orange County—behind the Orange Curtain, in L.A. parlance—when he got the phone call that would change his life. Four days removed from a nightmarish rookie season, Goff, the first-overall pick in the 2016 draft, was the embattled quarterback of a Rams team searching for a new head coach. So, when he saw the caller's ID—Kevin Demoff, the franchise's executive vice president of football operations—he answered immediately.

"Where are you?" Demoff asked.

"Irvine," Goff answered.

"We're in Marina Del Rey. How quick can you get here?"

Goff was 50 miles south, on a Thursday afternoon, with a notoriously crowded freeway, the 405, between him and his destination. He hurried. Sean McVay was in town for an interview, but only for another couple of hours, and Demoff wanted Goff to meet the 30-year-old candidate who'd already captivated him, general manager Les Snead, and owner Stan Kroenke.

It was a tense time. McVay was being wooed by two rival franchises, the Rams and the 49ers, and Demoff would soon come to believe he'd have to act fast to take McVay off the market. The meeting between prospective coach and franchise quarterback was top secret, but one interested party knew it was happening: Goff had texted me before beginning his drive to the Marina Del Rey hotel where the Rams were meeting with McVay, asking for intel on a young coach he knew that I knew. When I followed up with a text to McVay, telling him I thought he and Goff would get along, my phone rang immediately.

"You're not putting this out, are you?" McVay asked nervously. He was worried that if news of the meeting leaked, the Rams' decision-makers would peg him as the source and view that as a negative.

"Nope, laying low," I said. "I'll be very curious to see how this goes."

Their interaction went even better than I could have imagined. Goff was mesmerized by McVay's command of offensive principles and quarterback-centric mindset. Though he had enjoyed his previous head coach, Jeff Fisher, this was a different vibe. Fisher was a defensive-minded coach finishing out a long and distinguished career on a downturn, and his untested offensive coordinator, Rob Boras, had struggled mightily. By mid-December, the team's star running back, Todd Gurley, would derisively liken the Rams' scheme to a "middle school offense."

McVay, in that initial meeting, sounded more to Goff like the middle school prodigy who was already taking college classes. "We looked at some Washington film," Goff would say later, "and he walked me through some of their basic plays. I obviously was impressed; just the way he spoke and was able to convey his message. I thought, *That guy knows what he's talking about.* We talked about the previous year—what was good, bad, and indifferent—and he asked me some real questions, like what I felt needed to be fixed."

The answers Goff gave were encouraging to McVay. The former Cal star had become the Rams' starter in week 11 and struggled behind a poor offensive line, managing just a 63.6 passer rating, throwing seven interceptions and only five touchdowns, and losing all seven of his starts. Fisher had been fired with three games remaining in the season—after a blowout defeat to Dan Quinn's Falcons, with Kyle Shanahan and Matt Ryan on their late-season roll. Goff could have easily blamed the coaches who were no longer in the building. Instead, to McVay, he demonstrated accountability.

A week later, the Rams officially hired McVay, the first millennial to serve in such a role. As if to underscore the point, McVay brought his parents to his introductory press conference. The 49ers, who'd also been pursuing him, pivoted to Shanahan, coming to a de facto agreement with the Falcons' offensive coordinator five days later (though, as per NFL rules, it couldn't become official until after Atlanta's last game, which turned out to be Super Bowl LI). The two searches had been interwoven, with Anthony Lynn, who ultimately became the L.A. Chargers' head coach, also a strong contender for both positions. The Rams had tried to interview Shanahan in Atlanta, but their previous stop—in Providence, Rhode Island, where they visited with Patriots coordinators Josh McDaniels and Matt Patricia—was hit by a massive blizzard. With flights grounded, Demoff and Snead wouldn't be able to make it to Atlanta in time to talk to Shanahan before the Falcons' divisional-round game against Seattle—thus missing the end of the league-mandated window. They asked Shanahan if he wanted to talk to them via FaceTime instead, but he declined, instead devoting his focus to in-person meetings with Niners and Broncos decision-makers.

When McVay got his initial interview with the 49ers, he figured it was little more than a courtesy, an acknowledgment of his family ties. Because his grandfather, John, had been the team's general manager during the glory years of the '80s, McVay assumed that chairman Jed York felt almost obligated to meet with him.

If the interview had, in fact, been conceived as a "respectful tip of the cap," as McVay put it—and there's no confirmation that it was—things changed quickly. After the meeting, York described McVay's performance as "off the charts." It went so well that York ultimately gave McVay the phone numbers of Green Bay Packers executives Brian Gutekunst and Eliot Wolf, two of the Niners' top candidates to fill the vacant general manager role (with interviews taking place concurrently). The idea was that McVay would reach out and see what kind of connection he could form with one or both of them, as a precursor to a possible pairing. This was reported, and the Rams began to get antsy.

York, conversely, played it cool. He had fired coaches after three consecutive seasons: Jim Harbaugh, who'd taken the Niners to three conference title games and a Super Bowl, and then Jim Tomsula and Chip Kelly, a pair of one-and-done successors. Coming off a dreadful 2–14 season and saddled with a depleted roster, the owner knew he had to get this hire right, and he wasn't going to make an impulsive decision. As the process played out, he was interested in three young coaches with strong credentials on the offensive side: Shanahan, McVay, and Josh McDaniels. With the way things were playing out, York was fairly sure that at least one of those candidates would still be standing after the other teams made their hires. For that reason, he was content to wait. Ultimately, McDaniels withdrew from consideration. Once the Rams hired McVay, Shanahan was the last man standing.

Before Shanahan could officially become the Niners' coach, York, with his next coach's blessing, did something that shocked the league. On the Sunday before the Super Bowl, the 49ers confirmed a report that they were hiring Fox Sports broadcaster and future Hall of Fame safety John Lynch as their new general manager. The collective reaction around the league was . . . *Huh?* Lynch had no experience in scouting and had never worked in an NFL personnel department. The 49ers had interviewed at least nine experienced talent evaluators for the job, two of whom, George Paton and Terry McDonough, had met personally with Shanahan.

Earlier in the playoffs, during his final broadcast for Fox, Lynch had said Shanahan could come across as "arrogant"—a quality he spun as a positive for a head coach, adding, "I'd be hiring that guy in a second." Lynch reportedly reached out to Shanahan to offer his services, which set the process in motion. Mike Shanahan, who'd coached Lynch in Denver, where the torpedo of a safety spent the final four seasons of his playing career, played something of a matchmaking role.

Personality-wise, it was a very prescient match. Lynch, affable and comfortable with front-facing responsibilities, was happy to do some of the schmoozing that Shanahan detested. And his even temperament was a welcome contrast to Shanahan's impetuousness. Kwesi Adofo-Mensah, then the 49ers' director of football research and development, said, "They had me study great organizations, the Warriors and all these teams. One of the things you learn is there needs to be an absence of ego. That's not a lack of self-confidence, but somebody who's willing to defer. Every great team has somebody like that. To me, I'm not saying Kyle doesn't have that in him, but that's John. This guy's one of the smartest guys, a Hall of Fame safety, and he used to sit there weekly and have me teach him things. When you see that guy in a room, you wouldn't know he's John Lynch. He's just listening to people and taking notes and learning. He might know what you're talking about. He's just content."

Lynch's hiring reinforced several things. First, that it was exceptionally hard for minority candidates to compete on a decidedly non-level playing field. Comparisons were made to the Detroit Lions' infamous hiring of Matt Millen as GM and president in 2001. The former linebacker and popular television analyst had no front-office experience and proceeded to oversee the team for a dismal seven years, during which Detroit went a combined 31–81. No Black player-turned-broadcaster had ever been afforded similar on-the-job training at the highest level of an NFL organization; now, it was happening again. Second, the Niners' move underscored the reality that many high-profile NFL hires are spurred by preexisting relationships. And third, it revealed something about the power dynamic in San Francisco: Kyle Shanahan had essentially picked Lynch as his partner. Given that the coach had much more experience evaluating talent than Lynch, it wasn't hard to figure out who'd have final say. The move was also an acknowledgment by York that his decisions had helped put the franchise in a precarious place—and, perhaps, an attempt to will a new era into existence. Lynch and Shanahan each got six-year contracts, at least a year or two longer than most first-time hires typically received.

FOUR DAYS AFTER THE FALCONS' CRUSHING SUPER BOWL LI DEFEAT, Shanahan and Lynch were formally introduced at a press conference at Levi's Stadium. After opening remarks by York and Lynch, Shanahan told the assembled reporters, "It's a dream come true—not just the opportunity to be a head coach, but to be a head coach at a place like this." Referring his three years as a training camp ballboy during his father's stint as offensive coordinator in the '90s, Shanahan said, "It's always been a special part of my heart."

With Mike McDaniel and Mike LaFleur coming with him from Atlanta, Shanahan's offensive staff had its basic framework in place. His most significant hire would be defensive coordinator, and after a long search he settled on Robert Saleh, the coach who'd first introduced him to Matt LaFleur in Houston. It made some sense: having been with Quinn in Atlanta for two years, Shanahan now had a familiarity with the Seattle 3 defense. Saleh and Quinn had been together on Pete Carroll's 2013 staff when Seattle won a Super Bowl—Quinn as the defensive coordinator, Saleh as a defensive quality control assistant. Saleh then left to join Quinn's predecessor, Gus Bradley, who was in his second year as the Jacksonville Jaguars' head coach; Saleh would be his linebackers coach for the next three seasons.

"Kyle just wanted a defensive coordinator who would play a solid eight-man front and keep it manageable," recalled one coach who was familiar with Shanahan's thinking at the time. "He got Saleh, not understanding that what Saleh does can be taken apart—because of *him*. He didn't even truly realize what he did."

The two highly competitive coaches would clash. "Matt [LaFleur] was an antagonizer, [but] I was probably a very close second," Saleh said. "Kyle accused me to John Lynch of being insubordinate, just defiant. I was like, 'I'm not.' Kyle just challenges you, but I'm not just going to do something without being very confident in knowing everything. That's just the way I'm wired."

In other words, Saleh wanted to know the *why*. He'd have fit right in with McVay in L.A.; ensuring that everyone around him knew the reason for doing something was practically a crusade for the young coach. When it came to his own hiring decisions, McVay wasn't looking for yes men. He picked Wade Phillips, who'd had three previous stints as an NFL head coach and was nearing his 70th birthday, as his defensive coordinator. He brought in Matt LaFleur, in all his antagonistic splendor, as his offensive coordinator. Before doing the deal with LaFleur, McVay had tried—and failed—to hire an established coach and old friend for that role: Chris Foerster.

Foerster, who'd just finished his first season as the Dolphins' offensive line coach—he'd spent the previous campaign back with the 49ers as the line coach for Tomsula—was under contract. McVay hoped that the potential promotion would compel Miami to consider letting him go. It didn't quite play out that way: the Rams, per NFL policy, faxed the Dolphins, requesting permission to interview Foerster. Seconds after the fax arrived, Miami coach Adam Gase crumpled it up, called McVay, and said, "Don't even fucking think about it. He's way too valuable. I'm not losing him."

The conversation was amicable, and McVay quickly pivoted. Gase then walked into Foerster's office, showed him the balled-up fax, and started laughing. "Did you think you were leaving?" he asked, shaking his head.

Foerster, at the very least, wanted to get a raise out of it. At first, the Dolphins' front office resisted. A deal is a deal, and no one forced you to sign it, he was essentially told. He went to Gase and said, "This ain't right." Gase told him to write the deal he wanted on a piece of paper and place it on his desk. Foerster did, so the head coach delivered, and then some—the Dolphins gave Foerster what he asked for, adding a one-year team option to the proposed three-year contract. He was now the league's highest-paid offensive line coach, due to earn nearly $7 million over the course of the four-year pact.

He seemed to be set. In reality, he was nine months away from the lowest moment of his career, or perhaps any other NFL coach's.

⎯⎯⎯⎯

ONCE HIRED, McVAY QUICKLY BEGAN TRANSFORMING A RAMS FRANCHISE that had languished after returning to L.A. from St. Louis following the 2015 season. His enthusiasm and motivational skills would force a culture change; that part, however, seemed almost easy compared to the football component. The key to the whole operation would be unleashing Goff's potential—a tricky endeavor after the wretchedness of his rookie season.

"Very rarely do you see quarterbacks that go through that much failure the first year," Matt LaFleur said. "He started seven games, and I don't think they won a game when he started. I think that's why a lot of quarterbacks get scars in this league, and they don't get an opportunity to really develop. Once they lose confidence, its fucking over."

The best way to bolster Goff's confidence, McVay felt, was to make the quarterback's on-the-field existence as simple and clear-cut as possible. The Rams had an elite running back in Todd Gurley, the tenth-overall pick of the 2015 draft, and signed a standout left tackle, 11-year veteran Andrew Whitworth, in free agency. The initial idea was to build a strong running game rooted in the Shanahan-style outside zone scheme and run play-action off of that. McVay figured that he would largely use 12 personnel (one running back, two tight ends). He also viewed 21 personnel (two backs, one tight end) as a useful tool. Toward that end, the Rams would use a second-round draft pick on a tight end, Gerald Everett, who they felt they could pair with 2016 fourth-round selection Tyler Higbee. They even took a fullback, Sam Rogers, in the sixth round, signaling an intent to run at least some of the offense out of 21.

Yet, as the offseason wore on, another rookie—third-round pick Cooper Kupp, a rangy wide receiver from Eastern Washington—flashed more than any of the young skill players. The 6-foot-2, 208-pounder was a precise route runner who had a knack for getting open and a willingness to block downfield. L.A. had traded for speedy Sammy Watkins, the fourth-overall pick of the 2014 draft, and signed his former Bills teammate, Robert Woods, in free agency. Woods, too, was a strong and willing blocker. The more McVay, LaFleur, and the other coaches saw of Kupp, the more they reconsidered the plan. Lining up primarily in 11 personnel—with Kupp as the third receiver—would give Goff and the offense the best chance to succeed.

As in Washington five years earlier, when Shanahan transformed his offense to maximize the skill set and mask the limitations of then rookie Robert Griffin III, McVay was inclined to adapt and evolve. All three of his receivers were motivated to block, able to play fast, and well conditioned enough to pull it off. Running his version of Turbo out of 11 personnel would pay off in numerous ways. Opposing defenses would be kept off balance and unable to substitute. Most defensive coordinators were likely to play a basic nickel scheme, with five defensive backs, to maintain flexibility in such circumstances. Goff would find the defense's actions easy to predict. Defensive linemen would be more reactive and less likely to pressure the pocket. It also helped that the quarterback, who'd played in Sonny Dykes's Bear Raid no-huddle offense at Cal, was comfortable playing at a fast pace.

Best of all, having his players rush up to the line of scrimmage after the previous play would give McVay, in another coach's words, the opportunity to "play Madden," a reference to the popular video game. With coaches allowed to speak to the quarterback, via headset, until 15 seconds remained on the play clock (at which point the QB's in-helmet speaker is turned off), McVay could identify the pre-snap alignment and give Goff "alerts" about what to expect and where to go with the ball.

"Great coaches understand that they have to put the quarterback in position to be successful, and sometimes that requires you to adapt in ways you've never thought of," said Rich Scangarello, who was the 49ers' quarterbacks coach in 2017. "One of those ways to make it easier on play calling and visualization is to play with tempo, and to play at the line of scrimmage and be able to communicate through the helmet and take time—and put you as a play caller on the spot—to think what the defense is doing. Sean's very talented as a play caller in that way. It relieves tension for the quarterback. It empowers him and lets him play freely.

"Ultimately, that was an adaption that was required. It got the best out of everyone. It played to Sean's strengths and the quarterback's strengths, and the hand they were dealt with personnel and Cooper Kupp being arguably their best player. I think all that came together, and they were the first in the NFL to play with tempo in a way that could be played in the NFL. It got them success early on, by being a step ahead of everyone in the league."

The Svengali storyline would become annoying both to McVay (who thought it oversimplistic and insulting to his quarterback) and Goff (who didn't enjoy being portrayed as a puppet), but the system was clearly working to the Rams' advantage.

"I'm a second-year quarterback," Goff said in December of 2017. "Who, in my position, *wouldn't* want the benefit of a smart coach's input before the snap?"

McVay added another element to the Turbo concept, one that LaFleur, having been Shanahan's quarterbacks coach in Atlanta, understood on an advanced level. McVay started putting players in motion, augmenting the Gurley-driven ground game with jet sweeps to fourth receiver Tavon Austin, and expanding the concept to include Woods and other players in 2018. The mere threat of the jet sweep helped freeze defenders and open up passing lanes. Additionally, pre-snap reactions to the motion carried a predictive element that aided Goff immensely. McVay called the specific motions "man-zone indicators," designed to give Goff a tangible advantage before running the play.

Jedd Fisch, who joined McVay's staff as a senior offensive assistant in 2018, explained how McVay helped change the sport: "That's where Sean, in my mind, completely took the game to another level, when he started talking about man-zone indicators. When he started using formations to give them answers to the test. When he started talking about how motion was going to tell the quarterback ahead of time what to expect." Employing that tactic in a hurry-up attack, with time to convey the information to the quarterback before the in-helmet speaker was turned off, caught the rest of the league off guard.

McVAY AND GOFF'S FIRST TEST TOOK PLACE AT THE LOS ANGELES MEMO-rial Coliseum, a dilapidated, ivy-covered stadium that had hosted the 1932 and 1984 Summer Olympics and still served as home field for the nearby University of Southern California. The Rams would be stuck there for another three seasons until, at last, it was time for the grand opening of owner Stan Kroenke's palace in Inglewood, SoFi Stadium. Just over 60,000 fans showed up to see the Rams take on the Indianapolis Colts, far short of capacity. They were treated to a show: by the end of the third quarter, L.A. had a 37–3 lead. The Rams ended up winning 46–9, scoring more than a fifth of their 2016 point total in their first game. Goff threw for 306 yards, including an 18-yard touchdown to Kupp.

The Rams lost the next Sunday, 27–20, at home, to Washington—McVay's old team, still coached by Jay Gruden. Now 1–1, the Rams were besieged by residual skepticism. Soon, McVay and Goff made it all disappear. L.A. won back-to-back road games over the 49ers and Cowboys, scoring 41 and 35 points. The Rams put up 27, 33, 51, and 33 points during a four-game winning streak spanning October and November. McVay was clearly ahead of the competition on a schematic level, and he was quickly becoming Tinseltown's biggest football celebrity. People showed up at the Coliseum wearing "McVay Is the Way" T-shirts. Stories about his supernatural memory circulated. His "we, not me" mantra entered the lexicon.

About 350 miles up the coast, Shanahan was having a much different experience. The 49ers lost their first nine games that season, scoring more than 24 points in only one of those contests—the 41–39 defeat to the Rams in week three. Veteran Brian Hoyer, who'd played well for Shanahan in Cleveland before management benched him for Johnny Manziel late in the 2014 season, started the first six games. Then rookie C. J.

Beathard, a third-round draft pick, got the call, with similarly poor results. Shanahan understood that he'd taken over a team with a roster that needed drastic reshaping. He knew it would be a prolonged process. Yet watching McVay—his former quality control coach; a coordinator who'd ascended to head coach on the strength of his work with Kirk Cousins, the quarterback Shanahan had discovered and developed; a play caller using *his* Turbo package, aided by his former right-hand man Matt LaFleur—was a bit hard to take.

He and McVay weren't close friends, but they'd had a good relationship forged on mutual respect. Things were harder now. They'd have to play one another twice a year and compete for supremacy in the NFC West. Their dynamic had drastically shifted from mentor–student to peer vs. peer. As their mutual friend Raheem Morris said, "It's hard when you go at each other as much as they do, becoming head coaches at the exact same time, same division. At some point, you have to see—let's call it what it is—your 'enemy-friend.'"

Shanahan, too, was trying to change a culture. His approach was far different than McVay's. He wasn't caught up in slogans or following tried-and-true leadership practices. His approach was more straightforward: he demanded excellence and tried to avoid fluff. "I had six different head coaches," veteran left tackle Joe Staley said, "and you kind of know the filter of what's bullshit and what's actually authentic and real. Kyle, from day one, he's himself. He's real, and he allows people, including his coaching staff, to be the same way. He doesn't want you to be some stereotype of what a coach is, as long as you're getting results."

There was no greater example of this than McDaniel, who initially struck Staley as both weird and wordy. "He's not the stereotype of an offensive guru. I looked into his background, I was like, 'This is a "finance bro" just kind of living out a fantasy camp.' He's the same way as Kyle as far as the way he sees Xs and Os and manipulates formations. What was interesting, and what I got a front-row seat seeing, was how he developed in communicating with players. I remember his first year, in the first install meeting of the offseason, McDaniel gets up there. He's going over the run game and the run game install. We got through probably six out of 20 plays, because he just didn't stop overexplaining everything. He'd get distracted by some thought he had and he'd go down a tangent. Then he'd add a little bit of dry humor in there to get people to laugh—and then forget what he was talking about. Then he'd kind of come back to it. I remember going to the O-line coach, or Shanahan: 'Hey, can we have someone else do the install, because I gotta get through these plays? I don't want it to turn into comedy hour. I'm just trying to get some information here and get on with my day.'"

The comic material became less funny as the Niners struggled on the field. The rivalry with McVay was on, but in Shanahan's eyes, it wasn't yet a fair fight. That would start to change, thanks to an out-of-the-blue phone call from a legendary coach. For now, however, L.A. was the epicenter of football in California. As it turned out, Chris Foerster's career—and life— would be upended by events that happened in the area, too.

———

AS THE DOLPHINS PREPARED TO OPEN THEIR SEASON, AT HOME, AGAINST the Tampa Bay Buccaneers, Hurricane Irma loomed. The Category 5 storm swept through the Caribbean and barreled toward South Florida in September of 2017, causing the NFL to postpone the game, ultimately rescheduling it for November, when both teams had a bye. Owner Stephen Ross relocated the Dolphins' operation across the country to Southern California, using the Oxnard hotel and practice fields that served as the Cowboys' training camp headquarters. Miami's players and coaches would stay there for more than a week, leaving after the team's 19–17 victory over the L.A. Chargers on Sunday, September 17.

That meant Foerster had idle time—and an excuse to do some partying on the other side of the country.

Foerster knew a woman who lived in the area, and the two met for drinks one evening in Malibu, about 45 miles south of where the Dolphins were staying. She asked if he wanted to come to her place in Manhattan Beach, another 30 miles or so down the coast. Even assuming he'd be on the road early enough the next morning to avoid the nightmarish L.A. traffic, Foerster figured that was too far away. So, he passed, instead finding another party companion. This one happened to be an escort.

Though Foerster was thriving professionally, his life outside of work was a mess. He and his wife, Michelle, the mother of his three children, were essentially separated. He was behaving like a '70s rock star, albeit one who operated in the shadows. He owed back taxes to the IRS, a problem he solved via an arrangement with the Dolphins to divert salary toward paying down the debt. He owned a home in Tampa that he'd refinanced twice, and on which he'd taken out a second mortgage. The upshot was that Foerster, who'd purchased the home for $315,000 in 1998, now somehow owed $650,000. Generous toward his acquaintances and averse to cutting off anyone in his party circle—socially or financially—Foerster was focused on trying to have fun in the moment. He would worry about the consequences later.

The night with the escort became multiple nights, followed by ongoing communication and invitations to join him on the road—including in London, where the Dolphins faced the Saints on October 1. But the following Sunday night, hours after Miami's home victory over the Titans, a video surfaced that brought a permanent end to Foerster's self-destruction tour.

Foerster had sent a video to the escort, Kijuana Nige, in which he used a rolled-up $20 bill to snort white powder off his desk at the Dolphins' training facility. "How about me going into a meeting and doing this before I go?" he asked before doing the first line. He later said, "It's gonna be a while before we do this again, cause I know you're gonna keep that baby . . . but I think about you when I do it. I think about how much I miss you, how high we get together . . ." After snorting a third and final line, Foerster licked the remaining powder off his pinkie and made a sexually charged reference.

It didn't take long for his world to collapse. After Nige posted the video on her Facebook feed and it quickly began to circulate, Foerster got a late-night call from a Dolphins security official, informing him of the video's existence and that it had gone viral. The official told Foerster to come into the facility early in the morning. The next call Foerster received was from Shanahan, expressing his concern and offering support—something for which Foerster would forever remain grateful. Foerster's agent called, and then his son. He couldn't reach his wife until the next morning at 7 a.m. Her reaction was predictable. "What the fuck did you do?" she said. "You're going to treatment."

He wasn't in a position to argue. Similarly, Foerster could have tried to fight the Dolphins for some or all of the remaining money he was due on his contract, but he was a man defeated. The next morning, he resigned, then headed straight to rehab.

Foerster spent 60 days in a Florida inpatient facility, disconnected from a football world that continued without him. He was barely aware of the fallout from the video, which was abetted by Nige's appearance on Dan Le Batard's ESPN radio show three days after posting it. Nige said that Foerster "used me as his cocaine platter" and that the two had been "dating." She called the video "the tip of the iceberg," claiming there were numerous others like it. She described Foerster's cocaine usage as "a regular habit of his anywhere they go. It doesn't matter if they're in Miami, if they're in London, if they're in New York. I know about everywhere they went because I was invited everywhere they went. And everywhere they went, he was sending me other footage."

Then, in a twist few could have anticipated, Nige, who is Black, was asked why she chose to leak the video.

"My motive was to basically expose the inequalities in the system," she replied. "It's not just the NFL. The inequalities that come with being a minority compared with a white, privileged person in America in general. This is shining light on the inequalities we have as a country. We don't get paid the same amount as everyone else . . . How do we have someone who is paid millions to be a leader for a team doing blow when we can't have Blacks kneeling for the anthem? After I realized his habits and who he was and everything going on the system, he was going to get exposed."

It took some time for Foerster to get a clear sense of how far down the bottom was. Once, in a therapy session with about 20 other patients, Foerster tried to make the case that his situation wasn't as dire as the therapist was making it out to be.

"Let's put it up on the board," she said, an endeavor that a football coach could truly appreciate.

So, Foerster did, writing out his life circumstances. The more things he listed on the board, the more his audience was taken aback. Finally, Foerster took a long look at the board and understood. "Whoa," he said.

Late in his stay, Foerster had his breakthrough moment. He was taking a walk with his therapist on the grounds of the facility, and she asked, "How was your Thanksgiving?"

"Oh, it was good," he answered. "They had a little dinner for us, brought some food in . . . it was a good little setup."

"Bullshit," she said. Foerster frowned. "This isn't where you want to be for Thanksgiving," the therapist said. "Where would you have *really* wanted to be?"

Foerster thought for a moment. He tried to answer the question, but no obvious scenario came to mind. He was lost. And then it hit him: he'd devoted most of his time to pleasing others, as a coach and in social situations. He had yet to figure out what *he* wanted. Figuring out what he wanted to do for Thanksgiving was a metaphor; the real challenge was to figure out what he wanted out of life, from that point forward. He felt like a pathway to recovery had been opened, and he was determined to find his way through.

This wasn't a movie, however. There'd be no instant cure. After completing his 60-day stay, Foerster moved to a halfway house to continue his recovery, mostly surrounded by residents in their late teens and early 20s, many of whom had struggled with methamphetamine addiction. Each night, he'd go to sleep at 9 p.m. And each night, he'd be woken up at 11 p.m. and forced to blow into a Breathalyzer.

Tuesday mornings were the worst. Foerster's job in the halfway house was to clean the common bathroom, and the indignity was amplified on that specific day of the week. The reason? "What happened was, there were, like, four halfway houses nearby that this same guy managed," he recalled in 2023. "Drug testing night was Monday night, and we hosted it. All 50 guys that lived in those houses came through and did a pee test in the bathroom that I had to clean. Imagine 50 teenagers that are recovering addicts trying to piss in a cup, half of which went on the floor, and I'm in there Tuesday morning, scrubbing the floor."

Foerster's wife had insisted on a six-month stay at the halfway house, but he left after three and a half months. It wasn't a happy occasion: Michelle had been diagnosed with cancer and needed her husband's help. Taking care of her and their children became his primary focus. At that point, getting back to the NFL seemed as likely as being asked to join Dead and Company. But Foerster was committed to recovery and finally had his priorities in order.

─────

FOR SHANAHAN, IT WAS A ROUGH MONDAY MORNING. THE DAY BEFORE, in Philadelphia, the 49ers had fallen to 0–8 after suffering a 33–10 defeat to the Eagles, then flown back across the country in search of answers. Now he sat in his office, working on the game plan for the next week's opponent, the Arizona Cardinals.

He looked at his phone and saw a missed call. It was Bill Belichick's number.

The two coaches had formed a stronger connection in the wake of their Super Bowl LI meeting eight months earlier, when Belichick had called Shanahan to express admiration for his creative game plan. At Belichick's urging, they'd gotten together a few weeks later, during the NFL scouting combine in Indianapolis, spending several hours talking ball. Belichick and Mike Shanahan also had a good relationship, founded on mutual respect after numerous high-profile clashes between their teams over the years. It was because of Belichick's respect for Kyle Shanahan that he made this particular call, because the New England coach was dealing with a situation.

Tom Brady, the Patriots' legendary quarterback, had recently turned 40 and was in the final year of his contract. Brady's highly regarded backup and presumed successor, Jimmy Garoppolo, was nearing the end of his rookie deal, setting up a major decision following the 2017 campaign. Placing the franchise tag on Garoppolo to keep him as a backup would have stressed the Patriots' salary cap. He'd turned down a two-year bridge deal to stay on as Brady's backup, sensing opportunities elsewhere. Belichick, who could have commanded a first-round pick in return for Garoppolo following the 2016 season, had rebuffed trade overtures from the Browns and others, including the 49ers' Lynch. Brady, who didn't love the idea of a hovering backup waiting to take his place, had made his feelings known to owner Robert Kraft, with whom he was exceptionally close. Complicating matters further, Brady and Garoppolo had the same agent.

When Shanahan called back, Belichick got right to the point: with the trade deadline looming, the 49ers could have Garoppolo in exchange for their second-round pick in 2018—but he needed a quick answer. Some NFL coaches and personnel executives are convinced Kraft had ordered Belichick to move on from Garoppolo; others believe he simply assessed the situation and did what he felt was best under the circumstances. This much was clear: Belichick, who liked Garoppolo, was trying to do the quarterback a solid by pairing him with Shanahan. And Belichick preferred the idea of seeing a quarterback he'd drafted and developed succeed in Santa Clara—across the country, in another conference—to most other scenarios.

The proposal caught Shanahan and Lynch off guard. They quickly assessed their options. Kirk Cousins was likely headed for free agency after the season, having already been tagged twice by Washington—with the price of a third consecutive tag prohibitive. Shanahan remained extremely high on Cousins, who he knew was committed to running the offense as the coach intended. Before the 2017 draft, the 49ers had offered the second-overall pick for Cousins, as Mike Shanahan revealed to the *Athletic* in 2023. Washington rejected the offer and wouldn't engage in negotiations.

Later in 2023, Jay Gruden—who succeeded Mike Shanahan as Washington's coach—insisted during a radio appearance, "They would have given up way more than that," mentioning two first-round picks and a player as the realistic price. However, according to Gruden, owner Dan Snyder and general manager Bruce Allen "didn't like the Shanahans and didn't want them to get Kirk. It's a shame."

In short, the 49ers couldn't count on signing Cousins after the '17 season. Given Mike Shanahan's ugly exit in 2013, it seemed plausible that Snyder and Allen, out of spite, would try to keep him away from the 49ers at all costs. Said McDaniel, "I think they were thinking about sign-and-trade situations and that [Snyder and Allen] would take considerably less to make sure he didn't go to Kyle. So it was, 'Dude, we might not be able to get him.'"

If nothing else, the 49ers could take Garoppolo for a partial-season test drive and reassess. It seemed worth the risk. Shanahan and Lynch decided to go for it. For three weeks—a defeat, a victory, and a bye—Niners fans anxiously awaited the unveiling. Finally, with 1:07 left in a home game against the Seahawks that had already been decided, C. J. Beathard took a shot to the knee from Michael Bennett and left the game. In came Garoppolo, with the Niners trailing 24–6. He completed both of his passes, including a ten-yard touchdown to Louis Murphy on the final play of the game.

The 49ers, 1–10, turned to Garoppolo the following week in Chicago, his hometown. He threw for 293 yards and won. He put up 334 passing yards in a victory at Houston the following Sunday, then came home and threw for 381 in a home triumph over Tennessee. Shanahan and his coaches were shocked. Garoppolo didn't really know the offense, and yet he was thriving. He threw the ball better than they had imagined. His short- and medium-range passes were deadly accurate. His demeanor seemed cool and unflappable. "You could see it—he was like Aaron Rodgers," marveled Mike Shanahan. "He had a quick, quick release. Elite. You go, 'Holy shit.'"

The following Sunday, on Christmas Eve day, the excitement multiplied. The Niners were hosting the Jacksonville Jaguars, a team that boasted the league's top-ranked defense in terms of points allowed and which, a month later, would take a ten-point lead into the fourth quarter of the AFC Championship Game before losing to Brady and the Patriots. "We were way outmatched," McDaniel recalled. However, the Jags ran the Seattle 3 defense, installed by former coach Gus Bradley, and Shanahan knew how to carve it apart. "[Most teams] kind of adapted by that point, but they didn't change the rules," recalled T. C. McCartney, then a Niners offensive assistant. "Kyle knew what they were going to do before they did."

The 49ers, using a steady diet of play-action fakes, designed quarterback movement, and receiver and tight end motion, had Jags defenders swarming to the ball in defense of apparent runs, only to leave a fullback or tight end wide open on the backside. Shanahan's game plan didn't just gash the Jaguars' defense; it created an identity crisis—and an utter spectacle.

"It was humbling," then Jags safety Tashaun Gipson recalled. "We were the best defense in football that year, and it was just a mental mindfuck for us. We truly felt overmatched from a schematic standpoint. We were fighting each other on the sideline—about five fights in all—and tempers were flaring in our huddle. We didn't know what was going on."

The final act of humiliation came with 1:24 remaining, when backup running back Matt Breida sprinted 30 yards down the left sideline to clinch the Niners' 44–33 victory. It came on a misdirection play—a variation of

Taxi, a single-back run that attacks the outside of the line of scrimmage—
that was McDaniel's brainchild: Garoppolo faked a reverse handoff to wide
receiver Marquise Goodwin (who was running behind the quarterback,
from left to right) and abruptly tossed the ball back to Breida on his left,
who raced through a confused defense.

While the football nerds might have processed that game as a play-
calling clinic, most of the people in Levi's Stadium absorbed it as a Christmas miracle starring "Jimmy Jesus." With ten minutes left, the crowd
began chanting "MVP" as Garoppolo prepared to take a snap. After the
game, running back Carlos Hyde proclaimed that the 49ers would win the
following season's Super Bowl.

"Football's fun again!" Joe Staley told me after the game. "It's like having Tom Brady."

Later, I talked to Shanahan in his private dressing area. "He's doing
everything we hoped for, and more," Shanahan said of Garoppolo. "And all
the guys around him—I can't even explain to you how much better everyone is playing since he got here. He has rubbed off on everyone. It's too bad
we have to take a break here soon."

The 49ers had one more game, against a team that wasn't trying to win.
The Rams had already clinched the NFC West title, completing a stunning
transformation in McVay's first year. The Sunday before that Niners–Jags
game, the Rams had gone to Seattle and rolled to a 42–7 victory that had a
major changing-of-the-guard feel. Now, with little on the line in their season finale at the Coliseum, McVay was shutting it down. He rested most of
his key players, including Goff, Gurley, and All-Pro defensive tackle Aaron
Donald, and watched the Rams get steamrolled by the Jimmy G Express.
Garoppolo threw for 292 yards and two touchdowns in the Niners' 34–13
victory, propelling them into an offseason of optimism and anticipation.

The Rams, who'd just secured their first winning season since 2003
and first trip to the postseason in 13 years, got ready to host the Falcons in
a playoff game. McVay's impact had been astonishing, even to those who
thought highly of him: after scoring just 14 points a game in 2016, by far the
league's lowest output, L.A. led the NFL with an average of 29.9 points per
game. Goff completed 62.1 percent of his passes—up from 54.6 percent in
2016—for 3,804 yards, with 28 touchdowns and only seven interceptions.

His passer rating went from 63.6 as a rookie to 100.5. He and his coach were vibing.

"Every time a play comes over the headset," Goff told me, "you think, *We could score.* That's just because of the confidence he expresses, and the way we know we can execute it."

By the end of their first regular season together, McVay was convinced that Goff was the ideal quarterback for his team. "I think the thing that really starts to separate him, and shows week in and week out, is that this guy's a fearless competitor," he told me in December of 2017. "And one of his best traits is he's not afraid to fail. He doesn't let bad things affect him. He stays even-keeled at the tightest moments in the game. And this guy competes to win, which is what you want from your quarterback."

GOING INTO THE PLAYOFFS, THE FALCONS, AS THE THIRD-PLACE TEAM IN the NFC South, weren't nearly as confident as they'd been the previous year. Their offense, which had set records in 2016, ranked eighth in the league in yards per game and a middling 14th in scoring. Steve Sarkisian, hired by Quinn to succeed Shanahan as offensive coordinator, tried his best to keep the scheme intact. Raheem Morris returned as receivers coach. Almost everyone else on the offensive staff was new. Once the games began, the on-field product was like a blurred photocopy of the original. "Just trying to hold on to what we had," was how center Alex Mack remembered it. "Trying to hold on to that magic. We had a couple new people and we tried to keep the same stuff alive."

According to a source close to Shanahan, Quinn and other assistants contacted him at various times throughout the season in an effort to sharpen the Falcons' offensive operation. "They were calling Kyle still: 'How did you teach this? Tell me how you taught this run play so I can teach it to the offense.'"

The Falcons were underdogs heading into their playoff matchup with the Rams, but the evening before the game, Quinn was confident. "I wouldn't want to play us right now," he told me as we sat in a restaurant at the team's hotel near the L.A. airport. He was right: Atlanta's playoff experience and physicality prevailed, with the Falcons grinding out a 26–13 victory that ended McVay's storybook rookie season.

Despite the disappointment, McVay, who'd earn Coach of the Year honors, was excited about the immediate future. So, too, was Shanahan—given the unexpected bounce the Niners had gotten from Garoppolo. After going 5–0 to end the season, Garoppolo had won him over. In McDaniel's words, "He was making plays and we had a garbage team and we won five straight. And so, we were like . . . 'Imagine when he *knows* the offense.'"

In retrospect, even the smartest people in the organization were probably a bit too caught up in the general euphoria surrounding Garoppolo. Said one member of that San Francisco coaching staff, "It was so hard losing all those games at the start that, at least in the moment, we were all blinded by having success." The organization's blind faith translated to a five-year, $137.5 million contract extension that made Garoppolo the NFL's highest-paid player.

The Niners announced the deal at a festive news conference carried live by the NFL Network. Sitting between Shanahan and Lynch, Garoppolo flashed his newly minted smile and told his bosses—and a football-watching nation—"I'm excited for this next year, but like John said, we've got a lot of work to do. So, we're looking forward to it."

When the press conference ended, the 49ers had a party for coaches, talent evaluators, and other staff members at a Levi's Stadium restaurant. Garoppolo left early—and stayed gone for most of the voluntary offseason program, something almost unheard of when it came to franchise quarterbacks. Notorious for not returning calls and texts, Garoppolo extended that practice to the coaches' overtures, ghosting his bosses for an uncomfortable stretch. Recalled one member of that Niners staff, "Once he left that press conference, nobody heard from him for weeks and weeks. He didn't return calls, he didn't return texts—he basically just vanished. And we were looking at each other going, 'What just happened?'"

As another coach put it, "That was the wildest thing. We literally couldn't find our starting quarterback." McDaniel was more colorful, as usual: "That was the start of the [frustration] . . . Our nuts were on the line, and he [wasn't around]."

Even so, Garoppolo represented hope. Having found their quarter-back, Shanahan and Lynch felt they could accelerate their rebuilding pro-cess and compete immediately with the NFC's top teams, including the Rams. The rivalry was on. None of this was lost on McVay, who understood how special Shanahan was as an offensive mind and how much pain he could inflict upon opponents with a good quarterback.

A couple of months after the Rams' season-ending defeat to the Fal-cons, McVay and I got drinks in relative anonymity at Bungalow, a trendy Santa Monica bar across from the bluffs overlooking the Pacific Ocean. Chris Shula, his assistant linebackers coach and close friend from college, was there, as was Veronika Khomyn, McVay's future wife. Sitting at an outdoor table, the NFL's hottest coach was being treated like just another dude with a close-cropped haircut.

McVay had something on his mind—a loss he couldn't get over. At first, I figured he meant the Falcons game. I soon realized he meant the game that had taken place at the Coliseum six days before that.

"We had the division clinched and our playoff position set, and I did the smart thing and rested a bunch of guys," McVay said. "And Kyle and those guys came in and mauled us. It was miserable. I mean, it was just torture. I'll tell you this: that was the last time. I don't care if there's a game where we've clinched *everything* and there's zero reason to take a risk. If we're playing against Kyle, I'm playing *everybody*, and I'm playing to win. There's no way I'm going through that again, as long as I fucking live."

Chapter 13

Dueling Superpowers

L ate in the 2017 season, after Garoppolo had won some games and Shanahan was in a reasonably good mood, McDaniel, Mike LaFleur, and some of his other assistants were watching film of an opposing defense that had recently faced the Rams. At one point, they noticed a series of routes and blocking schemes, resulting in a Jared Goff completion to Cooper Kupp, that looked familiar.

Shanahan entered the room. McDaniel rewound the tape. "Look—Sean ran the same play, twice, in this game," he said drily. "And weirdly enough, it worked both times."

Shanahan rolled his eyes. Shanahan's weekly game plans, tailored to each specific opponent and crafted with care, were intricate and all-encompassing and unique. He rarely, if ever, repeated plays, because each one existed as its own separate tactic, designed either to gash the defense in question or soften it up for a later blow. It was an immense source of pride to the Niners coach.

McVay wasn't exactly rolling out a Cliff's Notes version of a Shanahan-style game plan, but his play sheet was streamlined by comparison. He felt he didn't need to overthink some things. If he found a way to manipulate a defense and use its own rules against it, and the strategy kept working, why not stick to it? Minus a major adjustment, a play that worked in the first quarter could work again in the third. Perhaps McVay would dress it up a little by changing the formation or accompanying motions—"the illusion of complexity" was a favorite phrase of his—or maybe it would be identical.

As long as his players had clarity and certainty about what they were doing, and as long as it put the opponent in a difficult position, he was fine going into a game with a more basic game plan than his former boss and now NFC West rival.

"I don't want to say 'the less you do,' because we did a lot, but still, the less you do, the more you know how they're going to defend you," said Jedd Fisch, a senior offensive assistant for the Rams in 2018. "The more you know how they're going to defend you, you now know how to attack it. If you're going to sprinkle a lot of different things out there, you can get a lot of different defenses. Kyle does a good job. Maybe he's not repeating the exact play, but you know what he's about to get to or how he's going to attack it. He's going to see how they defend the run, and then he's going to call the pass that plays off of that the way they defended that run. With Sean, it's like, 'OK, if I call this play, I know this is the defense I'm going to get. If I call this play again, and I get the same defense, why would I not keep calling it? Why would I not keep attacking? Why would I not keep getting into a rhythm where I'm forcing them to play left-handed because they have to play their second-best defense—because their best doesn't work against it.'"

Mike LaFleur, Shanahan's passing-game coordinator in San Francisco from 2017 until 2020—and, later, McVay's offensive coordinator—took a similar view: "Sean, really dating back to '17, '18, '19, I thought he was the best in the game of 'Dude, if it works, just keep running it.' Where that is different than Kyle—maybe not [as much] in the run game, but definitely in the pass game." LaFleur explained that McVay's approach is especially effective against defensive coordinators who are unpredictable, constantly varying fronts and coverages. "When you go against that from an offensive perspective, you have to have plays that make sense against all of their coverages," he said. "When you call a certain play, the next time you call it, you're probably not getting the same coverage"—meaning things are likely to unfold differently, with different openings and stress points. In that scenario, LaFleur explained, "You can repeat calls."

With McVay, there is always an inclination to try to distill football to its basics and avoid overly glamorizing the Xs and Os. Shanahan, conversely, makes it known that his endeavors are both uniquely intricate and non-replicable. He often scoffs at the notion that someone could steal his plays, as though to suggest as much is to betray a pathetically simplistic way of looking at the sport. It's not a playbook; it's a *system*, a collection of concepts and modes of attack that are pliable and adaptable. "It's funny how guys look at that, because everyone pictures [that] it's like [the Adam Sandler movie] *Waterboy*, like we're carrying around this yellow notebook with all our secret plays drawn up on it," Shanahan said in 2019. "You don't want to just be that person that wakes up on Monday and watches everyone else's offense and then comes in to the players and says, 'I have these 80 plays that are awesome. Let's run them!' It's [a question of] how does it fit into your team and what are you trying to do? Does this play set up another play? That, to me, is everything I do."

It's not hard to figure out which coach comes off with more humility. Not that Shanahan cares—he'd rather be *real* than unduly self-effacing. In his mind, he doesn't have time for fake. At least some of McVay's humility, however, is very real, and the accompanying vulnerability is one of his strengths.

———

IF ADMINISTERED TRUTH SERUM, McVAY WOULD CONCEDE THAT SHANA-han is strategically superior—to him, and quite possibly to everyone else. And he would also tell you, "I'm OK with that." What McVay believes sets *him* apart is an ultrapositive management approach that stresses connectivity and collective triumph, and the ability to lift up an entire organization through the sheer force of his personality. To him, motivating and captivating the people in the locker room, and all those who support them, is more important than outsmarting his peers.

To Shanahan, all of the motivational-speaker blather coming out of McVay's mouth is mere noise. The way to succeed as a football coach, in his eyes, isn't through intangible skills. You win the strategic battle and find the right players to execute the plan, and nothing else matters.

When I ran this contrast by McDaniel in 2019, he smiled. "Each of them *has* to feel the way he feels," he said. "Each guy has to believe, inherently, that he is the best, and that his superpower is what gives him that edge. To see it the other way around, for either of them, would be unthinkable."

If McVay's words—in speeches to the team, in interviews, and sometimes even in social settings—could sound like something out of a leadership book, that was no coincidence. He has devoured many of those books, constantly striving for a winning philosophy and message, and for the best way to convey it.

When he got to the Rams, he preached "we, not me" to everyone in the organization and never let up. Joe Barry, McVay's assistant head coach and linebackers coach from 2017 to 2020, explained it to me late in his first regular season with the Rams. "The way we build the 'we, not me' thing is, we tell the players, 'Hey, nobody is above being coached.' Every single time, he follows it with 'Especially and including myself.' He says, 'No one's bigger than the team—even me.' And he's incredibly hard on himself. The cool thing about it is, when you're around a guy like that, it kind of motivates you. You think, 'If this guy's crushing himself for something little, I've gotta pick my game up.'"

It helped that McVay's perfectionistic tendencies were often projected to those around him as self-perceived failure. In the words of Matt LaFleur, his first offensive coordinator in L.A., "I've been around this guy, there could be 70 plays in a game—if he makes 69 perfect calls and one call that doesn't go right, he's gonna beat himself up over it. He's got high expectations and standards for everyone, and it starts with himself. He's the first one to accept responsibility, even when it's not his fault. That's a pretty endearing quality." As LaFleur put it, "He lets people know it's OK to be vulnerable. And you know how many coaches *don't* do that."

McVay's approach would carry the danger of coming off as hokey or scripted if he weren't so magnetic. He has a true, inborn talent for walking into any situation, be it a crowded party or a one-on-one interaction, and winning the room. And he faithfully remembered and indexed those interactions, enabling him to stay connected with the many, many people who came into his orbit.

"I think people gravitate to [Sean's] energy," McDaniel said. "But you have to be your exact self, and if Sean wasn't that way, I don't think he'd be that cool and popular."

Helping McVay's credibility with players and others is his obsessive work ethic. "He's really good with the team," Barry said, "and he gets better every single time. And it's not that he wings it, although he could. He could bullshit his way through a team meeting and a [game-plan] installation; he's that talented. But every single meeting we have is so well thought out, and his presentation is phenomenal. He's got that *it* factor, but he also works his ever-living ass off. He works tirelessly at every single thing he does, whether it's a third-down play or a five-minute jolt speech he gives to the team every Friday morning."

Shanahan found a different way of reaching his players, one centered around the rawness of the delivery. No one could accuse him of being polished or political; he seemed to be blurting out his beliefs and feelings and projecting the *opposite* of "coachspeak." He often used video clips to drive home his messages to the team, letting players into his thought process and offering the proof behind his proclamations. They might not always have liked what they heard from him, individually or collectively, but they rarely felt they were being conned.

"Maybe McVay is a TED Talk, but Kyle ain't," Dan Quinn said. "His own way is his own way."

Like his father, who personalized his weekly battles with opposing coaches and players and explained to his own players, in graphic detail, how they could help him embarrass his counterparts, Kyle Shanahan exuded excitement about the impending humiliation. He spoke in a blunt, self-assured manner replete with f-bombs and colloquial phrases. On many levels, he was speaking his players' language.

Quinn, Shanahan's old boss in Atlanta, put it similarly. "When the leader says how it's gonna go down, and it does go down that way, you gain a lot of street cred. That's important."

McVay certainly spent more time worrying about how he might be perceived than did his rival. The perception of Shanahan as a nepo baby might have bothered him conceptually, but on a day-to-day basis, he didn't stress over what coworkers, players, or outsiders might read into his behavior. In the words of one former Shanahan assistant, "The reason people hate getting yelled at by Kyle is he's skinny, he's a brat, his dad was a famous coach . . . so it feels like he's entitled. And he'll say anything and make no effort to sugarcoat it, and the next day it's completely gone, like it never happened. *You* remember it—you have your fist balled up and want to have it out. But he's completely forgotten and moved on."

Another ex-Shanahan assistant, Rich Scangarello, described Shanahan's game-day venting as part of his process. "It's his genius. He does express himself outwardly. He is a *great* play caller. He sees the moves many steps ahead. But he has to release the negative energy from the play before, before he moves on. Hell, the next day, he probably doesn't even remember it. But if he carries that negative energy and doesn't express himself, he's not at his best."

Stories of Shanahan's releasing of energy have reached legendary status. Joe Staley, the Niners' left tackle during Shanahan's first three seasons, once caught a deflected pass during a game in which Shanahan was mic'd up by NFL Films. "We had talked about it 20 times leading up to that season," Staley recalled. "Kyle goes, 'Hey, offensive linemen, if you have a pass that's in the air, what do you do?' Everybody's like, 'Bat it down.' Then the moment hits me, and of course I catch it because *why not*? I remember seeing the mic'd up version of that, and Kyle's like, 'What the fuck is that idiot fucking doing?'"

Receiver Deebo Samuel, a second-round pick in 2019, was berated so frequently during his rookie season that, he recalled, "I used to go to practice with dark shields on my helmet, just so [Shanahan] couldn't see my eyes, cause I was cussing him out in my helmet."

Then there was the 2021 season opener in Detroit. In the third quarter, with the 49ers up 31–10 on the Lions, Jimmy Garoppolo dropped back and, under heavy pressure from a Detroit blitz, floated a high pass toward Samuel on the right sideline. Samuel, who had been told to run a stutter-and-go, was tightly covered by cornerback Jeff Okudah, but came back for the ball and caught it. "What the fuck was that? That's a terrible route! What is he doing?" Shanahan yelled over the headset at receivers coach Wes Welker. Even as Samuel cut back diagonally toward the middle of the field, Shanahan continued venting—complaining about Samuel's weight and forecasting that the wideout would be caught from behind because he was too heavy. While everyone on the 49ers sideline celebrated Samuel's 79-yard touchdown reception, Shanahan was disgusted.

For those who were used to his tirades—especially McDaniel, Robert Saleh, and Matt LaFleur—such moments were typically taken in stride. However, for the uninitiated, getting snapped at by Shanahan could be a jolting experience.

―――

T. C. McCARTNEY DIDN'T KNOW HIS WAY AROUND AN NFL LOCKER ROOM. He was 24 years old, with three years of experience as a graduate assistant at Louisiana State and Colorado—a young grinder trying to get to the next level. He had an advantage: he was more tech savvy than the average middle-aged coach. Because he knew his way around a laptop, McCartney got his big break.

The Cleveland Browns had filled out their 2014 coaching staff, with Shanahan as the newly hired offensive coordinator, Mike McDaniel as receivers coach (and unbilled run game coordinator), and Mike LaFleur as an offensive intern. Yet they soon discovered they had a problem: McDaniel needed a run drawer—someone to put the running plays that he and Shanahan conjured up onto cards that could be used during practices and installs. The preferred computer platform for such endeavors was Microsoft Visio, a diagramming and vector graphics program. Offensive line coach Andy Moeller, born in 1964, couldn't deal with Visio; he'd have had better luck figuring out how to post a Snapchat story. That created an opening for McCartney.

McCartney's year as an offensive assistant was illuminating. Shanahan didn't just come up with plays; rather, he seemed to be an all-knowing, all-powerful figure. In McCartney's words, "What you take from there isn't just specific plays. You take a way to think about the game. An 'ecosystem' is the best way to think about it. They have a great understanding about how everything fits together and why it fits together. They look at it as a whole, rather than an individual part. That's what makes it a lot different than anybody else."

McCartney's maternal grandfather, Bill McCartney, was a Rocky Mountain legend, having coached Colorado to unexpected prominence in the late '80s. Coaching was in McCartney's blood, and yet Shanahan, he felt, had exposed him to a masterclass. He wanted more, and after a one-year stint with the Jim Tomsula–coached 49ers in 2015 and another year at LSU in 2016, he returned: Shanahan, upon becoming the Niners' head coach, hired McCartney as a quality control assistant on the offensive side. Life as a QC is a notorious slog, but for the first month of the regular season, McCartney was happy to do it.

Then, on an early October night in Indianapolis, he was ready to throw it all away.

It was McCartney's job to prepare and print out Shanahan's laminated call sheets the night before games, and it wasn't as simple as it sounded. He needed the sheets printed on special card stock, measuring 11 inches by 17, with plays on both sides and aligned to flip in each coach's preferred direction. Shanahan's last game-plan task was to finish preparing his "high red zone" plays—calls for when the Niners' offense had the ball between the opponent's 11- and 20-yard lines. In Cleveland, Shanahan, as offensive coordinator, would submit those plays on Saturday evening, at which point there'd be a mad scramble to get the call sheets done before he met with the quarterbacks that night. Now, as head coach, Shanahan had more responsibilities and pushed things a bit later. For home games, McCartney knew that, if he rushed, he could meet the coach's deadline. On the road, things were more variable.

At the Niners' hotel in downtown Indy, the situation was not optimal. The printer was in a room on the basement level, two floors below the lobby, and cell service was spotty to nonexistent. It wasn't exactly a state-of-the-art setup. "It was like a Windows 98," McCartney recalled. "You click 'print' and it was, like, a 30-second walk to get around the corner to the printer. When you're trying to figure out if this printer is double-sided, is it [aligned] the right way, is it jamming . . . it's not easy. I had a whole team of people down there; the hotel staff was with me; we were just trying to get things done. It was literally a mad dash—I finally got it done and was running up the stairs when the texts started rolling through."

The texts were from Shanahan, and he wasn't pleased. McCartney recalled, "I was probably three or four minutes late to the quarterbacks meeting and he's like, 'What the fuck are you doing? Unfuckingbelievable, I've never had this happen in my entire fucking life.' This is, like, week five or six; I hadn't slept in forever and I just didn't take that style very well, and so I was heated. I was on another level. I was going to fight Kyle; nobody's going to talk to me like that. Nobody said anything in the quarterback meeting; I just threw [the call sheets] on the table and walked out."

McCartney retreated to the ballroom, where players and coaches were eating ice cream from a dessert buffet spread and decompressing from a long week of preparation. His fist was balled up under the table. The next thing he knew, Shanahan was rushing toward him. "Don't ever talk to me like that!" he told McCartney, fuming. McDaniel and Mike LaFleur, who were nearby, tried to head off a confrontation. "Hey, just stay away from T.C. right now." McCartney wasn't backing down. Yelling ensued.

Finally, Shanahan barked, "Fine—we'll do this without you!" and stormed off.

McCartney had been fired. The spectacle was witnessed by numerous players and coaches. Saleh, the defensive coordinator, had a bemused expression on his face as he sat at the table with McCartney.

"At that point," McCartney said, "I didn't give a fuck. I was on one." He took out his phone, went to the Southwest Airlines app, and started booking a flight home. Before he had completed the task, Shanahan reappeared. He told McCartney to follow him into a nearby room. The two had it out again, both men screaming, before finally reaching common ground. Remarkably, McCartney emerged with his employment status once again intact.

"That's what I respect about Kyle," McCartney recalled. "I just told him my point of view. Nobody handled it great in the moment. But he said, 'We'll be better from this.' That was it. There was an explosion, but we put it behind us. Some guys would hold on to that. But I don't think he ever did."

———

BY 2018, McCARTNEY WAS AN IMPORTANT PART OF THE OPERATION. LIKE everyone in the 49ers' organization, he was brimming with optimism that Garoppolo, in his first full season with the team, could elevate them to playoff contention or beyond. "We went into that offseason like, 'Oh my god, we got our quarterback,'" recalled Kwesi Adofo-Mensah, who was part of the 49ers' front office at the time. It was not to be.

Shanahan tried to warn me, noting a few days before the team's

season-opening game against the Vikings that Garoppolo "really hasn't
played much football," and that he and the quarterback were in the very
early stages of their partnership. In retrospect, I believe this was code for
"He blew off a bunch of the offseason program and isn't as far along as he
should be."

In the opener at U.S. Bank Stadium in Minneapolis, site of the previous February's Super Bowl, Garoppolo had a bad day. Against Minnesota's coach, Mike Zimmer, an esteemed defensive mind known for keeping
quarterbacks off balance, Jimmy G completed just 15 of 33 passes for 261
yards and a touchdown with three interceptions, including a pick-six. He
was also sacked three times in a 24–16 defeat. It was Garoppolo's first defeat
as an NFL starter—and his first at any level since December 13, 2013, when
his Eastern Illinois Panthers were toppled by Towson State.

Meanwhile, Shanahan had watched newly acquired Vikings quarterback Kirk Cousins—his former protégé—complete 20 of 36 passes for 244
yards, two touchdowns, and no interceptions. The following week, Garoppolo played well in a 30–27 victory over the Lions. Then the bottom fell out
of the Niners' season: late in a week three defeat to the Chiefs in Kansas
City, Garoppolo was flushed out of the pocket and ran down the left sideline. As defenders approached, he appeared to be drifting out of bounds.
However, at the last second, Garoppolo suddenly tried to plant and cut
back, taking an awkward step inside. His left leg buckled during a hard
collision with Chiefs cornerback Steve Nelson.

Garoppolo had suffered a torn ACL, ending his season. The Niners
trudged on, first with C. J. Beathard at quarterback, then with Nick Mullens, an undrafted free agent from 2017 who'd spent his entire rookie season on the practice squad. San Francisco was 1–7 when Mullens, pressed
into action when Beathard suffered a wrist injury, got his shot. In a *Thursday Night Football* clash against the Oakland Raiders at Levi's, Mullens
completed 16 of 22 pass attempts for 262 yards and three touchdowns in
a 34–3 blowout. His passer rating of 151.9 was the highest since 1970 for
a quarterback with at least 20 attempts in a debut. Mullens was also the
first player in 49ers history to throw three touchdowns in his first game
for the team.

Mullens didn't have exceptional arm strength or talent. Generously listed at six feet even, he was short by NFL quarterback standards. In one area, however, he was elite: his ability and drive to consume football knowledge. The 49ers used Strivr, a virtual reality training tool designed to simulate game reps. Coaches determined that Mullens led the league in most time spent on the program. It took them nearly two years to realize that, after each home game, Mullens would shower, get dressed, and return to the still-lit field, where he'd take that week's game script and replay it, one play at a time, going through his steps and visualizing it all as though he were the starting quarterback.

Then there were the oversized headphones that Mullens constantly wore in the locker room. Coaches wondered what Mullens was listening to before games. Country? Rock 'n' roll? Hip-hop? "We found out he was listening to tape recordings of Kyle calling plays so that he could get in the mode of hearing Kyle's voice," Mike LaFleur recalled. "For 98 percent of players, I'd say that's not going to work because you're stressing too much. But for Nick Mullens, it worked."

Later that season, it was discovered that Mullens was blaring crowd noise over the headphones while watching plays on his tablet. He and Beathard constantly created VR exercises for one another, simulating the receiving of play calls, the calling of plays, and their ultimate implementation.

Given his extreme preparation, Mullens's relative success wasn't overly surprising. Yet he couldn't save the season, or even come close to doing so. After getting rolled by the Rams in L.A., 48–32, on the final Sunday of the regular season—McVay, as promised the previous spring, played Goff and his other starters—the Niners were 4–12. Many fans wanted Saleh fired, citing the team's defensive woes during the coordinator's first two seasons. Some felt Shanahan would be coaching for his job in 2019, though owner Jed York stayed highly supportive, both publicly and privately. With all the money invested in Garoppolo, he'd clearly return as the presumptive franchise quarterback. However, those closest to Shanahan understood that the stakes were too high to stay blindly loyal to the QB. If Garoppolo had a poor start in 2019—and if the Niners weren't winning—Mullens loomed as a potential fallback. There was other work to do, too, in terms of the roster's reshaping, a stylistic defensive shift and some broad-based philosophical recalibrating. Shanahan had plenty of time to contemplate all of this, and he would do it in relative anonymity.

The rest of the football-watching world was preoccupied by the amazing rise of Sean McVay.

THE RAMS TOOK THEIR 2017 SUCCESS AND BUILT ON IT IN McVAY'S SEC-ond season, rolling to an 8–0 start and ripping through defenses with a hurry-up attack that somehow got even faster. A trade for speedy receiver Brandin Cooks, now deployed with Woods and Kupp in the Rams' favored 11 formation, allowed McVay to create more problems for opposing defenses. Even more so than in his rookie campaign, the coach seemed to be ahead of his peers.

"People want to say Sean's brilliance is memory," Fisch said. "His brilliance is his ability to see 22 people with knowledge of where they're supposed to be, not just the back of their jersey. That's just an added bonus of knowing what their names are. What he understands schematically is where people are supposed to go."

The Rams weren't always great on defense, but that didn't seem to matter. In mid-November, a Monday night game against the Chiefs that was supposed to take place in Mexico City was hastily relocated to L.A. due to poor field conditions at Estadio Azteca. Billed as a blockbuster, the game managed to exceed the hype. Both teams had 9–1 records and seemingly unstoppable offenses. Patrick Mahomes, a first-round draft pick in 2017, was in his first year as K.C.'s starting quarterback—and he was tearing up the league via an uncanny combination of arm talent, improvisation, intelligence, and composure. Goff, in year two with McVay, was in the midst of an incredibly prolific stretch as well. Kupp had suffered a season-ending torn ACL the previous week, but L.A.'s offense remained formidable.

It was one of the most entertaining regular-season games in NFL history, the first time ever that each team scored at least 50 points, with the third-highest combined total ever (105). There were 1,001 yards gained and six lead changes, including four in the fourth quarter. Goff (31 of 49, 413 yards, four TDs) clinched L.A.'s 54–51 victory with an exquisite 40-yard over-the-shoulder pass to tight end Gerald Everett down the right sideline with 1:49 remaining. "It was a crazy, crazy game," Mahomes (33 of 46, 478 yards, six TDs) told me afterward in the north end-zone tunnel near the locker rooms, speaking for a football-watching nation.

The exhausted Rams had a bye the next week, but then something strange happened. In a three-game stretch against the Lions, Bears, and Eagles, teams began defending them differently, playing more quarters coverage (four defensive backs dividing the secondary into quadrants), also known as a Cover 4 shell. This meant Goff had to process more *after* the snap, often after having his back turned following a play fake, and it muddled up play-action routes. Defenders flowed to the edges to cut off outside zone runs, and loaded fronts bottled up running lanes. Kupp's absence didn't help, nor did star running back Todd Gurley's increasingly problematic knee.

It turned out that Gurley, who'd torn his ACL in college, was playing through pain all season. Sometimes, he looked like his All-Pro self; other times, he struggled. Against the Lions, he carried 23 times for 132 yards and two touchdowns, and the Rams won by a 30–16 score. "It was the first time our offense didn't look like savages," recalled Ejiro Evero, the Rams' safeties coach that season. "Detroit played this 4–4 structure on us, where they're like, 'OK—you're not running the ball.' They put a cap on us for a play-action pass. They were forcing Jared to play quarterback. We weren't a great dropback team. We were a run and play-action team. Really, the only way to beat that defense is you have to throw the ball outside. We didn't play very well on offense, but we won the game."

The Bears were a more formidable challenge. Veteran defensive coordinator Vic Fangio was a Shanahan-like figure on the other side of the ball, constantly adapting his scheme to keep specific opponents off balance. He also had an abundance of good players for his schemes, including four Pro Bowl selections and three alternates.

In a *Sunday Night Football* clash at Soldier Field, the Bears swallowed up the Rams' attack in a 15–6 victory. L.A. gained just 214 yards. Defensive tackle Akiem Hicks, nose tackle Eddie Goldman, and the Bears' other interior defenders attacked the middle of the Rams' offensive line, exposing a weakness while maximizing their playmaking potential. Goff, under constant siege in the pocket, completed just 20 of 44 passes for 180 yards, throwing four interceptions. He was sacked three times—once in the end zone, for a safety—and fumbled once. "[Fangio] does a great job of never putting a player outside his range," Hicks said afterward. "Have I ever felt like he put me in a position of weakness? No. He always has a plan, and he inspires confidence."

The Rams were clearly unsettled. As he walked to the team bus, McVay called the defeat "humbling" and blamed himself for not putting players in position to succeed. "Vic is really, really good," he said, "but I was the main issue."

As Evero said, "Really, from that point on, we were never like the juggernaut on offense."

Predictably, the Rams saw more of the same the following week in a 30–23 defeat to the Eagles. Gurley, ineffective for a second straight week, sat out the team's final two regular-season games. McVay and Goff got the offense rolling again with December signee C. J. Anderson, a physical running back who'd starred for the Broncos in their Super Bowl 50 victory over the Panthers. They felt like they'd fought through a crisis, but that miserable night in Chicago would have lasting effects.

"I'll never forget that game," Mike LaFleur told me in the fall of 2023. "I tell Sean all the time, 'That game changed football.' Everyone copied that blueprint, and it got a lot of people hired in a lot of different spots."

How much were the Rams scarred? In January, a first-round playoff game between the Eagles and Bears at Soldier Field ended when Chicago kicker Cody Parkey famously missed a "double doink" field goal that secured Philly's victory. Watching in the staff room, McVay and offensive line coach Aaron Kromer erupted, relieved that L.A. would avoid a rematch with Fangio and the Bears in the next round.

———

FOR A FEW SURREAL SECONDS, I WAS LARGER THAN LIFE. THEN THE TERror set in.

Five minutes into the NFC Championship Game, the scoreboard operator at the New Orleans Superdome played a video clip from the NFL Network show *The Aftermath*, on which I was a regular cast member. It was of great interest to most of the 73,028 people in attendance, given that they were being called out as less rowdy than advertised.

After the Rams' divisional-round victory over the Dallas Cowboys in L.A. the previous weekend, I'd watched the Sunday games at Goff's Calabasas home with some of his friends and family members—and a couple of his Rams teammates. While the top-seeded Saints' victory over the Philadelphia Eagles played on the TV, the Rams players contemplated an NFC title clash in the notoriously cacophonous Superdome. They invoked their regular-season game there in early November, a 45–35 New Orleans victory. "The noise really wasn't an issue for us," one of them told me, and the others agreed. I filed it away, mentioned it on *The Aftermath* the next day, and carried on with my hectic playoff existence.

Now here I was, projected on a pair of massive video screens, saying, "One thing I can tell you is . . . spending some time with some Rams players yesterday, the noise didn't bother them the first time around. This is a direct taunt, apparently, to the fans in New Orleans who might have a few pregame beverages and crank it up a notch for the playoffs. But they thought the noise wasn't as bad as advertised. They operated fine."

Challenge accepted: the stadium erupted. The Rams, already trailing 3–0, were about to begin their first offensive possession. The Superdome felt like the inside of Angus Young's amp at an AC/DC concert. On his third play, Goff threw a ball that bounced off Gurley's hands and was intercepted by linebacker Demario Davis. The stadium seemed to be vibrating. So was my phone, with text messages from some of Goff's friends and family members, asking things like "What the fuck did you do?"

Soon, things got worse. The Saints took a 13–0 lead, and the Rams appeared overwhelmed. Gurley, coming off a 115-yard game against the Cowboys, looked completely ineffective, compelling McVay to ride with Anderson. Goff, whose helmet speaker had briefly malfunctioned, forcing him to borrow one from backup quarterback Sean Mannion during the first series, now had tape over the earholes in a vain attempt to mute the noise. Before most plays, he pressed his hands to the earholes to try to hear what McVay was saying; that only further encouraged the juiced-up fans.

"Loudest thing I've ever heard in my life," McVay told me later. Goff agreed. "The loudest thing I'll ever experience . . . disorienting . . . dizzying."

And yet the quarterback and his teammates kept it together. Early in the second quarter, the Rams faked a punt in their own territory and converted. Anderson's hard inside running helped steady the L.A. offense, and Goff asserted himself in the huddle.

"He took control in a way that I'd never seen before," veteran tackle Andrew Whitworth told me a few days later. "It was crazy loud, and a bunch of us kept trying to chime in and give input, and he just said, 'Hey! Everybody shut up. I'll get you guys into the right places. This is my show. I've got it.' First time I've ever heard him do that . . . and you know what? Everybody listened."

Added guard Rodger Saffold, "He said it with some bass in his voice. That was pretty cool. It was like, 'OK, Jared—I see you.' The noise was insane, but the fact that he was able to settle us down, show his leadership, and lead us . . . shows you how much he's grown these last three years. He had so much poise—and that's the biggest thing you need to know about Jared Goff: he has poise, win or lose."

On this day, Goff refused to lose. The Rams cut the Saints' lead to 13–10 at the half, overcame another ten-point deficit in the second half, and, after the Saints went back up by three, drove for a game-tying field goal at the end of regulation. The game would be best remembered for a brutal non-call that, if adjudicated correctly, would likely have sent the Saints to the Super Bowl. With 1:49 left in regulation and the game tied at 20, New Orleans quarterback Drew Brees threw a third-and-ten pass to receiver Tommylee Lewis, who was hit by cornerback Nickell Robey-Coleman before the ball arrived. Two obvious penalties seemed to have occurred: pass interference and a helmet-to-helmet personal foul. Either would have given the Saints a first down and the ability to drain the clock down to the final seconds before attempting a chip-shot field goal. Instead, the ball fell incomplete without a flag thrown. The officiating blunder was so egregious that, the following March, NFL owners would approve a rule change making such non-calls subject to replay review. (The rule, however, would prove to be misguided, and would be rescinded after a single season.)

New Orleans coach Sean Payton and his players were livid. After the non-call and subsequent Saints field goal, they'd watched Goff lead the team down the field for a tying field goal, only to lose the overtime coin toss. Then safety John Johnson came up with an acrobatic interception of a Brees pass, putting L.A. close to field goal range. Goff, on second and 13 from the Saints 45-yard line, had two players in his face on a repeat play call—one McVay questioned a second or two after the ball was snapped.

"I probably went to the well one too many times," McVay conceded afterward, his voice hoarse from celebrating. "That was the play we scored the touchdown on"—a one-yard toss to tight end Tyler Higbee that had cut the lead to 20–17 late in the third quarter—"and we'd run it a couple of other times, and [Saints defensive end] Cam Jordan—one of the best football players on earth—comes out unblocked and is in Jared's face and reaches up to block his throwing lane. And at that point, Jared basically was throwing blind—and his release was just miraculous."

The ball somehow found Higbee for a six-yard gain. After an incompletion that made it fourth and seven, McVay had a decision to make: have kicker Greg Zuerlein attempt a 57-yard field goal to win it, go for it, or punt. A Zuerlein miss would give the Saints the ball at their own 47, perilously close to being in range for a game-winning field goal of their own. McVay, who'd already called a fake punt, remained aggressive. Zuerlein proceeded to drill the longest game-winning kick in NFL history. After that, it got very quiet in the Superdome—other than the screams from the jubilant Rams players and coaches pouring onto the field.

McVay was headed back to Atlanta, his hometown, to coach the Rams in Super Bowl LIII, with a quarterback he believed was his psychic match. He scoffed at the depiction of Goff as a "system quarterback," telling me, "He makes 'the system' what it is—because he's great . . . He is unfazed. He has unreal poise and confidence that allows him to handle the success and adversity the same—which is a great characteristic for your quarterback to have."

Matt LaFleur—who, after a year as the Tennessee Titans' offensive coordinator, had just been hired as the Green Bay Packers' head coach, part of a leaguewide proliferation of all things McVay-adjacent—looked back on Goff's journey with a sense of wonderment. Upon arriving in L.A. after the 2016 season, he recalled, "Honestly, we didn't really know how it was gonna go, 'cause there were so many things he needed to improve upon."

Saffold, who'd spent all nine of his NFL seasons with the Rams—in the first six, they were still based in St. Louis—was giddy. "We were looking for a quarterback for *how long* on this team? To have one now, to have him come through time after time and get progressively better and better— think about that. It's scary to think about next year. He has so much poise, and he has Sean. These two are going to create a dynasty; I just hope I'm around to be part of it."

Now all McVay and Goff had to do was defeat the league's reigning dynasty, headed by Bill Belichick and Tom Brady. They had two weeks to prepare for the biggest test of their young lives.

They'd soon spend years wondering how it all went wrong.

Chapter 14

Friend of McVay

Kyle Shanahan didn't even try to conceal his disgust. A few months after Super Bowl LIII, while leading an offseason meeting, he decided to illustrate a point by showing some highlights—well, lowlights—from the Rams–Patriots game. Shanahan wanted his players to know that, even when coaches put them in poor positions, all was not necessarily lost. His message: When unexpected events happen, don't be a robot. Be a football player and figure it out.

In this case, Shanahan was spotlighting two head coaches he admired: Bill Belichick and Sean McVay. Shanahan showed a seemingly unremarkable first-quarter play in which Jared Goff, after taking a snap from under center and play-faking to Todd Gurley, threw incomplete to Robert Woods on a crossing route. From Shanahan's vantage point, the Patriots had been in quarters (or Cover 4) coverage, with four defensive backs splitting the back end of the field, whereas McVay and Goff had been expecting Cover 3, with a single high safety patrolling the deep middle. Goff, after turning his back to the defense, had thrown to the receiver that would be the logical target against Cover 3. That meant, to Shanahan, that Goff had decided beforehand who he would throw to. Had he not, he'd have seen Brandin Cooks open downfield for what looked like an easy touchdown.

"This dude has gotten so fucking used to not reading coverages," Shanahan told his players, "because they get up there, and they see it, and now he's predetermining it. So, he comes, his back's to the defense, now [he turns and] what coverage is it? Quarters. One, two, that's his progression. He should hit 'one' because it's quarters, but they made the [predetermined] call to three-deep. One hitch, it's a fucking touchdown."

Shanahan then drew attention to a Patriots defensive back who had bitten on the crossing route and undercut Woods, rather than following his assignment and sealing off Cooks on the back end. "Belichick's the fucking man. Like, The Man. [But] I can't believe how badly New England's coached on here. 'We schemed them, we'll fool them,' and you *did* fool them. But what if Goff was like, 'Fuck you, I just go through progressions.' Who the fuck is coaching this [defensive back]? In the fucking Super Bowl—they've been running quarters [in practice] for two fucking weeks, and that guy is cutting an obvious cross? How the fuck is this guy not flying back? This is a walk-in touchdown . . . Luckily, Goff wasn't ready for it."

I was able to spy on Shanahan's meeting, long after the fact, thanks to his father. Mike Shanahan wanted to show me the video to demonstrate his son's attention to detail and overall approach to making sure his players—and assistants—knew exactly what he wanted in various scenarios. Mike Shanahan also meant for me to see these specific examples of Kyle's commentary on the Super Bowl. In its immediate aftermath, I'd asked his opinion of what had gone wrong for the Rams, and he'd been eager to show me the visual evidence for some time.

"So, he's coming back with the same play," Mike Shanahan said of McVay, momentarily hitting pause on his iPad. "The exact same play."

He went back to the video from that 49ers meeting in 2019. Now, Kyle Shanahan called up a more memorable moment: the third-quarter deep ball that Goff threw to Cooks in the back of the end zone, which was broken up by cornerback Jason McCourty. Cooks had beaten his man and put his hand up as he crossed the Patriots 15-yard line with no one behind him, but Goff had taken several hitches before throwing the pass. McCourty, playing outside in quarters on the opposite end of the field, had come all the way across the end zone to break up the play.

"Belichick's definitely told that corner what to do on a crossing route," Kyle Shanahan told his players. "He must have fucked up. [McVay has] definitely told Goff, 'Hey, they're fooling us, so make sure you read it out.' Let's do it again. Single safety. Alright, fuck it. Single safety, let's do the same thing, get the high cross. It's quarters. Just read it out, you already missed it [on the earlier play]. Back foot hits. Where should he be throwing? Walk-in touchdown [if he throws it]. How they fuck did they not get this corrected? How the fuck is *that* [defensive back's coverage] not corrected? He takes two and a half hitches to make this read that he's already been given. Great play by that corner [McCourty]. Now, that [other] corner is fucking as bad at quarters as I've ever seen. All this shit is fucked up. That's what I'm saying: you put in a scheme and stuff to stop something, hell yeah. You still gotta [account for everything]. Read it out. It did stop the high cross. Three guys to stop the high cross? No, everything fucking matters. You have to look at fucking everything, and you can't just be like, 'Oh, we've got a scheme to stop that.'"

If Shanahan's regard for Belichick made the sequence particularly perplexing, there was something else in his tone, too: toward McVay, in that moment, he felt something akin to empathy. McVay had dialed up a good play call against Belichick—twice. On both occasions, there was an easy touchdown to be had. And yet McVay's quarterback, on the grandest stage, hadn't been able to get it done. By the following February, Shanahan would be able to relate to his rival in that way. It wasn't a very pleasant feeling.

———

FOR THE RAMS, SUPER SUNDAY HAD BEEN ANYTHING BUT. McVAY'S HIGH-flying offense was held to three points; as of this writing, no team has ever scored fewer in a Super Bowl. Remarkably, the Rams' defense did such a good job on Tom Brady and the Patriots that the game remained close throughout, with New England finally clinching its 13–3 victory on a field goal with 1:12 remaining. The Pats had taken a 10–3 lead midway through the fourth quarter before L.A. mounted its most impressive drive of the game. On first and ten at the New England 27, Goff threw a deep sideline pass to Cooks, who nearly pulled it in while racing toward the right pylon, but cornerback Stephon Gilmore seemed to grab his arm at the last second. Then, on the next play, Patriots defensive coordinator Brian Flores sent an all-out blitz, leaving his secondary in Cover Zero—everyone playing man-to-man, without even a single deep safety. Goff, under pressure, tried to throw the same ball to Cooks down the right sideline, but hung it slightly. Gilmore, who'd played off of Cooks this time (rather than pressing him, as he had the previous play), caught it for an easy interception.

At that point, it was all over but the self-flagellating. After the game, at his press conference, McVay blamed himself. "I'm pretty numb right now," he said. "Definitely, I got outcoached. I didn't do nearly enough for our football team . . . I just never enabled us to get into a rhythm offensively. Credit to them . . . they did a great job. It was a great game plan, and no other way to say it but I got outcoached tonight." He said the team's defeat "was mostly the result of me doing a poor job calling plays and not giving us a chance to win. I don't know how you ever get over this."

Later, after the Rams' locker room had already closed for the night, Goff brought me inside for his own finger-pointing session—also at himself. "What really stings for me, especially as a quarterback, is that our defense played so well—and I wasn't able to deliver," he said softly as we stood outside the cleaned-out coaches' lounge. "It was me. It was our offense. And we—well, *I*—couldn't do my part. It wasn't a game we needed 30 points to win. We needed *two touchdowns*, and I couldn't get it done. That's on me. I'm the guy who has to drive this offense."

The interception, in particular, was a deep source of pain and regret. "Obviously, I should have thrown it away," he said. "I knew it was 'zero'—of course I did—but I thought I could make a play. I didn't realize Gilmore was staring at me, and I threw too early. I put it in a bad spot. It was dumb. It was stupid. I *will* learn from it. But it really hurts right now."

As he prepared to head out of the stadium and into an offseason of regret, Goff's eyes were glistening. At 24, he'd been on the brink of glory, and now he'd hit a wall.

It wasn't just the coach and quarterback who'd underperformed, of course. Left tackle Andrew Whitworth, standing at his locker, still in full uniform long after the game, conceded the situation had been overwhelming to some people in the Rams' offensive huddle. "Guys were a little rattled. When you're not executing plays you normally execute, there's no other explanation."

Later on, and on more than one occasion, I tried to get McVay to explain to me what he felt he'd done poorly. The Rams had averaged 32.9

points a game during the regular season and couldn't even reach the end zone in the biggest game of all? In the previous year's Super Bowl, the Patriots had given up 41 points and 538 yards to the Eagles. How could things have gone *that* badly for the Rams' offense?

The answer, from McVay's point of view, invariably began with preparation. He'd put in the game plan the week before the game, and then, upon arriving in Atlanta for Super Bowl week, he kept watching tape and tweaking and tinkering in an effort to figure out new ways to outmaneuver the opposition and achieve something close to perfection—"chasing ghosts," in his words. He even watched tape of the Patriots' Super Bowl appearances from the previous two seasons. In retrospect, McVay wishes he'd spent that time drilling his players on the original plan and building in answers for possible Patriots schematic changes. That would surely have been helpful because Belichick, as is his custom, came up with a defensive plan far different from anything New England had shown all season.

"I think the main thing you learn is when you're playing on the biggest stage in the biggest game, and you've got two weeks to prepare, there's a difference between being thorough and indecisive," McVay said. "I changed a lot more as you're studying more and stuff like that, instead of being decisive and finalizing it."

Belichick and Flores had studied Vic Fangio's plan from the Bears' victory over the Rams in December and gone with a similar approach, but on steroids. The Patriots primarily played a 6-1 front—six defensive linemen and a linebacker. Safety Patrick Chung dropped down and served as the edge defender on the tight end side, with linebacker Kyle Van Noy deployed as the opposite edge, typically aligned in a manner to thwart outside zone runs. The Pats ran a plethora of stunts inside and mixed man and zone coverages—though they skewed more toward zone than in past games. They disguised coverages by having a safety creep toward the line of scrimmage and then sprint to the deep middle as the ball was snapped.

Making adjustments also proved to be a challenge for the Rams. That, again, came down to a lack of preparation, at least in McVay's eyes. "They came out and they played a defensive structure that didn't take long (to recognize). In the first drive, I said, 'They're doing what Chicago did.' We knew that. Then it's like, it's going fast, how much do you really say, 'Let me take a deep breath. Let's see what they're doing. Let's really talk and teach our players what it is. How do we really get to the right things that have the answers relative to the normal down and distance and the pass downs?'" McVay felt that the communication from coaches to players hadn't worked well enough, perhaps given the stakes and the anxiety that came with them.

Early on, after McVay and his assistants realized that the Rams were playing quarters in certain situations, they went with a play that wasn't on the call sheet—Foam X Pylon Post—that was designed to exploit it. However, Goff—who'd practiced all week in similar scenarios against man-to-man coverage or Cover 3, which is what the Rams expected from New England—didn't recognize that he was seeing quarters until it was too late. This was the first play that Shanahan later highlighted in that 49ers meeting. A touchdown there, in that context (the Rams trailed 3–0 at the time), would have changed the game.

At halftime, with the score still 3–0, McVay and his assistants did come up with a significant adjustment: they believed they had a formula for exploiting Chung's presence on the edge. The idea was to spread out their formations and force Chung to cover tight ends in space. However, less than a minute into the third quarter, Chung tackled Gurley on the edge while teammate Jonathan Jones torpedoed in—and Chung rolled over in pain, having suffered a broken right arm. So much for that plan. Now Hightower took Chung's place as the edge defender, and Elandon Roberts replaced Hightower as the single stack linebacker. McVay countered by rolling out more two-tight-end ("12") formations, which played into the Patriots' hands as well.

"We thought we were going to be able to take advantage of that defense," said Jedd Fisch, then a Rams senior offensive assistant. "Then it was like, 'Wow, now we've got a bigger body against the tight end.' Then it just became a big challenge."

Goff, under pressure all game, took four sacks but only turned it over once—the interception that essentially sealed L.A.'s fate. His numbers (19 for 38, 229 yards) weren't horrible, but he was now being criticized as a quarterback who struggled to read defenses—not necessarily a fair depiction, given that he'd been coached to expect certain receivers to be open in specific contexts. Over the next two seasons, McVay would come to sour on

Goff as a player, but the coach's belief that he, McVay, was most responsible
for the Super Bowl debacle was sincere.

As McVay saw it, on the biggest stage, against a legendary foe, he had
endured the unexpected—and he had frozen, unable to meet the challenge.
Fair or not, the self-loathing that resulted from the experience would drive
him in the years to come. "There's a lot of people that have jobs," McVay
said, "but I can confidently say that what I deem some of the [head coach's]
responsibilities, I didn't do a good enough job for us to be able to win that
football game. And I believe that in my heart."

IF SHANAHAN FELT FOR McVAY WHILE WATCHING GOFF STRUGGLE TO
recognize quarters coverage, it wasn't a prevailing emotion. Even with the
defeat, McVay was still the hottest name in coaching, the personable wunderkind who'd transformed a flailing franchise. He was still only 33. Surely,
he'd be back in the ring to take another swing—probably soon. If anything,
his self-excoriating in the aftermath made him more endearing and relat-
able. He was doing what the leadership books preach, taking accountability
and shielding his players—and his young quarterback—from some of the
attacks they'd otherwise have faced. For his part, Shanahan desperately
wanted to knock his former quality control coach off his perch.

Across the football world, the search for the Next McVay was proceeding conspicuously. There wasn't another one lurking out there, of course,
but that didn't stop franchises from trying. It had already started, in fact,
after the 2017 season, when the Tennessee Titans interviewed Matt LaFleur
for their head coaching job before choosing Texans defensive coordinator
Mike Vrabel, a former Patriots star. Vrabel then asked permission to interview LaFleur for a job as his offensive coordinator, a lateral move. McVay
denied it, believing LaFleur would have no interest. The next day, LaFleur
told McVay he wanted to explore the opportunity—it would give him a
chance to design an offense of his own and call plays on game day. McVay,
surprised but moved, changed his mind, and LaFleur got the gig. His first
and only year in Nashville was mixed. The Titans missed the playoffs after
losing a win-or-in game on the final Sunday night of the 2018 regular season, and Vrabel and LaFleur clashed stylistically—and, at times, person-

ally. There was enough tension that some GMs and coaches around the league believed Vrabel might fire LaFleur after the season. The problem resolved itself when the Green Bay Packers, conducting a coaching search for the first time in 13 years, chose LaFleur over eight other candidates without even proceeding to a second interview.

Around the same time, two Rams offensive assistants, quarterbacks coach Zac Taylor and tight ends coach Shane Waldron, landed interviews for the Cincinnati Bengals' head coaching job, with Taylor ultimately getting the gig. Then there was the curious case of Kliff Kingsbury, who'd just been fired as Texas Tech's head coach before resurfacing as USC's offensive coordinator. Before Kingsbury could get settled in L.A., the Arizona Cardinals and New York Jets each interviewed him for their vacant head coaching positions. It was strange to some, given his sub-.500 record at Texas Tech. Yet Kingsbury was young and personable and known to favor a fast-paced offensive attack. There was something else—he and McVay were occasional party buddies and confidants.

In a move that surprised many in the football community, and virtually everyone outside of it, the Cardinals hired Kingsbury. In the article on the team's website announcing the move, his personal tie to McVay was mentioned as a qualifying attribute: "Kingsbury is friends with Rams coach Sean McVay—the 32-year-old offensive genius who has become the blueprint of many of the new coaching hires around the NFL—and McVay reached out to Kingsbury after Texas Tech let him go to see if Kingsbury wanted to join the Rams' staff for the stretch run and postseason as an offensive consultant. Kingsbury considered it but ultimately joined USC." "Friend of McVay" became a recurring joke in coaching, media, and fan circles.

Nobody, at that juncture, was searching for the Next Kyle Shanahan, or looking into who he got drinks with. After two bad seasons with the 49ers, he would potentially be coaching for his job in 2019. He'd already fended off calls to fire his defensive coordinator, Robert Saleh, but changes were coming, and they would not be subtle. Shanahan wasn't just trying to catch up to McVay; he was intent on surpassing him. He wanted to build a juggernaut. And he felt he could finally do it in year three.

THE FIRST THING SHANAHAN DID WAS SWITCH UP HIS DEFENSIVE approach. After the 2017 season, Saleh had added a third-down pressure package to his Seattle 3–style scheme, but it clearly hadn't been enough. And a 4–12 campaign in 2018 meant everything was open to being questioned. It was time, Shanahan and Saleh decided, to change things up front. Specifically, they wanted the Wide 9.

The Wide 9, created two decades earlier by then Titans defensive line coach Jim Washburn, called for defensive ends to line up far outside of the last player on each side of the line of scrimmage (be it a tight end or offensive tackle) and aggressively penetrate upon the snap, with interior linemen simultaneously attempting to collapse the pocket. It was conceived as a means of countering the Titans' chief divisional rivals at the time, the Indianapolis Colts (both teams were then in the AFC Central), who feasted on stretch runs by star halfback Edgerrin James. It turned out that the Wide 9 had an ancillary benefit: the defensive ends had a better angle from which to attack offensive tackles, and a clearer path to the quarterback on passing plays. The Titans, coached by Jeff Fisher, reached the Super Bowl after the 1999 season on the strength of a ferocious pass rush.

Washburn had reintroduced the alignment while on the Philadelphia Eagles' staff in 2011, and the results were disastrous—and not for the teams' opponents. The Eagles loaded up on talent before the 2012 campaign, earning the premature and ultimately farcical nickname "The Dream Team," and proceeded to have a nightmarish season. Washburn, fired with four games remaining, later told a Philadelphia radio station, "I know the press didn't care for me . . . I was the Antichrist in Philadelphia." It turned out that the Antichrist was grooming a surrogate son of sorts: Kris Kocurek, a former Titans defensive lineman who became the Lions' assistant defensive line coach in 2009—after Tennessee defensive coordinator Jim Schwartz was named Detroit's head coach—and was promoted to defensive line coach the following year, serving in that role for the next eight seasons.

Saleh had become intrigued by the Wide 9 after the 49ers' 2017 defeat to the Eagles, when Schwartz was Philadelphia's defensive coordinator. That incarnation of the Wide 9 would prove to be much more popular in Philly, especially the following February, when the Eagles won their first Super Bowl. Over the years, Schwartz had proven to be Shanahan's nemesis. Saleh wanted to dig into why Schwartz's scheme caused so many problems for Shanahan's offense. Some of the answers were fairly obvious: while outside zone runs, and their accompanying countermoves, tended to be effective against reactive defensive fronts, the Wide 9 mucked things up, sealing off the edges to force immediate cutbacks and collapsing the pocket to limit the effectiveness of play-action passes. Saleh reached out to Kocurek, with whom he'd had a couple of casual conversations in the past, and asked for some intel about the scheme. Kocurek was happy to share, and the two began regularly corresponding, something that continued after Kocurek left Detroit to become the Dolphins' defensive line coach in 2018.

Knowing that Shanahan wanted a change and had positive thoughts about introducing the Wide 9, Saleh began lobbying for Kocurek. There was just one problem: the Dolphins' defense was a disaster in 2018, ranking 29th in the NFL. Kocurek's centerpiece player at the "Wide 9 technique" defensive end spot, Cam Wake, was 36 and far lighter than his listed weight of 269 pounds. It wasn't a great fit. At season's end, Kocurek was fired, and Saleh urged Shanahan to snap him up, and quickly, as four other teams were competing for his services.

Shanahan, however, had bolted to Cabo San Lucas, his frequent offseason refuge, and wasn't answering texts or calls. When he returned—with Kocurek still weighing his options—Shanahan, who'd been watching film in Mexico, called Saleh.

"Two things," he said. "First, our defensive line sucks. We need to figure that out, no matter what. Second—Miami's defensive line sucks."

Saleh laughed and stood firm. "You've just got to trust me," he said. "When you don't have good players, it's hard to be a good coach. This guy's good."

Shanahan made the hire—and then got Kocurek some very, very good players. First, the 49ers traded for Chiefs outside linebacker Dee Ford, signing him to a five-year, $87.5 million contract in the process. In Ford, who weighed 245 pounds, they had an ideal "LEO" defensive end (the weakside pass rusher in the Wide 9). The Niners would basically only get one year out of Ford, whose career was ultimately undone by back problems, but it was worth it.

They still needed a marquee defensive end to play on the strong side— and soon, thanks to a Friend of McVay, a phenomenal one would practically be gifted to them. The Niners owned the second-overall pick in that April's draft, with their NFC West rivals, the Arizona Cardinals, holding the No. 1 selection. The Cardinals had traded up in the previous draft to select UCLA quarterback Josh Rosen with the tenth-overall pick; it seemed inconceivable, at the time, that they would take another QB so early. For months, Ohio State defensive end Nick Bosa had been considered the likely No. 1 pick—he had speed, strength, power, agility, and a relentless motor, along with the right bloodlines. His father, John, had played defensive end for the Dolphins in the late '80s, and his big brother, Joey (also an ex-Buckeyes star), had been an immediate force for the Chargers after being picked third overall in the 2016 draft, earning Defensive Rookie of the Year honors and making the next year's Pro Bowl.

It stood to reason that the Cardinals would take Bosa—until they hired Kingsbury. Back in October of 2018, Kingsbury, then Texas Tech's head coach, had been asked about Oklahoma quarterback Kyler Murray, an electric player who was in the midst of a tremendous season. Kingsbury, who as Texas A&M's offensive coordinator had begun recruiting Murray in 2012—a connection that had persisted through various relocations by each party—answered, "Kyler is a freak . . . I would take him with the first pick of the draft if I could." Murray, also a talented baseball player, had been a first-round pick of the Oakland A's and had agreed to a $4.66 million deal with the organization. However, after winning the Heisman Trophy, he began to weigh his options. In January, the *San Francisco Chronicle's* Susan Slusser reported that the A's expected Murray to declare for the NFL draft, at which point Kingsbury's quote resurfaced, and people began to connect the dots.

Sure enough, come draft day, the Cardinals took Murray and traded Rosen to Washington, foisting him upon Daniel Snyder and Bruce Allen. In Santa Clara, after Commissioner Roger Goodell announced the Murray pick, Shanahan and Lynch didn't need the allotted ten minutes to decide what they were doing with theirs. They didn't need ten seconds, either: Bosa was the edge rusher of their dreams, and the perfect centerpiece for Saleh and Kocurek's Wide 9 rollout. In the draft room, Saleh began bear-hugging anyone in sight. He got so sweaty that he had to retreat to the locker room and take off his suit. "Drafting Nick Bosa was a godsend," he later said.

Suddenly, the Niners had a defense. Their tall and athletic defensive tackles, ex-Oregon teammates and fellow former first-round picks DeForest Buckner and Arik Armstead, now had more openings to wreak havoc up front. In March, San Francisco had signed free-agent linebacker Kwon Alexander to pair him with Fred Warner, a 2018 third-round selection who'd displayed exceptional playmaking and leadership skills. They drafted another linebacker in the fifth round, Dre Greenlaw, who would eventually become a minor star in his own right. And cornerback Richard Sherman—a former Seahawks star and longtime 49ers antagonist—was getting healthy and rounding back into form in his second season with the team.

That Shanahan and Saleh were open to the schematic switch set them apart from many of their peers. To future Vikings general manager Kwesi Adofo-Mensah, then the Niners' director of research and football development, it was further evidence that Shanahan is a "systems thinker. It wasn't just 'I was in Atlanta with Dan Quinn, so I'm going to run a Seattle Cover 3. No, we have to evolve. Why do we have to evolve? This is where I'm seeing the league going. Everybody's going to be running my system, so how do you protect your edges?' That's what I mean: It's every year that they're doing it. You can't be set in your ways. You think you have an edge—now, that edge goes away in this business, just like that. Every year you have to tweak, evolve, adapt."

Shanahan, in tandem with Saleh, had done something seismic—on the *defensive* side of the ball—that would reverberate through the football landscape.

"One of the great evolutions in a defense that happened is a credit to Kyle," said Rich Scangarello, the Niners' quarterbacks coach in 2017 and '18, and again in 2021. "His ability to see how great an eight-man front was, under the rules of the defense in the Seattle scheme, but to understand some of the flaws—and then to mandate a defensive coordinator to change to a nine-technique scheme, with crash nines, that would revolutionize the defense, because he understood how difficult it was to deal with and how to disguise things in the defense—really took it to the next level. And arguably, it has been the success of the 49ers—the defense has been so dominant. But it was the evolution that was mandated by an offensive coach because he understands defense on a level that most offensive coaches never will. And to have guys actually be hesitant about it, and then see him make it come alive and understand the *why*—honestly, it probably led to Saleh and DeMeco [Ryans] getting head jobs, and ultimately the Niners' longevity of success."

THE EVOLUTION OF SHANAHAN'S THINKING WASN'T LIMITED TO DEFENSE. If his offensive scheme had always revolved around the marriage of the run and the pass, the 2019 offseason was like a renewal of vows.

With Mike McDaniel leading the way, the 49ers began adding to their outside zone staples. There were counters, tosses, and power concepts; there was pre-snap movement and misdirection; there were receivers deployed in the backfield. Shanahan and McDaniel's runs had never been basic; now they were more complex than ever before. That season, the workload would be split between Tevin Coleman, who'd been with Shanahan in Atlanta, and holdovers Matt Breida, Jeff Wilson Jr., and Raheem Mostert. It didn't seem to matter who ran the ball—the holes were consistently there.

One reason the Niners would be so successful on the ground was the new level of detail Shanahan brought to his job, and to others. After the 2018 season, Mike Shanahan urged his son to instill a detailed approach—and the details themselves—in his position coaches and assistant position coaches with renewed urgency. Part of the elder Shanahan's reasoning was that, with success, the 49ers would lose assistant coaches to other opportunities, and this could ensure that the pipeline remained full. One such move with the pipeline in mind occurred after the 2018 season: Kyle Shanahan shifted defensive quality control coach Bobby Slowik, who'd worked in a similar capacity on his father's Washington staff early in the decade, to the offensive side of the ball, setting him up as another protégé.

Over that offseason, and in the months and years that followed, Kyle, in meetings with players and assistants present, became hyperfocused on giving intricate explanations of what he wanted from every player on the field—and explaining own his reasoning for each play, and why it should work against the defenses it was designed to attack.

In hammering home his points of emphasis, the younger Shanahan, like his father before him, would not be subtle. Kyle's bedside manner with his assistants wasn't always the best. As one put it, "Kyle thinks faster than anybody else, and when you can't keep up, he gets frustrated, and then he projects. It can wear you out as a coach."

As long as the players understood Shanahan's appreciation for them, he could live with everyone else's bruised feelings. Besides, John Lynch, his personable general manager, was there to assist. As Lynch told me in early 2020, "I don't want to make it seem like he's this hothead, but he can run hot from time to time, and I think we balance each other out. Kyle and I have a good yin and yang. And so, oftentimes there's a call or a text—'Can you come down and help out?' Sometimes it's just 'HELP.'"

Shanahan needed the best out of his team in 2019, and that meant nothing was sacred. Jimmy Garoppolo, returning from his torn ACL, had to play well—and win—or Shanahan would turn to backup Nick Mullens. It wasn't just about scheme anymore. The advent of Pro Football Focus, an analytics company, had helped level the playing field. Now, coaches all over the league had access, in real time, to well-organized videos of one another's play calls and outcomes in specific situations—and could study them and adjust accordingly. In the past, opposing coaches would typically have to wait until the offseason to slow down a new innovation. Such was the case with Washington's 2012 season, when Shanahan adapted his offense to allow Robert Griffin III to run it out of the pistol. Once PFF came along, coaches didn't have to wait. They could get cutups of, say, every team's red zone plays, or third-and-eight calls, and come up with countermoves before the next game. And, of course, Shanahan's shrewdest play designs could be lifted and borrowed by other offensive coordinators, too.

For these reasons and others, Shanahan was driven to create a Niners team that played with purpose from the very start and stayed one step ahead of the opposition. As training camp approached, Shanahan felt confident, but anxious. He believed he was on the verge of a breakthrough. It would be hard to confirm that belief, however, until the real games began.

———

THE SEQUENCE WAS SURREAL: A GLORIOUS MOMENT FOR THE NEW-LOOK Niners defense and, for Garoppolo, an 11-on-11 drill that would live in infamy.

During a training camp practice in Santa Clara, Garoppolo threw interceptions on five consecutive plays. Not five interceptions in a practice, which would be bad enough—five plays. Consecutive plays. Given that the practice was open to fans and media members, this wasn't something the 49ers could keep from becoming a public spectacle. Shanahan did his best to shrug it off, telling reporters, "You hope to never have a day like that, but I don't think it's never happened to anyone." Some people who'd been around the NFL a long time weren't so sure.

As Saleh recalled, "Even going into that year, defensively, we were beating the heck out of the offense—all throughout OTAs [and into training camp]. Jimmy throws five interceptions in a practice. Kyle's just yelling at everybody on offense. It's just a browbeating every day. I'm like, 'God, we either stink [as an offense], or we're going to be alright.'"

Immediately after the five-interception fiasco, the 49ers flew to Denver for joint practices with the Broncos in advance of their preseason game. It was a homecoming for Kyle Shanahan, who hosted a massive gathering for coaches and other team officials at Shanahan's, the popular steakhouse in Denver's Tech Center that bore his father's name. Once the 49ers' offense got to face an opponent other than their own defense, things started looking much better. Meanwhile, the Niners' defense continued to flash dominance. "We beat the heck of out them," Saleh recalled. "Then I'm like, 'Huh—maybe we're pretty good.'"

The 49ers would win their first eight regular-season games before suffering a narrow overtime defeat to the Seahawks on *Monday Night Football*—a temporary disappointment followed by two more victories. That early stretch of excellence included a 20–7 road triumph over the Rams in week five in which the 49ers' defense swallowed up McVay's offense after an unpromising beginning. The Rams, even with Gurley nursing a quad contusion on the sidelines, had gone up 7–0 on a seven-play opening drive that included zero passes. "They go right down the field," Saleh recalled, "and Kyle's just dog-cussing me. From that point on, the guys just strapped up, and Kyle controlled the shit out of the clock."

After that opening drive, the Rams would be limited to 48 net yards over their next *eight* possessions. They finished the game with 157 total yards, by far the lowest of McVay's tenure to that point. L.A. was 0-for-9 on third-down conversions and 0-for-4 on fourth downs—the first time in 31 years the Niners had skunked an opponent in those two categories. The Niners recorded their 12th takeaway in five games, after having forced seven turnovers all season in 2018, when they set an NFL record for futility. And Saleh, with his shiny pate and hyperactive sideline gesticulations, almost stole the show. After a second-quarter goal line stand on which the 49ers stuffed two running plays from the one-yard line, Saleh resembled a human corkscrew who looked poised to drill down into the Coliseum turf.

"Oh my god—that was amazing," Saleh told me afterward. "I thought I busted a blood vessel."

There was even talk that Shanahan was annoyed by all the attention his fist-pumping, gyrating coordinator was getting from the networks on their game broadcasts. The two of them remained combative at times—a pair of strong-willed men secure in their philosophies and obsessed with the *why.*

One thing was certain after that week five victory in L.A.: the head coach was quite happy with the on-field product. As I walked up the tunnel with Shanahan, toward the 49ers' team bus, I asked him why he'd stood by Saleh after two trying seasons, with so many people calling for a change. "Because I know football?" he asked rhetorically. "Look, Robert is very smart, he knows what he's doing, and he's a very good leader of men."

It was all coming together the way Shanahan had envisioned it would—even all the way back at the bleak beginning of his tenure. Early one morning in 2017, about midway through the 0–9 start in Shanahan's first season, left tackle Joe Staley went upstairs the coach's office to ask what he could do to help. "Kyle took an hour out of his day and just kind of gave me the whole vision of what he wanted to do with this franchise," Staley recalled. "[He went over] what he sees; [he was] breaking down Xs and Os as far as how he wanted to build the offense, the different kinds of players he wanted to bring in. He said, 'This is going to be a process. The first year, we're going to rebuild this offense and set a new culture, a new standard. Year two'—at the time, Kirk Cousins was the guy he wanted—'we're going to get the quarterback that I want, and that's going to completely transform what we're able to do in the passing game. Year two will be a hit-or-miss year because we still have to add pieces on defense, and it's a whole entire process. Then, year three, we're ready to take off. I don't see this thing slowing down.' It was what happened, to a T. We just exchanged out Kirk for Jimmy."

THE RAMS HAD BEEN SURPASSED, AND IT HAD HAPPENED QUITE SUD-denly. That defeat to the Niners dropped them to 3–3, and they struggled to find consistency, enduring even lower moments, such as a 45–6 home defeat to the Baltimore Ravens on *Monday Night Football* in late November. In that game, young Ravens quarterback Lamar Jackson, en route to an MVP season, vastly outshone Goff, who would throw a career-high 16 interceptions that year, tied for the fourth-most among NFL quarterbacks.

McVay hadn't seen it coming. A few months before the season, he'd told me that if I wanted to look prophetic, I should consider predicting Goff as the MVP. Five days before the regular-season opener, the Rams signed their 24-year-old quarterback to a four-year, $134-million contract extension, a sign of the coach's faith. By late December, after a 44–21 defeat to the Cowboys that saw L.A. slouch to 8–6, McVay had seen enough to know he'd be making big changes once the season ended.

At the same time, McVay kept hope alive—in the NFL, you never know. To have any shot of making the playoffs, the Rams would have to win the rematch against the 11–3 49ers on a Saturday night at Levi's Stadium. And three days before the game, even as he talked to me about the changes to come, he spoke excitedly about the possibility of pulling an upset. He had a plan. "I promise you this: I'm coming out swinging," he said. "We're gonna let our nuts hang and see what happens."

McVay's answer to the Wide 9 was to get Goff even wider. The quarterback, not known for his mobility, had operated almost exclusively from the pocket as a college player at Cal. Yet he had worked hard to improve his skills, specifically when it came to throwing on the run. Now, in front of an overflow crowd at Levi's that included his head coach's grandfather, John McVay, and a national TV audience, Goff put it all together in impressive fashion.

The Rams jumped out to a 14–3 lead and kept the pressure on all night, with Goff running a seemingly endless series of bootlegs—faking a handoff in one direction and then rolling out to the other while looking for an open receiver. Suddenly, the Niners' defense didn't look so potent. Saleh wasn't doing much fist-pumping on the sideline; he was too busy being screamed at by Shanahan.

Saleh! You've got to do something!

If Saleh wasn't prepared for McVay's plan, he had his reasons. "They ran 21 boots in that game," he marveled. "You don't run 21 boots in a *year.* From my understanding, the rumor is he actually called 28 of them, but seven of them got 'canned' "—that is, changed to alternative plays at the line of scrimmage.

The Niners somehow led at halftime, thanks to the one big mistake that Goff would make all night: a short checkdown pass that Warner intercepted and returned 46 yards for a touchdown in the final minute of the second quarter. Still, in the home locker room, Saleh was *stressed.* "At halftime, we put in these bullshit rules [to stop the bootleg] and came out and ran it [that way], kind of quieted it down a little bit," he remembered. However, the Rams kept moving the ball, tying the game at 31 with 2:50 remaining. Twice, it looked like L.A. would get the ball back for a potential game-winning drive; twice, Garoppolo coolly converted with pinpoint passes on third and 16, setting up Robbie Gould's game-winning field goal.

Afterward, with one regular-season game remaining—a Sunday night clash in Seattle that would decide the NFC West title—Saleh could barely celebrate. He needed to solve the boot problem, and he needed to do it quickly. The next day, he recalled, "We went to the lab and came up with a really cool system and just 'ruled' it out. Because of that game, we were able to develop, in my opinion, probably the greatest boot-rule system in football. [McVay] forced us to make so many different changes, and we made rules so that that never happens again." Eight days later, Saleh knew, the Seahawks would have Russell Wilson running similar concepts to see if the

Niners had adjusted. Sure enough, "first play of the game they boot, we run our rules and hit them right in the face. I was like, 'Hmmm—it worked.'"

The Rams left Santa Clara knowing they had one meaningless game left in an underwhelming season. It was a reminder that missed opportunities are especially painful in the NFL, because it is extremely difficult to replicate success, above all a run to the Super Bowl. Roles had been reversed: as the Niners competed for a championship, McVay would be the one plotting a strategy for getting back to the playoffs in 2020, with both the Niners and Pete Carroll's revived Seahawks now battling for control of the NFC West. After the season, McVay would decline to renew Wade Phillips's contract, bring in new coordinators on both sides of the ball, and get rid of Gurley, among other changes.

Simply put, McVay was disgusted. Three days before the Niners game, as we talked at the Rams' temporary training facility in Thousand Oaks, McVay had stated it this way: "When you prepare as hard as we do and put it on the line for three hours every week, every time you don't come away with a win, it makes you sick. Most people, when they experience that, are afraid to have that feeling again—but you can't fear failure. You have to fight through that and charge ahead and put it on the line the next week, over and over again. This year, it's been good for me. As sickening as it is, it's given me a new perspective and appreciation for what's important and who our core is. I've grown as a leader, because of the scars."

After falling just short against the Niners, McVay stuck with the theme, saying, "I'm proud of the way we battled and fought, but I'm sick that we didn't come out with the result, and I'm sick that we won't be in the postseason. Our season will end next week, and it's a sickening feeling, and one that will drive me—Every. Single. Freaking. Day—until next season arrives, and we finally get to come out and take another swing."

We talked about Goff's pick-six and Garoppolo's third-and-16 completions.

"It all makes me sick," McVay said.

Sicker than he felt after losing the Super Bowl the previous February? I asked.

"It might be worse," he said. "At least, right now, it feels that way. It's hard to say. Every single loss, you feel like you lose a piece of your soul."

McVay and I kept talking as he took the long walk from the visitors' locker room at Levi's to the tunnel behind the end zone, where the Rams' buses awaited him. I went upstairs to write my story; McVay headed for the airport. Before he got to his destination, the disgusted coach sent one more thought via text: *I promise this will only serve to drive an absolute maniac in me to be better.*

For the time being, McVay could only watch, along with the rest of the football world and much of the nation, the season-ending spectacle between his two division rivals on a surreal Sunday night in Seattle. With the Seahawks reeling from a wave of injuries at running back, Marshawn Lynch, central to their identity during Seattle's run of excellence earlier in the decade, had made a dramatic return from retirement. Lynch had parted with the organization on bad terms, spending two seasons with the Oakland Raiders before ostensibly stepping away from the game for the second and final time. Now, it was all love—and the storybook reunion almost ended in fairytale fashion. With the Niners up 26–21 and 22 seconds to go, the Seahawks moved the ball to the one-yard line. Given the heartbreaking ending to Super Bowl XLIX—Seattle a yard away from a touchdown that would have cemented a second consecutive championship, Lynch poised to score the winning TD, only to have Carroll call for a pass that would be intercepted by the Patriots—this was *too good*. Not giving Lynch the ball five years earlier had unraveled a potential Seattle dynasty. Now, a redemption of sorts beckoned.

Lynch would have gotten the ball this time. Alas, his time away did him in: unfamiliar with some new terminology, he was a little slow getting onto the field, and the Seahawks were called for delay of game and pushed back five yards. They would have to pass. Two incompletions later, it was fourth and goal. The division title would come down to Russell Wilson throwing over the middle to tight end Jacob Hollister, who, after catching the ball, was inches from crossing the plane of the goal line. Greenlaw, a rookie linebacker, somehow held firm and stopped him short. "Two inches from being *everything*," was how Carroll would later put it to me. Game over. Niners win. For Shanahan's team, those two inches were the difference between holding the No. 1–overall seed—and earning home-field advantage throughout the playoffs and a first-round bye—and being the No. 5 seed, with a much harder path.

Afterward, he and his defensive coordinator hugged. With everything on the line, Saleh's defense had saved the game. Now Shanahan—three years after 28–3—was two games away from getting back to the Super Bowl, this time as a head coach. And this time, he wasn't going to take any unnecessary chances.

Chapter 15

We Did It Again, Buddy

"Do you want to sound smart?" Mike McDaniel asked as we stood in the back of the south end zone at Levi's Stadium, about 45 minutes before the opening kickoff of the 2019 NFC Championship Game. He was leaning close to me, straining to be heard over the din of a crowd nervously awaiting the biggest game in the building's five-and-a-half-year history. The fans didn't want to entertain the prospect of losing, even though they feared such an outcome. Standing between the 49ers and a Super Bowl appearance was Aaron Rodgers—the Northern Californian who'd grown up a fan of the team, starred across the Bay at Cal, and seemed like the obvious choice to be the Niners' franchise quarterback when the team held the first-overall pick in the 2005 draft. San Francisco instead took Alex Smith, who'd had a fine career, much of it after leaving the organization. Rodgers, meanwhile, was already a certain first-ballot Hall of Famer after succeeding first-ballot Hall of Famer Brett Favre in Green Bay. Now, in the first year of his partnership with the Packers' rookie coach, Matt LaFleur, Rodgers had a chance to underscore just how bad that mistake had been.

McDaniel, the Niners' run game coordinator and Kyle Shanahan's most trusted assistant, wasn't worrying about Rodgers. Instead, he'd spent much of the previous week trying to get inside the head of a familiar foe. Mike Pettine, the Packers' defensive coordinator, had been the Browns' head coach who hired Shanahan and McDaniel in 2014, after they were let go in Washington, and they knew him well. The previous week, in a divisional-round playoff game at Levi's, the Niners had ripped through the Minnesota Vikings' defense with quick-hitting runs inside the tackles—a steady diet of power and counter runs. McDaniel's challenge was to figure out if a similar approach would work against Green Bay—or to find a better way to attack.

The problem with Pettine was that he had become wholly unpredictable. Most defensive coordinators had tendencies, especially when it came to pivotal moments in important games, and Shanahan and McDaniel were experts in isolating those tendencies, creating alignments that elicited an expected response and then exploiting it.

Yet the more film McDaniel watched of Pettine's Packers, the more exasperated he became. There were no rules—at least, not on a consistently trackable basis. In late November at Levi's, even as San Francisco rolled to a 37–8 victory over Green Bay, the Niners' coaches had frequently become frustrated during the team's offensive possessions. Now, as he broke down that film, McDaniel was still vexed by his inability to figure out why Pettine was making the calls he did at the times he made them. And so, finally, McDaniel stopped trying. He went to Shanahan with a radical plan: *Let's scrap everything and start from scratch.* They essentially drew up a new, streamlined running attack that discarded much of what they'd done during the previous 17 games and would instead mercilessly attack the edges, without many of the typical outside zone cues. Specifically, they'd use star tight end George Kittle, a ferocious blocker, and backup tight end Levine Toilolo to anchor the running game, forcing Green Bay's unrelated but equally imposing edge rushers, Za'Darius Smith and Preston Smith, to play 1950s-style football.

And now, as I prepared to cover the game for NFL.com, I was getting the answers to the test in advance. "Say this," McDaniel advised. " 'Based on what we saw against the Vikings last week, expect the 49ers to do a lot of running behind the tight ends—right at the Smiths—and to keep attacking the edges. How the Packers defense withstands it will be the key to this game.' "

McDaniel was displaying uncommon trust. The game represented a split within the Fun Bunch—and even among an actual family: Matt LaFleur's younger brother, Mike (another ex-Pettine assistant from that

2014 Browns staff), was the 49ers' passing-game coordinator, creating an awkward and conflicted Sunday for parents Denny and Kristi LaFleur, who had flown in from Michigan to watch the game with Mike's wife, Lauren. (It was all too much for Matt's wife, Bre, who stayed behind with the couple's two sons to watch with other coaches' wives in Green Bay.) Saleh, the Niners' defensive coordinator, would attempt to match wits with Matt LaFleur—the Packers' offensive play caller, and his best friend. During the week, McVay, whose Rams offense had performed in prolific fashion during that heartbreaking, late-season defeat to the Niners, got on the phone with Matt LaFleur to offer schematic insight, a clear indication of where his loyalties lay in this showdown between ex-coaching colleagues. There was a lot going on, and everyone knew everyone, and information was highly classified. Had Shanahan overheard my conversation with McDaniel, he might have threatened one of us with his job and the other (the guy with the pen) with his life. Yet McDaniel, with a trip to the Super Bowl on the line, was putting it all out there and seemingly already at peace with the eventual outcome.

"These guys [on the Packers' defense] are gonna have to play harder than they have all season, for three hours, because we're coming at them," he declared. "If they can do that, and they find a way to stop us, I can live with it."

McDaniel was barely known outside the NFL world, and still somewhat of a well-kept secret even in coaching circles. That was about to change. I'd watched him become increasingly confident in the years leading up to this moment, and I could tell by his tone he expected the game to go well. Something about facing the Packers and Pettine brought out the best in him. In October of 2018, the 49ers, then 1–4, had faced the Packers in a Monday night game at Lambeau Field. They didn't seem to have a great chance of winning. Jimmy Garoppolo had torn his ACL three weeks earlier and C. J. Beathard was now the Niners' quarterback. Running back Matt Breida was hobbled by a bad ankle, and the only other option at the position was fourth-stringer Raheem Mostert, a classic castoff who was barely hanging on to his NFL career. The Packers were favored by more than a touchdown, and that seemed conservative. And yet McDaniel had helped Shanahan come up with an effective run game approach that allowed the

Niners to put up an epic fight. Mostert gained 87 yards on 12 carries; Breida ran 14 times for another 61 yards. And the Packers' defenders were frequently caught in bad positions.

The Niners led 30–23 with two minutes remaining before a Beathard interception, a Richard Sherman illegal-contact penalty, and some Rodgers magic set up Mason Crosby's game-winning field goal for the Packers as time expired. The loss hurt, but McDaniel took pride in the performance. He'd put a lot of pressure on himself to come up with creative solutions in the wake of Garoppolo's injury. He wanted more responsibility, and he wanted to be noticed. Having confronted his issues with alcohol and gotten his life and career on track, he was sick of being the smart coach who got passed over by his peers, all while being perpetually yelled at by Shanahan. He felt like he'd developed the skills not only to game-plan, but also to call plays, should the opportunity arise. "This year, I felt like I tangibly could help the team win in ways that other people couldn't," he'd told me after that 2018 season. "And it was the first time that I've felt like I was in that groove. It was a cool year."

Now, in front of 72,211 fans and tens of millions of television (and streaming device) viewers, he was about to experience something even cooler. McDaniel's NFC title game plan played out with eye-popping precision, almost exactly as he'd told me it would. The Niners' starting running back, Tevin Coleman, left the game after suffering a shoulder injury in the second quarter—but it didn't matter. San Francisco ran for an incredible 285 yards, charged to a 27–0 halftime lead, and set football back 70 years in the process. Garoppolo threw only *eight* passes in San Francisco's 37–20 triumph, two of them after halftime. Kittle had one catch for 19 yards—and was the most impactful player on the field. And, in the greatest testament of all to McDaniel's schematic brilliance, Mostert carried 29 times for 220 yards and four touchdowns. Only Hall of Famer Eric Dickerson had ever run for more yards in a playoff game. Cut by six teams during the course of his career, Mostert had stuck in San Francisco as a special-teams standout who was never supposed to get meaningful carries. Now, he was an unstoppable force on the second-biggest football Sunday of the season. And all across the league, McDaniel was being penciled in as a potential head coaching candidate of the future.

THE PRIOR WEEK, IN FACT, HAD ALREADY SPARKED INTEREST ACROSS
the league. Eight days earlier, at Levi's, the Niners had gone old-school
in a 27–10 divisional-round victory over the Vikings, a game steeped in
significance for numerous reasons. For one thing, it featured a schematic
clash between two coordinators—Saleh and Vikings OC Kevin Stefanski—
who were the finalists for the Browns' vacant head coaching job. Stefanski
had been a prohibitive favorite from the start of the process, but Saleh, in
his first-ever head coaching interview, was so impressive that it became a
two-man race. In theory, the coach who shone on the national playoff stage
would gain a huge advantage—but this was the NFL, where the hiring process seldom makes sense. Because teams weren't technically allowed to hire
a coach whose team was still alive in the postseason, and because the scramble to hire assistant coaches was in full force, it was (and is) often actually
an advantage to be eliminated. By hiring a coach immediately, the Browns
could commence their latest rebuilding project at full speed, assembling a
staff that could join the front office in evaluating current players and prepare
for free agency and the draft. Or, Cleveland could wait up to three weeks,
lose out on some good assistants, and stay in a holding pattern.

In this case, winning was losing, and vice versa. That was bad news for
Saleh, whose defense would utterly smother Stefanski's Minnesota attack,
stifling Kirk Cousins and star running back Dalvin Cook. Late in the
fourth quarter, the Vikings had gained just 81 yards—the Niners would set
a franchise postseason record by giving up just 147. The next morning, the
Browns hired Stefanski. In this case, the move was especially infuriating to
those who tried to hold the league accountable for its racially imbalanced
hiring practices. Saleh, a Muslim of Lebanese descent, was a promising
minority candidate in a league where such men systemically didn't get a
fair shake relative to their white counterparts. To 49ers cornerback Richard Sherman, who'd also played for Saleh in Seattle, it was downright stupid. "That was one of the most ridiculous decisions I've seen," he told me
a few months later.

The game was significant for another reason. During the second half,
Shanahan made a decision to take the ball out of his quarterback's hands.
Garoppolo, who threw 16 passes in the first 35 minutes of the game, would

throw just three more over the final 25. His interception deep in his own territory late in the first half had allowed the Vikings to close to within 14–10. Early in the second half, another Garoppolo pass was nearly picked off—and Shanahan had seen enough. As he later said, "I'm gonna run it every fucking play, until I don't have to. I want to watch how this goes. And I call one pass and we throw it to their linebacker, he drops it."

So, Shanahan turned Garoppolo into a handoff machine. After Sherman intercepted a Cousins pass in the third quarter, the Niners, who led 17–10, had the ball at the Minnesota 44. Shanahan called eight consecutive running plays, culminating in Coleman's two-yard touchdown run. The game ended with Shanahan having called 47 runs, none of which gained more than 11 yards. That he would carry a similar mentality into the NFC title game against the Packers was not a surprise. The 49ers had lost three times that season—all on the final play. In his mind, a game plan mitigating the possibility of mistakes gave them the best shot of reaching the Super Bowl.

He wasn't wrong. Against the Packers, as the final minutes of the third quarter wound down with the Niners holding a 34–7 lead, Garoppolo asked Mostert, "How many yards have we thrown for?"

"Forty yards," the running back answered. "We've got 200 rushing, though."

Garoppolo shook his head in amazement and said, "Oh my god. But hey, I'm four-for-six."

To Garoppolo's credit, he was taking it well. Many quarterbacks wouldn't have been thrilled with the lack of action, let alone the lack of trust from their coach—and the perception, around the league and to fans and media members, that he hadn't earned that trust. Garoppolo, as usual, had the perfect temperament to shrug it off and seize on the positive: he was going back to the Super Bowl, this time not as Tom Brady's backup, but as the starting quarterback.

BECAUSE THE 49ERS WERE SO TALENTED, MATT LaFLEUR COULDN'T BE too crushed about the defeat—at least on an intellectual level. He could reflect on his season with pride. As a first-time head coach, he'd walked into a difficult situation, worked through a series of challenges, and thrived. Many in the coaching community, even his friends, worried about how LaFleur would fare as a neophyte in a storied setting, attempting to get a headstrong quarterback to adapt to a new system. They all agreed that it would really help if LaFleur could win early. And, ultimately, it went far better than anyone would have predicted.

The previous year in Tennessee, LaFleur's first as play-calling offensive coordinator, had been challenging. LaFleur and Titans coach Mike Vrabel weren't a great match. LaFleur was earnest, analytical, and prone to being an instigator. Vrabel, a product of the Patriots dynasty, was brusque, headstrong, and had little patience for nuance. He'd been a great player on an elite team and knew exactly what he wanted the Titans to be. Vrabel inserted himself into drills at practice, still a badass linebacker to the core. He viewed football as a test of toughness and will and had immense faith in his core beliefs, augmented by the massive success he'd enjoyed in his playing days. LaFleur, too, was secure in his beliefs, and not shy about sticking up for them. It was a clash of wills from the get-go, which wasn't unpredictable.

"It could have been a fucking disaster of a decision," LaFleur said. "A lot of people thought I was crazy for going. I remember, Raheem [Morris] called me when I decided to take the job and he's like, 'Coach—what are you *doing*? Do you know him?'"

Soon, LaFleur knew what Morris meant. Pretty quickly, he thought to himself, *What the fuck did I do?* He and Vrabel muddled through, barely missing out on the playoffs. It was unclear whether they'd continue for a second season—and then the Packers called.

After LaFleur got the job, McVay told Rodgers a story about his boss designed to shed light on LaFleur's personality. At that spring's league meeting in Phoenix, McVay was having a meal with LaFleur and some other coaches, one of whom admired the Rams coach's fancy new wristwatch. McVay explained that it was a Christmas gift from Veronika Khomyn, soon to be his fiancée, then started an amusing rant in which he referenced the couple's financial arrangement and griped about "this expensive new gift that I bought myself." His comic timing was impeccable, and it cracked everyone up.

Later that night, at an outdoor function attended by coaches, own-ers, general managers, and their family members, LaFleur held court and retold the story—with Veronika present.

"That's Matt," McVay said, recounting the story. "I wanted to strangle him—but you almost can't be mad at the guy, because it's like he doesn't even know he was doing anything wrong."

Upon arriving in Green Bay, LaFleur's guileless nature was on full display. Now employed in a city where they name streets after Super Bowl–winning coaches, he didn't even try to disguise his awestruck delight. "I didn't get into coaching to make money," he told me shortly after taking the job. "I got into coaching because I love football and I love working with people. And I wasn't talented enough to play anymore. So, the fact that [I'm] coaching in the NFL with the Green Bay Packers, I mean, like, are you kidding me? Like, I've almost got to pinch myself."

When I visited LaFleur in June, five months after he'd been introduced as Green Bay's coach, he broached a subject almost immediately upon my arrival, one that spoke to a classic clash between a system and a specific play-er's skill set, and something that was already being discussed in the league and beyond: "the audible thing," he called it. LaFleur was in the process of installing a Shanahan-style scheme, which didn't allow quarterbacks unlim-ited freedom at the line. Sometimes, a play call would be sent in with a corre-sponding "can" option, giving the quarterback one predetermined alternative based on what he saw at the line of scrimmage. Rodgers, conversely, had spent his career in a Mike McCarthy–directed scheme that allowed him carte blanche to switch to any play he preferred. Rodgers, an exceptionally intelli-gent and perceptive player with a sharp memory and unbelievable arm talent, had been one of the NFL's best players for more than a decade doing it that way—his way. He wasn't inclined to surrender that power easily.

Complicating matters was the fact that many of LaFleur's play calls would require pre-snap activity, such as players going in motion, that made any deviation from the script more difficult and drastically reduced the play-clock window within which Rodgers would have to operate. And some of the personnel and formations were so specific to certain play calls that it would be tough, if not futile, to change those calls on the fly.

"I think that has a lot to do with it," LaFleur told me. "We move a lot more. There's a lot more motion. There are a lot more moving parts. And so, if you just let the quarterback have that freedom to just get to whatever, I'm afraid it would slow our guys down. Now, he is a special talent and he's got an incredible mind, so as we move forward throughout this process, he's getting more freedom. It's just, where is that happy medium?"

"It's a conversation in progress," Rodgers said the next day, punctuating his words with a short chuckle. "I don't think you want to ask me to turn off 11 years [of recognizing defenses]. We have a number of 'check with mes' and line-of-scrimmage stuff. It's just the other stuff that really not many people in this league can do. That's not like a humblebrag or anything; that's just a fact. There aren't many people that can do at the line of scrimmage what I've done over the years. I mean, obviously, Tommy [Brady] can do it, no doubt. Peyton [Manning] could do it. Drew [Brees] can do it. [Patrick] Mahomes will be able to do it. Ben [Roethlisberger] has called the two-minute for years. There are a few of us who've just *done* it; it's kind of second nature. And that's just the icing on the cake for what I can do in this offense."

The "humblebrag" part of the quote got a lot of traction, fueling speculation that Rodgers was borderline insubordinate when it came to following his new coach's guidance. That was silly. However, there was a lot to work through, and the resolution wouldn't be instantaneous. As with Shanahan and Matt Ryan in Atlanta in 2015, year one would entail some choppiness and tension.

McVay urged LaFleur to loosen up, empower Rodgers, and take advantage of the quarterback's experience and acumen. He put it to me this way: "At the end of the day, there is one person that matters most, and it's the guy running the fucking show. Matt's job is to get him to buy into what he's doing and try to help him find the balance between trusting your coaches and empowering your player, who is the best in the world at what he does. You wanna know the best thing we do in L.A.? It's not scheme. It's not Xs and Os. It's emotional IQ. *That's* the fucking challenge. The challenge isn't Matt getting Aaron to respect him as a football mind. It's connecting. You're still in the selling process of getting guys to buy in and believe. This guy is *so* smart. He doesn't respect anybody unless they're on his level. But if you've got the ability to challenge him, on a level where he respects you and you're not infringing on Aaron Rodgers the person, it can be amazing."

Early on, it wasn't amazing. The Packers opened the regular season in Chicago, on a Thursday night. LaFleur's parents, Denny and Kristi, were among the group of four dozen family members and friends who showed up to cheer on the new coach. LaFleur took the field wearing a white quarter-zip, black Lululemon pants, and white Nikes. As he emerged from the tunnel and walked up the visitors' sidelines about an hour before the game, I snapped a photo and sent it to Shanahan. "Wow. He's copying my exact outfit," his former boss replied, adding the crying-with-laughter emoji for emphasis.

LaFleur's style was on point; his offense, not so much. It was, in LaFleur's words, "an ugly-ass game." The Packers gained just 213 yards and won, 10–3. Green Bay's only touchdown came after Rodgers, in a patented move, caught the Bears with 12 men on the field, quickly called for the snap, and parlayed the free play into an improvised scoring pass to tight end Jimmy Graham. "That was all Aaron—it was Aaron being Aaron," LaFleur said afterward in his private dressing area. "And no, I'm not mad about it."

Things got better as the weeks went on, but not in the way that LaFleur had hoped. The Packers would finish the season with the league's 18th-best offense, meaning they were in the bottom half of the league rankings. It was a testament to LaFleur's overall grasp of his new role that Green Bay, which had gone 6–9–1 the previous season, would finish 13–3 in 2019. Said McVay, "To me, that's a great reflection of the head coach: 'We figured out ways to win games and go 13–3. We didn't necessarily have to light you up.'" After defeating the Seahawks in the playoffs, the Packers had one team standing between them and the Super Bowl—and the 49ers proceeded to grind them into submission.

The ensuing offseason for Green Bay would be even more charged, with LaFleur and Rodgers confronting an unplanned and tumultuous threat to their budding partnership. In the meantime, LaFleur, for the second consecutive February, would watch one of his former bosses try to win a Super Bowl.

WHEN IT ALL UNRAVELED, IT WAS MATT LaFLEUR'S YOUNGER BROTHER who broke the ice. "We did it again, buddy," Mike LaFleur said to McDaniel in the upstairs coaches' booth at Hard Rock Stadium in Miami Gardens, Florida, his words tinged with gallows humor. It was a nightmare relived: for the second time in three years, the two coaches—and Shanahan—were on the wrong end of a team's dramatic Super Bowl comeback. In Super Bowl LI, the Falcons blew a 28–3 lead to the Patriots; this time, the Niners' ten-point fourth-quarter advantage had disappeared with almost as much drama. Seemingly on the brink of defeat, the Kansas City Chiefs outscored the Niners 21–0 in the final 6:13. After Kendall Fuller intercepted a desperate Garoppolo pass with 57 seconds remaining, that sick feeling returned in the coaches' box and on the sideline, where Shanahan was once again the poster child for spectacular Super Bowl collapse.

To those who knew him best, the stigma seemed particularly cruel. He had engineered one of the great single-season turnarounds in NFL history, constructed a team comprising tough and relentless competitors, and provided it with a peerless weekly blueprint for success. Even on the grandest stage—against Patrick Mahomes, the sport's most luminous young star—it seemed to be working, until it wasn't.

Mahomes, an MVP in his first season as a starter, had brought coach Andy Reid's unconventional offensive ideas to life, and this game had been framed as the young quarterback's likely coronation as the top performer in his sport. Shanahan and Saleh and their players, however, weren't having it. They led 20–10 midway through the fourth quarter and felt their advantage could have been greater. The Niners, who'd closed out their previous two victories in punishing fashion, were about to get the ball back and would surely run over the Chiefs, too, on their way to the franchise's first championship in a quarter century. In 1995, Mike Shanahan's cutting-edge game plan had propelled the 49ers to a blowout victory over the San Diego Chargers on the same field. As the Chiefs faced third and 15 from their own 35-yard line with 7:13 remaining, victory for his son seemed inevitable.

And then it all went to hell. Reid called 2–3 Jet Chip Wasp. Mahomes dropped back to pass and looked downfield, surveying his options. He kept backpedaling as Nick Bosa collapsed the pocket; Bosa looked ready to sack the quarterback, but left tackle Eric Fisher got his arm under the edge rusher's neck, a borderline hold that wasn't called. Defensive tackle DeForest Buckner rolled outside Bosa and hit Mahomes, who'd backed up even further, 14 yards deep, just as the quarterback released a pass downfield. Niners cornerback Emmanuel Moseley, stationed on the outside of a three-deep zone, had inexplicably vacated his area and run with K.C. wideout Sammy Watkins on a crossing route underneath, allowing the NFL's fastest receiver, Tyreek Hill, to get free on a post-corner route. Hill was all alone as he waited to catch Mahomes's pass, hauling it in for a 44-yard completion. The play changed the game.

That's when Shanahan started to worry—because, he recalled, "It was over to me if they didn't get that . . . Once they got that, I was like, 'Alright, this is a game now.' . . . And you could tell before that third and 15 that we had the momentum. You could feel that they kind of felt it. And that rejuvenated everybody."

Two quick K.C. touchdowns later, the Niners were still in it. Trailing 24–20 with 1:40 remaining, they faced third and ten on the Chiefs 49. Wideout Emmanuel Sanders broke free on a post route and flashed open inside the ten, but Garoppolo overthrew him by several yards, squandering what could have been a glorious moment. He'd had a sloppy game, having thrown an earlier interception and, on more than one occasion in the second half, having failed to spot tight end George Kittle in the middle of the field with room to run. "He was a little nervous for that Super Bowl game," McDaniel said of Garoppolo. "There were some plays that he had made routinely all season. He messed up, and then we were learning that he had some issues that could have been worked out if he attacked the offseason appropriately . . . so [he] wouldn't have those type of anxieties."

As Mike Shanahan put it, "And that's what separates the big boys."

Not long after Garoppolo's overthrow, Reid was finally hoisting a Lombardi Trophy after 21 years as a head coach, 221 previous victories, and one glaring Super Bowl defeat 15 years earlier, when Bill Belichick and Tom Brady had taken down his Eagles. He'd been the NFL head coach with the most wins who was still without a championship, and was thus a sentimental favorite, inside the football world and beyond it. To Shanahan, it all seemed surreal. The game had turned so abruptly, and the Niners' demise had occurred so rapidly, that he barely had time to process the devastation.

In the moment, he handled it well. He told his players in the locker room how much he cared about and admired them, moving some of them to tears. "Kyle held his head high," Niners defensive end Dee Ford told me afterward. "He told us, 'Of course it's not the result we wanted, but I'll line up with any player in here, anytime.' He told us, 'This team is special.' And it is."

Shanahan was gracious at his postgame press conference and was the last to leave the locker room, a captain going down with the ship. Long after the game, with the last of the team buses still waiting for the coach to board it, I got a text from McDaniel, describing his boss's behavior: "He is being an incredible leader right now, supporting all the broken hearts."

Once again, Shanahan had failed to achieve his ultimate goal in striking fashion. However, he'd already succeeded in accomplishing another objective. As his friend Raheem Morris, at that point the Falcons' newly named defensive coordinator after four years as a receivers coach, had put it to me in the days leading up to the game, "The goal is winning championships, yes. But for Kyle, it's also him just trying to make his dad proud."

Mike Shanahan's presence was a constant at the 49ers' facility, even when it wasn't physical. He regularly watched tape of practice and meetings; staffers were known to be admonished if he didn't get a prompt copy sent to him electronically, prompting jokes around the facility of a "Shanahan cam," or a "Shana-cam" in its shortened version. His work ethic and attention to detail could be felt throughout the building. Vikings general manager Kwesi Adofo-Mensah recalled his first encounter with the elder Shanahan, when he was the 49ers' director of football and research development. "You get why he's the founding father. I always tell the story, the first time we're in draft meetings together, he's in the gym at 5:30 a.m., getting a pump in. He's retired, by the way. He's up in meetings talking about 'Yeah, this guard's pretty good, but these other guys in free agency . . .' He'd already done the offensive linemen in the draft and free agency! By the way, he is retired—just helping out his son. It woke me up because it was like, you think your standard is championship-level and then you see that guy. That's championship standard in retirement. It really woke me up."

"Papa Shanahan, everything starts with him, for all of us," Saleh said. "If Kyle's a savant, he's Mr. Miyagi."

Mike knew his son as single-minded. "I actually believe each year he knows that if you don't win a championship, nothing else really matters." As Kyle and his wife, Mandy, boarded bus No. 7 outside Hard Rock Stadium on that February night in 2020, he knew there would be no quick fix for his agony, and nothing easy about his next steps. The quest for a Lombardi Trophy would continue, with McVay and Matt LaFleur intent on beating him there, and McDaniel and Morris and Saleh and Mike LaFleur and so many others pushing for the opportunity to do the same.

At that moment, it felt futile. Later that night, Shanahan walked to his hotel room with Bo Scaife, his former Texas teammate. As they neared the door, Shanahan said something that remains burned into his close friend's memory.

"I feel like God doesn't want me to win a Super Bowl."

Chapter 16

Hunkering Down

Many, many people suffered fates far worse during the COVID-19 pandemic than NFL coaches whose facilities shut down throughout the spring and early summer of 2020. Yet Kyle Shanahan, like so many others around the world, felt the sting of inactivity and detachment—during a time when he desperately wanted to move forward. As he'd say before the 2021 season, "I mean, no matter how tough of a deal you deal with in football, the cool thing about our job is, you get a chance to go practice and try to get better and prove yourself the next year. When that's taken away from you, that's tough."

There would be isolation, disruption, and uncertainty. As other leagues canceled their championships and seasons or created "bubble" atmospheres devoid of fans, it was unclear whether the 2020 NFL season would even take place. There'd be a virtual draft and offseason program as NFL commissioner Roger Goodell and his lieutenants tried to figure out a way to play the games. It was a tumultuous time in America that included civil unrest following a Minneapolis police officer's murder of a Black man, George Floyd, that was captured on video by a witness. Fear was a constant; emotions were raw. Throw in an upcoming national election that would test the limits of democracy, and an incumbent president making openly racist statements, and most Americans were on edge.

Relatively speaking, Shanahan and McVay weren't under extraordinary stress. Both coaches *did* feel a sense of urgency to redeem their Super Bowl failures. For Shanahan, having twice had his anticipated moment of glory snatched away, it was about prodding a very good team past the threshold. For McVay, it was about embracing a philosophical shift designed to confront the game's ever-evolving realities. Neither quest would prove to be smooth, or easy. And, naturally, each would start with the coach's connection to his starting quarterback, or lack thereof.

Not long after the Super Bowl ended, Shanahan was on the clock. Tom Brady, after 20 sensational seasons in New England, was an unrestricted free agent eager to relocate. Brady had numerous potential suitors, from the Raiders to the Chargers to the Dolphins to the Saints to the Bucs, but at least part of his heart was in San Francisco. A native of nearby San Mateo, Brady had grown up a rabid 49ers fan, witnessing in person "The Catch"—Dwight Clark's soaring snag of a Joe Montana pass in the 1981 NFC Championship Game that propelled S.F. to its first Super Bowl—as a four-year-old. There were some personal and professional links between him and Shanahan, including 49ers receivers coach Wes Welker, a close friend of Brady's who'd been one of his star receivers during his time with the Patriots.

Brady wanted to play in warm weather, ideally either in proximity to New York City (where Jack, his son from his earlier relationship with actress Bridget Moynahan, lived) or the Bay Area, where his parents still resided. He wanted a two-year, $50 million contract—not exorbitant, given his level of accomplishment—and a coach who valued collaboration. He wasn't necessarily chasing a seventh ring, but he wanted a team that was at least competitive. The Niners checked all the boxes. According to ESPN reporter Seth Wickersham, Brady reached out to Welker and told him that if they were interested, the 49ers could preemptively take him off the market—no free agency tour, no bidding war.

Shanahan, John Lynch, and others in the organization were skeptical at first, but they obviously had to assess the situation, given Brady's greatness. It was tricky, on many levels. Garoppolo, Brady's former backup in New England, shared an agent with the legendary quarterback. The 49ers had structured Garoppolo's contract in a way that would have allowed them to move on without much impact on their salary cap, and his trade value would have been decent. He was 28; Brady would be 43 before the scheduled start of the 2020 season.

In almost any other scenario, the notion of committing to a quarter-back that old would have been laughable. Brady, however, had defied all previous age-related precedents. He was still playing at a high level, having taken the 2019 Patriots, who were defending another Super Bowl championship, back to the playoffs after a 12–4 regular season. He'd thrown for 4,057 yards and 24 touchdowns, with eight interceptions. Putting him on a team with a Super Bowl–caliber roster didn't seem like too much of a gamble.

However, when the 49ers' offensive coaches broke down Brady's 2019 film, they weren't hugely impressed. Like others around the league who'd evaluated him during and after that season, they felt his arm strength had waned and that he finally appeared to be on the decline. They were wrong, of course—Brady would remain a force through his 45th birthday and beyond, and his arm somehow looked livelier in 2020 than it had in the previous season.

In the end, age wasn't the only consideration that gave Shanahan pause. As with Aaron Rodgers and Matt LaFleur in Green Bay, the Shana-han system wasn't a natural fit for Brady. For two decades, Brady had run a specific scheme. Like Rodgers when LaFleur arrived, he was accustomed to immense freedom at the line of scrimmage and wouldn't want to give that up, meaning he and Shanahan would have to figure out their own "audible thing."

The idea of moving on from Garoppolo was also unnerving. Yes, he'd missed some throws in the Super Bowl and had failed to come up big in the final minutes. And yes, he drove Shanahan crazy at times. He'd blown off the previous two offseasons and didn't see the field the way Shanahan wanted his quarterback to; he had a tendency, when pressured, to rely on his quick release and arm talent to make high-risk throws. Yet Garoppolo was coming off an impressive season with some indelible moments, includ-ing those third-and-16 completions that clinched that late-season victory over the Rams. He was popular in the locker room and, when comple-mented by a strong running game, looked capable of performing at a high level for years to come. Theoretically, he could get a lot better.

Ultimately, Shanahan and Lynch chose the status quo. They had a good thing going with Garoppolo and didn't want to make a potentially jolting move.

"It wasn't really a debate," recalled Mike McDaniel, then the team's run game coordinator. "We got to the Super Bowl, in part, because of Jimmy. And you just flip and fuck with your whole team chemistry? If you had known that [Brady] would do the unthinkable . . ."

No one knew—not even the Bucs, the team Brady eventually picked after the Niners politely passed. Nor did anyone know that Garoppolo, for the second time in three seasons, would be derailed by an early injury. For now, Shanahan was intent on running it back with Garoppolo, just as McVay had been the previous season with Jared Goff. That partnership, too, was about to endure a stress test.

———

THE FIRST SIGN THAT McVAY WASN'T PLAYING AROUND CAME IN MID-February, when word of his plans for the upcoming NFL scouting combine surfaced. McVay would only devote about 24 in-person hours to the week-long cesspool of energy and conversation, briefly hitting the bar scene after fulfilling his media obligations. Instead of scouting draft-eligible players on location, McVay would spend the bulk of his time with his newly hired coordinators on both sides of the ball—neither of whom would be going to Indy at all. The three of them were in the process of revamping the offense and overhauling the defensive scheme. There was much work to be done back home.

At the time, McVay didn't envision himself as starting a trend, though other coaches from the Shanahan ecosystem (including Shanahan himself, as well as Matt LaFleur and Robert Saleh) would come to adopt similar practices. McVay simply believed that he and his most important assistants would be much more efficient grinding away in L.A. and worrying about their evaluations of college players in the weeks to come—without the many hours of revelry in downtown Indy. And as it turned out, because of COVID, this would be the last communal gathering of its sort for a long, long time.

As McVay explained, "What is the best way to use that week? Is it really to go and sit there, have some in-person interviews? The simple fact was, you send your scouts and you can just get more done [at home] in an efficient manner when you take into account how long the travel is, and if we had a good season, how late we finished up. It's going in alignment with always asking the *why* and what's the best way to maximize our time?"

McVay moved on from defensive coordinator Wade Phillips after three seasons and replaced him with a hire that few saw coming: Broncos outside linebackers coach Brandon Staley, who four years earlier had been the defensive coordinator for a Division III school, John Carroll University. The two had developed an instant rapport in their initial interview, with McVay viewing the amped-up, intellectually curious Staley as "kind of like me, but on defense." It was no mystery why McVay was initially interested: Staley had been outside linebackers coach on the Bears' staff when the team stymied the Rams attack during that watershed 2018 regular-season game. Staley knew Vic Fangio's scheme inside and out, and had some ideas about how to put his own spin on it. McVay wanted that scheme—no matter what—and he decided Staley was the ideal person to implement it.

McVay, like Shanahan the previous year, was in the process of adapting his defensive philosophy by embracing a scheme that disrupted his specific offensive approach. For Shanahan, that meant bringing in Kris Kocurek as Robert Saleh's defensive line coach and implementing the Wide 9. In McVay's case, Staley would bring an approach that disguised coverages and limited explosive pass plays by playing quarters on the back end with match-zone principles (basically man-to-man with a caveat—such as a receiver in front of a defensive back or linebacker running underneath— dictating such coverage). Staley's defense made things tough on opposing quarterbacks by disguising its intentions. Often, pre-snap, Staley's defensive backs would line up in a very basic-looking two-high shell, with the safeties forming the top of an arc. Then, at the snap, safeties and corners frequently rotated to change the look, forcing the quarterback and his receivers to make quick decisions amid the chaos. For a quarterback who turned his back to the defense after faking a handoff, it was even more perilous. Obsessed with strategy, Staley favored Fangio's practice of crafting opponent-specific game plans designed to disrupt preferred routes.

At its best, the defense featured versatile, position-shifting players—

rangy edge rushers who could slow down perimeter runs (another similarity to the Wide 9), lighter defensive linemen and linebackers, corners with safety skills, and safeties with corner skills. In an increasingly explosive league, the Fangio defense strove to make quarterbacks settle for checkdowns and conduct long, time-consuming drives that could be derailed by mistakes.

McVay also wanted to freshen up his offensive approach and give Goff more hands-on help. After Matt LaFleur's departure, McVay had gone two seasons without an offensive coordinator. Now, he decided to hire one: Kevin O'Connell, a former quarterback—he was a Patriots third-round draft choice and backup to Brady—who, like Staley, had been a rapidly rising star in the profession. O'Connell, in his third season as a coach, had gotten a job as Jay Gruden's quarterbacks coach in 2017, partly on the recommendation of McVay, who'd just left to become the Rams' head coach. The two of them didn't know each other well, but McVay had heard good things and had explored a role for O'Connell on that first Rams staff, before Shane Waldron, Zac Taylor, and Greg Olson took up the available slots.

Now, things were a bit awkward: O'Connell had leapfrogged Waldron, the Rams' passing-game coordinator. Similarly, Staley had gotten hired instead of assistant head coach/linebackers coach Joe Barry, McVay's good friend and a former defensive coordinator in Washington during the 2015 and 2016 seasons, when McVay was his offensive counterpart. Suddenly, Barry was no longer McVay's closest confidant. In those early offseason weeks, it was just McVay, O'Connell, and Staley, trying to figure it all out together, with as little outside noise as possible.

The connection between McVay and Staley had been instantaneous, and soon enough, O'Connell and Staley were inseparable—a temporary state of affairs that would be exacerbated by the onset of COVID and the shelter-in-place orders that followed. As O'Connell recalled, "Brandon and I were just in a hotel together. There really wasn't anybody else staying there at the time. We spent a lot of time together, just kind of the new guys, dinner every night, just talking football, family. Before you know it, we were pretty close." It turned out they had a lot in common. Each coach had three kids of similar ages. Each had played quarterback in college and worn No. 7. Each married a former college volleyball player—Leah O'Connell and Amy Staley were the same height (5-foot-10) and had also donned the same jersey number (2). During the pandemic, Leah and Amy home-schooled their kids, together.

In one important way, however, Staley and O'Connell had had distinct journeys. In December of 2006, nearly three years after losing his mother to cancer, Brandon was finishing his first season as a Northern Illinois graduate assistant at the Poinsettia Bowl in San Diego. He was experiencing night sweats and flu-like symptoms and had a growth in his chest. Doctors discovered a grapefruit-sized tumor on his right lung and diagnosed him with Hodgkin's lymphoma. He steeled himself for what turned out to be an eight-month treatment ordeal, one that would trigger a renewed urgency to attack his life goals. "It gave me a chance to compete against something," Staley said. "And that's the way I looked it was, it was gonna be a chance for me to show what I was made of."

Defense wouldn't be the Rams' problem in 2020, even as Staley installed his scheme with the players over Zoom. Rather, it was their strength. The disconnect between L.A.'s head coach and quarterback would prove to be the fatal flaw.

MANAGING THE COACH–QUARTERBACK RELATIONSHIP WAS A CONSTANT challenge, as Matt LaFleur would learn during the strange 2020 offseason. And in this case, the Packers' front office was a big part of the problem.

In most franchises, the head coach and general manager are presumed to work in lockstep when it comes to the draft, important roster decisions, and other key moves, such as contract extensions, that could shape the direction of the franchise. In some cases, as in San Francisco, the coach technically had more power; in others, the general manager had the final say over the 53-man roster. In yet others, the coach is also the GM, or the owner effectively is. In any event, alignment is the supposed goal. Even when the coach and GM disagree, it is important that each of them properly communicate his perspective and that they remain at least partially on the same page.

Then there were the Green Bay Packers—an organization that, in the 21st-century NFL, existed as its own separate world, with its own rules. For one thing, the Packers didn't have an owner: they've been a publicly owned, nonprofit corporation since 1923. The NFL now prohibits such arrangements, but had granted the Packers an exemption because their structure predated the rule. The franchise was run by an executive committee, elected via the board of directors, with the committee's elected president as its only compensated officer. That president, Mark Murphy, had served in the role since 2007, operating as the de facto owner without some of the usual pressure points. Perceived as "small market" due to Green Bay's small population, the Packers' franchise was actually sitting pretty: because so much of the NFL's revenue is shared, including the massive national broadcast deals, the Packers weren't at a financial disadvantage. In reality, they had an advantage, precisely because of their corporate structure. At various times throughout their existence, the board had conducted stock sales that filled the franchise's coffers without surrendering any power.

Unlike a typical sale of common stock, the Packers' sale terms conferred none of the traditional rights associated with being a shareholder. That meant no equity interest, no dividends, no trading privileges, and no protection under securities law. Stockholders didn't even get a leg up on purchasing season tickets; all they got were voting rights, an invitation to the annual meeting, and the chance to purchase exclusive merchandise. An example of how it worked: beginning in late 2021, the franchise offered 300,000 shares at $300 apiece, the proceeds of which could then be used for stadium renovations and other club-related expenditures.

Yet, perplexingly, the Packers were among the league's least aggressive teams when it came to player acquisition. Unlike the McVay-era Rams, who never shied away from big-ticket free-agent signings or high-risk trades that would cost them draft picks, the Packers perpetually played it safe. For nearly two decades—first with Ted Thompson as general manager, and later with Brian Gutekunst—the Packers had favored a draft-and-develop strategy that included few, if any, big risks. The Packers' leadership got away with it, in part, because they were enjoying what proved to be an NFL anomaly: an uninterrupted three-decade run of future first-ballot Hall of Fame quarterbacks—first Brett Favre, and now Rodgers. Both players were so transcendent that they covered up the team's weaknesses and kept them highly competitive. Many skeptics, however, believed the Packers had underachieved, and it was hard to argue with them. With Favre and Rodgers, two of the best QBs ever to play the position, they'd appeared in a grand total of three Super Bowls in 29 seasons, winning two.

Coming off a lopsided NFC Championship Game defeat, Rodgers, now 36, was tired of the prevailing model. He'd long been frustrated with the franchise's caution, dating back to the middle of the 2010 season, when Green Bay could have traded for Rodgers's friend and former Cal teammate—future Hall of Fame running back Marshawn Lynch—but passed, despite the quarterback's urging. Rodgers, it turned out, would go on a postseason tear that ended with him winning Super Bowl MVP and hoisting the Lombardi Trophy, but he'd since lost three conference title clashes. Gutekunst had been surprisingly active in free agency the previous year, his first as the team's GM, and the players he'd signed (including edge rushers Za'Darius Smith and Preston Smith) had played a big role in the team's 2019 success. This time, Rodgers wanted more help, especially on offense.

What he got was, in his estimation, a kick in the nuts.

Typically during the draft, an organization's top decision-makers—along with, depending upon the franchise, assistant coaches, personnel executives, and scouts—gather in a "war room" at the team facility and conduct their business over the event's three nights in a communal setting. Because of the pandemic, that would not be happening in 2020. The "virtual draft" had people spread out in their respective residences, doing business via cell phone and on Microsoft Teams. That meant the existing communication issues between the Packers' powerbrokers—Murphy, Gutekunst, and executive vice president/director of football operations Russ Ball—and LaFleur and his assistants was further exacerbated.

So it was that LaFleur, sitting in the downstairs bar area of his home, learned of Gutekunst's franchise-defining move just seconds before the rest of the draft-obsessed world: The GM swung a trade with the Dolphins to move from 30th to 26th in the first round, then used that selection on Utah State quarterback Jordan Love, an intriguing prospect who lacked high-level college experience.

LaFleur liked Love as a player and a project, but obviously understood that a message was being sent. In 2005, Rodgers, passed over by the 49ers, endured a conspicuous freefall that finally ended when Thompson—not in the market for a successor to Favre, but shocked that such a player was available—took him with the 24th pick. Rodgers sat behind Favre for three seasons before the incumbent quarterback retired, unretired, and finally provoked a tumultuous departure in the summer of 2008. For the Packers, that had worked out well in the end, and Love was raw enough that he stood to benefit from some time as Rodgers's backup. In theory, planning for the future made sense.

However, Rodgers saw the Love selection as a clear sign that he was no longer wanted. In the current era, quarterbacks drafted in the first round either played immediately or soon. The plan, Rodgers assumed, was to give him one more season as the starter and then move on. There was also the issue of opportunity cost—picking Love meant the Packers were forgoing a chance to make their 2020 team better. Amazingly, the selection of Love marked the first time in the 15 years since Rodgers had been drafted that Green Bay had used a first-round selection on a skill-position player. To Rodgers, this was additionally insulting: rather than arming him with, say, another receiver to pair opposite All-Pro Davante Adams, Gutekunst was telling Rodgers his time in Green Bay was nearing its end.

LaFleur texted Rodgers seconds after he learned of Love's selection, attempting both to reassure him that he remained the team's quarterback of the present and to send a not-so-cryptic signal that he'd been blindsided, too. Rodgers wasn't too worried about the former concern—"No matter who you bring in, they're not going to be able to beat me out anytime soon," he'd said in the lead-up to the draft—and though he wasn't totally convinced about LaFleur's professions of ignorance, he knew how the Packers' power dynamic worked. Though Rodgers would remain in Green Bay for another three seasons, the same amount of time that Favre had held him off a decade and a half earlier, his relationship with his Green Bay bosses would never be the same.

Looking back, perhaps LaFleur, sincere to the core and mesmerized by the opportunity to coach the Packers, had been naive about the job he was accepting. This was how things worked in Green Bay. After the 2020 draft, the coach's only move was the make the best of it. "Obviously, Aaron Rodgers is the leader of this football team, and my expectation is that he will be for a long time," LaFleur told me the morning after the pick. "I sincerely love the guy, and I love working with him, and it's a hell of a lot of fun. I'm really excited about where we can take this, and that hasn't changed one bit."

In some ways, the pandemic would turn out to benefit the Packers. It was harder to get players to spend time in Green Bay during the offseason than in other NFL cities. Rodgers, in particular, had become increasingly prone to skipping voluntary activities—unusual for a franchise quarterback not named Jimmy Garoppolo, though Rodgers, at least, had earned it. Now, no one around the league could participate in in-person OTAs, leveling the playing field. Just as the lack of crowd noise would give Rodgers a massive advantage on the road during a regular season played largely in empty or near-empty stadiums—one less element to keep him from carving up opponents—the virtual offseason became an equalizer for his coaches.

Left to their own Zoom devices, LaFleur, offensive coordinator Nathaniel Hackett, and quarterbacks coach Luke Getsy began breaking down their entire attack with Rodgers and recrafting it as a joint venture. Some plays and concepts were thrown out. Others were inserted. The coaches wanted to create an offense that Rodgers owned, operated, and embraced. Hackett, whose schematic foundation had been forged in the West Coast offense (his father, Paul, had been a key assistant for Bill Walsh's 49ers), helped bridge the gap between Rodgers's past preferences and LaFleur's present sensibilities. LaFleur reflected, "The first year, I know we won a lot of games, but we weren't a well-oiled machine on offense. Any time you introduce a new system, it takes a legit year for that offense. I look at what we did in Atlanta in '15; it was not great. In '16, we were unbelievable."

In Atlanta, LaFleur, according to Tom House, had been the "taint"; now, Hackett was in that role. He turned out to be ideally suited for it, especially given the challenges of the times. Hyperenergetic, unfailingly upbeat, and refreshingly unconventional, Hackett had a knack for keeping Rodgers engaged. He also loved technology and teaching and embraced the challenge of creating learning tools that could be used virtually, and he would help make things lively for Rodgers and the Packers' other offensive players in the coming months.

Hackett felt a great deal of loyalty to LaFleur, who he believed had "saved" him after a massive career disappointment in November 2018, when he was fired as the Jaguars' offensive coordinator. Less than a year removed from a season in which Jacksonville had nearly reached the Super Bowl with the embattled Blake Bortles at quarterback, Hackett felt he'd been scapegoated by Jags coach Doug Marrone and was planning to leave the profession. "I was gonna be done with coaching," Hackett recalled in June 2022. "I had no use for it, after what happened in Jacksonville. Matt kept me in. I owe him everything."

Because of his familiarity with the dropback passing game, Hackett felt he could help merge those principles with LaFleur's preferred modes of attack: outside zone runs, and the bootlegs, rollouts, and play-action passes that served as their accompaniments. He asked LaFleur for more responsibility in game-planning, and LaFleur gave it to him, telling Hackett what he wanted to accomplish and allowing the coordinator to craft a plan accordingly. "Hackett played a big part in [that 2020 season], just being a bridge for those two guys," said Ejiro Evero, a close friend of Hackett's since their days as UC Davis teammates, who was the Rams' safeties coach in 2020.

A little more than a year into the job, in a charged atmosphere he hadn't caused or asked for, LaFleur was evolving, setting the stage for one of the great regular seasons in the history of quarterbacking.

▬▬▬

WHEN LAFLEUR GOT TO GREEN BAY IN JANUARY OF 2019, ONE OF THE things he wanted to replicate was the brotherhood that Dan Quinn had preached as his mantra in Atlanta. The closeness of those Falcons teams, LaFleur believed, had propelled them to the Super Bowl and the brink of the franchise's first championship.

Now, more than three and a half years removed from the squandered 28–3 lead against Tom Brady and the Patriots, the operation was collapsing. Quinn, who'd saved his job in 2019 by recovering from a 1–7 start to finish 7–9, wouldn't be so fortunate in 2020. After Atlanta lost its first five games, owner Arthur Blank fired Quinn and general manager Thomas Dimitroff—and turned to Raheem Morris as his interim coach.

Morris, by his own measure, was a much better coach now than when he'd become an NFL head coach at 32. During his fourth season as the Falcons' receivers coach, amid that disastrous 1–7 start, he'd gone back to his roots, becoming the team's secondary coach and then taking over as Quinn's defensive coordinator following the 2019 campaign. Now, he had a chance to run the whole operation. With 11 games left, Morris hoped to force the removal of the interim tag and stay on as head coach. When Blank was asked about that possibility during the press conference to announce Quinn's firing, he responded, "If Raheem ends up 11–0, then he'll certainly be a candidate."

It was another regrettable moment for minority coaches struggling to overcome the systemic racism that had denied them so many opportunities. Undaunted, Morris proceeded to win three of his first four games—the only defeat coming when running back Todd Gurley, now on the Falcons and with a chance to ice a game against the Lions, accidentally scored a touchdown in the final two minutes; intending to stop short of the goal line to set up a game-winning field goal, Gurley's momentum carried him into the end zone. The Lions drove down and won on Matthew Stafford's 11-yard touchdown pass to tight end T. J. Hockenson (and the ensuing extra point) with no time remaining.

Morris had placed a renewed emphasis on accountability and precision, instituting a "corrections period" at the end of practice. Following a 24–9 defeat to the Saints in his fifth game as interim coach, he scrapped the next day's scheduled virtual meeting, instead gathering players in the expansive field house at the team's facility for "Tell the Truth Monday." As Morris explained to me at the time, "We wanted everyone to be able to look each other in the eye and talk about what we didn't do well and fix it. We didn't cut corners; we didn't beat around the bush; people were accountable, coaches and players."

It worked. Six days later, the Falcons rolled to a 43–6 victory over the Raiders. Morris called me on his drive home up I-85; it was now realistic to ponder him landing the job on a permanent basis. His Tampa stint, he said, "seems like a lifetime ago. Hey, trust me: 32-year-old Raheem Morris is nothing like the guy coaching now." Then Morris laughed, amazed at his own self-importance. "Did I just refer to myself in the third person?" he asked.

The Falcons lost their final five games, the first four of them by five points or fewer. Morris got an interview for the head coaching job after the season, but he assumed it was a courtesy. Blank instead hired Arthur Smith, who'd succeeded LaFleur as the Titans' offensive coordinator—technically, another member of the Shanahan coaching tree. However, Morris had proven something—to himself, at the very least. If and when his next real opportunity to be an NFL head coach came, he knew exactly how he'd approach it.

IF SHANAHAN HATED THE COVID-19-IMPACTED OFFSEASON, THE START of his 2020 regular season was even worse. After losing their opener to the Cardinals in an empty Levi's Stadium, the Niners flew east for consecutive games against the Jets and Giants, both on the MetLife Stadium turf. They won both, but the dubiously sticky FieldTurf, newly installed that summer, derailed their plans: against the Jets, star edge rusher Nick Bosa and defensive tackle Solomon Thomas tore their ACLs on consecutive plays in the first quarter, ending their seasons. Garoppolo suffered a high ankle sprain that would keep him out the next two weeks; in early November, a reaggravation of the ankle injury would shelve him for the year. Star tight end George Kittle, running back Raheem Mostert, wide receiver Deebo Samuel, edge rusher Dee Ford, and cornerback Richard Sherman also missed significant time during the season. The decimated Niners couldn't withstand it. Football is a physical sport with a high rate of attrition, but it was one of the most unlucky seasons any NFL team had endured in recent memory.

There were some uplifting moments, including consecutive victories over the Rams and Patriots that pushed San Francisco's record to 4–3, briefly instilling a sense of hope that the 2019 magic could be replicated. It couldn't—the Niners lost their next three games, headed into their bye week with a losing record, and prepared for a moment of reckoning. For the second time in three years, Garoppolo had been felled by injuries, leading to a lost season. Shanahan was coming to the conclusion that he could no longer count on his quarterback to stay healthy.

The Niners rallied for a last show of strength, and an unlikely one at that. Playing at the Rams' newly opened palace, SoFi Stadium in Inglewood, with Nick Mullens at quarterback, S.F. didn't seem to have a great chance of winning the two teams' November 29 rematch. The Rams, 7–3 coming in, had yet to lose in the building. They were about to suffer more than one defeat: by day's end, McVay would lose faith in *his* quarterback, too.

Six days earlier, Goff had played well in a 27–24 *Monday Night Football* road victory over Tom Brady and the Buccaneers, offering coach and QB a measure of redemption. Goff's month had also begun in Florida, in horrific fashion: subjected to what seemed like an endless succession of Zero blitzes by the Dolphins—whose head coach, Brian Flores, clearly felt the Rams' QB wouldn't be able to handle the pressure—Goff had a disastrous day, throwing two interceptions and losing two fumbles. O'Connell, new to the growing McVay/Goff divide, was so rattled by the experience that, following his first season as the Vikings' head coach, he would hire Flores as his defensive coordinator. "The Miami game was tough on all of us," O'Connell said in the fall of 2023. "That's one of the reasons why Brian Flores is in this building now, just remembering the feeling of that and kind of the mentality that they had defensively that day."

Going into the season, both McVay and Goff had expressed confidence that they'd rebound from the disappointments of 2019. That September, when I visited Goff at his home in Hidden Hills—Kardashian country—he conceded that he'd tried to do too much the previous season and said he planned to channel his frustration into something positive. "Sometimes," he said, "you need a punch in the face, a kick in the face, like, 'Oh, man, I can be better than that.'"

He possessed what Rams left tackle Andrew Whitworth called "a new edge" that seemed directly traceable to the team's emotional bonding sessions—over Zoom—in the wake of George Floyd's murder. Race, police brutality, and other topics were discussed freely, and much of it was illuminating to Goff, who'd grown up in Novato, a largely white suburb north of San Francisco. "I think this offseason, specifically with what's gone on, has definitely hit me differently than anything before," Goff told me. "I would imagine it's centered around hearing stories from my own teammates about some of the ways they've been treated, actually hearing that firsthand."

When it came to football, Goff was excited by the evolution of McVay's offensive approach. During the latter part of the 2019 season, as he explained, "we really started involving more of our offense. We weren't so live and die by one thing, right? Didn't live and die by a certain personnel grouping; didn't live and die by a certain type of run or pass or anything . . . I think that's the best thing about Sean is his humility, and as good a coach as he is, he's the first one to look inward. And I think that trickles through the whole team."

Previously, McVay himself conceded, Fangio, Bill Belichick, and other great defensive minds could play their base defense with a surplus of big bodies up front and essentially dare the Rams to throw. "And so," McVay continued, "we had answers, but those answers didn't really go in alignment with the philosophy that I think has given us a lot of success. And that's really the gist of it, is not letting people dictate terms on you, based on how they match. You can always dictate the terms, if you've got multiple personnel groupings you can activate."

Sometimes in 2020, Goff and the Rams dictated and thrived. Other times, he and the team struggled. In training camp, going against Staley's cutting-edge defense, which featured wrinkles such as cornerback Jalen Ramsey being deployed all over the field in a trendy new position known as "Star," had proven to be a major challenge.

Goff's uneven training camp performances would make more sense at season's end, when the Rams' defense ranked at the top of the league. By then, however, McVay and Goff were in a dark place.

One McVay assistant believes the coach's frustrations with Goff dated back to his struggles against the Bears and other teams late in the 2018 season, which precipitated the quarterback's poor Super Bowl performance. "Before that, it was this scheme and his innovation that was scoring points, and then people started to figure it out," the coach said. "We're like, 'OK, well, the quarterback's got to play, and make reads and make decisions and make throws.' I think Sean got frustrated with Jared not being able to see the game the way he sees it."

During that 2020 season, McVay was either unable or unwilling to conceal his frustration—or both. In one game, according to a witness, he called in a play over the headset and added, "This'll work if Jared doesn't fuck it up." McVay likely didn't intend for Goff to hear the comment but had neglected to turn off the communication channel. Goff, already up toward the line of scrimmage and preparing to call out his pre-snap cadence, was stunned.

Over the course of the year, other Rams players and coaches picked up on the tension. It boiled over in that second 49ers game. McDaniel, flummoxed by Staley's lack of predictability—as he had been with Mike Pettine's in the previous January's NFC Championship Game—crafted a straight-ahead power-rushing plan designed to attack whatever front the Rams' coordinator threw at them. The Niners ran 33 times for 112 yards, and Mullens completed 24 of 35 passes for 253 yards, leading a pair of late scoring drives. For his part, Goff threw a pair of interceptions—one of which was returned 27 yards for a touchdown by Niners defensive tackle Javon Kinlaw—and lost a fumble. That gave him ten turnovers in his prior four games and 14 overall, tied for second in the NFL. After the Niners won, 23–20, on Robbie Gould's 42-yard field goal as time expired, McVay was furious. "Our quarterback has got to take better care of the football," he said in his postgame press conference, an uncharacteristically strong assignment of blame to someone other than himself.

Looking back, McVay conceded that the loss to the Niners was painful—partly because of his rivalry with Shanahan, and partly because so many of his team's mistakes were self-inflicted. "That was the one that was maddening," he said. "Some of the turnovers and the defensive touchdown . . . that's one where you're really reflecting on it afterwards."

Three weeks later, the Rams would suffer another 23–20 defeat at SoFi—to a Jets team that had been 0–13 coming into the game. They'd found a new bottom. The next week, they'd travel to Seattle for a game that would decide the NFC West title. It would also give McVay the opening he now craved.

DESPITE THE EMOTIONAL VICTORY OVER THE RAMS, THE NINERS HAD BIG problems. The day before the game, on their hour-long flight to L.A., Shanahan and others learned that new COVID-19 restrictions had been issued in Santa Clara County that would essentially ban gatherings, including practices and games, for at least three weeks. Would they have to finish their season elsewhere? Family members placed frantic calls while players were still in the air.

After the victory, the 49ers flew north and the news became official. "We win that game and it was all roses," recalled Mike LaFleur, the team's passing-game coordinator at the time. "Then, on the plane, John [Lynch] tells us we're getting kicked out [of Santa Clara]. What a kick in the face that was. Kyle was like, 'You've got to pack up. You're moving for six weeks. Enjoy your family for a couple of days.'"

The team would spend the final five games of the season in Glendale, Arizona, staying at a hotel across the street from State Farm Stadium, the Cardinals' home field. The Niners proceeded to lose four of those five games, the lone exception being a "road" game against the Cardinals in the mostly empty home the two teams were temporarily sharing. That came on the day after Christmas—one that, for most people in the organization, had not been especially merry. People missed their families, were stressed about their loved ones' welfare, and knew there would be no forthcoming glory at the end of the ordeal. Some players openly cried. The fourth quarter of Super Bowl LIV, which had begun with the Niners on the verge of a championship, had taken place in February of the same calendar year. To many players and coaches, it felt like another lifetime.

At one point, Lynch, mindful of the drudgery, suggested to Shanahan that they liven up practices. The GM said, "We might have to go high school a little bit." At the end of each practice, Lynch and Shanahan instituted daily competitions. There'd be coaches running the receiver gauntlet drill, offensive linemen catching punts, strength coaches pushing golf carts, and other amusing contests. "Then you always had to one-up it," LaFleur said. "It was like, 'Goddamn, what are we going to do now?' Kudos to Lynch and Kyle. It was fun for all of us, just to have something to laugh about. And, of course, we videotaped everything."

There was one other uplifting element of the 49ers' exile in the desert: Chris Foerster was back among them, engaging in the pursuit he loved most.

———

BEFORE FOERSTER GOT SOBER, AN EXTENDED STAY IN ARIZONA DURING the season could have sent him careening. However, the coach who was with them now—technically as a game-plan consultant, but also an uncredited assistant to offensive line coach John Benton and a run game collaborator with his old friend McDaniel—was focused only on his craft and on rebuilding his relationships with his wife and kids. He was grateful. Most of all, he was indebted to Shanahan.

It wasn't just that Shanahan had called him to offer his support almost immediately after the infamous video surfaced in October of 2017. Shanahan had kept in touch with him during his recovery and, ultimately, had given him a lifeline. In the immediate aftermath of the video's posting, the notion that Foerster could coach again at the NFL level seemed improbable. Shanahan, however, believed in second chances—and in his friend and former colleague.

Foerster's first foray back into football was in predraft training. In early 2018, his agent hooked him up with a one-week gig at a Bay Area training facility, where Foerster taught aspiring NFL linemen techniques of the trade. The trip, his first outside of Florida since the incident, required him to leave his halfway house. He moved in with a former colleague, Clyde Christensen, who was the Dolphins' quarterback coach at the time, spending the next six months bunking in a spare bedroom. He got a few more side gigs as a private coach—training players from Fort Lauderdale's St. Thomas Aquinas High School, working out some Dolphins offensive linemen, and sometimes using equipment stashed in the trunk of his car.

"I didn't know if I'd ever get back in," Foerster said. "At some point in that process, I said, 'If I never coach again, if all I do is prep players for the combine, work with college kids, work with high school kids—eh, I deserve this. I did this to myself.' In the same sense, I just had this branch out there, and it was Kyle. He had a plan for me."

While Foerster was out in Northern California, he had dinner with Shanahan, who was intent on helping. "Figure out some things you can do from home," Shanahan told him. The 49ers paid him $25,000 to help them scout some players—"just enough for four or five house payments," recalled Foerster, whose money and IRS problems had put his family in a tough spot.

Foerster, at Shanahan's invitation, showed up at training camp in 2018—"all under wraps," he recalled. He met with 49ers owner Jed York, whose franchise had twice employed him previously, and tried to convince him he was a new man and was ready to return to the NFL. It was a big ask, and a premature one. However, Shanahan continued to throw assignments Foerster's way that fall. Then, at season's end, the head coach reached out with a different thought.

"Come out here," he told Foerster. "Do the same thing. You're [still] a consultant, but come to the building." It wasn't totally Shanahan's call alone. York and Lynch both had to sign off on bringing him back. The potential for relapse and embarrassment to the organization were concerns. The 49ers had just released linebacker Reuben Foster, a 2017 first-round draft pick, following a November 2018 arrest for domestic violence. Lynch was dubious. However, Foerster got some help from a very unlikely source.

In 1988, Foerster was an assistant offensive line and special teams coach at Stanford, where John Elway's father, Jack, was the head coach. After that season, Elway was fired. In what at the time was a major anomaly, Foerster and the other assistants had all been given two-year contracts and thus were technically still employed, though their fates were in limbo. They were given a choice by school officials: stay on and keep recruiting while the search for a successor played out, or stay home and keep getting paid. "I'm 20-something years old," Foerster remembered. "What am I gonna do? I'm gonna go on the road. I had Dallas, Vegas, Orange County, San Diego . . ."

One of the prized recruits in the San Diego area was a three-sport star from Torrey Pines High School who hoped to be the next great Stanford quarterback: John Lynch. Foerster called to set up a home visit with Lynch and his parents, who were skeptical, given that the team didn't have a head coach. Said Foerster, "They're like, 'Really, coach, you want to come by?'" Foerster insisted. For one thing, Stanford *really* wanted Lynch. And his pitch, once in the meeting, was simple: "You don't come to Stanford for the head coach. You come to Stanford because it's Stanford, no matter who the coach is."

The message worked. Lynch committed, showed up at Stanford to play for new head coach Denny Green, and, when it didn't work out at quarterback, switched to safety before his junior season. After Green was fired, Lynch, who'd been drafted by the Florida Marlins, planned to leave school and pursue a baseball career. Green's successor—Bill Walsh, who'd come out of retirement three years after stepping away from the 49ers following his third Super Bowl victory—talked him into returning for his senior season, insisting Lynch could be a Pro Bowl safety in the NFL. Walsh was wrong: Lynch would become a Hall of Famer.

Foerster, it turned out, had made quite an impression during that home visit. Thirty years later, as Lynch pondered the possibility of bringing Foerster into the organization, his mother, Cathy, recalled how nice Foerster had been and lobbied for a second chance. As Lynch recalled, "My mom even said, 'John, I think that would be wonderful. Chris is a good man. He made a bad mistake. Maybe numerous of them.' So, then we set parameters."

"Amazing," Foerster said upon reflection. "John and Kyle together brought me along."

As a consultant in 2019, Foerster was prohibited by NFL rules from working on game day. He was allowed to be on the practice field during the week, but Lynch nixed that idea. Halfway through the season, Shanahan tried to persuade Lynch that Foerster should be at practice, telling the GM, "This is ridiculous. He's here."

"No," Lynch replied. "It's better." Foerster's return had been reported on during training camp, but it hadn't generated much attention in the months that followed. The 49ers were winning, and the GM didn't want to introduce a potential distraction. So, Foerster sat in his cubicle at the team facility, breaking down film during the week and watching games from his office.

When the 49ers won the NFC Championship Game, it meant Foerster would be going back to South Florida, where his career almost ended. After one of their practices during the week, the 49ers posed for a team photo, and Lynch insisted that Foerster be part of it—a moment that left the coach choked up. He was less touched by his Super Sunday experience: Foerster sat in the locker room, helplessly watching the fourth-quarter collapse.

In 2020, though his title remained the same, Foerster essentially became Benton's assistant. It wasn't just a courtesy. He was deeply involved in the evolution of the offense. Recalled Foerster, "We made changes to the footwork of the backs. We were watching [Titans star running back] Derrick Henry." In 2011, Foerster and Kyle and Mike Shanahan had crafted a new blocking scheme, updating the former teachings of Alex Gibbs, Mike's legendary line coach with the Broncos. Yet they hadn't matched it up with the way they were coaching their backs, who were still taking deliberately wide steps before planting their foot and cutting back. Said Foerster, "The reason [Gibbs] did his footwork was, it was the illusion of run outside the cut inside. The old footwork worked because the backs we had were really fast, so they were able to catch up. We had Raheem [Mostert]. We had [Matt] Breida. I said, 'Why don't we look at changing the footwork, because it fits better with how we run our system?' And we did. We ended up tossing out the old way."

From that point on, the Niners' backs got out of their breaks more quickly. Foerster, for his part, was out of the shadows. His value to Shanahan was undeniable.

After the 2020 season, Saleh was hired as the New York Jets' head coach, with the understanding that he'd take either McDaniel or Mike LaFleur as his offensive coordinator—it would be up to Shanahan, who, unsurprisingly, wanted to keep McDaniel at all costs. And Saleh also hired Benton as his offensive line coach and run game coordinator, a move that almost certainly would not have happened without Shanahan's signoff.

He signed off, of course, because Benton's replacement was already in the building. Foerster was all the way back.

———

JARED GOFF WAS HAVING A TERRIBLE, HORRIBLE, NO GOOD, VERY BAD day in Seattle—and then it got worse. In the third quarter of the late-December game between the Rams and Seahawks that would decide the NFC West title, Goff banged his thumb on the helmet of Seattle defensive end Benson Mayowa after releasing a pass. The thumb bent in an unnatural direction, clearly dislocated. Goff popped it back into place and finished out the game—a 20–9 Seahawks victory. He soon learned that his thumb was also broken.

The Rams were still in playoff contention, but it appeared Goff's season was over. He had surgery the day after the Seahawks game and kept hope alive, sitting out L.A.'s season finale against the Cardinals. Goff's unheralded backup, John Wolford, threw an interception on his first NFL pass, and Arizona quickly scored to go up 7–0. However, Cardinals quarterback Kyler Murray hurt his ankle and missed most of the first three quarters, and Staley's defense produced a touchdown and a safety. Wolford, who threw for 231 yards and scrambled for 56 more, was serviceable enough to secure the victory.

Afterward, in a reaction that surprised even some of his coaches, McVay celebrated the backup's efforts as though he'd just discovered the next Kurt Warner.

Wolford, undrafted out of Wake Forest, had played in the Alliance of American Football before landing on the Rams' practice squad in 2019. After winning the job of Goff's backup in 2020, he was still unknown to all but hardcore fans. Listed generously at 6-foot-1 and with an average arm at best, Wolford had the type of intangibles that coaches love. "Look," one Rams assistant told me, "John Wolford is a *great* kid. He works hard, he goes the extra mile, he hustles. He's good energy. You love having him around. Now, as far as him *playing*? He's a guy that, if you absolutely have to put him in, you're just hoping you have a lead and you can get through that game. You do not want to see that guy on an NFL field on a long-term basis."

McVay, however, viewed it differently. When I spoke to him a few hours after that game against the Cardinals, he was practically giddy.

Yes, Wolford had shown some spunk in a crucial situation. To McVay, however, his greatest attribute seemed to be that he was not Jared Goff. For McVay's first-year coordinators, O'Connell and Staley, watching that once healthy coach–quarterback relationship disintegrate was jolting.

"It was tough," Staley said. "Looking back on it, and having time to reflect, the NFL's really tough. No matter how good of a player you are at quarterback or how good of a coach you are, you're going to have losses where it doesn't go well at all. It's part of the NFL. When you're a perfectionist and you have these expectations that you can win and should win every game, and play it the way that you want it played, that's where I think it can go sideways. You can start to press. You can grow apart. Instead of going together, you grow apart."

To McVay, there seemed to be no path forward. He was all in on Wolford, even though Goff believed he could gut out his postsurgical thumb pain and play in the team's playoff opener the following Saturday: a rematch with the Seahawks in Seattle. Goff, whose thumb lacked flexibility, wouldn't be at his best. The desire was there—except, McVay wanted Wolford. He told Goff Tuesday that because he was unsure about how well the thumb would hold up, and because Wolford had gotten so few reps throughout the course of the season, he needed to make a decision and stick with it. Wolford would start; Goff would back him up. Goff wasn't happy. He was even less thrilled when he got a grand total of zero practice reps throughout the week. Instead, he worked off to the side of his teammates, running plays "on air," getting every mental rep he could.

Before the game, Fox broadcaster Terry Bradshaw—apparently acting on information someone at the network had gleaned from McVay—stated that one reason the coach was so high on Wolford was that he reminded him of himself as a quarterback. To those mystified by McVay's affinity for Wolford, this wasn't great news. McVay, who'd starred as a high school option quarterback before being switched to wide receiver at Miami of Ohio, seemed to be off-kilter.

On game day, as Wolford trotted out on the field with the first-team offense after the opening kickoff, Goff stood on the sideline, tortured. "Yeah, it was extremely hard," he told me that night as he sat on the team plane at SeaTac Airport waiting to fly back to L.A. "It was one of the hardest things I've had to handle. The week was tough. I knew I had to prepare to be ready to play, in case they needed me. And I'm happy I did."

That's because, on the Rams' second drive, Wolford took off running into the secondary—showing little field awareness, a function of his inexperience—and got absolutely blasted by Seahawks safety Jamal Adams. He was down and out, officially listed with a neck injury, soon to be transported to a local hospital for precautionary reasons. Newly signed third-stringer Blake Bortles—the former Jaguars starter—was inactive. The Rams would have to go back to Goff.

To everyone not named Sean McVay, what happened next was inspirational. After missing his first four passes, Goff floated an underthrown ball to the sidelines that Cooper Kupp came back for and turned into a 44-yard gain. Staley's defense came through again, with cornerback Darius Williams intercepting Seahawks quarterback Russell Wilson and racing 42 yards for a touchdown to put L.A. up 13–3. Goff later scrambled on a third-and-nine play and deftly flipped a pass to running back Cam Akers, who rambled forward for a 44-yard gain of his own. Two plays later, Akers scored to give the Rams a 20–10 lead they would take into halftime. Goff's 15-yard fourth-quarter touchdown pass to Robert Woods, after freezing the Seahawks' defense with a crafty play fake, secured the 30–20 victory.

The Rams were moving on—headed for a divisional-round matchup with the top-seeded Packers at Lambeau Field—and Goff was excited for a showdown with Rodgers in what would be a battle of ex-Cal quarterbacks. McVay, however, wasn't into it. He told assistants that, if Wolford were cleared, the plan was to start the backup over Goff again. Some of them were stunned—he was that down on Goff. Wolford was ruled out medically, which decided things.

For another week, at least, the McVay–Goff partnership would remain intact. They had an elimination game to play on the "frozen tundra" of Lambeau Field, against a coach and quarterback who'd soon go through their own crisis. Elsewhere in California, Shanahan, too, was done with the status quo.

PART III

NO MORE MESSING AROUND

Kyle Shanahan ponders another Super Bowl heartbreak as he leaves the field following the 49ers' overtime defeat to the Kansas City Chiefs in February 2024.

Chapter 17

Deal

The 20-mile corridor between Cabo San Lucas and San José del Cabo is lined with award-winning resorts and spas, championship golf courses, and acclaimed culinary offerings. Nestled on the southern tip of Mexico's Baja California peninsula, Los Cabos—or Cabo, as most visitors call it—serves as a quick and embracing getaway for West Coast elites and rowdy college kids alike. By January of 2021, it had become an offseason refuge for some of the NFL's most accomplished coaches and players.

When Sean McVay showed up at the Chileno Bay Resort a few days after the Rams' divisional-round playoff defeat to the Packers in Green Bay, he was stressed, seething mad, and searching for answers. He needed to relax, and this seemed like the perfect spot.

He had no idea how much shit was about to go down.

McVay, out of necessity, had started Jared Goff against the Packers, and the quarterback—19 days removed from surgery to the thumb on his throwing hand, playing in the bitter cold—had performed commendably under the circumstances. By that point, however, it didn't really matter. McVay was done with Goff. Shanahan had beaten McVay twice in 2020, once with his backup quarterback. LaFleur had just ended McVay's season with a quarterback who'd soon be named the league's Most Valuable Player for the third time; even when LaFleur made *bad* calls, Aaron Rodgers turned them into gold. In his press conference after the game, asked directly about Goff's status with the team, McVay replied, "Yeah he's our quarterback—right now." The next day, McVay declined to guarantee that

Goff would be on the team's roster in 2021. And general manager Les Snead, in his meeting with local reporters nine days later, was similarly noncommittal, saying Goff was a Ram "at this moment."

It is highly unusual for a coach and GM to convey so little public confidence in a supposed franchise player. That they did was an indication of how much McVay wanted to replace Goff, a player he'd urged owner Stan Kroenke to sign to a four-year, $134 million contract just 16 months earlier. The question was: How would he do it?

Even if the Rams were able to find another quarterback, getting rid of Goff was a tricky proposition. Cutting him would cause tens of millions of dollars to count immediately against the Rams' salary cap, making it hard to field a competitive roster. His trade value was low—partly because of his contract, and partly because it was increasingly obvious that McVay didn't want him. McVay needed a creative solution. In a matter of days, right there at the Chileno Bay Resort, that solution would literally walk into McVay's world.

BEFORE McVAY COULD EVEN THINK ABOUT DECOMPRESSING FROM THE season-ending playoff defeat, there was additional drama. The day after the game, veteran left tackle Andrew Whitworth hosted a football-watching gathering for various teammates and assistant coaches, including first-year offensive coordinator Kevin O'Connell. As Tom Brady led the Buccaneers to a road playoff upset over Drew Brees and the Saints, setting up an NFC Championship Game matchup with the Packers, news broke that Brandon Staley, the Rams' first-year defensive coordinator, would be hired as the Los Angeles Chargers' next head coach.

McVay was caught off guard. A year earlier, when he'd hired Staley—an anonymous Broncos outside linebackers coach—the near-universal reaction was "Who?" Now, after one impressive season as the coordinator of the league's No. 1 defense, Staley—who, five years earlier, had been a Division III defensive coordinator—was an NFL head coach. McVay had expected Staley to get some head coaching interviews; seeing him get hired to coach L.A.'s other NFL team less than 24 hours after the Rams' season ended was a surprise.

Staley himself wasn't shocked: Late in the season, he and McVay had discussed the scenario in which he got a head coaching job and the assistants he'd be able to take with him. Staley, who'd grown exceptionally close with O'Connell, believed that he and McVay had an understanding: if Staley was hired somewhere, O'Connell would come run his offense. Though technically a lateral move, this would be an obvious upgrade for O'Connell—while McVay was the Rams' primary offensive game-planner and play caller, Staley would let O'Connell run the show. Throw in the fact that the Chargers had an emerging star in quarterback Justin Herbert, who'd just completed a stellar rookie season, and it would be hard to ask O'Connell to pass up that opportunity. In a similar scenario three years earlier, McVay had allowed then OC Matt LaFleur to leave for Tennessee and run the Titans' offense under Mike Vrabel, a defensive-minded head coach. Now, seconds after the news broke that he'd be the Chargers' next coach, Staley was calling O'Connell to tell him, "I can't believe we're going to get to do this together."

McVay couldn't believe it, either—literally, in this case. Replacing one coordinator, for the second consecutive year, would be challenging; replacing *both* seemed untenable. A couple of minutes later, he called O'Connell, too. "Hey," McVay told him, "we need to have a conversation."

The other people at Whitworth's house knew something was up. "All the offensive linemen were there, and the quarterbacks," O'Connell recalled. "They could tell—the second that news got announced, I got up from the couch and was on the phone basically for the next hour. Then I got out of there, and they were all kind of wondering what was going on."

O'Connell talked to his wife and his agent; he talked to Staley and McVay again, too. "Most of it, for me, was just trying to manage relationships," O'Connell said, "and making sure people knew, 'Hey, I care about everybody involved here. Let's just figure this out together.'" It wasn't easy. The fight over O'Connell caused a rift between McVay and Staley—one they'd eventually repair, but which made things uncomfortable at the time.

From O'Connell's perspective, it had all happened so quickly. McVay had asked him to break down film of other quarterbacks who might be available after that season; at the same time, O'Connell had begun preparing his postseason review process for Goff, mapping out the quarterback's offseason. "It was a crazy, crazy month," O'Connell recalled.

McVay had the final say—he was allowed to block O'Connell, by rule, and he did so. First, however, he had a frank conversation with his OC, during which he explained to O'Connell how much value the coordinator had to the franchise, and what he thought they could accomplish together in 2021.

Now, McVay and Staley shared a predicament: They needed to hire the most important person on their respective staffs—a defensive coordinator in McVay's case, an offensive coordinator in Staley's—and they needed to do it quickly. Staley's pivot was intriguing. For his part, once he gave up on prying O'Connell from the Rams, Staley turned his gaze northward. He wanted Mike McDaniel.

Timing, again, worked against him. A few days earlier, the Jets had settled on Robert Saleh as their head coach. As expected, with Kyle Shanahan's blessing, the outgoing Niners defensive coordinator took Mike LaFleur as his offensive coordinator and John Benton as his offensive line coach—paving the way for the expected promotions of McDaniel (to offensive coordinator, after four seasons as run game coordinator) and Chris Foerster (to offensive line coach). The 49ers announced those moves the day after that Bucs–Saints game. *That's that,* Shanahan thought. Then, Staley reached out to McDaniel, who understood the magnitude of the opportunity: rather than continuing to set the table for Shanahan, albeit with a better title, he could head to L.A. and work with one of the league's most promising young quarterbacks—and run his own kitchen.

Shanahan had blocked McDaniel once before, in 2019, when newly hired Cardinals coach Kliff Kingsbury, who ran his own offense, asked permission to interview McDaniel to be his nominal offensive coordinator. Yet McDaniel felt that the Chargers opportunity was special enough that he went to Shanahan and asked if he could pursue it. He eventually spoke to Niners GM John Lynch, and even CEO Jed York. All basically told him the same thing: *You agreed to a deal, we announced it, we can't let you go.* As McDaniel remembered, "It was a quick no. I didn't fight it. I wasn't gonna do that to people who had [helped me so much]. It was weird timing. I would've definitely done it if they had been like, 'A play caller spot? That's great for you.' Then, yeah, I would've gone."

Staley ended up going outside the Shanahan/McVay world and hiring Saints quarterbacks coach Joe Lombardi, an arrangement that would only last two seasons. McVay, meanwhile, knew exactly who he wanted as Staley's replacement—and his timing, at least, was impeccable.

RAHEEM MORRIS WAS AT A STEAKHOUSE NEAR THE TPC SUGARLOAF Country Club in suburban Atlanta, dining with his wife, Nicole, when he saw McVay's number flash on his iPhone. Old friends from their days on Mike Shanahan's staff, they didn't have to cut through a lot of BS. Morris got up from the table to take the call in a quieter area. As he walked, McVay got right to the point. "What are you thinking?" he asked Morris, who'd interviewed for head coaching jobs with the Falcons (for whom he'd just served 11 games as interim head coach) and Jaguars. The Falcons were in the process of hiring Arthur Smith; the Jaguars had cut a deal with Urban Meyer, a star in the collegiate coaching world who'd won a combined three national championships at Florida and Ohio State. The twist was that Meyer, after learning he was in line to get the job, then called Morris on a Friday to ask him to be his defensive coordinator. "Why don't you come out here Tuesday?" Meyer asked. Morris had made a silent fist pump—that bought him time to explore other options. It was a sign that Meyer was clueless when it came to the NFL and how the competition for assistant coaches played out.

Now, three days later, McVay was about to make things more interesting. Morris had believed that the Chargers would hire Bills offensive coordinator Brian Daboll—who'd have brought Morris as his defensive coordinator—but Staley had gotten the job instead. During the season, Matt LaFleur had put out feelers to Morris to see if he'd come to Green Bay, should LaFleur decide to move on from Mike Pettine (he eventually did, but not until after the NFC Championship Game). And Shanahan, Morris's close friend—who had tried unsuccessfully to pry him from Atlanta and make him his first 49ers defensive coordinator in 2017, only for head coach Dan Quinn to block the move—had already decided to promote from within, naming inside linebackers coach DeMeco Ryans as Saleh's replacement.

So, here was McVay, with an opening, not even pretending there'd be an interview process if Morris were to express interest. Because Morris is Black, there would be no need, under the terms of the "Rooney Rule," to interview at least two minority candidates before hiring him. (The rule was changed later that year to prevent any preemptive hires, regardless of race.) "This could be awesome," McVay said. The two talked about which coaches from the current staff would be good to keep and how they could be developed; they also pondered some potential additions, among other exploratory topics. Morris told McVay he'd give it some thought, but that he planned to fly to Jacksonville in the morning to interview with Meyer.

Morris went back to the table and spared his wife the details. He was still taking it all in. Later, a little after 10 p.m. Eastern time, they were lying in bed when McVay FaceTimed. "Are you *really* going on this interview in Jacksonville?" McVay asked, urging Morris to reconsider. "Why don't you just come here? Let's do this."

By the time Morris hung up, he was convinced. "I guess we're going to L.A.," he told Nicole, who was implicitly on board with the decision ("Where he goes, I go") but still completely stunned. As she'd recall in May of 2023, "I'm planning for us to live on the beach, and I have, like, five houses in Jacksonville to look at. I've worked with a realtor; my flight is booked." What happened next, by now, should not be a surprise: Morris put "his phone back on the charger on the nightstand and lays his head down on the pillow and starts snoring within two seconds. And I'm up all night, staring at the ceiling. I'm like, 'Oh my God—we're moving across the entire country.'"

Morris's hiring would become official before the week's end—the same day that Rodgers, preparing for the Packers' NFC Championship Game matchup with Brady and the Bucs, told reporters, "My future is a beautiful mystery, I think." The quote didn't cause a major stir at the time, but in retrospect, it presaged a tumultuous offseason. It also lodged in Les Snead's psyche. Five days later, in a virtual interview with reporters, the Rams' general manager twice decided to drop the phrase. There would be more intrigue to come, much of it taking place in Mexico.

By then, in Green Bay, things weren't so beautiful. In the NFC title game, the Packers' Super Bowl dreams ended abruptly. They came out and played a shaky first half that ended with them giving up an unconscionable 39-yard touchdown pass with one second left to fall behind 21–10. The lead grew to 18 points in third quarter before the Packers finally got rolling, with Rodgers directing a pair of touchdown drives—one punctuated by a dropped two-point conversion, which would haunt them later—and Green Bay intercepting Brady on three consecutive possessions.

Late in the game, the Packers, trailing by eight, drove to the Tampa Bay eight-yard line, but, after three consecutive incompletions, faced a fourth and goal. With just over two minutes remaining, LaFleur—in a move that would be relitigated for months and years to come—called for a field goal. After Mason Crosby's 26-yarder cut the Bucs' lead to 31–26, they got the ball back, recorded three first downs, and ran out the clock, sending Rodgers and the Packers into an offseason of uncertainty.

Looking back, LaFleur doesn't regret having taken the ball out of Rodgers' hands on that fourth-down play eight yards from the end zone. "I still stand by it today," he said in the spring of 2023. "I thought that was the best opportunity. Our defense was playing really well. They had already picked off Tom three times. It didn't work out. We had three shots from the eight-yard line. We got no yards. There aren't many good plays on fourth and goal from the eight-yard line. I thought the percentage of us kicking a field goal, getting a stop, and then going for the win [was better than] going for the tie in that situation. We had the two-minute warning and we had all our time-outs, so I was like, 'Fuck, we can get the ball back.'"

It didn't take long, after the loss, for LaFleur to pivot to a new problem: Would Rodgers come back? At his virtual postgame press conference— COVID-19 restrictions were still in place—Rodgers told reporters, "A lot of guys' futures are uncertain, myself included. That's what's sad about it most . . . getting this far. Obviously, there's going to be an end to it at some point, whether we make it past this one or not. Just the uncertainties, [it] is tough, and the finality of it."

Rodgers, then 37, called the defeat "gutting." It was also galling. Whereas the Packers' passivity in player acquisition had been a constant annoyance during his time as a starter, the Bucs had prevailed after employing the opposite approach. After landing Brady, who turned 43 before the start of the season, Tampa Bay general manager Jason Licht had gone all in, acquiring a slew of accomplished veterans—including tight end Rob Gronkowski, wide receiver Antonio Brown,and running backs Leonard Fournette and LeSean McCoy—in pursuit of a championship. In the draft, Licht had used the 13th-overall pick on a player who'd made an immediate impact and made Brady's life better, a player who thus might have been, to Rodgers, the anti-Jordan Love: right tackle Tristan Wirfs.

After 16 seasons with the franchise and 13 as its centerpiece, Rodgers, soon to be named MVP, was seemingly at his breaking point. Upon the Packers' selection of Love the previous April, Rodgers believed 2020 would be his final season in Green Bay. But because he'd performed at an incredibly high level, he felt that deadline might be pushed back a tick. He was about to make it clear to his bosses just how unhappy he was.

CALLING ME FROM CABO A FEW DAYS AFTER THE BUCCANEERS' VICTORY at Lambeau, Sean McVay wanted advice. His responses to questions about Goff's future had fueled a torrent of speculation about the quarterback potentially being replaced, the contract situation notwithstanding. McVay didn't love the optics or the way he'd come across. He asked for my thoughts and didn't like my answer: I felt he'd inflamed things by being intentionally vague and that Snead, his general manager, had been equally culpable in his end-of-season press conference, with his references to Rodgers's "beautiful mystery" line.

"I just don't want to lie, or ever be accused of lying after the fact," McVay said. "I really don't know how it will play out, and I'm just conveying that."

It seemed pretty clear that McVay would try to move on from Goff. That he would do so only a few days after our conversation, however, seemed highly unlikely. In truth, the events that followed caught McVay off guard, too. And they played out in a manner that appeared even shadier than anything that had already happened.

McVay and his then fiancée, Veronika Khomyn, had joined Whitworth and his wife, Melissa, for an annual end-of-season getaway at Chileno Bay, where the Whitworths owned a vacation residence. Whitworth, who was also close to Goff, was a bit surprised when McVay told him he was intent on finding another quarterback. One obvious target was Matthew Stafford, a former No. 1–overall pick who'd spent his entire 12-year career as the Detroit Lions' starter. Now Stafford had asked for a trade, and the Lions—whose newly hired general manager, Brad Holmes, had come from the Rams' front office—told him they'd oblige. Tall, strong-armed, tough, and more able to make off-schedule plays than Goff, Stafford, in McVay's eyes, would give him a chance to expand his options on offense. Stafford was someone who could operate from the pocket, drive the ball on out-breaking routes, and, when things broke down, improvise and make plays on the move. He was an expert at fitting the ball into tight windows, and his wealth of experience made him more adept at reading defenses.

Technically, Stafford couldn't be traded until the start of the league year in mid-March, but teams could make non-binding agreements in principle. McVay wasn't sure when and how the Stafford sweepstakes would be decided, but he figured it would be sometime after he returned to L.A.

Kyle Shanahan happened to be in Cabo, too, though not at the same resort. He also had interest in acquiring Stafford, having decided that, among other issues, Jimmy Garoppolo could no longer be counted upon to stay healthy.

Someone else pertinent to the situation was vacationing in the area and staying at Chileno Bay: Matthew Stafford.

There are different stories about how McVay and Stafford came to share drinks poolside at the resort a few days before the trade was made. Whitworth told me in February of 2022 that he set up a golf outing that included Stafford—whom he knew from a mutual friend—Saints coach Sean Payton and Brees. Yes, there were a *lot* of NFL luminaries in Cabo.

In Seth Wickersham's 2023 ESPN.com profile of McVay, he wrote of the coach returning to his hotel room after hanging at the pool with Stafford and, "a few tequilas in," hopping on a FaceTime with the Rams front office and going on a now-legendary rant: "Here's the fucking deal, OK? We can sit here and exist, and be OK winning nine to 11 games, and losing in the fucking divisional round and feel like, 'Oh, everything's OK.' Or, we could let our motherfucking nuts hang, and go trade for this fucking quarterback, and give ourselves a chance to go win a fucking world championship. You ready to fucking do this or what?"

According to Wickersham's retelling of the story, laughs followed, not pushback. McVay knew he was being high-maintenance. He'd insisted on Goff getting the big contract extension before the 2019 season. Now he was demanding that ownership trade for Stafford (and eventually pay him) *and* figure out a way to get out of the team's deal with Goff. Doing all of that was going to cost a lot, in terms of draft capital—and the Lions knew it.

There was always a suspicion among Shanahan and other 49ers decision-makers that the trade might be in the bag for the Rams, given Holmes's relationship with Snead, his former boss. Holmes had a favorable enough opinion about Goff's abilities that he was open to the idea of acquiring him as the Lions' next starting quarterback—though, of course, he would insist upon the Rams paying a premium. At one point, the Carolina Panthers believed they were very close to making a deal to land Stafford. The Niners were also in the mix.

Given that Stafford's perspective was being taken into account by the Lions, those poolside drinks with McVay undoubtedly didn't hurt the Rams' cause. "I truly ran into him organically, whether people believe that or not," McVay told me in the summer of 2023. "You're thinking that's gonna be a couple-weeks process. I still don't know exactly how involved [the 49ers] were in that." Later, he and Shanahan would circle back on that topic, and it was not a pleasant conversation for Shanahan.

What we know is this: on Saturday night, January 30, the Rams agreed to trade Goff, two first-round picks, and a third-round selection to the Lions for Stafford. The story broke fast—so rapidly that Goff learned of the news from McVay only seconds before it was reported. Not long after taking that call from his coach, Goff saw another call coming in from his father, Jerry, who'd been alerted to the news. Goff, stunned and disgusted, told McVay, "I've gotta go," and clicked off to talk to his dad.

The next morning, Goff was pissed. "I'm just excited to be somewhere that I know wants me and appreciates me," he told me, choosing his words carefully. "I'm moving forward and couldn't be more excited to build a winner there. I'm excited about Dan [Campbell, the team's newly hired coach] and the whole staff." He'd been blindsided, but he also sounded like a weight had been lifted off his shoulders. He'd gotten calls from Campbell, Holmes, and offensive coordinator Anthony Lynn Saturday night, and he'd heard the excitement in his new bosses' voices and felt heartened by their support. Clearly, he hadn't experienced the same from McVay for some time.

Shanahan was also upset—partly because of the way things had played out, and partly because he knew how good Stafford and McVay could be together. In Mike McDaniel's words, McVay now had a chance to emerge from a two-year stretch in which it felt like each opposing "defense has all the answers for whatever you're trying to do, which set Sean back years [of] his life." Now, because of Stafford's skill set and veteran savvy, McVay could evolve and dictate terms to his foes; even when Rams receivers were tightly covered or the play call wasn't perfect, Stafford's golden right arm could make it alright.

McDaniel, as Shanahan's newly named offensive coordinator, was going to feel *his* boss's wrath in the aftermath. Said McDaniel, "We knew [the Rams] had their nuts squeezed with that Goff contract. The fact that they not only got an elite thrower [in Stafford] but got rid of [the Goff contract], it's like a double 'fuck you,' within the division. So, yeah, that was miserable."

That summer, McVay and cohost Peter Schrager had Shanahan as a guest on their *Flying Coach* podcast, and the rival coaches broke down the madness of that Saturday night in Cabo.

"You don't want to get me started, dude," Shanahan said, with real disgust in his voice. "That was frustrating."

He proceeded to share his version of that night's events. Until the 2020 season ended, Shanahan hadn't really studied Stafford closely since the quarterback was coming out of Georgia and entering the draft. The film Shanahan saw blew him away. "I remember looking through it because everyone was telling me [a trade] was a possibility, and Stafford's The Man . . . He's actually underrated to me . . . I know how good he is at play-action. I know how smart he is. Not only does he have a big arm, but he's got touch and he knows where to go with the ball, so I was trying to get involved in it."

Shanahan had been in touch with Stafford's agent, Tom Condon, who was in close communication with the Lions. The coach conceded that he also had other intel—"someone who had knowledge of the situation"—who told him at approximately 7 p.m. on the night in question, "No, nothing's happening at the earliest, till tomorrow, so you can finish your night.' So, I'm like, 'Alright, I'm done.' Put my phone down, talked to Mandy, I'm like, 'Alright, let's go out to dinner, let's have some drinks.'"

For most people, blowing off one's phone while on a romantic date with one's spouse in a Mexican beach town would be a perfectly natural move. For Shanahan, it turned out to be a nightmare.

"Half an hour later," Shanahan continued on the podcast, "my buddy calls me, he's like, 'I'm just telling ya, if you want Stafford, you need to get a hold of him right now' . . . and, like, ten minutes later, it was all over. What fun."

Well, it was fun for the crew over at Chileno Bay, where McVay, Stafford, and Whitworth were able to celebrate over dinner and drinks, capping one of the most bizarre trade sequences in NFL history, and instilling McVay's chief coaching rival with an even greater sense of urgency to find an elite quarterback.

Chapter 18

Hidden Horsepower

I f Kyle Shanahan felt like the football gods were taunting him that night in Cabo when he put down his phone and lost out on Matthew Stafford to McVay, the sensation intensified eight days later. In the Super Bowl, Brady and the Bucs rolled to a 31–9 victory over the Chiefs, terrorizing K.C.'s injury-decimated offensive line and harassing Patrick Mahomes incessantly. It seemed as though each time a Chiefs defensive back even breathed on a Bucs receiver, the officials threw a flag. Brady, as great as he was, apparently always got the calls. The previous year's Super Bowl, by contrast, had been officiated much more loosely. Football was infuriating sometimes.

In the year since the 49ers had blown their fourth-quarter lead over the Chiefs and lost Super Bowl LIV, Shanahan had suffered many indignities, including a wave of injuries that torpedoed his team's 2020 campaign and a forced relocation to Arizona for the final five weeks of the season. He also had plenty of regret. In retrospect, the decision not to get rid of Jimmy Garoppolo and sign Brady had been the wrong one. Brady's arm strength turned out to be better than what Shanahan and others had assessed; the quarterback obviously was still playing at an exceptional level, even at 45. And Garoppolo had been derailed by injuries for the second time in three seasons.

Now, Shanahan had seen enough. He was done with Garoppolo; he needed an upgrade. Stafford had been one option, but there were others. The status quo would not be one of them.

Joe Staley, a locker room leader who concluded his long run as the 49ers' left tackle after Super Bowl LIV, put it this way: "As the seasons went on, I think Kyle got frustrated with the way that Jimmy couldn't really take that next step, where he couldn't take complete ownership of the playbook and what the Xs and Os were, what the plan was for the game or the season. I think Kyle always felt like he was starting over every single week and not building something. When he first got there, he used Matt Ryan as an example of what he wanted—he was like, 'The first year I was just calling [plays for him]; the second year, [when] he won that MVP, [it] was like he completely understood. He understood why I was calling something the second quarter—it was to set up something in the third—so you had to go through this read. He saw the game the same way I did.' Whereas Jimmy, I think he always felt like he was just out there running the plays and not being a part of the process."

The fact that Garoppolo was so difficult to reach during the offseason exacerbated the coach's frustration. Many of Garoppolo's teammates had a similar reaction. "Jimmy was always great in the moment," Staley said. "We used to always joke that Jimmy was a great face-to-face guy. If you're not seeing him, he's the worst. You can't even have a relationship with him. Jimmy was around; he just wasn't communicating with everybody. That was *everyone*. It was weird."

Shanahan wanted a partner. He wanted a grinder. He wanted someone who saw the game the way he did and executed his plan accordingly. McVay had found his guy. Now Shanahan was intent on doing the same. He couldn't have Stafford—but maybe, just maybe, he could get someone even better.

IT WAS CLEAR AFTER THE PACKERS' NFC CHAMPIONSHIP GAME DEFEAT that Aaron Rodgers was pondering an escape. The now-three-time league MVP was still under contract, but he could try to force the issue. It made sense that other teams would poke around in the wake of Rodgers's "beautiful mystery" comments. The 49ers and Rams had both made inquiries; the prospect of landing such a rare talent was enticing. The Rams were now out of the picture, but the Niners had even more incentive to get Rodgers.

The situation was complicated, on many levels. At the same time the Niners were gauging such a deal, the Packers were desperately trying to bring their semi-estranged quarterback back into the fold. CEO Mark Murphy and general manager Brian Gutekunst flew to L.A. to meet with Rodgers at his offseason residence, in the hope of addressing his concerns. LaFleur also made a trip out west. Rodgers's agent, David Dunn, went to Green Bay to try to reach agreement on a contract extension that would clarify his client's status as the starter for multiple years to come. None of this was necessarily working; all three of the Packers' power brokers, however, were dead set against Rodgers playing for another team.

Time wasn't on Shanahan's side. He had to look into other options at the position. Deshaun Watson, a young star with the Houston Texans, wanted out, and the 49ers explored a possible deal. However, they backed away as more than 20 civil lawsuits alleging sexual misconduct piled up against Watson.

As Shanahan homed in on Rodgers, there was also the tricky matter of his relationship with LaFleur. Friends competed and clashed over various things like this all the time in the NFL, but this was more charged. Rodgers was a generational quarterback who'd helped LaFleur reach consecutive conference title games in his first two seasons as a head coach, with the expectation of more potential championship runs to come. Because Shanahan and LaFleur had such an established connection, they communicated on a level of implicit trust. In a sense, Shanahan had what amounted to inside information about a very sensitive situation that was of the utmost importance to LaFleur. Potentially using that information to help pry Rodgers away was to threaten their relationship.

If the Niners could somehow pull it off, Shanahan's life would be much better—and LaFleur would be crushed. Unless and until that happened, Shanahan and Lynch needed to pursue a parallel path to salvation.

THE WORST THING THAT CAN HAPPEN TO AN NFL FRANCHISE WHEN IT comes to quarterbacking is to get stuck in the mediocre middle. If a team is going to pay premium money to a veteran QB—and have that eat up a sizable chunk of its salary cap—that quarterback had better be good enough to cover up for the accompanying weaknesses such a commitment might entail. Rodgers and Brady were those type of quarterbacks; it was the Jay Cutlers and Joe Flaccos and Tony Romos and Ryan Tannehills of the world who could get you into trouble. They were better than their potential replacements, but not good enough to carry a team.

Or, conversely, a franchise could opt to take advantage of the artificially deflated contracts given to incoming players, via the "rookie wage scale" agreed to by the owners and players union during the 2011 lockout, which was now part of the collective bargaining agreement. Rookie deals for quarterbacks picked in the first round lasted four years, with a team option for a fifth. The contract for any rookie quarterback could not be renegotiated until after his third season. That created a window during which a team could spend big at other positions.

Given that Lynch and Shanahan had built an excellent roster, drafting a quarterback made a lot of sense. And when they took a look at the incoming draft class, the two decision-makers became even more convinced that going young at quarterback might be their best move, for the present *and* the future.

Five quarterbacks were shaping up as potential first-round picks, an unusually large group. The Jaguars, picking first, were almost certain to take Clemson's Trevor Lawrence, a tall and strong-armed passer who'd looked the part during his impressive collegiate career. The Jets—with former Niners defensive coordinator Robert Saleh as coach and ex-S.F. passing-game coordinator Mike LaFleur running the offense—seemed locked in on BYU's Zach Wilson, whose arm talent was said to be striking. After that, things were more fluid. Justin Fields, an athletic and prolific Ohio State star, was an enticing prospect. Mac Jones, who'd led Alabama to a blowout victory in the national championship game over Fields's Buckeyes, had obvious skills as a pocket passer. And Trey Lance, a big, mobile late bloomer out of North Dakota State, was believed by many scouts and talent evaluators to be the most intriguing of them all.

The Niners, though, had the 12th-overall pick, where they couldn't feel secure about landing any of the quarterbacks. All five could be gone by then—or, certainly, the one or ones they wanted most could be off the board. The 49ers could try to draw things out until draft night and make a move in real time, or they could go for the preemptive trade—as Washington had in 2012, when Dan Snyder and Bruce Allen swung that blockbuster deal with the Rams to land the No. 2–overall pick they would use on Robert Griffin III.

Lynch started making calls to teams who picked above the Niners. The Dolphins, with the third-overall selection, were eager to talk. Miami had drafted Tua Tagovailoa, Jones's predecessor at Alabama, fifth overall the previous year and wasn't looking for another quarterback. It made sense for the Dolphins to trade down—but the price would not be cheap.

On March 26, 2021, nearly five weeks before the first night of the draft, the 49ers agreed to send Miami three first-round picks (their own selection in the current draft, plus first-rounders in 2022 and '23) and a 2022 third-round pick for the third-overall pick. Shanahan was quite obviously looking for a franchise quarterback to replace Garoppolo. And clearly, he was sold on at least three of them. At the time the news of the trade broke, Lynch was at BYU's Pro Day, watching Wilson throw.

Doing the deal that early was a curious move by the 49ers, who could have continued to evaluate the quarterbacks and tried to manipulate the situation to their satisfaction. The aggressiveness made sense, however, in the context of Shanahan's recent experience. A few months later, he admitted to me that a series of moves by the Niners' chief division rivals, the Rams and the Seahawks, had influenced his decision to take a swing. The Rams, among other proactive moves, had gone big to acquire Stafford and All-Pro cornerback Jalen Ramsey. The Seahawks had traded two first-round picks and a third-rounder to the Jets to land star safety Jamal Adams before the 2020 season.

The question was: Which quarterback did Shanahan prefer? The Niners were now on the clock. The whole football world was watching. And, right away, those who knew Shanahan best surmised that Jones was his target.

That, to many outsiders, was surprising. Jones, listed generously at 6-foot-3 and 220 pounds, didn't have exceptional size. His arm wasn't viewed as potent, at least by the standards of NFL starters. Shanahan had concerns about his ability to throw the deep ball. Jones wasn't known for his mobility. And yet, those who studied him closely noticed that Jones had some elite traits that a more discerning eye could perceive: he had uncanny pocket skills, especially out of the shotgun formation, and foot-work. His ability to slide in the pocket to either side and react quickly to onrushing defenders, even unblocked ones, was notable. He was able to throw accurately from all kinds of angles. He came from a tennis-playing family and had spent some time on the hardcourt as a kid, which seemed to correlate with his footwork. His steps seemed to be in sync with his throw-ing motion, an important part of Shanahan's system. And Jones's football knowledge was impressive—though each of the draft's five top passers was believed to be intelligent, according to the NFL's rather silly measurements of such things.

"People think Mac Jones is the least athletic," one coach close to Shanahan told me. "But when you think about the box that surrounds the pocket, in that confined area, he's the most athletic of the three (not including Lawrence and Wilson, who were likely to be taken first and sec-ond). Under duress, he's the best I've ever evaluated. He can throw it from any angle, no matter what's going on around him, like Drew Brees. And if something is going on below him, at his legs, he doesn't see it . . . but he can *feel* it . . . like Brady. It's just uncanny."

If Shanahan viewed Jones in this way, he *had* to be excited about the idea of drafting him. And yet, because the trade happened when it did, he left himself a lot of time to rethink, overthink, and question his ini-tial impulse. He kept his circle tight and his thoughts mostly to himself, but Lynch, assistant general manager Adam Peters, and owner Jed York had ample opportunity to share their thoughts—and none of them was believed to be as enamored of Jones as was the head coach, to whom they would ultimately defer come decision time.

There was noise out there. There was a *lot* of noise. In a draft-obsessed culture, Shanahan's potential Jones pick (floated publicly by me and others) was being shouted down with great disdain and vehemence. First, there were the cries from the Upside Police: *How could you trade all the way to three to take an unremarkable player like Jones? Lance or Fields, with their conspicuous physical traits, have a "higher ceiling" and are thus more wor-thy of the pick.* Things got louder after a locker room photo of Jones with his shirt off and a cigar in his mouth—while celebrating the Crimson Tide's victory in the national championship game—appeared on social media.

The quarterback's physique did not impress. Race also entered the conversation: Shanahan, some critics charged, had never been comfortable with a Black quarterback, with McNabb and Griffin cited as examples. In NFL circles, this wasn't viewed as a legitimate criticism, yet some close to the situation wondered: Was Shanahan hearing all of these things and talking himself out of following his instincts?

As the predraft process played out, it became a two-man race. Shanahan soured on Fields, who in college had a tendency to hitch at least once before unleashing downfield throws—even when there was no reason to do so. He also had trouble finding secondary receivers running underneath routes. Some evaluators viewed those shortcomings as a function of Ohio State's relatively simple offense, the amount of time he had in the pocket, and the superior athleticism of Fields's receivers; he hitched because he *could*. To Shanahan, it was a bad habit indicative of a general sloppiness that might not translate well to the NFL level, especially in his offense.

Lance, though, was something else. He was 6-foot-4, 226 pounds, and threw an effective deep ball. He was an accomplished runner who was perceived to have high-level speed, though that was a matter of some debate. There was no scouting combine in 2021, and Lance didn't run a 40-yard dash at either of his Pro Day workouts. In March, Lance told the NFL Network's Mike Garofolo that a GPS tracker had measured his top speed on a touchdown run in the 2020 Football Championship Subdivision (FCS) national championship game at 21.54 miles per hour, which would have ranked 12th in the NFL that year among all ballcarriers and first among quarterbacks. One of Lance's trainers claimed he regularly clocked him in the 4.5 range, yet the quarterback had run a 4.92 coming out of high school, which was among the reasons he didn't receive offers from programs in the Football Bowl Subdivision. Instead, Lance raced past defenders in the lower-ranked FCS, tearing up such Missouri Valley Conference opponents as Murray State, Western Illinois, and Youngstown State. It remained to be seen how fast he'd look against NFL players.

If you went with Lance, you were betting on potential. Not only had he played against lesser competition, but he also hadn't played that much. Lance had stepped into what was an FCS dynasty, following NFL quarterbacks Carson Wentz and Easton Stick. He'd spent only one season, 2019, as a starter. North Dakota State's 2020 campaign, due to COVID-19, had consisted of one early-October game against Central Arkansas that was essentially staged as a predraft audition for Lance.

So, the body of work wasn't vast. Lance, playing in a run-first offense, threw just 318 passes in college. His completion percentage was under 60 percent, which raised questions about his accuracy. He'd run a two-minute drill—once. Picking him, let alone picking him third overall, would be a leap of faith. As one NFL coach who was evaluating the quarterbacks that year asked, "How can we know?"

Shanahan, however, was warming to the idea of drafting Lance. Looking back, he'd missed out on the possibility of drafting Mahomes (who'd beaten him in Super Bowl LIV) and Watson (who'd also become a star) in 2017 because he focused on landing Kirk Cousins in free agency the following year. He'd since watched mobile quarterbacks like Lamar Jackson (Ravens) and Josh Allen (Bills) ascend to the top of the sport—and shine in games against the 49ers. Allen, in particular, seemed like a legitimate comparison to Lance: he was big (6-foot-5, 237), amazingly athletic, had a strong arm, and had struggled with accuracy in college. Allen had played at the FBS level, but for Wyoming, a middling program in the Mountain West Conference—not exactly Alabama or Ohio State.

Mobility was of more and more importance to Shanahan, given the proliferation of his offensive concepts around the league, with McVay, Mike and Matt LaFleur, Arthur Smith, and others now running similar schemes. That meant their teams' defenses practiced against those players every day; it meant their upcoming opponents studied those plays and preferences on film more regularly. In the constant quest to adapt and evolve, Shanahan saw a natural opening: if he could get a Mahomes- or Allen-type quarterback, it could keep him a step ahead of the competition.

Like many others, Shanahan viewed all of the incoming quarterbacks as intelligent—"That's why it was an easy thing to fall in love with all of them at different times," he'd tell me after the fact. Lance, he felt, was next-level. To confidants, he described Lance's scores on the brain-function tests administered by the 49ers and other teams—AIQ (Athletic Intelligent Quotient) and S2 Cognition—as freakishly high. "Super smart," McDaniel said of Lance in 2022. "He's [got], like, elite intelligence." And though he couldn't interact with prospects in the usual way because of COVID restrictions, Shanahan had a gut feeling, based on his in-person interactions with Lance, that the quarterback had the right makeup to handle the most important role on his roster.

As the draft approached, Pro Days were playing out on individual campuses. Because of the unique circumstances, Jones, Fields, and Lance each put on two workouts open to NFL coaches and talent evaluators, and televised by the NFL Network. Lance's first Pro Day, in Fargo—scripted by his personal quarterbacks coach, Quincy Avery—hadn't gone especially well from the Niners' perspective. About a week and a half before his second one, Niners quarterbacks coach Rich Scangarello provided Lance with a blueprint for the throws the team would like to see him attempt in that workout; he did the same thing for Fields.

On April 14, in Columbus, Ohio, Fields, according to one witness, seized the moment "like an alpha," adapting to Scangarello's script and taking charge. Five days later, in Fargo, Lance tried to do the same—and, again, it didn't quite work. On the flight home, however, Shanahan rationalized Lance's performance and continued to speak highly of him—prompting some in the organization to presume that he had shifted his preference from Jones to Lance. The 49ers had no real reason to keep their target a secret; presuming the Jags and Jets stuck with their respective plans, they'd get their guy no matter what. Yet Shanahan was intent on maintaining silence, and, clearly, was struggling with the decision in his own mind.

Several people close to Shanahan are certain he went against his initial instinct, to select Jones, and pivoted to Lance late in the process. Publicly, Shanahan would later insist the 49ers had made the trade with no specific quarterback in mind and were simply positioning themselves to conduct a more thorough evaluation. That claim seemed dubious, and not especially flattering to his own organization—why go all in without any certainty?

When I ran it all by Shanahan early in training camp that summer, he framed the decision as a struggle. "I mean, that [going back and forth on which player to pick] was for months. We did [the trade] so early, so we were never gonna be, like, 'Hey, this is the guy—we're sticking with it.' We really wanted to get up to that spot so we could do the right process with everyone. I always would [bounce back and forth]. You do it to check yourself. I mean, you make sure you see someone for everything they're good at. Then, the next day, you try to see them for everything they're bad at. And you keep going back and forth."

At that point in our conversation, Shanahan made an amusing analogy. "I kind of compare it to how my wife and I try to buy houses. She falls in love with everything, and I talk about how bad it is, and then I end up loving it because I realize, 'It wasn't that bad.' But it's just a process and how you get to the final answer."

When I asked Shanahan if there'd been a moment when he'd achieved clarity on Lance as his guy, he replied, "Towards the last couple of weeks, going to see him again, being able to talk to him in person . . . just being around him, everything you see on tape, then being able to get around him and feel it in person . . . I mean, there was a lot of good. Just the skill set that he brought, some of the things that we thought we could do with him, and just to see, really, the hidden horsepower I feel like he has. He hasn't played a ton of football, and I think he's only gonna get better as he gets older and the more reps he gets."

Gambling on "hidden horsepower" was a hell of a thing, especially because Shanahan and Lynch had constructed their roster to take advantage of Garoppolo's far different skill set. Receivers Deebo Samuel and Brandon Aiyuk and tight end George Kittle were adept at catching accurate, short and medium-range passes in tight quarters and gaining yards after the catch, something that aligned with Garoppolo's strengths. With Lance, that approach was likely to change dramatically.

When the transition would actually happen remained unclear. The Niners still had Garoppolo under contract and were prepared to keep him as their starter in 2021—if Lance couldn't beat him out in training camp—to give the raw rookie a year to acclimate. That was the plan, at least; it would change in many unforeseen ways over the coming years.

After the fact, many would try to ascertain what had prompted Shanahan to settle on Lance, a question only he could answer. One person who worked closely with him had a theory. "The smartest guys in football are usually the worst evaluators. They think they need to see things no one else can see. That's good when it comes to late-rounders. When you pick late, you look for traits that fit your system, and you figure out how to bring those out. When it's a top 30 pick, it's more obvious [who is really good]. But you tend to ignore the obvious and look for something no one else can see."

SHANAHAN HAD EVERYTHING HE WANTED AS THE DRAFT APPROACHED. The greatest suspense surrounding the event concerned the Niners' selection at No. 3, and no one besides him, York, and Lynch knew which quarterback they would draft. The Niners' choice would be the talk of the football world.

And yet, he wanted more.

Things had degenerated between Rodgers and his Packers bosses; the quarterback had asked for a trade, and he wanted to be dealt to the 49ers. And yes, despite the predraft drama, Shanahan and Lynch were very much open to the conversation. Sure, they'd swapped three picks for the chance to select a new franchise QB, but that could be sorted out later. The Niners could include the No. 3 pick in a trade with Green Bay, or flip it to another team on draft night and recoup some of their losses, or pick a different player at another position, or pick Lance anyway and have him sit behind Rodgers. It didn't matter: if Shanahan had a chance to get a future first-ballot Hall of Famer, he would jump at the opportunity.

The key was to create the opportunity. Rodgers, according to Paul Allen of KFAN in Minneapolis, believed the Packers had told him early in the offseason that they'd accommodate a trade request and had since reneged. As the draft approached, Murphy and Gutekunst were digging in and saying they wouldn't deal him to any team. The day before the draft, Shanahan called LaFleur and asked about the possibility of a trade, saying later, "I didn't want to wake up the next day . . . and see Aaron Rodgers, one of the best quarterbacks in this league, traded without doing any due diligence on it . . . And Matt told me I'd be wasting my time if we had Lynch call [Gutekunst]."

Yet the quarterback still harbored hope. Trey Wingo, a longtime ESPN personality who'd recently left the network, tweeted as the first night of the draft approached that "per sources: as of last night Rodgers was convinced he was headed to San Francisco." Two hours before the start of ESPN's draft broadcast, the network's "insider," Adam Schefter, reported that "Rodgers is so disgruntled with the Green Bay Packers that he has told some within the organization that he does not want to return to the team."

The Rodgers news had hijacked the predraft hysteria, and LaFleur was incensed. To him, the timing felt coordinated and insidious—an attempt to put the Packers in a vulnerable position with a ticking clock that worked against them. He had some suspicions. Rodgers and Lynch, the 49ers' GM, shared an agent in David Dunn. LaFleur was repped by the same firm, Athletes First, though not by Dunn directly.

LaFleur felt betrayed by his longtime friend, Shanahan. With Rodgers gone and Jordan Love at quarterback, LaFleur believed the Packers would struggle to avoid finishing last in their division. With Rodgers, the reigning MVP, they were Super Bowl contenders. This was coaching life or death to him, and he viewed Shanahan as a force working toward his demise.

If Shanahan was oblivious to LaFleur's fury—well, he figured it out a few minutes before the start of the draft as a surreal scene played out: McDaniel was sitting in his office, talking to his former Niners colleague Mike LaFleur, now the Jets' offensive coordinator, via FaceTime. Jets coach Robert Saleh was in the room with LaFleur, chiming in at times; McDaniel's door was open, and some other Niners coaches walked in and joined in the lighthearted banter. Then Shanahan entered McDaniel's office. With the Jets set to take Zach Wilson second overall, Shanahan joked to LaFleur, "I hope you guys don't take a different QB and cross us up. We haven't looked hard enough at Wilson."

"What do you mean? You've already got your quarterback," LaFleur replied. "Aaron Rodgers."

Shanahan tried to brush off the comment as a joke. "Hey," he said, "tell your brother to call me. He hasn't returned my calls."

"Can you blame him?" LaFleur asked.

At that point, Shanahan became visibly upset and left the room. He didn't appreciate the insinuation; he didn't like being cast as a villain in his own building. Clearly, blood was thicker than water for Mike LaFleur.

The draft began. The Jags, as expected, picked Lawrence. The Jets, as expected, took Wilson. The Niners were up. Shanahan, in the team's draft room, got a call from Saleh amid the suspense. "Can you tell me now?" Saleh asked, referring to the intrigue over which quarterback the Niners would pick. Shanahan misunderstood and thought Saleh was probing for other inside information. He snapped, "What the fuck is the deal with you guys? Really? While I'm about to pick?"

"Hey—easy," Saleh protested.

Shanahan hung up. The Niners took Lance. The Bears traded up from 20 to 11 to select Fields; the Patriots stayed at 15 and drafted Jones. That lent credence to the predraft presumption held by some that, if Jones had truly been Shanahan's target, the Niners could have stood pat and gotten him with the 12th pick. It wasn't necessarily true, however. The Patriots might well have traded up to take Jones before the 49ers could pounce; similarly, the Panthers (who took cornerback Jaycee Horn eighth overall) had interest in Jones at that spot, but traded for Jets quarterback Sam Darnold a few weeks before the draft—partly because they believed the 49ers would take Jones at three.

The only remaining mystery was whether the Packers would try to bridge their divide with Rodgers. "I just have this feeling that our front office will size up the moment and recognize how important this is and make a gesture that shows Aaron how valued he is," one Packers coach told me shortly before the draft began. "Like, if we traded up to take a wide receiver—that would be a way of trying to make it right."

I responded skeptically. "I think they might surprise us," he said, as though willing it to happen.

Later that night, the Packers stayed put at 29—and selected cornerback Eric Stokes from Georgia. It was a typical Green Bay pick, and the exact opposite of a conciliatory gesture to their estranged quarterback.

"Unreal," another team's longtime general manager told me that night. "It's almost like they're rubbing Aaron's nose in it."

━━━

WHEN LAFLEUR VENTED TO McVAY ABOUT THE 49ERS' PREDRAFT POWER play for Rodgers, and the role that he perceived Shanahan as having played, McVay told his friend to take it down a notch. *It's just football,* McVay assured him. *We're all competitors. This is part of it.*

Then again, at that moment, McVay was especially unbothered. "So easy for him to say after they just made a trade for Stafford," Mike LaFleur said, laughing, when reflecting back on that wild offseason. "Life was great. All he's doing is scheming it up. Sean's sitting in the weeds with Matthew in Cabo, just having the time of his life."

It hadn't all been cheery, however. Before moving forward with his new quarterback, McVay needed to have a long and uncomfortable conversation with his former one. Goff, blindsided by the trade, may have hung up abruptly on McVay in late January. However, as the reality sunk in, the quarterback wasn't content to pack up his things and head to Detroit. First, he wanted to meet with his former coach.

Days after the trade, Goff went over to former teammate Andrew Whitworth's house to debrief. Then Goff, according to a *Los Angeles Times* profile, told Whitworth he planned to meet with McVay at the Rams' facility. "I'm like, 'Wait, what?'" Whitworth recalled to the *Times*'s Sam Farmer. "And he's like, 'I told Sean I still want to do our exit meeting.'" Whitworth told Goff he was crazy and asked why he'd want to do such a thing. Goff's answer: "I want him to tell me right to my face what I did wrong. I want to hear it from him. How do I get better?"

Said Whitworth, "He wanted the full breakdown of why."

Goff had helped McVay ascend to the top of the profession, and now he was being replaced. As he retraced their final season together, Goff came to feel as though he'd been in a bad relationship that at times bordered on the emotionally abusive. McVay regretted how he'd handled things and how abruptly the trade had been presented to the player. "I got some answers and gained a lot of closure," Goff told Farmer, referring to that exit meeting. "He was forthright."

McVay felt he owed it to Goff to explain the *why*, at least belatedly. "There were a lot of really good times that we had together, significantly more good times than the challenging ones," McVay told me. "If you have to make tough decisions, there's never really a smooth way for that to go down other than just being direct and to the point. How do you do that in a way that doesn't lack empathy, appreciation, and gratitude? That's a hard thing."

It wasn't just the abrupt goodbye, however, that McVay regretted. The coach's own frustration had failed him, his disapproval and reproach seeping into his quarterback's psyche and contradicting the ultrapositive vibe that had built the McVay-era Rams. Said McVay, "With Jared, were there times when I can reflect and say, 'Man, I feel really good about trying to help and being the best advocate and influence and instill the belief'? Yes. Were there times that I could have done better and didn't do good enough for what he deserved from me? I can say yes to that as well."

The exit meeting helped McVay, at least. The conversation may have been awkward, but it left the coach feeling better about the breakup than he had before. He was excited to rebuild his offense around Stafford's strengths and obsessed with getting back to the Super Bowl and winning it. Yet he felt a void within himself that he couldn't quite describe. He was less of the ebullient optimist that he'd been when the Rams hired him. He was possibly burned out. A Lombardi Trophy, he believed, would cure all that. He'd later describe that sentiment in stark terms: it was a lie.

Chapter 19

Ain't Losing to This Guy Anymore

The ball hung high above the SoFi Stadium turf, floating slowly toward its unintended target. Watching it from the visitors' sideline, Kyle Shanahan's mind was racing. It was all happening; this was his moment. The Rams had cut the 49ers' lead to 17–14 with ten minutes left in the NFC Championship Game, and now Matthew Stafford, backed up near his own end zone, had served up what should have been an easy interception at a terrible time. The ball sailed well past receiver Van Jefferson, and S.F. safety Jaquiski Tartt stood alone at his own 35, arms outstretched, preparing to haul it in with room to run. Shanahan could see it all playing out: the 49ers with the ball at midfield, or better. A decisive, punishing drive that showcased their superior physicality and stamina, culminating with a game-clinching touchdown. Then, there would be celebration. A Niners team that had been written off at midseason was about to complete a stirring run to the Super Bowl by once again vanquishing its rival. Shanahan would capture his seventh consecutive victory over McVay; his ownership of his former protégé would be undisputed and complete.

It was all *right there* for the taking—and then, in an instant, it all fell apart. Shanahan saw the ball bounce off the top of Tartt's chest, hit the safety's face mask and elude his grasp. Then Tartt was face down on the turf, his hands clasped around the top of his helmet. It was as if he'd dropped the Lombardi Trophy—and Shanahan, who had some metaphorical experience in that department, might as well have been right there alongside him.

Suddenly, the Rams were driving for a game-tying field goal. Then

L.A. got the ball back, marched into field goal range, and took a 20–17 lead. Jimmy Garoppolo had one last chance to keep the Niners' dream alive, but on third and long, his desperation pass bounced off a running back's hands and headed toward Rams linebacker Travin Howard, who didn't drop it. And then it was all over: McVay hugging everybody in sight as blue, yellow, and white confetti fell; Shanahan walking off the field in a daze, his expression blank, seething inside and unsure how once again he'd gotten so close, only to watch it so cruelly slip away.

The season had begun with so much promise. And then, for a disturbingly long stretch, it looked as though Shanahan's Niners had lost their way. A six-week slump created what Mike McDaniel described as a "high-octane pressure situation" that shrank Shanahan's margin for error to almost nothing—and brought out the best in him. He made a pair of shrewd scheme adjustments, created a new identity for the team on the fly, and led it on a stirring regular-season charge bookended by victories over the Rams. Then, in the playoffs, the Niners had gone into Dallas and Green Bay and asserted themselves in a truly inspiring fashion.

He'd fully expected to beat the Rams a third time, go back to the Super Bowl, win it, and achieve his life's dream. Now, he'd have to watch McVay do it. He felt sick. Long after the game, as he walked back across the field toward the tunnel near where the 49ers' buses were parked, Shanahan was almost too angry to speak. It was understandable. There was nothing really to say.

MUCH OF THE BOUNDLESS OPTIMISM IN THE NINERS' TEAM FACILITIES had started that offseason with Trey Lance. The idea was to ease him into his pro career, given how raw he was, how little he'd played, and how vast the difference was between North Dakota State and the NFL. If Lance could beat out Garoppolo in training camp, fine; if not, he could watch and learn while being situationally subbed into games as a change-of-pace weapon. The mere hint of a "Trey Lance Package" would be a bother to opposing defensive coordinators, who, in a given week, would have to account for Lance's mobility and big arm while also game-planning against a more traditional pocket passer. Said Mike McDaniel, "Picture the love child of

Josh Allen and Lamar Jackson—and now imagine you have to deal with that on a random third and three in the second quarter . . ."

Shanahan seemed to have achieved the best of all possible worlds. Garoppolo had reacted to the drafting of his eventual replacement by altering his approach. Jimmy G had been a fully engaged participant in the off-season program, and he showed up for training camp looking much better, and with a much stronger grasp of the offense, than in previous years.

During that first week of camp, Lance was also good. In fact, he seemed to have picked up the system so seamlessly that Shanahan and his assistants were openly wondering if naming him their starter might give the Niners the best chance to win in 2021. Niners fans were all for it; many had already declared that the Bay Area was now the "Trey Area." The hysteria reached fever pitch in the Niners' preseason opener against the Chiefs at Levi's Stadium when Lance, on the first play of his second series, faked a handoff, rolled to his left, and unleashed a deep ball down the right side of the field to Trent Sherfield, who hauled it in and kept running for an 80-yard touchdown.

Things leveled off pretty quickly, however. Lance began struggling with some of the more intricate elements of Shanahan's scheme—understandable, for any rookie—and noticeably lost confidence. The Niners headed south for joint workouts against the Chargers in advance of their preseason meeting, and Lance struggled against Brandon Staley's defense. Garoppolo, meanwhile, had a strong camp and easily won the job.

Soon, the Trey Lance Package lost its luster, too. Lance broke a finger on his throwing hand in training camp and it hadn't healed properly, forcing him to deliver passes without being able to bend the finger. His accuracy had been a concern beforehand; now, he was missing layups. Inserting him into games broke Garoppolo's rhythm and proved to be too much of an adventure for Shanahan's taste. And when Lance, pressed into starting duty during an October game against the Cardinals because of Garoppolo's calf injury, suffered a sprained left knee, the idea of using him for cameo appearances became even less appealing.

By then, the 49ers had even bigger problems. After winning their first two games, both on the road, they proceeded to lose four in a row, and five out of six. The low point came on November 7 at Levi's Stadium. The Cardinals, who'd beaten them four weeks earlier in Arizona, showed up and shellacked S.F. 31–17, with 35-year-old backup quarterback Colt McCoy shredding the secondary. Worse, the Niners looked lifeless. It was their eighth consecutive home defeat (though three of those games had been at the Cardinals' home stadium during the previous season's COVID-induced relocation) and they seemed to be going nowhere. They were on the verge of benching Garoppolo and looking toward the future with Lance. S.F. was now 9–16 since holding that ten-point lead in the middle of the fourth quarter of Super Bowl LIV. The players hadn't yet given up hope, but it was trending that way. The chances of an abrupt turnaround seemed remote.

"Yes, it can be done," center Alex Mack told me as left the field after the Cardinals loss. "But it's got to happen soon—like, very soon. We're running out of time."

That evening, another veteran player put it this way: "Good teams have an identity. Ours—what is it? We've just got to keep pressing to find it."

They had to do it right away. The Rams, remade around Stafford, were coming to Levi's eight days later for a Monday night clash.

EARLY ON, LIFE WITH STAFFORD WAS EVERYTHING McVAY HAD HOPED for—and more. He altered and expanded his offense to take advantage of Stafford's potent arm, playmaking ability, and experience, and opposing defenses mostly looked rattled and reactive. The Rams won seven of their first eight games and were 7–2 when they headed north for that game against the reeling Niners. S.F. had swept the series in each of the previous two regular seasons; this time, however, L.A. looked like the stronger team.

There was already lot of talk about Stafford as a potential league MVP, but it was also clear he'd have some strong competition—from the reigning MVP, who'd captured that honor for the third time in 2020. Aaron Rodgers, after all the offseason drama, had gone back to Green Bay with a new contract. Upon his arrival, Rodgers held a press conference, aired out most of his past and current frustrations, and proceeded to resume his role as a ruthless destroyer of opposing defenses. Year three of the Matt

LaFleur–Rodgers partnership was even more impressive than the previous one had been, with offensive coordinator Nathaniel Hackett again playing a pivotal part.

One of their signal wins had come against the Niners, in a game at Levi's in late September. The Packers stormed out to a 17–0 lead, which S.F. cut to 17–7 when Shanahan—on the final play of the first half—inserted Lance and called the quarterback's number on a one-yard touchdown run. The 49ers kept battling, ultimately taking a 28–27 lead on Garoppolo's 12-yard touchdown pass to Pro Bowl fullback Kyle Juszczyk with 37 seconds remaining.

Rodgers, with no time-outs left, coolly completed passes of 25 and 17 yards to star receiver Davante Adams, setting up Mason Crosby's game-winning 51-yard field goal as time expired. The only thing that momentarily cooled the Packers' elation was LaFleur's chilly, no-look handshake with Shanahan near the middle of the field—a sign of the bad feelings that followed the potential Rodgers trade to S.F.

"I thought we blew the game," LaFleur recalled. "Mason made a huge kick, and Aaron and Davante made some unbelievable plays. That was a pretty cool moment. That's one of the games I'll remember forever."

While things between LaFleur and Shanahan remained fraught, McVay, too, was locked in a battle—with himself. McVay, who felt he'd "lost my humanity a little bit" after the Super Bowl LIII defeat and had become increasingly obsessed with winning it all, had "let the frustration of the expectations be more about me than I'd ever want anyone to know." The coach internalized much of his stress and, during the 2020 season, began spending more time in his home office, something he found to be more efficient. People couldn't poke their heads in and run things by him; it was easier for him to block out the world and grind.

As the Rams prepared to head north for their early-November game against the 49ers, they looked to the outside world like a thriving operation. McVay, however, was experiencing "constant torment . . . Like, you have a fucking problem and you've got to fix it, but you don't know how to fucking fix it. Nobody puts more pressure on themselves than I do of me, but I think a lot of that pressure is a result of when I lose sight of what matters."

Shanahan, as that Monday night game approached, didn't have the luxury of self-reflection. The only thing that mattered was finding a way to win. Something had to change, and it had to change immediately.

THE FIRST MOVE WAS A RADICAL ONE. THE 49ERS NEEDED BALANCE, which meant they needed to run the ball. Their running backs, at least the ones who were healthy, weren't getting it done. So, Shanahan turned to his most productive receiver—Deebo Samuel, who, after catching passes in stride, barreled down the field like a nimble bowling ball—and basically asked him to solve the problem by simultaneously playing two positions.

Samuel wasn't just a skilled runner; he was all attitude, a tone-setting player whose violent style fired up teammates. He could get the ball on jet sweeps and blast forward with a running start; he could also line up in the backfield, or motion there from the line of scrimmage, and take pitchouts and handoffs. His positional versatility would also open up schematic options for Shanahan to prey upon opposing defenses, allowing the coach to use pre-snap shifts to alter his formations and create mismatches. Using Samuel as a de facto halfback—or "wide back," as Deebo christened it—was classic Shanahan: a surprising idea that, at its core, was beautiful in its simplicity.

On the eve of that meeting with the Rams, Shanahan told his players at the team's hotel near Levi's Stadium, "If we get 30 runs, we're gonna win the game." It turned out his math was off. The 49ers would run it 44 times against the Rams, with Samuel carrying five times for 36 yards, and roll to a 31–10 victory. "That's kind of when our offense shifted," Juszczyk recalled. "It's not like he can snap his fingers and call 30 runs in a row; you've got to *earn* those calls by converting on third down and sustaining drives and playing great defense. Him saying that instilled a nastiness and a physicality that became our calling card."

Shanahan and his first-year defensive coordinator, DeMeco Ryans, made a similarly seismic move on the other side of the ball. It involved 6-foot-7 defensive tackle Arik Armstead, who served as a base defensive end in defensive line coach Kris Kocurek's Wide 9 scheme—setting the edge on first and second downs, primarily as a run defender—and shifted inside on obvious passing downs. Armstead, whose contributions often went largely unnoticed by ordinary fans, was now being viewed in a more critical light. His close friend, former University of Oregon teammate and All-Pro defensive tackle DeForest Buckner, had been traded to the Indianapolis Colts following the 2019 season; with only so much salary cap space to go around, the 49ers' front office had chosen Armstead over Buckner, given him a five-year, $85 million contract extension, and used a 2020 first-round pick on Javon Kinlaw to fill the void left by the departing star. Kinlaw, who'd had knee issues in college, made a limited impact as a rookie and was shut down five games into his second season after suffering yet another knee injury that would require reconstructive surgery. Now, Kocurek wanted Armstead, who'd had ten sacks in 2019 after managing just nine in his first four seasons combined, to affect the game in a bigger way.

Instead of putting Armstead out on the edge, where teams often ran away from him, Kocurek, after conferring with Ryans and Shanahan, suggested moving him inside full-time. Like Samuel had, Armstead essentially said, *Whatever helps the team.* The change helped him, too: Armstead had five of his six sacks that season after the switch and finished with a career-best 63 tackles.

After that Monday night mauling in Santa Clara, McVay was miserable. He'd now lost five consecutive games to Shanahan, and memes were starting to circulate throughout the football world. A popular one involved a Photoshopped version of a Shanahan family picture, with McVay's face in place of Kyle's son Carter's, as Kyle's right hand is pressed lovingly against the boy's chest. Things got worse after L.A.'s bye week, with the Rams' 36–28 defeat to LaFleur and the Packers at Lambeau Field. McVay's team had now lost three straight, and the honeymoon with Stafford was ending. The quarterback, who'd thrown four interceptions in the Rams' first eight games, served up five during those three defeats. Stafford would finish the regular season with 17 interceptions, tied with rookie Trevor Lawrence for most in the NFL, including an astounding four pick-sixes. By comparison, Jared Goff had also thrown four interceptions for touchdowns—in his *five seasons* with the team.

McVay, whose mood had turned increasingly dark, was aware of his role as a "thermometer"—players, coaches, and others in the Rams' facility tended to feed off his energy, good or bad. Worried that his dismal moods would rub off on others, he retreated, spending even more time in his home office and leaving his players to muddle through the misery without him. As he'd recall after the season, "It was a fucking joke how pissed and how—I can't even articulate. The disgust. The sickness. The constant pit in your gut. You have to fight what you're feeling."

Back at the Rams' facility, coaches and players wondered why their leader and tone-setter was so distant. For Rams players to turn things around, they needed to *feel* McVay. By that point, there was only one person in a position to tell him the truth.

———

WHEN RAHEEM MORRIS CAME ABOARD AS McVAY'S DEFENSIVE COORDI-nator in January, some people were thrown off by the hire. Schematically, it wasn't a natural fit: McVay wanted to keep running Brandon Staley's system, based on Vic Fangio's principles, which had helped the Rams' defense to a No. 1 ranking in 2020. Morris had been trained in Monte Kiffin's Tampa 2 scheme and had later implemented Dan Quinn's Seattle 3 principles in Atlanta. None of it made sense, except to McVay and Morris.

"Scheme is scheme," was the way Morris put it to me. McVay's version: "Raheem is so smart. Raheem knows football. I think that the best coaches have an agility and an adaptability and a flexibility. When you come into a situation where you had done pretty well the year before, Raheem doesn't have an ego in terms of the schemes. We had continuity with the position coaches at all three levels—Eric Henderson, Chris Shula, Ejiro Evero. What I thought was great was, he's coming in, he's really saying, 'Alright, let's figure out our verbiage, our vernacular. What do we want to be, identity-wise? Then we'll have our foundation and our philosophical approach,' which he believed in based on studying the tape, who our players were, our personnel. Now, how do we build it and how do we tweak?"

More important to both men was their shared history and their implicit trust in one another. Though running backs coach Thomas Brown had the "assistant head coach" title, Morris, in McVay's eyes, was something even more: a close friend with head coaching experience and an upbeat temperament that smoothed over his own edges.

As the Rams' long November continued and McVay walled himself off from his peers and players, Morris was the one who pulled him back. He confronted McVay about the head coach's dark mood and penchant for self-alienation. To McVay, Morris was like a big brother. His words carried weight.

"Sometimes, people need you," Morris told McVay. "Sometimes when your voice is around, you give people comfort, make them feel better. You make them want to go play."

McVay became more present and engaged; so did the Rams. Despite Stafford's turnovers, L.A. went on a five-game winning streak and closed in on a division title. The Rams were all in on winning a championship. That was clear on November 1, just before the trade deadline, when they sent second- and third-round picks to the Broncos for star pass rusher Von Miller, who was in the final year of his contract and would turn out to be a short-term rental. A week and a half later, L.A. signed electrifying wide receiver Odell Beckham, a three-time Pro Bowl selection who'd been released by the Cleveland Browns after clashing with quarterback Baker Mayfield.

The addition of Miller allowed Morris to make some shrewd strategic adjustments. Adding the MVP of Super Bowl 50 to a mix that already included defensive tackle Aaron Donald—possibly the NFL's most dominant player—and talented pass rusher Leonard Floyd opened up some possibilities, and Morris tweaked the scheme to maximize their talents. He began using more five-man rush packages, limiting teams' ability to double-team Donald, Miller, or both. Because he trusted his pass rushers to get to the quarterback quickly, Morris also called for tighter coverage on the back end. That led to more big plays, especially in big moments. "Just watch the way that he called it as we got more comfortable with our players," McVay told me in 2023. "Our defense in '21 doesn't get enough credit for crunch-time stops. I think that was the thing that separated that team—in general, they made plays when they had to. I don't get caught up in the stats. I just know that when we had to have stops, or we needed turn-overs or we needed to be able to make plays, the defense seemed like they delivered in every single situation and scenario in crunch-time moments."

Morris's presence came with another benefit for McVay: he knew Shanahan as well as anyone in the profession. Morris understood the way Shanahan thought about football, attacked defenses, and tried to use a defense's rules against it. That didn't necessarily mean he could come up with foolproof plans to shut down Shanahan's teams, but it allowed him to make things tougher for the Niners. And as the Rams prepared for their regular-season finale between the two teams at SoFi, beating Shanahan had never felt more urgent.

It was one thing for McVay to be lampooned as Shanahan's son in a meme. It was another thing to have a chance to take out your rival—and complete the task. The 49ers, at 9–7, needed to win to make the playoffs. The Rams had plenty of incentive, too: they led the Cardinals by a game in the division and could clinch the NFC West with a victory. As the Rams' players and coaches prepared during the week, they were well aware of how badly McVay wanted this game. He and O'Connell crafted a game plan that threw out many of the tried-and-true strategies the Rams had employed during their five-game losing streak to the 49ers. They felt they finally had some answers for a scheme that DeMeco Ryans, in his first year as Saleh's successor, had fine-tuned.

That confidence was borne out in the game's first 24 minutes, after which L.A. held a 17–0 lead on the strength of two Stafford touchdown passes to Tyler Higbee. Following the second one, McVay was so jacked up that he ran the length of the Rams' sideline and joined the tight end and quarterback in an end-zone celebration. It was an image that Shanahan and his players would later recall with no small amount of joy. No one on the 49ers' sideline believed it was over. They'd won six of eight games following that home defeat to the Cardinals. SoFi Stadium was filled with red; fans of the visitors had shown up in force in what was billed as a "49ers Takeover."

Shanahan's team would live up to that phrase in dramatic fashion.

THERE WERE A LOT OF TIMES THAT SHANAHAN GLARED AT GAROPPOLO AS though he wanted to strangle his quarterback with a headset cord. This Sunday afternoon was not one of them. Seventeen days earlier, in a 20–17 defeat to the Titans, Garoppolo had suffered a torn ligament in his right thumb. After sitting out the next week, Garoppolo—who felt a searing pain every time he threw a pass—sucked it up and returned. For the franchise quarterback whose boss had decided he wasn't good enough, it hadn't been the easiest season. As one Niners assistant put it, "Jimmy had a hard adjustment in 2021. You go from being coached like 'Hey, what did you see here? How can we fix that? What's your process? Let me help you . . .' to 'Why the hell did you do that?' It's not unique to Jimmy; it's the nature of the NFL. But it was a hard adjustment." On some level, the way Garoppolo handled all of it—his displacement, the 49ers' ugly first half of the season that left them on the brink of elimination, and now the thumb injury—resonated with Shanahan. As Shanahan's former defensive coordinator Robert Saleh said, "I think Kyle has a heck of a lot more respect for Jimmy than people realize. Kyle loved his competitiveness."

This regular-season finale at the stadium 49ers fans would come to call "Levi's South" was San Francisco's season in miniature. At halftime, with the Rams' lead at 17–3 after Robbie Gould's field goal on the final play of the second quarter, things looked pretty grim. In the second half, Samuel's 16-yard touchdown catch sparked a comeback. But with 2:29 remaining in the game, Stafford's scoring pass to Cooper Kupp put L.A. back on top, 24–17. Garoppolo and the 49ers had one possession to save their season. Roughly a year after Shanahan had decided, once and for all, that he was done with Jimmy G, he now needed his quarterback more than ever.

As he leaned over and prepared to snap the ball to Garoppolo on the drive's first play, Alex Mack—now 36, having just been selected to his seventh Pro Bowl—understood the urgency of the situation. He'd been with Shanahan in Cleveland, when organizational dysfunction had derailed a promising season. They'd been together in Atlanta, coming so close to winning it all, with Mack battling the Patriots on a broken leg and Shanahan heading west after that ignominious Super Bowl collapse. Now, they needed a touchdown to keep hope alive.

When it came to comebacks, Mack's position coach certainly could speak from experience. Chris Foerster, now four years removed from the infamous cell phone video that seemed likely to cost him his career, was very much a part of the 49ers' success, working in tandem with Mike McDaniel on blocking schemes and running calls and helping Shanahan's offense hum. Mack, who said he had "butted heads" with Foerster on some occasions, had become a believer in his approach. "I really wish I could have had him seven years prior," Mack said. "I didn't think at year 13 I had much more to learn, but I learned a lot. I've always wanted to know the *why*. I always liked to ask the question of 'What are we trying to do? Why do you say this? Is there another way you can phrase it so it hits my brain in a way that makes sense?' The good coaches will have a reason why."

Also boasting what Joe Staley called "the beautiful mind" of McDaniel, the 49ers—by that second Sunday in January—had many, many ways to attack a defense. With the season on the line, it all had to work.

Garoppolo's game-tying drive, which began from the Niners 12-yard line, was a masterpiece: a pinpoint pass over the middle to Brandon Aiyuk, who charged ahead for a 21-yard gain; a short pass over the middle to No. 3 receiver Jauan Jennings for five more yards; a gorgeous spiral down the right sideline to Samuel, who'd slipped behind star cornerback Jalen Ramsey and charged forward after the catch for a 43-yard gain. If anyone is an argument for players over plays, it is Deebo Samuel—yet that game-changing moment was truly about play design: two tight ends leaked to the outside while both receivers started as though they were going upfield before cutting hard to the corners. Ramsey, forced to make an instant decision, guessed wrong, dove, and missed the ball; Samuel made the kind of inside cut only he could make, and kept running to the 19-yard line. After an offside penalty and an incompletion, S.F. faced a second and five from the L.A. 14 with 26 seconds to go. Samuel, in the backfield, went in motion, confusing the Rams' defenders. Jennings, wide open over the middle, caught Garoppolo's pass and cruised into the end zone for his second touchdown of the day.

The game would go to overtime. Garoppolo got the ball and took the Niners on another long drive; they settled for Robbie Gould's 24-yard field goal at the end of the 12-play march. Now, only 2:45 remained. The Rams could tie the game with a field goal or win it with a touchdown. They did neither: Stafford's underthrown deep ball for Odell Beckham was picked off by rookie cornerback Ambry Thomas at the S.F. 20, clinching the second-biggest comeback victory of the NFL season.

The Niners were alive. The Rams would win the NFC West anyway, thanks to the Seahawks' 38–30 victory over the Cardinals, but there would be no celebration. Recalled O'Connell, "They're putting up on the 'Oculus' [double-sided video board] at Sofi Stadium: 'L.A. Rams: 2021 NFC West Champions.' We go in the locker room, and there weren't shirts. There weren't hats. We just knew we might play them again, and we would probably have to if we wanted to lift a Lombardi Trophy."

<hr>

ONCE INVITED TO THE POSTSEASON PARTY, THE 49ERS BARGED THROUGH the door and took over the joint. They started with a road game against the third-seeded Dallas Cowboys, champions of the NFC East, and emerged with a 23–17 victory. Six days later, in Green Bay, the Niners showed up with swagger and a belief that they couldn't be toppled, even by the top-seeded Packers. Garoppolo had suffered a sprained right shoulder in the second quarter of the game against the Cowboys, making his passes even more painful—but he stayed in the lineup. It turned out he'd suffered a torn capsule in the back of the shoulder that would require offseason surgery; between that and the thumb injury, he was operating far below peak performance.

It would take a full-team effort for the 49ers to beat the Packers and Rodgers, their soon-to-be-four-time-MVP quarterback; only Peyton Manning, with five, had won more. Shanahan, however, had constructed the 49ers to prevail in such circumstances. Back in September, they'd put up 28 points against the Packers and lost. This would be a much different type of game.

Quietly, the chill between Shanahan and LaFleur had thawed. At the repeated urging of Saleh, now the head coach of the Jets, and with the help of another third-party intervention (via a mutual friend from their days together with the Falcons), LaFleur had reached out with a text message to Shanahan, and now they were at least communicating again. "Life's too short," LaFleur told me. "We ended up talking and just hashed it out. I shouldn't have; I should have waited till after the season. Maybe we would have beat their ass in the playoff."

It looked like an ideal night for the Packers, with Lambeau Field covered in snow. Green Bay got the ball first, marched 69 yards in ten plays, and went up 7–0 on A. J. Dillon's six-yard scoring run. Then the Niners' defense stiffened, and the game turned into a rock fight. The 49ers didn't complete their first pass, or record a first down, until six and a half minutes remained in the second quarter. It was 7–0 at halftime—the Packers had a field goal blocked on the final play—and 10–3 early in the third quarter. The 49ers kept hanging around. As in the Dallas game, a recent Shanahan/McDaniel innovation—lining up All-Pro left tackle Trent Williams in the backfield, putting him in motion across the formation and having a halfback run behind him—would prove crucial in short-yardage situations. Finally, with 4:41 remaining, S.F. broke through. Jordan Willis blocked a punt, and rookie safety Talanoa Hufanga scooped up the ball and scored from six yards out.

Now it was 10–10, and the Packers couldn't recover. "You could feel the momentum change," LaFleur recalled. "I could feel it from the look in our guys' eyes. I'm like, 'Guys, it's a fucking tie game. We get the ball. There's four minutes left. Let's go win this fucking thing.' We didn't get it done. It was like a perfect storm. We shit the bed."

The Packers went three and out after the blocked punt, with Rodgers making an impulsive decision on third down—he had receiver Allen Lazard uncovered in the middle of the field, but instead forced a deep incompletion to Davante Adams, his favorite target. "We had Allen wide-ass open," LaFleur said. "But it is what it is. It's players, not plays." The 49ers took over at their own 20 and drove to the Green Bay 38, where Samuel, on third and seven, ran nine yards for a first down. That set up Gould's 45-yard field goal as time expired, bringing another Packers season to yet another sudden end, and vaulting the Niners into the NFC Championship Game.

The next day, they would find out whether they were headed to Tampa, to face Brady and defending champion Bucs, or back to SoFi. The Rams had rolled the Cardinals in their playoff opener, and they started out their divisional-round game against the Buccaneers like a team possessed. With seven minutes left in the third quarter, L.A. led 27–3, and some people assumed the game was over. Shanahan—he of the 28–3 Super Bowl scar—was not one of them. Sure enough, the Rams started turning the ball over, and Brady brought the Bucs all the way back, tying the game on Leonard Fournette's nine-yard touchdown run with 42 seconds remaining.

On the next possession, Stafford took a one-yard sack on first down. Then Buccaneers defensive coordinator Todd Bowles—true to his aggressive nature—gave L.A. an opening by calling a blitz. Stafford grooved a deep ball over the middle to Kupp for a 44-yard gain, setting up Matt Gay's walk-off 30-yard field goal. The Rams had survived, partly thanks to the brilliance of McVay's chosen quarterback. Now, to get back to the Super Bowl, the coach would have to do something he hadn't been able to accomplish since the end of the 2018 season: defeat Shanahan. In the days leading up to the game, both men were asked if Shanahan was in McVay's head. Neither loved the question. McVay loved it least.

McVay had reached a breaking point. "He was super confident that week, actually," recalled Evero, the Rams' secondary coach and passing-game coordinator that season. "He was just like, 'We're gonna fucking win this game. We're gonna kick some ass. We ain't fucking losing to this guy anymore.' He was determined. He was driven. He was willing it to happen now. I know, too, that even if the Rams don't make the playoffs, and he's watching, he can't stand to watch Kyle have a run. We were always gonna be rooting against the Niners. It's like, 'Hey, anybody else.' Andy Reid can win ten Super Bowls, but Kyle can't have one."

ON THEIR SECOND TRIP TO SOFI IN THREE WEEKS, THE 49ERS AGAIN enjoyed something akin to a home crowd. Garoppolo threw touchdown passes to Samuel (44 yards) and George Kittle (16), and the Niners took a 17–7 lead into the fourth quarter and looked ready to close. McVay, however, remained confident that his offense would break through. Stafford's 11-yard touchdown pass to Kupp cut the lead to three with 13:30 remaining. The 49ers quickly drove into Rams territory and had second and one at the L.A. 44. Then came the game's pivotal sequence.

Halfback Elijah Mitchell was stuffed on a run up the middle, losing a yard. In the upstairs coaches' booth, however, it was presumed to be third and one, which was what was conveyed to Shanahan, rather than third and two. He called for a run—with Williams going in motion from left to right—blurting out, "Man, that's pretty far" on the headset shortly before the ball was snapped, as if he'd like to have the play call back. Garoppolo gave the ball to Juszczyk, who tried to fool the Rams by sneaking inside while Williams blocked on the edge, but was stuffed for no gain. Shanahan resisted the urge to go for it, and his decision to punt was seemingly validated when Stafford floated the badly overthrown deep ball that was headed straight for the 49ers' strong safety.

When Tartt dropped it, the game didn't end. The 49ers still led, 17–14, and the Rams faced second and ten from their own 15 with 9:47 to go. Yet, when it was over, after Garoppolo threw his last-gasp interception and Stafford took a knee three times to kill the clock and McVay had finally broken free from Shanahan's stranglehold, the Niners appeared stunned by the way they had collapsed over those final ten minutes, as if they'd never recovered from the dropped interception.

Mike McDaniel was teary-eyed and visibly shaken. He spoke hoarsely, in hushed tones, with none of his usual dry humor. Of Garoppolo, McDaniel said, "He played through so much shit, and all the shit in his head. Most of the time, when you draft somebody high, people fold. He got better, and that started in the offseason. Everyone noticed. It was really cool." When Shanahan emerged, he was fuming. "We should have been able to close it out," he said while pulling a suitcase behind him, never breaking stride.

Near the spread of to-go food set up near the team buses in the stadium's southeast tunnel, I caught up to Garoppolo. He took a deep breath, gave me a confessional look, and said, softly, "Now I can tell the truth."

Specifically, he acknowledged that his thumb and shoulder had hampered him during the 49ers' playoff run. "Every play, I feel it," he said. "I can't believe this shit held up, to be completely honest with you. The thumb, the shoulder . . . all of it. It was one thing after another . . . every time I threw. It was a *lot*."

He talked about the way he'd reacted to the 49ers' drafting of Lance. "I think the competition, or whatever it is, it pushes you. When [the trade] happened, I think it kind of just sent me to a different zone. And I think that paid off this year. It paid off for this team. And good things came from it."

Garoppolo grabbed a plate—"I'm starving," he said, laughing—and answered one last question about his future. Surely, this would be his final game with the 49ers, or so it seemed. "All through this, I haven't even thought about it. It'll hit me on this plane ride, and probably tomorrow a little bit. But we'll figure that out when we figure it out."

He gestured toward the rest of his teammates, most of whom were waiting on the bus, and politely excused himself. "I want to enjoy this time, with these guys," Garoppolo said softly. "For as long as I can."

Chapter 20

What Else Could You Want?

Three years after emerging shell-shocked from his loss to Bill Belichick, McVay was going back to the Super Bowl under optimal conditions. The game would be played at the Rams' home stadium. McVay would be facing a team, the Cincinnati Bengals, coached by one of his former assistants, Zac Taylor. In Matthew Stafford, he had an experienced quarterback who wouldn't be rattled by the moment. The Bengals were a strong team with an emerging superstar in second-year quarterback Joe Burrow, but this felt more like a coronation.

The Rams, derided by cynics for their go-for-broke philosophy, were on the verge of having it all pay off. They hadn't used a first-round pick since taking Jared Goff first overall in 2016 and didn't have one until 2024 at the earliest; they had squeezed as many contracts under the salary cap as mathematically possible and would have to make some tough decisions later. Those were worries for another time. One more victory, and McVay could finally exhale.

Except, even as he neared the end of his fanatical quest, McVay didn't feel like he was on the verge of fulfillment. He had ground himself down, but it wasn't just that. Something about the single-minded obsession with winning a championship, and the behavior he had rationalized along the way, had cost him a piece of his identity. The past three years had taken a toll on him—part of what he'd later call "a slow creep away from the person that you want to be." Hoisting a Lombardi was still the goal, but it was suddenly a strain to think about what came next.

Would McVay walk away after winning a Super Bowl—or not winning it? Inside the Rams' training facility, it was an open secret that he might. "He had mentioned it at times," said Ejiro Evero, the Rams' secondary coach and passing-game coordinator that season. "He has a hard time stepping away from it, which is a blessing and a curse, obviously."

There was a logical and lucrative escape route, too: the salaries for top NFL television analysts were exploding, with CBS having signed former Cowboys quarterback Tony Romo to a reported ten-year, $180 million deal in 2017. Amazon Prime would soon be competing for talent; ESPN was looking for a star analyst to be its new *Monday Night Football* centerpiece. McVay had suitors, and options—and stood to make even more money broadcasting than he would coaching, with $10 million per year likely the starting point for negotiations. At 36, he could recharge, try his hand at a new venture, and plot a potential return to coaching down the road.

Eventually, news of McVay's possible departure became public. At a press conference two days before the Super Bowl, he was asked about his future. Normally, a coach would squelch the speculation, to head off any potential distractions before the biggest game of his players' lives. McVay kept the mystery alive. If still coaching at 60, he told reporters, "I won't make it." Asked why he felt that way, McVay initially said he'd been joking. He then spent a minute and a half talking about his inner struggle. "I love this so much that it's such a passion, but I also know what I've seen from some of my closest friends, whether it's coaches or even some of our players. I'm gonna be married this summer . . . I want to have a family, and I think being able to find that balance, but also be able to give the time necessary . . . I have always had a dream about being able to be a father and I can't predict the future, you know? . . . I don't really know."

McVay and fiancée Veronika Khomyn had twice postponed their wedding because of COVID-19-related complications, with a third date scheduled for that June. McVay had seen his father, Tim, avoid coaching, after growing up as the son of an NFL coach and general manager who spent a lot of time away from home. Said McVay, "One of the things that prevented [Tim] from getting into coaching was, 'Man, I had such a great relationship, but my dad missed out on a lot of the things,' but didn't want to do that with me and my little brother. So, I always remembered that, and at some point, I want to be able to have a family. So, that's why I say that.'"

So, yes, McVay was the biggest story heading into Super Bowl LVI. However, as he and O'Connell formulated their plan for attacking the Bengals' defense, they had a sense that Odell Beckham Jr. would quickly seize the moment. Beckham, an immensely talented receiver who'd become an immediate star with the New York Giants in 2014, was now on his third team. A few months earlier, he'd been released by the Cleveland Browns and picked the Rams over several other teams. "I remember thinking to myself about three days before the game, 'I think Odell Beckham's going to be the Super Bowl MVP,'" O'Connell recalled. "Just knowing how they would defend Cooper [Kupp], knowing he would get some one-on-one matchups. I remember thinking we had a great game plan."

Sure enough, Beckham scored the game's first points, hauling in a 17-yard touchdown pass from Stafford with 6:22 left in the first quarter and moonwalking in celebration. He had a 35-yard reception early in the second quarter as the Rams went on another touchdown drive. Then, with 3:50 left in the half, Beckham ran a short crossing route and, as Stafford's pass arrived, suddenly went down without being touched—never a good sign. He grabbed at his left knee; he was done, his ACL torn, a huge blow for him personally and a major limiting factor for the Rams' attack.

L.A. led 13–10 at halftime, but with Beckham out, McVay and O'Connell worried about the Rams' ability to keep scoring. Defensive coordinator Raheem Morris, mindful that the Rams might pivot to a more conservative plan on offense, knew his unit had to lock down Burrow and the Bengals.

Before the game, one of Morris's major concerns was defending the Bengals when they went "empty"—with no player lined up in the backfield other than Burrow. By inserting an extra pass rusher, Morris felt he could compel Cincinnati to move away from that formation and add more pass protectors. At halftime, Morris initiated a switch to a 5–0 formation—a variation of their dime defense, with six defensive backs on the field. The other five players would be pass rushers (defensive linemen and linebackers coming off the edge), with no linebackers roaming the middle of the field. This would often force the Bengals' five offensive linemen into one-on-

one matchups with the pass rushers when Burrow dropped back to throw, something that worked to the advantage of All-Pro defensive tackle Aaron Donald and elite edge rusher Von Miller. And playing a five-man front on running downs also helped bottle up Cinci's ground game.

Morris would go down as one of the Rams' Super Bowl LVI heroes, a result that seemed unlikely after the first play of the second half. Burrow lined up under center, faked a handoff, stepped up in the pocket to avoid pressure, and heaved a deep sideline pass to wide receiver Tee Higgins inside the Rams 40, with star cornerback Jalen Ramsey in coverage. As the pass came down, Higgins used his left hand to pull Ramsey's head around, grabbing the defender's face mask in the process—but no flag was thrown. Ramsey fell down and Higgins caught the ball and cruised into the end zone, giving Cincinnati a 17–13 lead.

On the Rams' first snap of the half, Stafford threw over the middle to wide receiver Ben Skowronek, Beckham's replacement. The ball bounced off Skowronek's hands and was picked off by Bengals cornerback Chidobe Awuzie for Stafford's second interception of the game. Now the Bengals had a chance to extend their lead, and Beckham's absence meant the Rams would have to manufacture yards and points. The Bengals took over at the Rams 31 and drove to the 11, but on third and three, Donald got a favorable matchup and sacked Burrow. Cincinnati settled for a field goal and a 20–13 lead. "One of the things that I thought was as big a deal as anything was, we ended up getting a crucial sudden-change stop right there," McVay recalled.

Said Evero, "We knew we weren't getting much from the offense. Give Raheem credit: he had a good plan. We talked about the five-man front for [defending] the run game. Our guys adjusted well and played their asses off in the second half."

After that field goal, the Rams' defense was dominant. The Bengals, in their five remaining possessions, managed just four first downs. Miller had two sacks, and rookie linebacker Ernest Jones (often blocked by a running back, thanks to Morris's scheme shift) and defensive tackle A'Shawn Robinson had one apiece. The Rams cut the lead to 20–16 on a third-quarter field goal and then embarked on a 15-play touchdown drive from their own 21 with 6:13 left in the game. Three plays in, the Rams faced fourth and one from their own 30. McVay kept his offense on the field, a high-risk move. The call was for Stafford, lined up under center, to hand the ball to Kupp, who had motioned from the left slot and was running to his right. The play had been a disaster in practices leading up to the game, Stafford and Kupp fumbling the handoff several times. The quarterback and receiver had tweaked the play design to make it more efficient; McVay signed off on the adjustment, but the Rams had never repped the new version. No matter—Kupp took the handoff and cut inside for a seven-yard gain.

Five plays later, on second and seven from the Bengals 46, Stafford hit Kupp on a no-look pass that went for 22 yards, bailing out what McVay later described as a horrendous play call. "If you said, 'What's the worst coverage that you could get for this high-low concept, that concept we hit Cooper Kupp on . . . there's like two coverages where you're saying, 'That should be a dead play.' Well, one of them, we got . . . when basically [safety] Vonn Bell's dropping right into that area that's where that point of attack is, and what happened? Matthew Stafford and Cooper made it right."

Helped by a defensive holding call on Stafford's third-and-goal incompletion to Kupp, and a pass interference penalty on another attempted hookup between the pair, the Rams finally reached the end zone: on a one-yard pass to Kupp, the eventual Super Bowl MVP, with 1:25 remaining. "It just felt like the never-ending drive that culminated in us giving a fade ball to Cooper," O'Connell said. "That was going to be Odell in the [original] plan. We're shifting formations on the goal line. Sean called a great, great drive."

Down 23–20, the Bengals quickly moved to the L.A. 49, where they faced second and one. However, after an incompletion on a deep ball from Burrow to Ja'Marr Chase and a Samaje Perine run for no gain, it was fourth and one. The Bengals called time-out. McVay paced back and forth on the Rams' sideline—his back to the field, his voice almost gone—imploring his defensive players to end it. "Hey!" he croaked. "What else could you want? What else could you want? Right now! Let's go! Let's go!" McVay looked at Donald, a three-time NFL Defensive Player of the Year and a Ram since 2014, when they were based in St. Louis: "Hey, Aaron, this is the moment. Right now."

As Burrow prepared to receive the snap, McVay put his hands on his knees and said into the coaching headset, "Aaron Donald's gonna make a play." He was prescient. Donald burst through the line and got to Burrow almost instantly, spinning the quarterback around as his desperation pass fell incomplete. It was over. McVay was a Super Bowl champion. The quest was over.

That night, at an airplane hangar at the Hawthorne airport, the Rams staged a massive victory party. "I got a chance to spend a lot of time with Sean that night in a reflective kind of mode, which was very, very special," recalled O'Connell, who'd already agreed to become the Vikings' next head coach. "There was nothing that gave me more joy than spending those few hours with Sean late into the night after that game, knowing that I was moving on. We had accomplished what he had brought me there for, and we had overcome some things that will always stay between him and I . . . all the ebbs and flows that some people know about and some people don't."

McVay, displaying what O'Connell called his "competitive stamina," partied deep into the morning while seemingly retaining every morsel from every conversation. The next day, when he began sorting through the barrage of congratulatory text messages he'd received, the victorious coach got a nice surprise. "The thing that shows what a stud and what a class act he really is, is one of the best text messages I got after the Super Bowl was from Jared Goff," he told me on my podcast, Open Mike, later that spring. "The further we get away, the more appreciation we'll have for the great four years we did have together because it was a lot of really good times . . . I wish I had handled [his departure] better as a leader for him."

The celebration continued three days later during a championship parade that traveled from the Shrine Auditorium to the L.A. Memorial Coliseum, the franchise's twice-former home. General manager Les Snead wore a T-shirt with the slogan "Fuck Them Picks" emblazoned over his own image, an ode to the popular meme about the Rams' win-now approach. At a subsequent rally outside the stadium, McVay seemed to be telegraphing his intentions. He led fans in a chant of "Run it back" during Donald's speech, a reference to the defensive tackle's own uncertain future and a plea for him not to retire. Later, McVay told fans, "I can't say enough about this team, the resilience, the mental toughness—Super Bowl champs. This shit will never ever get old!"

Not too long after the parade, McVay decided not to retreat to the TV booth—although the impending increase to his coaching salary certainly helped. "There were still too many people that it affected that I cared about that I didn't want to affect in a negative way," McVay said. "I think it was more like it was flattering to have those opportunities or discussions. It was just the financial ramifications, and really, sometimes your ego; you're like, 'OK, I'm going to step away on top.' If I had done that, I would have still gotten in trouble. The reason why you get into coaching is you love influencing and affecting guys and stuff like that."

Clearly, McVay was still struggling. For three years, he'd been convinced that getting back to the Super Bowl, and winning it, was his sole purpose. He hadn't just made sacrifices in that pursuit; he'd made rationalizations and compromises. Who was he, really? What did he stand for? What had he proven? What next? He now felt an emptiness he hadn't expected. "The lies I told myself were, 'Once you're fortunate enough to be part of a team that finishes that job, then it'll be kind of like you're complete.' Well, that's the wrong way to look at it."

Finding a better way would prove to be a process. Running it back would prove to be a fantasy.

———

ONE OF THE PERKS OF COACHING A TEAM TO A SUPER BOWL VICTORY typically comes a few weeks after the game, when the newly minted champion gets to spend seven or eight days in downtown Indianapolis, parading around the NFL scouting combine like a conquering hero. From the convention center hallways leading to Lucas Oil Stadium to the well-lit corners of Prime 47 steakhouse, the victor soaks up the admiration from peers in a relatively stress-free environment.

McVay, however, wasn't in Indy—and he was dealing with a ton of stress. Khomyn, his fiancée, was immersed in the terror of an existential threat to her home country: Russia had invaded Ukraine, where her parents still lived, in late February. Since then, she and Sean had gone to bed each night dreading the possibility of a middle-of-the-night phone call that could shatter their world. McVay skipped the combine entirely.

By early June, Ukraine's resistance had stiffened, and the terror had slightly subsided. As McVay put it, "What a perspective when you say things are getting better when the bomb sirens only go off a couple of times a day, instead of ten to 15 times a day."

Amid the difficult backdrop, Sean and Veronika staged a festive wedding at the Beverly Hills Hotel that featured many associates from his coaching past (including Matt LaFleur, Brandon Staley, O'Connell, Jedd Fisch, and Jay Gruden) and present. Raheem and Nikki Morris's children, aged three and six, played roles in the ceremony. Andrew Whitworth, Matthew Stafford, Cooper Kupp, and Aaron Donald—now firmly committed to returning for the 2022 season—were among the players who attended. Odell Beckham crashed the event, and everyone seemed happy to see him.

Shanahan wasn't there, and his absence was a topic of conversation among many of the other coaches present. It was assumed that McVay hadn't invited him. The two coaches were friendly and had a ton of mutual respect, but there was a distance between them exacerbated by how frequently their teams clashed on the field.

To his credit, Shanahan was up front about all of it. At the annual league meeting in March, the first time he had seen McVay since their NFC Championship Game showdown, Shanahan told McVay he'd had a hard time watching the Rams' Super Bowl victory two weeks later. "My wife hates you more than me," Shanahan told him, laughing, "but that was fucking hard to watch you guys win." Shanahan added that he was drunk during the game, for obvious reasons, telling McVay, "I can't watch that fucking game."

None of this detracted from McVay's post–Super Bowl matrimonial glow. Four months after winning a Super Bowl ring, he and his wife went on a honeymoon. The Rams' honeymoon would last only slightly longer.

THE FIRST SIGN OF TROUBLE CAME IN TRAINING CAMP, WHEN STAFFORD stopped throwing in team drills. He'd experienced issues with his throwing elbow all offseason, at one point receiving an anti-inflammatory shot.

He hadn't participated in OTAs and began training camp on a "pitch count" before McVay started holding him out of the more significant practice sessions—and, at times, all of them. Publicly, the coach and quarterback downplayed the situation, explaining that Stafford would be good to go on Thursday night, September 8, when the Rams would host the Buffalo Bills to open the 2022 regular season. Privately, coaches were concerned.

The Rams, it turned out, were *not* good to go on September 8. They looked like a team overwhelmed by the occasion. The offensive line was a mess. Stafford got sacked seven times—the most in the McVay era—and hit on 16 other occasions. Buffalo rolled to a 31–10 victory. It would not prove to be an aberration. In early October, during a 24–9 road defeat to the 49ers on *Monday Night Football* that dropped them to 2–2, the defending champs looked far from potent. Stafford forced the ball to Kupp and tight end Tyler Higbee, who combined for 33 of his 48 targets, while wide receiver Allen Robinson, a high-priced free-agent signee, made little impact. The Rams were 3–3 coming out of their bye week before everything collapsed, beginning with a 31–14 defeat to the Niners at SoFi that set off a six-game losing streak. By the end of November, Kupp (ankle), Stafford (spinal cord contusion), and Donald (ankle) had all been shut down for the season.

In a sense, McVay, too, was shutting down. Early in the regular season, he had been more present at team facilities, and in his interactions with players, coaches, and other Rams staff members. Now, as he had the prior year, he retreated to his home office, especially on Mondays and Tuesdays. Sometimes, he withdrew emotionally. Other times, he let everyone around him know how miserable he was. He was often in a bad mood, and he vented accordingly. Even his trademark slogan, "we, not me," began to ring hollow. As one Rams assistant put it in 2023, "There wasn't a whole lot of 'we' last year. There was a lot of 'me.'"

Before an October game against the Cowboys, McVay, who was sick and working from home, floated the idea of giving up play calling to newly hired offensive coordinator Liam Coen. This was after the lifeless performance in that Monday night defeat to the 49ers, and some of the other Rams assistants perceived this suggestion as McVay setting up Coen as a fall guy. At the very least, the optics weren't good. Some coaches asked Morris to talk to McVay about the wisdom of such a decision; eventually, assistant head coach Thomas Brown did so. McVay relented and decided to keep calling plays, even admitting to players in a team meeting that he'd had a "moment of weakness," but that "I'm here for you now." Later in the season, McVay did cede play-calling responsibilities to Coen before reclaiming the job after a 26–10 defeat to the Chiefs.

McVay was shaken during this dismal stretch by the death of his grandfather. John McVay, the 49ers' legendary general manager during their '80s dynasty, was 91 when he passed away on October 31, 2022. Sean had long admired his grandfather's grace and inherent kindheartedness, qualities not always associated with highly successful men in that unrelenting profession. As he grieved, McVay wondered whether he was measuring up.

He did so in the only way he knew: by working. McVay achieved a measure of clarity about the 2022 Rams, recognizing some poor dynamics between coaches and players that would help him make decisions on which staff members to move on from after the season. Most of all, he learned how much he hated not calling plays. "The great thing was, trying it made me realize, 'No, I definitely don't want to do that.'"

Still, the thought that he should have perhaps taken a broadcast job creeped in. One realization that hit McVay that fall was just how good he'd had it since arriving in L.A. in 2017. Four years before he was hired by the Rams, he'd watched his boss, a two-time Super Bowl–winning head coach, get swallowed up by organizational toxicity in Washington and spit out into retirement. What Mike Shanahan navigated during that 2013 season—and, really, throughout his four years as the coach of Dan Snyder's franchise—had been illuminating and instructive to his young tight ends coach. Had McVay, after his immediate success with the Rams, forgotten how cruel the profession could be?

McVay also seemed to need a reminder that his path to becoming an NFL head coach wasn't exactly paved with potholes. "You try to work as hard as you can to earn everything you get. You really just think about what other people have gone through. When you talk about being a beneficiary of timing and things working out to your favor, it's a joke how lucky I've really been."

ONE REASON McVAY FELT FORTUNATE WAS THAT MORRIS WAS THERE TO help him. As in 2021, the unfailingly upbeat defensive coordinator served as a steadying force for his longtime friend and encouraged him not to remain isolated during times of despair. Morris, McVay recalled, was "steady as hell. If you were to say, what's one of Raheem's best traits that I think is the separator in life, it's his mental toughness. He just doesn't let shit bother him."

Schematically, McVay also experienced a reckoning. With Stafford sidelined, the offensive line struggling, and Kupp responsible for a disproportionate share of the passing attack, McVay the strategist couldn't simply come up with a cure-all game plan. He'd always had so much faith in his system—and, perhaps, a misplaced conviction in the ability of scrappy backup quarterback John Wolford's ability to run it—that the Rams' current offensive ineptitude seemed almost unthinkable. Eventually, he would have to confront Wolford's limitations and bring in a more accomplished alternative.

After that late-November defeat to the Chiefs in Kansas City, which made it five losses in a row, McVay called a meeting with his assistants during which he fervently implored them to raise their standard and focus on teaching and developing players. The Rams lost again the following Sunday, with Wolford emerging from a 27–23 defeat to the Seahawks with neck soreness. The next day, the Carolina Panthers released Baker Mayfield, Beckham's old nemesis in Cleveland. The No. 1 pick in the 2018 draft, Mayfield was seen by many as a bust, though he had guided the Browns to a resounding playoff victory in Pittsburgh just two seasons earlier. The Rams pounced, claiming Mayfield on waivers. He arrived in L.A. on Tuesday night, roughly 48 hours before the Rams would host the Las Vegas Raiders on *Thursday Night Football*. The notion of Mayfield assimilating an unfamiliar offense and playing in that game was absurd by NFL standards—yet that's exactly what happened.

On the game's second series, with the Rams already trailing 10–0, Mayfield took over for Wolford. Hours later, with 1:41 remaining in the game, it was 16–10 Raiders when L.A. got the ball back at its own two-yard line. Mayfield, who'd already led a scoring drive earlier in the fourth quarter, took the Rams on an epic march that ended with him throwing a game-winning 23-yard touchdown pass to wide receiver Van Jefferson. Nine seconds remained. McVay celebrated like a man who'd just been told by doctors that his terminal diagnosis was mistaken. "That game was like an exorcism," McVay said.

Mayfield started the season's final four games, with McVay placing a renewed emphasis on the running game and play-action passes that flowed from it. L.A. would lose three of those games—the lone exception a 51–14 thrashing of the Broncos on Christmas Day, a result that would trigger the firing of first-year Denver coach Nathaniel Hackett, Matt LaFleur's former offensive coordinator in Green Bay—but McVay was starting to emerge from his malaise. Rams chief operating officer Kevin Demoff and Snead had given McVay the option of taking a one-year sabbatical in 2023. That was one possibility; quitting outright was another. At season's end, McVay considered his choices for about a week before deciding, emphatically, that he would return.

By May of 2023, as he presided over an OTA practice full of players with whom even the most rabid Rams fans were unfamiliar, McVay had convinced himself that he once again was headed in the right direction. He was "still growing and figuring things out and learning from my mistakes. I think when you're forced to grow up professionally in front of the world, I'm not afraid of those scars that occurred—especially last year." The one-time wunderkind was entering a new phase of his journey. Veronika was pregnant, and McVay looked forward with a fervor that matched his previous pursuit of a Lombardi. "We're having a boy," he said, "and she's due on the very day that my grandfather passed away last year. Isn't that wild?"

He smiled like a man who wasn't sure what parenting entailed, but who couldn't wait to get started. Soon, he'd be a father. He knew to his core that, most of all, *that* was the person he wanted to be.

Chapter 21

The Liberation of Mike McDaniel

It was petty. It was punitive. And for Mike McDaniel, it was ten seconds of pure bliss.

He was back in Levi's Stadium for an early-December game against the 49ers, this time on the visitors' sideline. A battle between two scorching-hot teams was about to commence, and the rookie head coach of the Miami Dolphins had a surprise for his longtime mentor and sometime tormentor, Kyle Shanahan.

He chose to make a statement on the first play from scrimmage. McDaniel figured Shanahan's second-year defensive coordinator, DeMeco Ryans, would go against tendency and open the game with a blitz—as a means of showing McDaniel, his former colleague, that he wouldn't just sit back in predictable coverages and let a coach who knew Shanahan's scheme better than anyone but Shanahan himself pick it apart.

McDaniel was a step ahead. He felt he could further bait Ryans into blitzing by trotting out a personnel grouping the Dolphins hadn't used all year. He lined up Tua Tagovailoa in the shotgun and dialed up one of the young quarterback's favorite plays: a jet-motion RPO (run-pass option). Running backs Raheem Mostert and Alec Ingold were split behind Tagovailoa. Star receiver Tyreek Hill motioned left across the line of scrimmage, cut back to his right, and sprinted toward the sideline as the ball was snapped. Ingold, after selling a play fake from Tagovailoa, ran a scissors (crossing) concept with Mostert, a former 49ers standout. Sure enough, Ryans blitzed one linebacker (Dre Greenlaw), while two others (Fred Warner and Azeez Al-Shaair) cheated up toward the backfield. Another Dolphins receiver, Trent Sherfield, leaked down the right seam to the area Warner had vacated, caught Tagovailoa's crisp pass in stride, and cut diagonally to his left, with safety Tashaun Gipson caught flat-footed amid the confusion.

And then, suddenly, Sherfield, who'd spent the 2021 season with the 49ers before following McDaniel to Miami, was racing down the left sideline for a 75-yard touchdown while his head coach left his feet to do a celebratory, back-facing body slam with an assistant on the sideline.

It was the moment when the younger brother finally manhandles big bro on the backyard basketball court.

While McDaniel's revolt proved short-lived—the Niners, with the league's No. 1 defense and a team in the middle of what would be a 12-game winning streak, came back to win, 33–17—he'd still made his old boss feel his presence. Their reunion would prove to be significant to Shanahan for other reasons. Less than four minutes into the game, the Dolphins had knocked out Jimmy Garoppolo, the quarterback suffering a season-ending foot injury after being sacked by linebackers Jaelan Phillips and Jerome Baker. In came the 262nd and final pick of the 2022 draft, who proceeded to play with poise, precision, and savvy far beyond his meager pedigree. Brock Purdy was now the 49ers' quarterback of the present—and future.

To that point, however, the NFL's most stunning quarterback story of 2022 had McDaniel's handprints all over it. His revival of the embattled Tagovailoa had already shocked NFL coaches, talent evaluators, and fans in 2022. Yet as much as McDaniel sincerely credited Shanahan for so many things—giving him chances (and second and third chances) to succeed in the profession, teaching him an offensive system and philosophy, anointing him as an indispensable confidant and collaborator—McDaniel had some hard feelings. At various times during the two coaches' decade-and-a-half-long, mostly uninterrupted run together, McDaniel had felt held down, passed over, exploited, censured, scapegoated, silenced, and manipulated. Shanahan had blocked McDaniel from being interviewed for other jobs (though that is not uncommon in the profession) and tried to convince him he wasn't ready for the pressure and scrutiny that came with such promotions. He'd yelled at him frequently and profusely, sometimes blaming him for things beyond McDaniel's control.

And the previous January, when the career assistant's dream of becoming an NFL head coach was finally in sight, Shanahan—in the eyes of some people close to McDaniel—had tried to derail it.

Shortly after concluding a 9–8 season, Dolphins owner Stephen Ross fired coach Brian Flores, a surprising end to the three-year tenure of one of the NFL's more promising Black coaches. Part of that had to do with Flores's brusque leadership style and abrasive interpersonal skills. The Dolphins began a search for a kinder, gentler successor, and eventually McDaniel, in his first year as Shanahan's nominal offensive coordinator, surfaced as a person of interest.

After the 49ers won the road playoff game against the Cowboys to advance to the divisional round, the Dolphins were allowed a preliminary discussion with McDaniel the following week. It was his first-ever head coaching interview, and it would take place on Zoom, four days before the Niners were to face the Packers at Lambeau Field. McDaniel, immersed in game prep, chose a window that wouldn't conflict with practice or meetings.

However, as the meeting approached, Shanahan abruptly changed the Niners' schedule, moving practice to coincide with McDaniel's interview slot. McDaniel's agent (Richmond Flowers, his former assistant-coaching colleague in Washington) called the Dolphins, apologized, and nailed down a new time. Then, with little warning, Shanahan changed the schedule *again*. That meant the interview would be pushed back to Wednesday, January 19—three days before the game, making it the equivalent of a Thursday in a normal week of prep. The Dolphins, with many other candidates and interview slots to juggle, weren't thrilled. Neither was McDaniel, who experienced even more stress than he normally would during the postseason.

"I was just getting pulled on both ends," McDaniel told me the following June. "I wasn't gonna shortchange the team, though. But then I also really wanted the opportunity. So, they did it at the hardest [time], when I'm most depleted. Everybody that's ever worked with me knows on Thursday after practice, I'm just, like, [the most mentally exhausted]. It was right after that practice, when I was, like, in zombie mode."

McDaniel actually left the field shortly before practice was over, after the day's last offensive period. He still had to prepare for a meeting with Shanahan later that day to go over the runs in the game plan, a significant part of his week. He showered, put on a suit, and was spirited from the team's training facility to an upstairs suite at adjacent Levi's Stadium—"a fucking location I'd never been to." The interview lasted 50 minutes, and McDaniel—whose dry sense of humor and nuanced communication style tend to play much better in person—believed he'd bombed.

If the Dolphins had been annoyed over twice rescheduling McDaniel's interview, they also viewed it as a good sign. To team president and CEO Tom Garfinkel, it was an indication of how much Shanahan valued McDaniel.

"I think Kyle would do *anything* to try to avoid losing Mike," one 49ers veteran told me as the drama was playing out.

Some NFL coaches, including Bill Walsh, took pride in their assistants getting more prestigious gigs elsewhere and actively nurtured new branches of their coaching trees. Shanahan wasn't exactly known for that. When Matt LaFleur became the Packers' head coach in 2019 and wanted to hire his younger brother as his offensive coordinator, Shanahan said absolutely not—though it would have been an obvious promotion for Mike LaFleur, then the Niners' passing-game coordinator. A year earlier, newly hired Cardinals coach Kliff Kingsbury had "put in a slip" requesting to interview McDaniel (then the Niners' run game coordinator) for offensive coordinator. McDaniel learned of this not from Kingsbury, or from his agent, but from Shanahan.

"Kyle called me directly," McDaniel recalled, "and he said something that was pretty funny. He called me and said, 'Yeah, Arizona just put in a request for you.' I was like, 'Really?' He goes, 'Yeah, I blocked that shit so fucking fast. Ha ha.'"

What a dick, McDaniel thought.

After the 2020 season, when newly hired Chargers coach Brandon Staley was interested in McDaniel as his offensive coordinator—an opportunity for autonomous control of an attack featuring an emerging star in second-year quarterback Justin Herbert—the 49ers squelched that, too.

McDaniel's promotion to offensive coordinator had been announced days earlier by the 49ers, and Shanahan was averse to losing him.

Shanahan, per NFL rules, didn't have the power to keep McDaniel from pursuing the Dolphins job. Though it's likely Shanahan didn't accurately gauge the Dolphins' interest. Additionally, he felt he had an insurance policy. Though not yet known publicly, the Dolphins had a secret plan. Six days after McDaniel's Zoom interview, with the Niners now preparing to face the Rams in the NFC Championship Game, Sean Payton stepped down after 16 years as the New Orleans Saints' coach. Eight days later, Tom Brady, following the Buccaneers' divisional-round playoff defeat to the Rams, announced his retirement. The Dolphins, via back-channel communications with both parties, were prepared to bring both men to Miami as a package deal, with Brady receiving a small ownership stake. Miami would have had to compensate both the Saints and Bucs as part of the plan, so there were a lot of moving parts. Shanahan, who'd heard about the scheme, felt confident he wouldn't lose his offensive coordinator.

Then, just hours after Brady's retirement announcement, everything changed. Flores filed a class-action lawsuit against the NFL and three teams, including the Dolphins, alleging racism in hiring practices. The Dolphins, now on the defensive, scrapped their plan to hire Payton, who is white, and continued their search. McDaniel, considered a minority via NFL policy because he is three-eighths Black, was deemed worthy of a second, in-person interview. (McDaniel's biracial status had not been known to the general public until the spring of 2021, when he talked about it with NBC Sports Bay Area's Matt Maiocco—just months after the NFL enacted a policy awarding teams compensatory picks when minority coaches or GMs they'd cultivated were hired by other organizations.) The Dolphins waited out the NFC Championship Game and, because the 49ers lost, were allowed to bring in McDaniel the following week.

McDaniel, slim, short, and ironic, knew he didn't fit the archetypical mold of an NFL head coach. He also had his past issues with alcohol to address. He'd never been a play caller. His sense of humor and presentation were an acquired taste. He knew the Dolphins were high on other candidates, including Bills offensive coordinator Brian Daboll (who would be hired by the New York Giants as head coach before Miami concluded its search) and Cardinals defensive coordinator Vance Joseph. "I'm not sure, going into it, if I was the crowd favorite or not," was how he'd drily put it to me the following June as we sat in a Fort Lauderdale restaurant.

It wasn't hard to see why the Dolphins would be intrigued. "I told people who asked us, 'He might be Belichick,'" recalled Vikings general manager Kwesi Adofo-Mensah, who was the 49ers' director of football research and development during McDaniel's first three seasons there. "I don't use the word *genius* lightly, but he might be one. He's unique. I'm glad that the genuine self, people have accepted. He is, and I'm not kidding with this, he's me—the analytical brain—with Kyle's football sense. That is a dangerous combination for a coach. You talk about a players' coach. I have players that I come across, to this day, who tell me, 'He's my favorite coach. He knows how to get the best out of us. He cares about making me a better player.' His players love him."

All McDaniel wanted was a chance to have a chance to impress in person; now, thanks to Flores, he would have it.

BY THIS POINT, McDANIEL HAD MADE A DECISION. INSTEAD OF FIXATING on the fact that other coaches his age (McVay, Matt LaFleur, and now Mike LaFleur, who'd become a play-calling offensive coordinator with the Jets) had seemingly leapfrogged him, McDaniel would just put his head down, work on his craft, and—most of all—remain true to himself.

The catch was that he wasn't the most polished candidate when the Dolphins came calling—though, in his eyes, that ended up being an advantage. "What's tricky is then you get, 'Oh hey, this team wants to interview you,'" he said. "Well, I just spent a lot of time *not worrying* about the interview. So then, all of a sudden . . . and it's during the playoffs . . . and I didn't have time to really overthink the whole thing."

Because this was his first and only head coaching interview, McDaniel figured it represented a chance to practice. "I was looking at it like this: from a historical perspective, a guy gets an interview, OK, now you've got a real shot the next cycle. So, that's the way I was approaching it. So, I did an interview over Zoom, then they asked me for a second one, and then I got my feet on the ground . . . and I met the people in the building, and [general manager] Chris Grier was giving me a tour, and I had a bunch of background information from people that had worked for the Miami Dolphins, a lot of coaches have come through . . . and I'm realizing, live speed, 'This is everything I've ever wanted.' I'd been in six different organizations, and I'm recognizing that this place has all the utility and just needs a head coach to fit within . . . People don't understand, a lot goes into a football team. And you have to have synergy from coaching staff and players, but also all the support staff—and those are the ones that deal with players every day. And I've been in organizations where they have been a huge root of a problem, whether it's training staff, video department, equipment. And I'm like, 'Whoa, this is perfect.'

"So now, I'm like, 'Oh, I can't mess this up.' It was hyperfocus—like, 'OK, you just worked 39 years; you've got about eight hours, dude.'"

As McDaniel pursued what he now realized was his dream job, Shanahan remained unprepared for the imminent departure of his long-time right-hand man—at least, that's how Mike LaFleur would frame it to me later on. "Isn't that wild that Kyle didn't even know the scope of what was going on because he doesn't pay attention to shit except for his team? From afar, I was like, he's going to get this Miami job. Kyle has to know. McDaniel's like, 'I don't think he has any idea.'"

Soon, everyone would know. McDaniel aced the second interview, largely by being himself. He was deemed to be the opposite of the former guy—Flores, a former Bill Belichick assistant in New England, had been domineering, paranoid, combative, and very, very hard on Tagovailoa, among other things—which is always a bonus in such situations. Flores came from a defensive background, another contrast to McDaniel. While Flores's lawsuit had merit, many people in the coaching community, and in the Dolphins building, had come to a consensus: he surely did not deserve to be fired based on his solid three-year record or coaching aptitude, which is significant; however, given the way he comported himself, including when dealing with his bosses, it didn't seem outlandish that owner Stephen Ross made the move.

Shanahan was stung by the loss of McDaniel. The sole consolation had been that the Dolphins were the team to poach his longtime right-hand man. The plan had been for Foerster to come along as McDaniel's offensive coordinator, but given that coach's unfortunate history in the Dolphins facility, a move back to Miami was a nonstarter. Instead, Shanahan was able to keep him in San Francisco, promoting him to run game coordinator. Then again, Mike LaFleur isn't convinced Foerster would have followed McDaniel anywhere. "Mike might *think* he was coming with him. There's three people that aren't getting out of that San Francisco building: [defensive line coach Kris] Kocurek and Foerster, and Nick Bosa."

As he embarked upon his new journey, McDaniel had to assemble a staff, import and install an offensive system, collaborate with Grier on key personnel decisions, and resuscitate the flagging career of an embattled quarterback, among many other challenges. McDaniel was immersed in the grind, but he wasn't buckling under the pressure of the tasks at hand or the win-now expectation that hung over it all—worse than usual in Miami, given that he'd inherited a 9–8 team. Yes, he had more responsibility than ever before. He also seemed more relaxed.

There was a lightness to McDaniel that belied his circumstances, but it made sense. Yes, he had a lengthy to-do list.. He also had . . . freedom. Shanahan wasn't there to yell at him for things beyond his control, to prod him relentlessly. McDaniel owed many of his opportunities to Shanahan, and could thank him for much of his career. And certainly, while fighting through his issues with alcohol, McDaniel had needed Shanahan's support to stay in the game. Yet when would it end? In the words of Joe Staley, the 49ers' starting left tackle for more than a decade, "Kyle needs someone he can 'Bad dog!' That was McDaniel. It almost made you feel responsible, like, 'I've got to play better, so this poor guy doesn't get berated.'"

Matt LaFleur, as someone who was once the frequent object of Shanahan's ire, understood better than almost anyone. "Mike's been around Kyle more than anybody, going back to frickin' Denver [as an intern for Mike Shanahan], even if it wasn't in that type of role. Obviously, he's been with him the longest. Kyle was hard as shit on Mike. I think anybody that's been around him and can endure that is going to be better for it, too. It's not the worst thing when people are hard on you. Honestly, it raises your own level of expectation that you have for yourself."

McDaniel, no longer subject to constant backlash, quickly found a comfort zone. Fans and media members were getting his jokes and digging his vibe. In February, a local sports anchor had ended an interview on the Dolphins' practice field by asking McDaniel to play "Kiss, Marry, Kill" (a PG-13 variation of the popular hypothetical game) with former colleagues Kyle Shanahan, McVay, and Matt LaFleur as his options. McDaniel, wearing a blue suit and red tie, went with the bit, complete with deadpan delivery and explanations. "I'll start with Matt, I'd kiss him because he's, uh, most endearing. I would marry Kyle because I've spent the most time with him, so I should marry him, and I would kill Sean because he just was the last team that I played and he beat me."

IF McDANIEL EXPECTED TO HAVE ANY SUCCESS AS A ROOKIE HEAD coach, much of that would depend upon his quarterback. Tagovailoa had been an instant star in the college ranks, coming off the bench at halftime of the national championship game in January of 2018, as a true freshman, in relief of future NFL star Jalen Hurts, with Alabama trailing 13–0. He sparked a comeback that culminated with his walk-off touchdown pass on second and 26, giving the Crimson Tide an overtime victory over Georgia. Two years later, the lefty from Oahu entered the draft as the holder of numerous NCAA records. Quarterback Joe Burrow, who'd won a national championship with LSU, went first overall to the Bengals. The Dolphins, with the fifth pick, could choose between Tagovailoa and Oregon's Herbert, who was bigger, taller, and more athletic. Miami selected Tua. The Chargers took Herbert with the next pick. In week two of his rookie season, Herbert made an emergency start when a Chargers team doctor mistakenly punctured Tyrod Taylor's lung while giving a pregame pain-killing injection. With literally 60 seconds of notice, as Taylor was being rushed to the hospital, Herbert took over, played like a seasoned pro, and nearly defeated Patrick Mahomes and the Kansas City Chiefs. The next week, Herbert looked the part again. Soon, he was a star.

Tagovailoa, meanwhile, got benched by Flores on more than one occasion late in the 2020 season, with the Dolphins fighting for a playoff berth. Things degenerated in 2021 as Miami sputtered to a 1–7 start. As the November 2 trade deadline neared, Flores pushed hard for the team to acquire Texans quarterback Deshaun Watson, who was embroiled in a scandal involving alleged sexual misconduct during numerous private massages. The trade would have happened had Watson been able to settle all 24 of the outstanding civil lawsuits against him, but because at least two plaintiffs refused to do so, Ross nixed the deal.

Still, even as Miami rallied to win seven consecutive games to get back into playoff contention, Tua's time as the team's franchise quarterback looked as though it would be fleeting. It was as if he had *Not Justin Herbert* on the back of his jersey. Flores's notoriously bad bedside manner and obvious desire to replace him didn't help Tagovailoa's flagging confidence.

McDaniel's first mission was to prop him up. After accepting the job, McDaniel flew back to South Florida from Northern California on Ross's private plane and, with the team's in-house camera crew documenting the moment, hit up Tagovailoa on FaceTime. McDaniel, wearing oversized AirPods, knew his half of the conversation, at least, was likely to be shared with the masses, and his enthusiasm was manifest. "One thing I know about you is you have the ambition to be great," he told the quarterback as McDaniel's then 16-month-old daughter, Ayla, fussed in the background. "My job is to coach you to get all that greatness out of you." Toward the end of the brief conversation, McDaniel seemed to be hamming it up, telling Tua, "It's on, bro. If you don't have any eye black at home, you better go get some eye black. 'Cause we're going."

That McDaniel exuded positivity was nothing new, and it wasn't specific to Tagovailoa. Since I'd known him, when discussing virtually any player, his first impulse was to highlight that player's redeeming qualities, almost with a sense of wonderment. So many NFL coaches, striving for perfection in a chaotic sport, tended to complain about the inability or unwillingness of the men they coached to perform as directed. McDaniel was more likely to begin and end his evaluations with "Let me tell you what this guy does that's amazing . . ."

To Jets coach Robert Saleh, now McDaniel's AFC East rival, this mentality could be traced not to Kyle Shanahan, but to the exacting coach who gave McDaniel his first break: "Papa Shanahan's method was 'I don't want to hear what the player can't do. Tell me what he can do, and then tell me how you're going to implement it on the football field.'"

While Tagovailoa lacked height and athleticism, it wasn't as though he didn't have talent. His ability to release the ball quickly, decisively, and accurately into tight windows had been apparent at Alabama; if nothing else, McDaniel believed he could turn Tua into the NFL equivalent of a point guard, and scheme accordingly. That is, if Tagovailoa's confidence and self-esteem hadn't been completely dismantled by the prior regime, and all the noise that he was a colossal bust.

As he looked deeper into Tagovailoa's psyche, the first thing McDaniel saw was a reflection of himself. "I found it was hard for me to not look at him and think of my experience," he said. "And in my experience in the world, I'm a head coach now and I know where I came from. How did I even have a chance to even fulfill this overly ambitious vision, or drive, or dream that I had? And I knew I would've had no chance had I not been built up by my mom, to 'You know what? You can do anything. You are the smartest . . .' Everything a single mom would tell a child.

"And so I saw Tua like that. Like, how can we even approach the idea of we know what this player is, when I don't know from my vantage point? Who does this guy have who believes in him? So, we have to start with, he has to know that someone's 100 percent in his corner—which I see as that's what a coach is—and that 'No, dude, you can do it.' So, I had to convince him that I believed in him so that he could in turn allow himself [to believe]. Because I've been through it."

As free agency approached in mid-March, McDaniel held the conviction that to unleash Tua, the Dolphins needed explosive players in the passing game. They'd drafted one such player—wide receiver Jaylen Waddle, Tua's former teammate at Alabama—sixth overall the previous year. McDaniel believed strongly that Miami needed another difference maker, the faster and more explosive the better.

In meetings between Grier and his personnel staffers, along with McDaniel and his assistants, a legitimate philosophical divide emerged. McDaniel knew "that Tua needed skill-position players that were dynamic with the ball in their hands, 'cause I saw him as, 'This dude is a point guard.' He has a gift that way. And then, so, the people in personnel were like, 'You know what? No. We need to spend money on offensive linemen.' And I could feel that—I *knew* that I disagreed with it. But I hate the 'Hey everyone, no, 'cause I said so.' So, I'm like, 'OK, cool, take in the information, let me go back to the office.'" What McDaniel proceeded to do was watch and cut tape of Dolphins pass plays during Tagovailoa's tenure, intending to demonstrate that Miami's receivers struggled to get open. "I'm watching the different skill positions," he recalled, "and as I progress through this tape, I start to notice this trend."

His pulse quickened. He sat up straighter in his chair as he watched play after play. It was, he'd recall, a "Marvel sesh," referring to the popular superhero movies. "And it's like, 'Wow, that's like the seventh different outbreak that I've watched Tua throw to the field.'" As McDaniel explained, "an outbreak to the field, I see once or twice from a particular quarterback in a season. Because the receiver's running away from you, meaning the ball's in the air longer, which is a higher risk for defenders to make up that ground, undercut, and pick-six for a catastrophic turnover. This is a high-risk throw that quarterbacks are very nervous to make." Not Tua. "So, like, let's say the ball is on the left hash," McDaniel said. "The receiver, from where the ball is snapped, the receiver on the right is running an out route, to the field. And he would make pinpoint throws that are down-the-field ten-yard throws, but are literally 40-yard throws."

McDaniel started compiling tape at around 6:30 p.m., his excitement growing by the minute. "I'm, like, freaking out, and I'm, like, I'm sitting on this. I know for a fact from this night of study that this is the best quarterback for our offense that I've had a chance to coach. And I'm, like, freaking out, right?"

He had to share his revelation. McDaniel called Anne Noland, the Dolphins' senior director of football communications, and told her to mark the date—March 7, 2022—and commemorate the moment. "This is *crazy!*" he said. His next call, at midnight, was to Grier. "Dude," McDaniel said, "I've just gotta tell you, I've gone through, like, 700 different passes, and I cannot believe what I'm seeing. This guy is doing stuff that, I just haven't focused all my attention on this quite yet, and . . . We are sitting on a gold mine. We need to do everything—everything we do moving forward should be [getting] skill-position players that have the ability to do stuff with the ball in their hands, because this guy, if they're open, he'll get it to them."

McDaniel continued to cut his tape, finally leaving the office at 1 a.m. He went home and tried to sleep, but his mind was racing. He knew, from his time with the 49ers, how players skilled at gaining yards after the catch ("YAC," in NFL terminology) such as Deebo Samuel, Brandon Aiyuk, and George Kittle could thrive in an offense featuring a quarterback who could fit the ball into tight windows. By 3 a.m., McDaniel was back in his office, refining the tape, unable to contain himself.

I need to show the whole organization this tape TODAY!

At 5:21 a.m., he sent Noland a text: *Call me when you feel like hearing genius.*

He waited until daybreak, when he figured Grier would be awake, and called the GM again. "Dude, sorry, but can we have a staff meeting at 8 a.m.?" McDaniel asked. "When are the scouts gonna be in? We're gonna have everybody in there, right? I need to show this tape. I have to get this off my chest."

A couple of hours later, McDaniel presented the tape to the entire staff, his excitement palpable as he ran through 150 clips that illustrated his point. He also included some plays from his 49ers days to suggest the offense's potential. By that afternoon, the team's analytics department had created charts for all available free-agent skill players, detailing their ability to separate and gain yards after the catch.

"And the whole organization saw it," McDaniel recalled, "and we just moved in the direction of, 'Alright, we're empowering Tua. Let's go.' "

McDaniel *knew* he was right. Now he had to convince his quarterback. Not long after he made the tape, the coach called Tagovailoa into his office and played it for him. If the tape had represented an epiphany for McDaniel, Tua's reaction was far more measured. The previous season had been so trying, he later revealed, that he would look in the mirror and ask himself, "Do I suck?"

"It was interesting," McDaniel recalled, "because it was like the most extreme case of a person not knowing how to take a compliment. You could tell he was not used to anything but overly constructive negativity. So, he didn't know how to take it. It was a slow momentum-building meeting that probably, clip 75, he starts participating. He's reading the room, like, 'This isn't a trick, right? This isn't a setup?' I can feel him get up in his chair. And then I'm making the pitch: 'OK, well dude, you were doing all this incredible stuff, and in my estimation, people aren't open enough. This is what it *should* look like.' . . . Showed him some stuff, he gets fired up, and by the end of it he's like, 'WE NEED PLAYMAKERS!'"

The eventual results would surpass even McDaniel's optimism. A week after the start of free agency, the Dolphins swung a blockbuster trade for Kansas City Chiefs All-Pro Tyreek Hill, the NFL's fastest receiver and most dangerous breakaway threat. Frustrated by his attempts to negotiate a new contract with the Chiefs, Hill had asked for a trade, with the Dolphins and Jets emerging as the most ardent suitors. Hill ultimately picked Miami, and the Chiefs, unwilling to meet his contractual price, honored his wishes. The Dolphins traded five draft picks, including their 2022 first-round selection, to land the six-time Pro Bowl receiver, giving him a massive contract extension in the process. They were all in.

For all the talk about McDaniel's past success in crafting the running game, his Dolphins offense would center on explosive plays. After Hill arrived in the building, McDaniel showed the receiver the Tua tape and explained his vision. "I was only going this direction if I was without a doubt positive in what I was saying. I wasn't gonna ruin my credibility with the organization or Tyreek Hill or anything. I showed him that, and then immediately Tyreek's like, 'Oh yeah, totally.'"

Hill's enthusiasm was reinforced during OTAs, when Tua began to develop at least a little swag. In McDaniel's words, "You could see a guy viscerally, in front of you, like, 'Maybe I *am* good.'"

As Dolphins offensive coordinator Frank Smith recalled, "If you didn't study the tape, you would've thought he can't do this, can't do that. But then when you watched him throwing to real NFL targets, you're like, 'He's good.' And he plays with timing, anticipation, and good fundamentals. But when you talked to him, he didn't even know why he was doing it. It was this lump of clay that didn't even realize his potential. So, we invested. We knew we had to give him players, so we tried to make sure that we invested in playmakers and tried to develop the talent we [already] had, and it worked out."

Recalled Tagovailoa, "Well, having someone that, first off, believes in you makes all the difference. Having someone that calls me randomly, just telling me how much I mean to him and the things that he's trying to accomplish and we are trying to accomplish as a team . . . yeah, it's cool . . . Love that guy."

On the practice field, Tagovailoa's teammates started to notice the change. In June, Hill was asked to compare Tua to his former teammate Patrick Mahomes, the NFL's brightest young star, already a Super Bowl winner (with another Lombardi Trophy, and third Super Bowl appearance, to come the following February). "As far as accuracy-wise, I'm going with Tua all day," Hill declared. The statement went viral, with a predictable outcry. To most fans, having watched Tagovailoa struggle for two years, it was as though a prominent rapper had declared that Lil Uzi Vert was a more skilled lyricist than Kendrick Lamar. To McDaniel, it made perfect sense.

IN MID-AUGUST, THE DOLPHINS STAGED JOINT WORKOUTS WITH THE Tampa Bay Buccaneers. Watching Tua shine against another team's defense further convinced the coach that he wasn't crazy. Still, nobody outside of the Dolphins' facility suspected what was coming.

"I felt like I was sitting on a secret forever," McDaniel recalled. Once the regular season began, he noted, "It didn't take long."

In week one, Tagovailoa completed 23 of 33 passes for 270 yards, with one touchdown and no interceptions, in a 20–7 victory over the Patriots. The next week, the Dolphins faced the Ravens in Baltimore and found themselves trailing 35–14 in the third quarter—and then the world shifted. Tua threw four touchdown passes *in the fourth quarter*, the last of which, a seven-yarder to Waddle with 14 seconds remaining, gave Miami a stunning 42–38 victory. On the day, he'd thrown for 469 yards and a franchise record–tying six TDs, including 48- and 60-yard strikes to Hill, who finished the day with 190 receiving yards on 11 receptions. Waddle was right behind him, with 171 yards on 11 catches.

Phew, I was right, thought McDaniel, who later noted, "And that's when people kinda stopped the 'Mike McDaniel's crazy' [talk] . . . they started to listen."

In week three, the Dolphins hosted the Buffalo Bills, considered by many at the time to be the league's best team. With the game tied at 14 late in the second quarter, Tagovailoa took a late hit from Bills linebacker Matt Milano after releasing a pass to Waddle, fell backward, and hit the back of his head on the grass. When he got up, he appeared wobbly. He shook his head repeatedly and seemed momentarily to adopt the "fencing" posture, with both hands pulled up toward his face mask. A few seconds later, he fell to the turf again.

To the naked eye, it certainly appeared as though Tagovailoa had suffered a concussion. He was taken to the locker room and evaluated; it was reported that he'd suffered a back injury. According to the Dolphins, doctors decreed that Tua's back had locked up after the hit by Milano and caused his "gross motor instability." The doctors cleared him after performing a concussion check, and he played the entire second half, with Miami prevailing, 21–19.

Understandably, there was intense skepticism surrounding the injury. McDaniel, only three games into his coaching career, defiantly insisted that the Dolphins had done everything according to protocol and would never subject their quarterback to undue risk. Four days later, they played a nationally televised game against the Bengals in Cincinnati, and things got much worse: Tagovailoa was sacked in the second quarter, again hitting his head on the turf. This time, while flat on his back, he clearly adopted the fencing posture. It was a scary sight. He was taken away on a stretcher and ruled out with a concussion, and McDaniel and the Dolphins were castigated by numerous critics (including Ravens coach John Harbaugh) as insensitive to the perils of head trauma, a controversial subject for a league that had paid out hundreds of millions of dollars in a class-action lawsuit brought by impacted former players.

The Dolphins, who lost that game to the Bengals, suffered two more defeats with Tagovailoa sidelined. He returned and resumed his stunning revival, playing at a high level while leading Miami to five consecutive victories. At that point, he was being talked up as an MVP candidate.

In early December, against the 49ers, Tagovailoa zipped that touchdown pass to Sherfield on the first play of the game. McDaniel had no way of knowing it at the time, but that would be the quarterback's high-water mark. The Dolphins lost that game, and their next four after that. Worst of all, following a three-interception performance in a Christmas Day defeat to the Packers, Tagovailoa reported symptoms—including memory issues—that led to another concussion diagnosis.

His season was over. In the ensuing days, weeks, and months, there was a lot of talk about Tua's football future—and, specifically, questions about whether the Dolphins could count on him as their quarterback going forward. McDaniel never wavered, even when the Ravens' star quarterback, South Florida native Lamar Jackson, showed interest in joining his hometown team via a trade during a contract dispute the following March. Over the offseason, Tagovailoa took jiujitsu classes in an attempt to learn how to protect himself when falling. He switched to a new helmet theoretically designed to provide better protection.

To McDaniel, Tua's ability to stay healthy was the only remaining impediment to a great NFL career.

"It was amazing how much growth that human being had in a calendar year," McDaniel told me after the season. "More so than anything I've ever seen in my life. Ever."

McDANIEL GREW ON THE JOB, TOO. AS ROOKIE SEASONS GO, HIS WAS filled with more drama than most. With backup quarterback Teddy Bridgewater also injured, McDaniel was forced to start a rookie third-stringer, Skylar Thompson, in the final game of the season, against the Jets. The Dolphins, at 8–8, were still in playoff contention, but had been fading. There was even a report by veteran Dolphins beat writer Armando Salguero that McDaniel could be fired if Miami were to lose its finale. That seemed implausible, and no one in the building gave it much credence. Still, it was another example of his unusually eventful journey in season one.

In October, the Jets had crushed the Dolphins, 40–17, with Thompson playing almost the entire game. Both the Dolphins and Jets carried five-game losing streaks into the January rematch—and Miami eked out an 11–6 victory, sneaking into the playoffs after the Patriots suffered a 35–23 defeat to the Bills.

The seventh-seeded Dolphins now went to Buffalo to face the second-seeded Bills, with Thompson once again making the start. Few gave

McDaniel's team a chance to win, and Miami fell behind 17–0. Yet the Dolphins rallied, ultimately losing 34–31. And they could've won. They were at least partly done in by communication issues between coaches and players that slowed down the play-calling process in key moments—surely a byproduct of an inexperienced third-stringer at quarterback.

McDaniel received some criticism for the confusion, and he hadn't been able to pull off the massive upset. Nevertheless, he'd managed to win respect among the NFL coaching community, especially because of Tagovailoa's remarkable transformation. To McDaniel's credit, he'd seen it coming.

Back in June, as we sat at a Mediterranean restaurant overlooking Fort Lauderdale Beach, McDaniel insisted he was looking forward to the challenges he'd face as a first-time head coach. "Oh, that's actually what I'm most excited about. 'Cause I think, within every game and within every season, there's a point . . . every season I've ever been a part of . . . where you're like, 'Oh fuck' . . . and there's uncertainty and there's stress and . . . and in my opinion, that's when head coaches actually earn their money. So, I'm excited for the fact that I know that shit's gonna hit the fan or there's gonna be pressure, and I think that I'm more built to thrive in that."

After years of sublimating his ambition, McDaniel now felt like he'd rediscovered an essential part of himself. The "psycho ballboy" who refused to let the Broncos believe it was acceptable to jog off the field; the guy who wrote up the 32-point presentation that helped get Shanahan out of Cleveland; the coach who told players he would help get them paid and then tried to scheme it into existence—*that* dude was now in charge of an NFL team.

McDaniel was grateful, and he was confident. He referenced the "high-octane pressure situation" the 49ers had faced the previous season, when they'd started 3–5, saying, "I'm excited for what those moments are like, that there's gonna be a fuck-ton of adversity somewhere," McDaniel continued. "And I think that I'll thrive in it. I've always been good at scheming football. But now I get to lead people and stuff. I knew at the beginning of my career, I'd be an elite head coach. And I knew a lot of people didn't see me that way or whatever, but then, as my career went along, I just stopped thinking about it and I've been kind of revitalized, like, 'Oh yeah, this is what fucking 20 years ago I set out to think that it would be, this is what I'd be best at in life.'"

Some first-time head coaches mimic their mentors. Perhaps most infamously, Josh McDaniels wore a Belichick-style hoodie, and embraced a similarly imperious and paranoid leadership style, during his ill-fated run as the Broncos' head coach following Mike Shanahan's firing. There was little risk that McDaniel would try to be a mini-Kyle. If anything, he relished his liberation and leaned into his oddness. Partly because he was following the dictatorial Flores, partly because he was great at scheming up explosive plays, and partly because he is actually funny in a way that few in his profession have ever been, McDaniel's authenticity was well received.

The authenticity resonated with his bosses. "This is a league of copycats and insecure job preservationists," Garfinkel told me in October. "Mike is different from other coaches. He's brilliant, he's funny, he's grateful, he's mature, he's secure in who he is, and he's positive."

A representative moment came in early November, during a 35–32 victory over the Bears in Chicago. Bears quarterback Justin Fields ran 15 times for 178 yards, breaking the NFL single-game record for most rushing yards by a quarterback. At one point, Fields finished a scramble by running out of bounds on the Dolphins' sideline, a few feet away from McDaniel. As Fields walked back onto the field, McDaniel approached him from the side and exclaimed, "Stop it!"

That would not be McDaniel's most discussed sideline moment, though. In January, during the playoff game in Buffalo, the CBS broadcast zoomed in on him before a play. Wearing thick black gloves on a chilly Western New York afternoon, McDaniel put his hand to his mouth and appeared to be vaping. It was nicotine, and McDaniel—caught on camera—quit cold turkey afterward.

After his rookie season, McDaniel wasn't seduced by his relative success. He fired defensive coordinator Josh Boyer and landed a massive prize, former Broncos head coach Vic Fangio, as his new DC, with McDaniel beating out numerous other suitors. Unlike Shanahan, he had no prior connection with Fangio, but he was able to convince one of the most gifted defensive minds in the sport to come aboard.

Beginning in 2022, for the first time in a long time, McDaniel didn't have to listen to Shanahan, either the exacting coach's random venting or forewarnings about leaving the nest. He had proven that he was fully capable of paving his own path and handling the pressure that came with it. There was no one quite like him in the profession, and he wasn't afraid to reveal his personality to the outside world. If anything, he was prepared to show *more* of it—and no one could convince him that was a bad thing.

Chapter 22

You Don't Let Him Out

The conversation began with a question about accuracy, a sensitive subject for Kyle Shanahan in the summer of 2022. His newly anointed starting quarterback, Trey Lance, looked inconsistent during the first week and a half of training camp, missing easy throws and sending errant passes into the hands of 49ers defenders. It had been a trying offseason for the second-year quarterback, who tweaked his mechanics, shortened his throwing motion, and experienced arm fatigue that caused concerned coaches to hold him out of drills. Now, in summer practices open to media members and fans, Lance looked less like a franchise QB than a work in progress. That "hidden horsepower" Shanahan had been intent on releasing remained concealed, if it existed at all.

It was one thing to miss an open receiver on a rollout swing pass. Missing on a quarterback drafted third overall, especially when it had taken three first-round picks to acquire that selection? That could be ruinous for a coach, and for a franchise. The 49ers were all in on winning a championship in 2022, and seemingly all in on Lance. His predecessor, Jimmy Garoppolo, was still technically on the team. However, Garoppolo had already said goodbye in an emotional farewell press conference in early February. Given his $24.2 million salary and its impact on the team's salary cap, the presumption was he'd be traded or released before the start of the regular season. In the meantime, Jimmy G, still rehabbing from the offseason surgery to his throwing shoulder that had derailed earlier trade scenarios, was spending his late-July and early-August days throwing passes to Cam Bustos, who worked in the team's health and performance department. Garoppolo conducted his daily hour-long routine on a turf field behind a set of bleachers, west of the practice fields where the rest of the 49ers were getting ready for the season. It was a literal sideshow. At times, curious fans at the top of the bleachers turned their backs to the action and instead observed Garoppolo zipping balls to Bustos, shouting their encouragement. Teammates coming to and from practice walked right past their former starting quarterback, dapping him up as he got his arm ready for his next NFL home.

It was Lance's show, and Shanahan didn't really have a Plan B. The 49ers had signed former Eagles backup Nate Sudfield to a fully guaranteed one-year, $2 million contract in March, but it was clearly Lance or bust. And so far at camp, there were plenty of moments that suggested "bust." That the second-year player might not fulfill his promise wasn't a popular opinion in those parts. The fan base had embraced Lance's potential with a protective fervor, even before he was drafted, and many reacted angrily to any suggestion of his struggles. When I'd reported over the offseason about the young quarterback's arm fatigue issues, the blowback on social media and elsewhere had been intense and sustained. Shanahan, it could be reasonably surmised, also was not a fan of such storylines. Yet, when I caught up to him as he walked to his office after a spirited training camp practice, he confronted the accuracy question without deflecting or equivocating.

Yes, Shanahan conceded, Lance's accuracy was a concern. The coach attributed much of the problem to the fact that Lance was often asked to throw on the move in high school and college. The faster one travels, Shanahan explained, the trickier it is to make the ball go where you intend it to go. He didn't portray the issue as insurmountable, but he also didn't act like it wasn't a thing. What Shanahan said next opened a portal into his mind, revealing something foundational about how he viewed the game. All quarterbacks, he said, have weaknesses that must be navigated and mitigated. The key is to build a team around the quarterback capable of reducing his massive burden, and of compensating for his failings in key moments.

The conversation veered into an assessment of how much is put on an NFL quarterback and how many obstacles appear—especially in the postseason, when games tighten up and every play can feel monumental. In those settings, Shanahan felt, asking the quarterback to "do everything," to be the primary driving force whose actions determine victory and defeat, is typically not a winning strategy. He referenced the previous January's 13–10 playoff victory over Matt LaFleur and the Packers at Lambeau Field, and how much of Green Bay's operation revolved around Aaron Rodgers. "That's why they don't win," he said. Similarly, Peyton Manning, a quarterback he believed had the greatest-ever command of the position, had suffered a slew of postseason disappointments during his career, albeit while capturing two championships. "There are just too many variables you have to deal with that are difficult to predict," Shanahan said, citing Bill Belichick's strategic blueprint for consecutive Patriots playoff victories over the Colts in 2003 and '04—when he had defenders play tight, hyperphysical coverage on Indy receivers and dared the officials to penalize them repeatedly—as an example. "It's too much on one guy. There can be [bad] weather, injuries, so many things . . . The only quarterback who has ever been able to handle all of it, in my opinion, is Tom [Brady]. For anyone else, you need to give him some help."

The overarching point was this: Shanahan was accustomed to managing his quarterback's imperfections and crafting a plan to overcome them. He fully anticipated having to do so with Lance, but for critics to focus only on the second-year player was to ignore how Shanahan had navigated the previous four and a half seasons with Garoppolo, who sometimes struggled going through his progressions, seeing the field the way Shanahan wanted him to, and throwing deep, among other shortcomings. The 49ers had been to a Super Bowl and come close to reaching another because of Jimmy G *and* in spite of him. Shanahan and Lynch had constructed a talented, well-rounded team whose players valued attention to detail, selflessness, and relentless physicality and effort. Because of the two decision-makers' belief in the soundness of that approach, they'd pivoted to a model of trusting a young quarterback on a rookie contract to be good enough to allow the 49ers' comprehensive excellence to prevail. It wasn't a bad plan, assuming Lance could find some consistency. And if he couldn't? Well, the model was still sustainable. The coach and GM would be proven right, though in a way they never could never have anticipated during training camp.

THE FIRST PUBLIC CLUE THAT SHANAHAN WAS LOSING FAITH IN LANCE
came in late August, when the 49ers made the shocking announcement
that Garoppolo was coming back. It was a fulfillment of what the *Athletic*'s
Tim Kawakami had dubbed "The Garoppolypse," in reference to the uni-
verse's seeming unwillingness to keep this franchise and this quarterback
apart. Shanahan and Lynch tried to spin it as a signing of convenience:
lacking more enticing options, Garoppolo had agreed to a revised one-year
contract that reduced his base salary to a fully guaranteed $6.5 million
(with up to another $8.95 million in incentives) and included a provision
that he couldn't be traded or given the franchise tag after the season. Spin
aside, the 49ers' interest in approaching Garoppolo with an offer clearly
represented a change of thinking, given that the team's former starter
hadn't been asked to attend meetings or film-watching sessions during the
preseason and had yet to even *meet* first-year quarterbacks coach Brian
Griese. Jimmy G's return to the roster as a backup was sure to put more
pressure on Lance, but Shanahan clearly wasn't averse to taking that risk.
It was, quite plainly, a hedge. It aligned with something that a former 49ers
assistant coach had predicted to me months earlier: "I think Kyle is just
trying to figure out some way to bring Jimmy back, somehow, because he
knows it could go really bad with Trey."

The day after the Garoppolo news broke, in a move that attracted far
less attention, the 49ers included Sudfeld in their final roster cuts to reach
the 53-man limit. Garoppolo's return may have made such a transaction
seem inevitable, but there was a twist: Shanahan and Lynch kept three
quarterbacks on the roster, which had not been their intent at the start of
training camp. The third was a rookie they'd planned to release and then
bring back onto the practice squad, allowing the Niners to keep the young
quarterback in the fold while paying him very little, and to use the valuable
roster spot on a player at another position. However, the rookie—whom
the 49ers had selected with the 262nd and final pick of the draft—had
impressed Shanahan from the moment he arrived in Santa Clara. More
to the point, he'd unleashed a few bold and savvy passes during the preseason that Shanahan feared would be noticed by other teams' coaches
and scouts. Shanahan felt that cutting the kid and sneaking him onto the

practice squad was too risky; another team could claim him and sign him to its active roster.

So, Shanahan and Lynch decided to keep Brock Purdy on the team.

Purdy's ascent may have appeared unlikely to outsiders, but in the locker room, most people got it. He'd made a good impression in OTAs and minicamps, and, once training camp began, had made the most of his limited opportunities. Because of that, his opportunities increased. He was ultraprepared, went through his progressions faithfully, saw the field well, and exuded calm in a manner that belied his status. Best of all, he had what is known in 49ers internal parlance as "some shit in his neck." Nearly from the outset, the 22-year-old acted like he belonged, and then some. It helped that Purdy was used to being underestimated. Growing up in Queen Creek, Arizona, he was a sports-loving kid who dreamed of playing major college football despite the improbability of that actually happening. Earning a scholarship was important to him, and not just symbolically. In 2008, the Purdys, like so many American families, had their lives upended by the housing crash caused by the subprime mortgage crisis. His father, Shawn, a former minor league pitcher, and mother, Carrie, struggled to make things work while prioritizing the athletic pursuits of Brock, younger brother Chubba, and older sister Whittney.

"At the time, I didn't really understand what was going on," recalled Purdy, who was eight. "But I knew we lost everything, and we were moving from house to house, and my dad had to open up his business in another name. And all that stuff, I didn't understand any of it. When I got through high school and [started to understand], I was like, 'Maaaan.' You look back and [think], 'They put everything into us, still, even with all that.' No matter what their situation was, they still gave all that they had to us, in terms of the time spent, my dad coaching us—everything. They showed me what sacrifice was. They showed me what real love was."

On the recruiting trail, love was harder to come by. Purdy, who stood 6-foot-1, didn't have an overwhelmingly strong arm and wasn't exceptionally athletic. He got no attention from big-time programs until late in his senior season, when he threw 57 touchdowns and earned Arizona Gatorade Player of the Year honors. He finally attracted interest from some

Power Five conference schools: first Iowa State, and then mighty Alabama, though coach Nick Saban wanted him as a "preferred walk-on." Shortly after Saban pivoted and offered a full scholarship, Texas A&M extended a similar overture. As things heated up, Arizona State, and then Arizona, came in belatedly.

Sometime after the initial signing day in December of his senior year, Purdy got a text from a Sun Devils staffer, something that once would have caused him to hyperventilate with excitement. He wasn't sold on its sincerity; it felt like a face-saving measure. "It was respectful," Purdy remembered, "but it wasn't like, 'We want you to be the guy,' or anything like that. It was more like, now I had offers from Alabama and A&M and 'the whole state's telling us to sign you.'"

Purdy politely passed. In February, he signed with Iowa State because Cyclones coach Matt Campbell had made him feel wanted in a way that others hadn't. "There were a handful of teams at the end that offered me. But Coach Campbell called me and said, 'Man, I want you. We're not trying to recruit any other guys. If you come here, great. If not, we're set with who we got.' That, to me, was like, 'Man, this guy really believes in me.' Whereas all these other schools, if they didn't get their guy, they were gonna go get another guy. Campbell didn't do that. And then, from day one, once I got there and started playing, that dude gave me the keys to the program and trusted me and believed in me."

The belief was validated the following October, when Campbell turned to Purdy and the true freshman led Iowa State to high-profile upsets of Oklahoma State and West Virginia. By the time his four-year career was done, he held 32 school passing records. He believed he was ready, again, for the next level of competition. And yet, once again, it seemed that very few people believed him capable of meeting that standard, especially after he ran a relatively slow 40-yard dash (4.84 seconds) that didn't properly showcase his pocket elusiveness.

Before the 2022 draft, Purdy was realistic. He knew he had no shot of going in the first three rounds, so he set his sights on day three. His mom wanted to host a big party at the house, but Brock, nervous and overwhelmed, insisted that the gathering be kept small unless and until he was actually drafted. Carrie Purdy persisted in her optimism, preparing enough food to feed a small village. As the final four rounds played out, it appeared as though there'd be a whole lot of leftovers.

The morning of the draft's third and final day, Purdy got a call from 49ers headquarters that raised his hopes. Griese, who'd succeeded John Elway as Mike Shanahan's starting quarterback in Denver, and assistant QBs coach Klay Kubiak—whose father, Gary, had given Kyle his first opportunity as an offensive coordinator in Houston—told Purdy the team might select him at some point during the day.

The 49ers had become intrigued after area scout Steve Slowik—brother of Bobby, the team's passing-game coordinator—alerted them to Purdy's abilities and to Campbell's glowing praise; as the coach put it, "This guy changed our program." Griese had initiated some Zoom sessions between him, Kubiak, and Purdy to discuss scheme, the quarterback's processing style, and his backstory. All of that was cool, but hardly a guarantee that the 49ers would actually select him.

So, Purdy watched anxiously and waited. And waited. Finally, sometime during the sixth round, he retreated to his childhood bedroom and slept, exhausted from the stress. "That last day was just so tiring, so draining," he recalled. "Throughout the day, I was following the Niners, and any time they didn't pick me, I would be, like, drained in a sense. So, I remember my dad and I literally took a nap at some point in the sixth round. I was so tired from all of it."

Shortly after waking up, he got another call from 49ers headquarters. "They said, 'Hey, we have one more pick in the seventh round and we're gonna try to take you—it's between you and a safety.' I said, 'Alright, sweet.' I hung up and Googled what pick they had, and it was the *last* pick. I was like, 'You've gotta be kidding me.'"

The wait seemed endless, especially given all the compensatory picks that lengthened the seventh round. Purdy hoped another team might swoop in and snap him up before the Niners were on the clock. As he watched that hope evaporate, he and his agent fielded calls from various teams angling to sign him as an undrafted free agent. Purdy jotted down notes from those conversations, assessing his options and anticipating the mad scramble for such players that occurs upon the draft's completion. At that point—at least logically—going undrafted was a preferable outcome.

That way, Purdy could choose the team that best suited him and theoretically optimize his chances of sticking around in the league. However, it wasn't the outcome Purdy craved.

Finally, as the round neared its conclusion, the 49ers called again: they were taking Purdy at 262. A wave of joy engulfed him; bedlam ensued. "I was the last pick," Purdy said, "and we celebrated like I was the first pick." *Now* Carrie had the green light to host the party. "We had almost everybody from my life in football and family friends come over," Brock said. "Probably over 100 people within the next hour. We were all excited."

<hr>

IN 1976, FORMER USC AND NFL WIDE RECEIVER PAUL SALATA COINED THE term "Mr. Irrelevant," bestowing that moniker upon the final pick of the draft and feting him with a series of events during "Irrelevant Week" in Newport Beach, California, including the awarding of the "Lowsman Trophy"—a play on the Heisman Trophy, only this time with the bronzed player fumbling a football. It became an annual tradition. It was kind of funny at first, then bemusing. By 2022, it was played out. Realistically, it hadn't been amusing for at least a couple of decades.

As thrilled as Purdy was to hear his name called on draft night, he wasn't particularly captivated by the spoofing of that pick and the opportunity to play along. On a conference call with reporters covering the draft at Levi's Stadium, Purdy chafed at the Mr. Irrelevant queries, saying, "For me, I'm looking at it as an opportunity. I got my foot in the door. A team believed in me, and now I get my opportunity to go and play football . . . From the outside looking in, yeah, I guess it's a funny thing."

Fighting for a roster spot was a serious matter, and Purdy intended to win one. In Shanahan's eyes, he was a younger version of Nick Mullens, the scrappy backup quarterback who'd once worn headphones around the facility, listening to the coach call plays so that it would all seem familiar on game day. When Purdy showed up for rookie minicamp, he was a bit awestruck, overwhelmed by the 49ers' aura, "the history of it with the Super Bowls and the quarterbacks—and obviously, I'd grown up watching Kyle Shanahan coach." He had to quickly digest one of football's most intricate playbooks and become versed in Shanahan's scheme. He shone in OTAs and got his head coach's attention early in training camp.

About a week into camp, Shanahan, while walking off the practice field, approached CEO Jed York and told him, "I think our third-string quarterback is our best quarterback." York gulped. As he'd later explain, "One thing that owners don't love to hear when they've invested money and/or draft picks into people is that the last pick in the draft is the guy that we think is the best. That's generally not great news." When pressed, Shanahan told York he had no plans to change the depth chart, "but I think Brock will end up being our quarterback."

By the second week of camp, Purdy's fearlessness and penchant for playmaking had started to become a thing. The day before the 49ers hosted the Packers in their preseason opener, two of their best players, linebacker Fred Warner and offensive tackle Trent Williams, were walking off the practice field together. "Man," Warner said to Williams, "I can't wait to watch Purdy play tomorrow." They didn't realize it, but Purdy was walking behind them, within earshot, thrilled that such accomplished teammates even knew his name. Recalled Warner, "Even though [Purdy was playing with] the third team, he had command of the third team. I just kind of admired him from afar—just little things he did out there."

Purdy made some eye-catching plays during the preseason, fitting balls into tight windows between linebackers and defensive backs, but he also drove Shanahan, Griese, and Bobby Slowik crazy at times by trying to do too much. Purdy got a taste of Shanahan's temper, too, including once when he deviated from the coach's script during a training camp drill. "I remember there was this one play, it was a play-action. I rolled out, and we had [tight end] Ross Dwelley leaking backside and I ran for, like, ten yards. On the jog back [to the huddle], I'm like, 'Alright, that was a good play.' [Shanahan was] just cussing at me through the mic: 'Are you kidding me? This is not how I taught it!' He was heated."

On cutdown day, however, Purdy felt the warm embrace signified by a roster spot. To some people, possibly including Sudfeld, that was a surprise. To one very accomplished offensive strategist, it made all the sense in the world.

MIKE SHANAHAN SAT ON A COUCH IN ROOM 753 OF THE J. W. MARRIOTT IN downtown Chicago, about ten miles east of the Oak Park neighborhood where he was born. Like everyone in the 49ers' traveling party, he was anxious to see how Trey Lance would do the following afternoon in his first regular-season game as the team's starting quarterback, especially with driving rain in the forecast. That was one of many topics of discussion the proud father was eager to discuss. Something made the elder Shanahan a little more serene than he should have been—the presence of a quarterback whose virtues he'd been openly extolling for months.

"When you have a guy like that on your team, a guy with the traits he has," Shanahan said, "you don't let him out of your building."

Mentally, at least, I did a double-take. We were talking about Brock Purdy, and this two-time Super Bowl–winning coach was doing so in a tone normally reserved for elite and accomplished passers from his past. It made sense, though, given our previous conversations in May and June, during which Shanahan had made numerous unsolicited mentions of the 262nd pick's many positive attributes. Like Slowik, Griese, and Kubiak, Shanahan had watched Purdy's college tape before the draft and become intrigued. Once the retired coach got his hands on the 49ers' OTA film, that intrigue morphed into intense adulation.

Whether Mike Shanahan was serving as a shadow GM for his son (that was probably overstated) or simply staying involved in the game during his golden years was a matter of some debate; he told me the main reason he liked watching practices and meetings was to keep abreast of his son's cutting-edge schematics, which had evolved a great deal since the Washington days. Whatever the case, Mike, from afar, saw something early in Purdy that even Kyle hadn't yet spotted. What stood out most was Purdy's comfort and recognition of what he himself was seeing on the field. "He's *played*," Shanahan said, referring to Purdy's 48 starts at Iowa State. In that sense, Purdy was almost the anti-Lance. Could it be that the Niners had taken a massive swing and miss—and that they'd get away with it because of the equivalent of an infield hit on an errant pitch that nicked the back of the bat?

The early returns on Lance as Garoppolo's successor weren't promising. Against the Bears, he sailed a first-quarter deep shot beyond the grasp of backup tight end Tyler Kroft, who'd been beautifully schemed open by Kyle Shanahan. The Niners, with a seemingly comfortable 10–0 lead midway through the third quarter, gave up a couple of big plays—including a 51-yard broken-play touchdown pass to Dante Pettis, a former 49ers wide receiver who'd been cut after landing in Shanahan's doghouse—and fell behind 13–10. On cue, the rain started coming down hard, increasing the degree of difficulty as Lance tried to mount a comeback. He failed, and after the Niners' 19–10 defeat, it was clear that Lance would not receive an unlimited grace period. Star tight end George Kittle, who sat out the game with a groin injury, said afterward, "We're going to do everything we can to play well around him. But he's a grown man. I know he's young, but he's *played* football."

The stress ramped up the following week as the 49ers prepared for their home opener against the Seahawks. Another poor effort from Lance would increase the calls from media personalities and fans for Shanahan to replace him with Garoppolo; some players and coaches were privately wondering if that would be the best course of action. Late in the first quarter, Shanahan called an inside run for Lance, a strategy partly stemming from the realization that the quarterback wasn't as fast as the 49ers believed when they drafted him, and thus wasn't effective on the NFL level as an outside runner. Why run him inside? They had to run him *somewhere*, because he wasn't a polished pocket passer. Sandwiched between a pair of Seahawks defenders, Lance crumpled to the ground with a significant break and dislocation to his right ankle. The next day, he'd have season-ending surgery. For all the intense focus on Lance in the months leading up to the season, in football, everything can change in an instant.

Garoppolo, pressed into service without any practice reps, came in and smoothly operated the offense. Following the 49ers' 27–7 victory, though empathetic toward Lance, many of Garoppolo's teammates and coaches marveled at how good he'd looked. There was a lightness in the locker room for the first time, perhaps, since the 2019 season. As terrible as it was to say aloud, the 49ers appeared to be a better team with Garoppolo at quarterback. Two people—one player, one coach—affirmed that thought in the aftermath, telling me, "I can't say it, but you can."

The following Sunday night in Denver, Garoppolo had a lousy game. He fumbled a snap, threw an interception, and stepped out of the back of the end zone for a safety in an 11–10 defeat to the Broncos. After the interception, Garoppolo was shown on camera voicing his frustration, and amateur lip readers concluded that he was telling Shanahan, "All your plays suck, man." Three weeks later, the injury-ravaged Niners got thumped by the Falcons in Atlanta, falling to 3–3. Patrick Mahomes and the Chiefs were coming to Levi's the following Sunday, the stiffest possible test for a reeling team. It looked like the middle of 2021 all over again.

The 49ers needed a jolt. A year earlier, facing an even more daunting crisis, Shanahan had provided it by turning wide receiver Deebo Samuel into a part-time running back. That had gone well in the moment; after the season, when Samuel wanted to be rewarded for his sacrifices, not so much. Eventually, after Samuel publicly requested a trade, Shanahan and Lynch paid him almost as much as he was asking for. It didn't help the team's cause that, in an offensive meeting a couple of days before one of the 49ers' 2021 playoff games, Shanahan addressed the receiver in front of his teammates, saying, "Deebo, I've coached some incredible players, guys like Julio Jones. You're the best football player that I've ever been around." Samuel hadn't forgotten that. Now paid accordingly, Samuel's versatility remained a key component of Shanahan's offense. However, opposing defenses were catching on and adjusting. The coach needed another wrinkle. Twelve days before the trade deadline, Lynch gave Kyle Shanahan the greatest gift imaginable for a coach like him.

IN NOVEMBER OF 1998, AS MIKE SHANAHAN'S BRONCOS WERE IN THE midst of a second consecutive championship season, I wrote a *Sports Illustrated* feature story on Denver wide receiver Ed McCaffrey that bore the headline "White Lightning"—a reference to his "deceptive" speed, a clichéd tag for white athletes. The story included a scene from the McCaffrey home in which Ed's wife, Lisa, watched the couple's young sons race through the kitchen. Lisa, whose father, David Sime, won the silver medal in the 100-meter dash at the 1960 Olympics, cracked, "That's why Ed and I got together—so we could breed fast white guys."

She wasn't lying. Christian McCaffrey, two years old at the time of that utterance, grew up to become an All-American running back at Stanford, finishing second in the Heisman Trophy voting as a sophomore. Drafted eighth overall by the Panthers in 2017, McCaffrey soon achieved NFL stardom as a dual-threat back, becoming the third-ever player to gain more than 1,000 yards rushing and receiving in the same season. However, a host of injuries forced McCaffrey to miss 23 of 33 games over the 2020 and 2021 campaigns, creating the perception that his body was breaking down. Carolina, which fired coach Matt Rhule after a 37–15 defeat to the 49ers on October 9, was in rebuilding mode. Several teams called the Panthers about the possibility of trading for McCaffrey, with the 49ers and Rams emerging as the strongest suitors.

It was yet another Shanahan–McVay showdown, and the mentor would defeat the student. The 49ers, without first-round draft picks anytime soon because of the trade for the pick that became Trey Lance, got it done via a package that sounded like a dance step: a two, a three, a four, and a five. It was a gamble, given the possibility that McCaffrey's body wouldn't hold up. But the upside, if the player could stay healthy, was immense. Not only was McCaffrey an explosive and gifted running back, but he was someone whose unique skill set, attention to detail, and football aptitude made him the ultimate fit for Shanahan's offense. As former 49ers assistant T. C. McCartney put it, "His value is higher with [Shanahan] than anybody else." McCaffrey, he explained, gave Shanahan another "positionless player," along with Samuel and fullback Kyle Juszczyk, that the coach could use to manipulate opposing defenses at the line of scrimmage. One or more of those players could be motioned to and/or from the backfield to alter the 49ers' formation and keep defenders off balance. For example, what had been a "three-by-one" look (three receivers on one side of the formation and one on the other) could quickly be transformed to a two-by-two, or vice versa. Similarly, a defense designed to stop a team in 21 personnel could suddenly find itself confronting 11 or 12. Explained McCartney, "So now, you're messing with the defense's rules, just because of who people are and where they line up."

When McCaffrey arrived two days before the 49ers–Chiefs game, he changed everything. After making a cameo appearance in a 44–23 defeat that dropped the Niners to 3–4, he started learning the offense and torturing opponents. The 49ers were about to go on another run, beginning with a game in which McCaffrey would become the fourth player since the 1970 merger (and first since Hall of Famer LaDainian Tomlinson in 2005) to throw, run for, and catch a touchdown. A classic Shanahan flex, it happened at SoFi Stadium against McVay's Rams, in a 31–14 victory.

The new-look Niners were rolling. They'd won four in a row by the time Mike McDaniel and the Dolphins came to town for that early-December showdown in which Miami scored on its opening play. Garoppolo was playing at a Pro Bowl level and exuded the breeziness of a man who'd been cast aside by a coach who now needed him more than ever. He was unbothered, and his boss respected it. "Every quarterback has to be able to block things out," Shanahan told me in the days leading up to the Miami game. "But Jimmy does it as well as anyone I've ever been around, and it's a big reason why this works."

———

AS THAT DECEMBER 4 NINERS-DOLPHINS CLASH APPROACHED, MATT LaFleur was in Green Bay, confronting the imminent end of an era. The Packers were 4–8 and on the brink of playoff elimination. Aaron Rodgers, who'd signed a three-year, $150.8 million contract extension in March, appeared disengaged and psychologically prepared to finish his career elsewhere. A little more than two and a half years after the drafting of Jordan Love, after all the conflict and drama and the two painful playoff defeats, Rodgers and the Packers were done. "I thought we got it all worked out [in 2020]," LaFleur said in 2023. "It never quite goes how you think it's going to go. He would always make comments about how we drafted his replacement and this, that, and the other. Turned out to be true. He always talks about manifestations, speaking it into existence."

In March, the quarterback and team had pledged to give it one more go—appropriately, at a wedding. When David Bakhtiari, the Packers' star left tackle, married Frankie Shebby at the Rosewood Miramar Resort in Montecito, California, Rodgers, his status still in limbo, served as the officiant. LaFleur came to the event unsure whether Rodgers wanted to stay in Green Bay, force a trade, or retire. During the reception, Rodgers let it slip to offensive coordinator Adam Stenavich, newly promoted from offensive line coach after the Broncos hired Nathaniel Hackett as head coach, that he intended to return. However, Rodgers decided to torture LaFleur by insinuating the opposite. His then girlfriend, actress Shailene Woodley, helped sell the prank.

"I'm surprised you're talking to me," Woodley said to LaFleur.

"What are you talking about?" he said.

"Oh, he didn't tell you yet?"

Recalled LaFleur, "She's an actress. I was all paranoid. I [thought], *He's leaving*. They were messing with me a little bit, which I think was a cruel joke."

"Dude, we're good," Stenavich finally assured LaFleur, who tried to mask his inner panic.

"Hey," LaFleur replied, "he's got to do what's best for him."

Soon, however, it became clear that 2022 would be worse for everyone. With Davante Adams, perhaps the NFL's top receiver, headed for free agency and seeking a massive deal, the Packers traded him to the Raiders. The plan was to use the resulting draft capital to find younger replacements, and Green Bay picked receivers Christian Watson (second round), Romeo Doubs (fourth round) and Samori Toure (seventh round). Typically, it would be crucial for a franchise quarterback to develop timing and chemistry with such newcomers during the months that followed. Rodgers, though, blew off most of the offseason program, instead engaging in activities that included a three-night ceremony in which he drank ayahuasca tea, a psychedelic drug, under the guidance of a shaman. In retrospect, *everyone* was tripping. LaFleur, at first, tried to spin the quarterback's absence as a positive because it would allow Love, now heading into his third season, to take all the reps and further develop. In hindsight, it was actively harmful to the Packers' 2022 prospects. "Unfortunately, it was one of those things I had to go through to realize how detrimental that was," LaFleur said. "Football, it's not a one-man sport. It's 11 men on the field at once. They didn't have the rapport built in the offseason, which is when you've got to do it. I didn't realize the significance and how much that would hurt us. And it did hurt us."

Rodgers saw it differently, later insisting that any progress made during OTAs is "very nominal." He rejected the premise that him staying away had hurt the team's chances, saying, "When I'm in, I'm all in, and you wanna ride with offseason workouts? I won MVP without doing offseason workouts. Like, was my commitment any less then? I'd say not at all. The way that I come back to work—not just physically in good shape, but mentally refreshed—is the best thing for me to have the season I wanted to have . . . I think that's just a cop-out written to try and find something to disparage me about that, honestly, when you know what offseason workouts are really about, it's completely ridiculous."

By early December, LaFleur knew he and the Packers had erred. For one thing, he hadn't realized the true magnitude of losing Adams. Rodgers and the young receivers were struggling to connect, and the quarterback was openly showing his frustration. Hackett, the former offensive coordinator with whom Rodgers was close, wasn't there as a buffer. The first-year Broncos coach had his own problems, presiding over a disastrous situation in Denver, where newly acquired star quarterback Russell Wilson was regressing horribly. Hackett would lose his job after just 15 games.

Rodgers, who'd appeared close to checked out to his bosses, turned it on at the last possible juncture, when Green Bay was 4–8. He got more engaged, raised his level of play, and helped spur a four-game winning streak. To LaFleur, that almost made it *worse*. Had Rodgers been that focused from the time he signed his extension, the Packers might have been legitimate contenders. It wasn't totally over; the Packers were in position to make the playoffs on the final night of the regular season. All Green Bay had to do was defeat the Lions at Lambeau in a battle of 8–8 teams. Detroit had been eliminated from contention earlier in the day and was playing only for pride. Rodgers had owned the Lions during his career, beating them 18 out of 25 times, often in embarrassing fashion. Yet, on this night, in a battle of former Cal quarterbacks, Jared Goff was the best passer on the field. The Packers lost, 20–16, and there were plenty of lowlights. Midway through the first quarter, with Green Bay facing a fourth and one at its own 32-yard line, LaFleur elected to go for it and called a quarterback sneak. It likely would have worked, as no Lions defender lined up over center Josh Myers. However, Rodgers inexplicably audibled, calling a jet sweep to Allen Lazard. The receiver was stuffed for a one-yard loss, setting up a Lions field goal.

Instead of traveling to Santa Clara for a playoff matchup against the 49ers, the Packers were headed into another uncertain offseason. LaFleur had to confront some hard facts. The defense had played well enough to defeat the Lions; the offense, led by Rodgers, had failed. There would be no begging Rodgers to stay in 2023, and no renewal of vows with a half-committed quarterback.

LaFleur, who'd gone 47–19 in the regular season (a .712 winning percentage) and 49–22 overall, would turn to an untested quarterback and wouldn't get much of a grace period. He knew what was at stake: a bad season could cost him his job. Worst of all, he knew the Packers had missed a window to win a championship. In each of the previous two seasons, that had been there for the taking; now, it was time to confront the reality that the Lombardi Trophy, for the foreseeable future, appeared well beyond their grasp.

THERE WAS A TIME WHEN ACQUIRING RODGERS HAD BEEN SHANAHAN'S dream. At other moments during his six-year tenure as the 49ers' coach, he'd envisioned Matthew Stafford, Kirk Cousins, Mac Jones, Deshaun Watson, Trey Lance, and, of course, Garoppolo as the answer at quarterback. Now, in a surreal development, he and Garoppolo were back together by necessity. Things were going well, until they weren't: four minutes into their December 4 game against the Dolphins at Levi's, Garoppolo got sacked by Dolphins linebackers Jaelan Phillips and Jerome Baker, and his foot bent in a gruesome direction and broke.

In that moment, Shanahan's football journey was sent on a new and incredible course. Thrown into the game against the Dolphins, Purdy looked poised and precise in a 33–17 victory. As upcoming opponents would soon learn, it was not a fluke. The next Sunday, at Levi's, a quarterback from nearby San Mateo showed up intent on putting on a show for the 83 family members and friends who sat together on his dime in the stadium's upper southeast corner. Tom Brady *needed* to do Tom Brady things, with the 6–6 Buccaneers fighting for a playoff berth. Was he auditioning? Brady, now 45, would be a free agent after the season. Should he choose to continue his seemingly endless career, it was fair to wonder whether Brady might be a viable option for the Niners.

Purdy wasn't playing along with that storyline. He was busy authoring his own improbable script. He completed 14 of his first 18 passes for 185 yards, throwing two touchdowns and running for another, as the 49ers went up 28–0 before halftime and won 35–7. Purdy even suffered a broken rib in the first quarter, but played through it, fueled by adrenaline and a realization that players drafted 262nd overall don't often get second chances to leave a first impression. Fans chanted his name as television cameras caught his father, Shawn, crying in the stands. Brady threw a pair of interceptions and looked utterly miserable. After the game, Niners linebacker Dre Greenlaw, who'd intercepted one of the passes, approached the seven-time Super Bowl–winning quarterback on the field and asked him to sign the ball. Brady complied, headed to the locker room, and left the stadium without showering. "Some things I don't give a fuck about, at this point," Brady explained as he headed toward the team buses. "Fuck that. I'm going home."

To most of the viewing public, Purdy's performance had been a major surprise—people didn't even know who he was. In the 49ers' locker room, players and coaches at least had an inkling he might shine on the big stage. For months, Purdy had impersonated opposing quarterbacks in practice with a little more presence than the average third-string rookie seventh-round pick. "When I got to the scout team," Purdy said, "I took it as a challenge. Like, man, I want to see how good I am with Nick [Bosa] coming off the edge and Fred [Warner] dropping back and covering whoever. There were times when I did well, and there were times when they shut me down and I learned some different things about the pocket and all that."

Still unconvinced, Shanahan needed a contingency plan. With a team built to win now, substandard play at quarterback would not be acceptable. Shanahan and Lynch put out overtures to a pair of highly accomplished quarterbacks who had recently retired: Ben Roethlisberger (who wasn't interested) and Philip Rivers (who was). The stakes were high when, four days after beating the Bucs, Purdy faced the Seahawks on *Thursday Night Football* with his broken rib. Minutes before the game, it appeared as though Shanahan would have to turn to veteran Josh Johnson, signed nine days earlier, as his emergency starter. Purdy had attempted a couple of wobbly warmup passes before shutting it down because of the rib pain on his left side. Then, as Shanahan went into the locker room and started altering his game plan, the pain-blocking meds kicked in, and Purdy told Griese he could give it a go. He didn't feel as though sitting out was an option. "I know opportunities don't come like this all the time, especially for guys in my shoes, being a later pick. It sort of gives me a perspective of 'Make the most of this opportunity. Don't go down the road in life and look back and be like, "I wish I would have," or regret anything.' So, that's where I was at, at the time of the broken rib."

Shanahan called a careful first couple of drives, trying to limit Purdy's downfield throws and eliminating rollouts to the left side of the field. But Purdy was not meant to be a so-called game manager. Late in the first quarter, with the game scoreless and the 49ers facing a second and eight from the Seattle 28, Shanahan dialed up a play called Hollywood that would have made Shailene Woodley proud: Purdy took a shotgun snap and looked left toward receiver Ray-Ray McCloud, who had motioned behind the quarterback just before the snap, and pump-faked as if to throw a screen. Then Purdy spun back to his right and sold another pump-fake to McCaffrey, who was slowly drifting toward the right flat. Now it was the Seahawks' defenders whose heads were spinning, and Purdy pounced: Kittle, who had pretended to be a blocker for the screens-to-be, snuck upfield, caught Purdy's perfect pass over the middle, and rumbled into the end zone.

By the time the 49ers' 21–13, NFC West–clinching victory had been secured, Shanahan was convinced. Purdy was a *dude*. He had his quarterback. Even given the Lance debacle, he and Lynch could still take advantage of a quarterback on a rookie deal (this one even cheaper). Purdy, he felt, had the skills, brains, and toughness for the job. Recalled Shanahan, "He talked to me the whole way through it and was accurate the whole time. And he didn't make excuses for himself, either. He did have bad plays in there, and you never heard, 'Oh, it's because I'm hurting.' He wasn't that type of guy. And I think that's why the players really believed in him, too. The poise, the competitor, everything. It was all real. To me, it was, 'Alright, this dude you can trust.'"

———

THE 49ERS CLOSED OUT THE REGULAR SEASON WITH THREE MORE VICTO- ries, running their winning streak to ten. Nothing about their performance was subtle. By season's end, they'd made NFL history in an arcane way: their opponents, after playing the 49ers, went 0–15 the following week. (Only the Chiefs, who had a bye between games, won the next time out.) "Honestly, I don't think I've heard of a cooler stat," Juszczyk said. "It's a fucking gangster stat, a savage stat. We're out there to be physical as hell. Teams are gonna have to bring everything to beat us, and it's gonna be hard to recover."

To the outside world, Purdy was enjoying a fairytale run. To Shanahan, it was a slasher movie. Critics had always complained that what the coach really wanted was a robot—a quarterback who'd run the offense the way Shanahan instructed him to, throw it to the receiver that the coverage dictated he should, and generally just stick to the plan. This was different. Certainly, Purdy's youth and inexperience made him more prone to following Shanahan's instructions without deviation, but there was something else going on: his feel for the pocket was unexpectedly advanced. That allowed Purdy, when things broke down, to make something out of nothing—in contrast to Garoppolo, among others. And Purdy didn't perpetually choose the careful option. He had the audacity to believe he could place balls into tight spots between defenders, and the accuracy to get away with it.

Late in the season, Shanahan began checking in weekly with his former passing-game coordinator, Mike LaFleur, who was having a tumultuous second and final season as Saleh's offensive coordinator in New York. It wasn't like Shanahan to do so; he is known for shutting down most communication with people outside the facility during the season, and LaFleur took it as a sign of his former boss's unusual comfort in the situation. That, and what LaFleur saw on tape, convinced him of Purdy's legitimacy.

"He doesn't talk to anybody during the season," LaFleur recalled, "and now I'm talking to him every week because he's just in a good place—because he loved his roster and he loved the team and he loved his quarterback. I'm like, 'Dude, watching you call this is like 2016 [in Atlanta] all over again. You're calling it to shred people.' [Purdy's] phenomenal. It's amazing how some people, good football minds, are like, 'Well, is he [legit]?' Guys, watch the game and then watch his processing. Watch how quick he is in and out. He doesn't need to be a 4.5 guy. In that ten-yard little area back there, he's fast as shit and he processes fast. He feels all that. Watch the plays that Kyle calls. Kyle's smart, so now he gets to call it in an attacking way because he trusts his quarterback."

Any worries that Purdy might shrink in the postseason spotlight were dispelled when the 49ers destroyed the Seahawks in a first-round game at Levi's, with the rookie quarterback throwing for 332 yards and three touchdowns. The next week's divisional-round clash with the Cowboys would be much more challenging. Dallas defensive coordinator Dan Quinn, Shanahan's old Falcons boss, sent waves of pressure at the young quarterback and diminished his windows of opportunity. Quinn knew that matching strategic wits with Shanahan would be a challenge, especially now that McCaffrey had been added to the mix. He so revered the "positionless player" concept that he'd applied it to his defense, deploying second-year star Micah Parsons at numerous positions (edge rusher, inside linebacker, outside linebacker, interior defensive lineman) and using free safety Jayron Kearse at buffalo nickel (a hybrid linebacker position) and cornerback in the team's dime package. "[Shanahan] got my wheels spinning: 'Who can be multipositional players in the NFL?'" Quinn explained. "They've got potentially their best receiver as one of their best backs, and their best back is potentially one of their best receivers. I've tried to flip that defensively to do the same, much like a basketball guy, like [finding] a 'five' who can carry the ball."

The 49ers prevailed over the Cowboys, 19–12, setting up a third trip to the NFC Championship Game in four seasons. It would be on the road, in Philadelphia, against an Eagles team that had gone 14–3 in the regular season and had an emerging star in dual-threat quarterback Jalen Hurts. Shanahan and DeMeco Ryans, his second-year defensive coordinator, had a plan for that: they'd instruct their defensive linemen to push the pocket, protecting the interior A and B gaps rather than trying for sacks, in an attempt to pen Hurts in and make him decipher disguised coverages in the secondary. Shanahan also strongly believed his game plan for attacking Philly's potent defense with quick passes and a variety of run concepts, with Purdy executing it, would succeed.

Three decades into his NFL coaching career, Chris Foerster, in his first year as Shanahan's run game coordinator and third stint as the 49ers' offensive line coach, had never been part of a run like this: a 12-game winning streak heading into a conference title game was unique. Along the way, Foerster had molded a mostly untested offensive line, with three new starters inside the tackles, into a force. The 49ers appeared unbeatable and seemed to be getting better every week. It was like 2019, but even better. This time, Foerster and virtually everyone else in the building believed, they would extinguish all doubt and finish the job.

GEORGE KITTLE SAT IN A CHAIR AT HIS LOCKER INSIDE LINCOLN FINANCIAL Field, his head slumped forward, his body full of welts, his spirit broken. "Sometimes life just punches you in the face, multiple times," he said softly. "In football, and in life, balls don't always bounce your way. Today they bounced just about every way away from us."

It was hard to process everything that had gone down on a miserable January afternoon in Philly. The 49ers had been soundly defeated, 31–7. Purdy had been knocked out midway through the first quarter with an injury to his throwing elbow. (It would turn out to be a torn ulnar collateral ligament, an injury that had the potential to imperil his 2023 season, and possibly even his career.) Then, early in the second half, the Eagles had knocked out Johnson, too, forcing Purdy—who could barely throw a screen pass—to finish out the farce. The sense of stability that Shanahan had about his young quarterback and his team for the next season and beyond was shattered; another potentially tumultuous offseason awaited.

How had it all gone so bad, so abruptly? Shanahan, sitting in his private coach's locker room, tried to retrace the steps. On the first drive of the game, the Eagles went for it on fourth and three from the S.F. 35, and Hurts scrambled left and launched a long pass down the sideline. Falling backward, receiver DeVonta Smith made a leaping one-handed catch. He was seemingly in bounds, but just barely, and it wasn't clear whether he had secured the ball on his way to the ground. The Eagles rushed to the line to snap the ball, meaning Shanahan had only seconds to decide whether to use one of his replay challenges. He chose not to, which proved to be unfortunate: the play likely would have been overturned. The Eagles scored two plays later and went up 7–0.

On the 49ers' next drive, Purdy, on second and six from midfield, faked a handoff to McCaffrey and dropped back to pass. Edge rusher Haason Reddick didn't go for the play fake and was singled up on Kroft, the team's backup tight end. Reddick, who had 16 sacks during the regular season, tied for second in the NFL, took advantage of the mismatch. As Purdy extended his arm to attempt a pass, Reddick raced in and bent it backward, forcing a fumble (initially ruled an incompletion, but overturned after a challenge by Eagles coach Nick Sirianni) that Philly recovered. The Niners' defense forced a three and out, but Shanahan had bigger problems. "I can't throw," Purdy told him on the sideline, and the coach's head dropped.

Shanahan's players stayed resilient, and for a sublime stretch, they thought they might win anyway. With 8:29 left in the second quarter and the ball at the Eagles 23, McCaffrey took a handoff from Johnson, stepped to his right, and was confronted by a flash of green barreling toward his knees. Then, in his words, he "went blackout," jumping nimbly to avoid onrushing safety Marcus Epps, cutting back inside, juking one defender, charging forward, and running through two more. McCaffrey beat a fifth Philly player to the pylon and spun the football in celebration while being mobbed by his pumped-up teammates. The game was about to be tied at seven; standing on the sideline, Purdy and the rest of his teammates believed they'd somehow find a way to prevail.

Wild possibilities began spinning through people's heads. The 49ers had held out hope that Garoppolo could make it back from his foot injury at some point during the postseason. The Super Bowl was two weeks away. Could Jimmy G come back and reemerge—yet again—as the Niners' starting quarterback? Garoppolo, standing next to Purdy on the sideline, was convinced he'd be good to go. Shanahan had other ideas, thinking to himself, *Are we going to have to get Philip Rivers for the Super Bowl?*

Soon enough, reality set in. The Eagles, benefiting from some dubious penalty calls against the 49ers' defense, drove for a go-ahead touchdown, recovered a fumble, scored another, and went into halftime with a 20–7 lead. On the first possession of the third quarter, Johnson found Kittle for a 22-yard completion on third and 13. Two plays later, Johnson took a hit from veteran defensive tackle Ndamukong Suh while releasing a pass, fell backward, and hit his head hard on the turf, suffering a concussion. The 49ers were finished. Purdy reentered the game, basically as a human handoff machine. *This isn't fair*, Purdy thought. Late in the game, Shanahan got choked up. A year earlier, he'd walked across the field at SoFi Stadium, overcome with anger. This was different. He was crushed. Lynch, still enraged by the calls that had gone against the 49ers in the second quarter, unloaded at officials as he left the field.

The aftermath wasn't fun. Doctors suspected Purdy had suffered a torn UCL, an injury commonly experienced by baseball pitchers, requiring Tommy John surgery (named after the former Los Angeles Dodgers pitcher on whom the procedure was pioneered in 1974) that typically knocked them out a year or more. He hoped for a better outcome. Members of the team's medical staff told him he might have a strained ligament that would take six to eight weeks to heal. On the flight home, Purdy grieved for his veteran teammates whose Super Bowl hopes had been dashed, and waited to see what the next morning's MRI would bring. He found out the results while sitting on a training room table at Levi's Stadium, and when he learned that his UCL was indeed torn, his "stomach dropped. I was just like, 'You've got to be kidding me.' I just asked myself and sort of asked God, 'Why? Why take me through all this? Isn't it supposed to be a story-book ending kind of thing? We were supposed to win the Super Bowl, and I'm the last draft pick, I got thrown in—we're supposed to go all the way.' And none of it panned out like that."

At Shanahan's season-ending press conference, he was asked about the preponderance of QB injuries during his 49ers tenure (to Garoppolo, Lance, and now Purdy and Johnson) and the coach's potential culpability. He did not react kindly to the suggestion, incorporating sarcasm into his answer: "I think if you looked at the injuries, common sense would answer that question. How have they gotten hurt? I'm sorry Josh got a concussion when he hit the ground, so that's the fourth one you're talking about. I'm sorry [Purdy] got his elbow bent backwards on a normal dropback pass. I'm sorry [that] on a dropback pass, someone rolled up on Jimmy's ankle. And then we have a dual-threat quarterback [Lance] who got hurt running the ball. So, to throw all those four in that category? No quarterbacks got hurt when we had to hand it off the whole second half, so we can look into that."

That was the end of the press conference, and the beginning of another offseason full of ambiguity and angst over the sport's pivotal position. There was a lot to ponder, with possibilities ranging from Brady to Rodgers to Matt Ryan to even less sexy alternatives. It wasn't a pleasant conundrum, but soon enough, the coach would be happy to dig into it.

Once Shanahan had a chance to assess the situation, it didn't seem so dire. He'd just coached a team to within a game of the Super Bowl on the strength of a rookie quarterback who, nine months earlier, no one—not even the 49ers—believed capable of playing at that level. Purdy's strong sense of self had helped him overcome those doubts. Soon, Shanahan would get his swagger back, too.

Chapter 23

Ten Years Gone

He was mystified. He was mortified. And most of all, as he entered the home locker room at Levi's Stadium at halftime, Kyle Shanahan was *pissed.*

On this afternoon in late-January 2024, Shanahan had to be honest with himself about what was happening. His top-seeded 49ers trailed the Detroit Lions, 24–7, and were staring at their third consecutive NFC Championship Game defeat—and that wasn't even the worst of it. The 49ers' season was on the verge of ending not because of ill-timed injuries or one missed opportunity, but because they were getting beaten into submission on both sides of the ball. They'd given up 280 yards of offense—280 yards!—and looked like the vastly inferior team. Shanahan actually felt bad for his players. They were momentarily down, bereft of answers. He wasn't mad at them *or* the football gods; he was infuriated by the clarity he possessed and the larger truth it revealed.

We don't deserve it.

For Shanahan, this made things simpler. The situation couldn't be rectified merely by making schematic adjustments or correcting mistakes. This was a matter of will. As the 12-minute halftime break progressed, he saw the unwavering resolve return to his players' faces. "There wasn't one guy who looked at all like we weren't gonna turn it around," he'd later recall. "You could see that in their eyes, and you knew they believed it. So, it gave us a chance."

Shanahan had a few adjustments, and one significant philosophical shift, in mind. He harkened back to the mantra he'd learned from Matt Ryan during his two seasons as the Falcons' offensive coordinator. He repeated it now, to his offensive assistants, as they tried to conjure a feasible path toward the Super Bowl: "Players over plays."

Standing atop an escalator at the Hilton Lake Las Vegas Resort and Spa 11 days after the fact, Shanahan broke it down for me. "I mean, when you have players who can make plays, the whole thought of a play is how to get the ball *to* those players," he said. "It's not 'come up with a cool play.' If a play has to be cool to get somebody open, and to get someone in space, then hell yeah, you do that—but you're never just trying to come up with a cool play so it looks like a cool play. It's 'How do I get this guy in this spot to make a play 'cause this guy's that good?' And I guess that's how I look at it."

In that moment, with a season—and perhaps a championship window—on the line, Shanahan felt he didn't have much of a choice. Brock Purdy, his second-year quarterback, was coming off a poor divisional-round playoff game against the Packers and was now being asked to become Joe Montana, who was upstairs in CEO Jed York's luxury suite. Shanahan, a coach who craved that every game be played on his terms, no longer had that luxury. He was going to empower Purdy to deliver the ball to Deebo Samuel, Brandon Aiyuk, Christian McCaffrey, and George Kittle, and live with the results. If the 49ers' defense didn't drastically improve its performance against Jared Goff and the Lions, it wouldn't matter, anyway.

LOSING TO THE LIONS, AT HOME, WOULD BE AN EMBARRASSMENT FOR Shanahan. That was one way to look at it. However, a lot of smart football people were nonetheless blown away by what the coach had managed to do: spend three first-round picks to get in position to draft a franchise quarterback, talk himself out of his initial impulse, pick a raw prospect (Trey Lance) who'd turn out to be a bust, and coach up the 262nd and last pick in the next draft expertly enough to remain among the NFL's elite. To other coaches, Shanahan's credibility had never been higher, almost because of the Lance debacle. He wasn't doing this with Patrick Mahomes or Josh Allen or even Jimmy Garoppolo. Purdy, one of the least likely MVP finalists in football history, was the quarterback charged with bringing Shanahan's plays to life.

None of this had been promised, even after Purdy's impressive two-month stint as Garoppolo's replacement during his rookie season. The torn UCL Purdy suffered in the 2022 NFC Championship Game, and the resulting Tommy John surgery, created legitimate doubts about whether he could be counted on in 2023 and beyond. Even before Purdy underwent the procedure and began what doctors hoped would be a six-month rehab, Shanahan and general manager John Lynch had some big decisions to make. The status quo was untenable. Garoppolo was an unrestricted free agent, and Shanahan was done with him; Lance, coming off two ankle surgeries, hadn't come close to convincing his bosses that he could thrive as an NFL starter. Shanahan was sold on Purdy, and on the model of having a quarterback on a rookie deal and surrounding him with high-priced standouts. However, because of the uncertainty surrounding the quarter-back's recovery, he needed a hedge.

Aaron Rodgers, his relationship with the Packers increasingly strained, was a potential trade target. Yet that would require a multiyear commitment to the 39-year-old that would force the 49ers to make some hard salary cap decisions. Matt Ryan, coming off a miserable season as the Indianapolis Colts' starter, was 37 and looking into broadcasting jobs. There was another, much older option in play, and he made the most sense: Tom Brady, 45, had just retired for a second time without contractual obligation and was thus there for the taking. Shanahan and Lynch had passed on the Bay Area native three years earlier and had quickly regretted it. They took another swing, viewing him as a one-season, Super Bowl-or-bust stopgap before they handed things back over to Purdy.

Purdy didn't have the surgery until March 10; the procedure was delayed because of continued inflammation in his elbow. Before then, Shanahan assured him that, if healthy, he'd be the team's starter in 2023—unless Brady played ball. "That meant so much to me," Purdy recalled. "I remember [Shanahan] saying, 'If we can get Tom Brady, we're going to try to get him.' And I was like, 'Yeah, he's the GOAT. I get it.' But something deep down inside me was sort of like, 'Dude, I just showed you that I can play well in this system. And we were one game away from the Super Bowl.' More than anything, I was like, 'OK, now let's go.'" As Shanahan recalled, "I actually thought it was giving Brock the biggest compliment. I let him know he's our guy long-term. No question. And if Tom Brady wanted to come here and start for one year, that's the only way you're not starting when you're healthy this year . . . But how cool would it be if Tom Brady would be the quarterback here for one season? How cool would it be for you to learn from him?"

Brady passed. The contingency plan became Sam Darnold, the third-overall pick in the 2018 draft, a talented thrower who'd washed out in stints as the Jets' and Panthers' starter. Darnold, still only 25 at the time of his signing in March, was someone Shanahan was convinced he could rehabilitate. That became clear when I spoke to the coach on the first day of training camp in July and he compared Darnold to a passer his father had once helped propel to greatness. "I mean, Steve Young took a while to get going, and he's one of the best quarterbacks of all time. I don't like to compare anyone to Steve, 'cause of how good he is, but why can't Sam be like that? He's got that type of ability. He is that type of person. And I'm just pumped that we could get a talented guy like him here." Another quarterback on the roster, former Bengals backup Brandon Allen, had also made a strong impression with Shanahan. The coach had run out of quarterbacks in his most recent game, the NFC Championship Game disaster in Philly; now, he seemed to be overcompensating. "If you have three quarterbacks good enough to make teams in the NFL," he said, "you always keep 'em. And then that's what I'm happy about, 'cause I think we've got four right now. You don't see many people keep four, but it's been done before."

I didn't think Shanahan would actually keep four QBs, but the conversation revealed a great deal about his assessment of Lance. In August, before joint workouts with the Raiders in Las Vegas, Shanahan told Raiders coach Josh McDaniels and general manager Dave Ziegler he was concerned about facing the Raiders' defense with an injury-depleted offensive line "because I've got two starting quarterbacks" that needed to be protected. It was pretty obvious that Purdy and Darnold were those players.

Purdy had exceeded even the most optimistic medical projections and was cleared to return at the start of camp. The 49ers built in some scheduled off-days for him, but those soon evaporated. On August 25, shortly before their preseason finale against the Chargers at Levi's, Shanahan and Lynch traded Lance to the Cowboys for a fourth-round pick, essentially admitting a cataclysmic mistake that ranked among the worst trades in NFL history. Yet, as long as Purdy kept playing the way they expected him to, there'd be no recriminations, internally or from outsiders.

For most of the 2023 season, Purdy was even better than Shanahan expected. He and McCaffrey both established themselves as MVP candidates, beginning as early as October 8, when the quarterback threw four touchdown passes in a 42–10 pummeling of the Cowboys on *Sunday Night Football*. At that point, the 49ers were 5–0 and looked like a superteam. Then, they endured a mini-crisis.

———

FIRST, THEY WENT TO CLEVELAND AND WERE STYMIED BY THE BROWNS and defensive coordinator Jim Schwartz, a longtime Shanahan nemesis. The following Monday night, in Minneapolis, Shanahan encountered another blast from his past: Vikings quarterback Kirk Cousins shredded the S.F. defense in a 22–17 victory. The tension on the 49ers' headsets was significant. At one point, Shanahan, after a heated exchange with Chris Foerster, told the veteran offensive line coach, "You're done talking. From now on, if anyone talks, it's [assistant line coach James] Cregg." Foerster stayed quiet for a short time and then ignored the decree, without further incident.

By halftime, Shanahan's ire was directed toward defensive coordinator Steve Wilks. With 16 seconds remaining in the second quarter, and the Vikings up 10–7 with the ball at their own 40-yard line, Wilks called a Zero blitz that left the deep middle of the field exposed. It almost turned out to be a brilliant call: Cousins threw a ball over the middle that cornerback Charvarius Ward nearly intercepted at the 35, but receiver Jordan Addison ripped it out of his hands and raced untouched to the end zone.

Shanahan—who felt he had absorbed an unfair share of the blame after Super Bowl LI, given that Falcons coach Dan Quinn had the ultimate green-light authority over his calls—wasn't shy about scapegoating Wilks. "He knows he messed up," Shanahan told reporters two days later.

The following day, Wilks held a mea culpa press conference of his own. Three days later, at Levi's, Bengals quarterback Joe Burrow embarrassed the 49ers in a 31–17 victory, completing 28 of 32 passes for 283 yards and three touchdowns, dropping S.F. to 5–3 heading into its bye week. Before the Niners' next game, Shanahan announced that Wilks would move from the upstairs coaches' box to the field at his discretion.

The hiring of Wilks had been a curious experiment, and it wasn't going well. Some of Wilks's fellow assistants felt he'd been set up to fail. After DeMeco Ryans, who'd coordinated the league's top-ranked defense in 2022, was hired as the Houston Texans' head coach, Shanahan wanted to keep both the existing scheme (including the Wide 9) and the bulk of his incumbent defensive staff intact. Wilks, coming off a relatively impressive stint as the Panthers' interim coach, had never before run the Seattle 3 system first installed by Robert Saleh and later carried on by Ryans, who in 2023 would coax the Texans toward an unlikely division title (while his Shanahan-trained offensive coordinator, Bobby Slowik, helped guide quarterback C. J. Stroud to a record-setting season and the NFL Offensive Rookie of the Year award). Wilks, a well-respected leader who'd joined Brian Flores's class-action lawsuit against the NFL for racial discrimination in its hiring practices, was a semifrequent target of Shanahan's ire, which was jarring to some of the people who witnessed it. As one 49ers assistant said, "It wasn't pleasant from time to time. No one likes being talked to like they're an idiot."

The 49ers regrouped after the bye and won six in a row, including one game that meant quite a bit to Shanahan and his players. On December 3, they returned to Lincoln Financial Field to face the Eagles, who were 10–1 at the time. It had been ten and a half months since the NFC title game. With a minute left in the first quarter, a familiar theme appeared to be playing out: the Eagles had put together a pair of 12-play drives, while the Niners had minus-six yards to their credit. Purdy was 0-for-4 and had been sacked once by Haason Reddick, who had injured him in January, and harassed by the edge rusher on numerous other occasions. The score was 6–0, but it felt like 100–zip. Things got heated on the headset before Shanahan took a deep breath and reset. "Just calm everybody down," he told his position coaches. "We're good."

They were better than good. The 49ers snapped out of it and rolled to a 42–19 victory that asserted their superiority in the NFC and caused an identity crisis among the Eagles that they would never recover from. The game's signature moment came with 9:27 left in the third quarter, when 49ers linebacker Dre Greenlaw, after a hard sideline tackle, got into a physical altercation with Philly's longtime security chief, Dom DiSandro—a cult hero whose Big Dom clothing line could be purchased at the stadium. Greenlaw was ejected for grazing DiSandro's face with his finger, and when Shanahan realized that someone who wasn't a player or coach was involved in the incident, he lost his mind. "What I couldn't accept was who taunted him," Shanahan told me later as we sat in his private dressing area next to the 49ers' locker room with his son, Carter, enjoying an indelible go-to-work-with-your-father moment. "When we lose one of our best players 'cause he's getting into it with someone who's not [involved] in the game, that was kind of hard to accept at the time."

By game's end, the 49ers looked unbeatable. They weren't, though. On Christmas night, at Levi's, the Baltimore Ravens crushed them by a 33–19 margin, intercepting Purdy four times. His Ravens counterpart, Lamar Jackson, essentially won the MVP trophy that night, as Baltimore emerged as the NFL's team to beat heading into January. The Niners rebounded six days later, winning a road game against the Washington Commanders and—because the rest of the NFC was collapsing—clinching the No. 1 seed and the first-round bye that came with it. That meant it would be three weeks before the 49ers would play another meaningful game, in the divisional round of the playoffs. The time off would show.

———

LAMAR JACKSON COULD HAVE BEEN A DOLPHIN. THEORETICALLY, THE star quarterback was free to try to sign with any team in the spring of 2023. Locked in an acrimonious contract dispute with the Ravens, he publicly requested a trade, a sentiment he'd conveyed to his bosses in early March. The franchise had responded by placing the nonexclusive franchise tag on Jackson, meaning any team could negotiate with him and sign him to a contract, while the Ravens would have the right to match, or to receive two first-round draft picks in return. Given the extent to which things had degenerated, the Ravens might have been persuaded by a motivated suitor to take less compensation than that.

The Dolphins, Jackson hoped, would step up and make it happen. He'd grown up in South Florida and loved what Miami's offense had accomplished in Mike McDaniel's first year as coach, with breakaway threats Tyreek Hill and Jaylen Waddle transforming them into one of the most feared offenses in the league. McDaniel and general manager Chris Grier had a high opinion of Jackson, but felt committed to incumbent quarterback Tua Tagovailoa, who they believed could avoid the concussion issues that had plagued him in 2022. They expected to be even better in 2023. Less than a month into the season, the Dolphins did something that had only seemed possible in a video game.

On September 24 at Hard Rock Stadium, they dropped 70 points on the Denver Broncos, piling up 726 yards of offense in the process—even though Waddle missed the game while recovering from a concussion. It was only the fourth time in NFL history that a team had hit the 70 mark—and the first in 57 years. The Dolphins were within three points of the all-time record (the Bears' 73–0 victory over Washington in the 1940 NFL Championship Game) with eight minutes remaining. After driving into field goal range late in the game, McDaniel opted to take a knee. "It felt like chasing points, chasing a record," McDaniel explained afterward. "That's not what we came here to do."

The league took note. "It's unreal," Mike LaFleur, two games into his tenure as the Rams' offensive coordinator, told me the following day. "I'll never see that again in my lifetime. You just won't." Said Dolphins assistant quarterbacks coach Chandler Henley, "You remember when I told you that McD would just get better each year 'cause he's a cyborg and keeps evolving? That's what's happening."

"Their schematics are almost revolutionary in what they do," Bills coach Sean McDermott said of his AFC East rivals. Analytics experts feverishly broke down the "Cheat Motion"—as christened by Shanahan, who quickly appropriated the tactic—the Dolphins were employing to make Hill even more dangerous off the ball. The receiver, starting from a tight split, would burst toward the sideline just before the snap and cut upfield as the center released the ball, simulating a running start. Whereas almost all motions in the NFL went outside-in, this went inside-out. "Guys are fascinated by our offense, the way that Coach got me motioning around," Hill told reporters in September. "They are like, 'Bro, where does that come from?' I'm like, 'You know what, I have no idea.'"

The Dolphins looked like legitimate Super Bowl contenders. Tagovailoa would, in fact, start all 17 games, defying the skeptics who believed his history of head trauma would derail him, and lead the league with 4,624 passing yards. Yet something wasn't quite right. Though Miami rolled to a 9–3 start, it didn't have a single victory that stood out. Beating a mediocre Broncos team badly didn't quite count. At 11–4, the Dolphins traveled to Baltimore for a pivotal showdown with Jackson and the Ravens—and got rolled, 56–19. Vic Fangio, one of football's great defensive minds, wasn't meshing with McDaniel. It didn't help that the Dolphins endured a slew of injuries to key defensive players, but the McDaniel–Fangio pairing would turn out to be a one-year arrangement, with Fangio moving on to join the Eagles after a mutual parting of the ways at season's end.

The Dolphins lost their regular-season finale at home, to the Bills, ceding the AFC East title to Buffalo in the process. That meant they'd have to go to Kansas City for their playoff opener, with the defending Super Bowl champion Chiefs and a hellacious cold front awaiting them. The Dolphins did not score 70 points in that playoff game; they managed just seven, with Hill burning his former team for a 53-yard touchdown in the second quarter. It was four degrees below zero at kickoff, with a minus-27 wind chill, and McDaniel—for all his revolutionary contributions during his first two seasons—went home facing increased scrutiny after a second consecutive late-season fade. The NFL could be brutal, and seemingly impossible, no matter how smart you were.

———

THE DAY AFTER THE DOLPHINS WERE ELIMINATED, MATT LaFLEUR GUIDED the Green Bay Packers into a first-round playoff game against the Cowboys—with Jordan Love at quarterback. An era had ended the previous March when Rodgers, the team's starter since 2008, emerged from a four-day darkness retreat in Oregon and declared he wanted to be traded to the Jets. Yes, the same Jets coached by LaFleur's close friend Robert

Saleh, who had just fired LaFleur's younger brother and replaced him with former Packers offensive coordinator Nathaniel Hackett. All of it could have been awkward for Matt LaFleur, but by then he didn't care. Just as Rodgers had done during Brett Favre's later years, Love had just spent three seasons as a backup and was now deemed ready to run Green Bay's offense. LaFleur knew his partnership with Rodgers had run its course, and moving forward with Love had its advantages. Rather than having to tailor his offense to Rodgers' preexisting preferences, LaFleur could now install the system—closer to Kyle Shanahan's template than anything run by Shanahan's other protégés—he really wanted.

Once the Jets formalized the trade for Rodgers in late April, the pressure intensified in the Big Apple. Saleh fed into it, telling reporters in May, "In my opinion, 32 coaches stand in front of their teams every year, talk about winning a championship, and then realistically, there's maybe six or eight teams that have an actual chance to do it, and I do think we are one of those teams." LaFleur was stunned. "I can't believe he said that," he told me. "It's one thing to say that to your team. It's another thing to say it publicly. I'm like 'Dude, why would you put [yourself in] the crosshairs?' It always comes with the job, but you don't need to say it. He's obviously one of my closest friends. He's smarter than fuck. That, to me, was not one of the smartest things."

As it turned out, the Jets had no chance. On their fourth offensive play of the regular season, Rodgers tore his Achilles tendon. Dysfunction followed, leading to huge pressure on Saleh (who nonetheless survived to coach a fourth season) and further damaging Hackett's reputation in the wake of his disastrous one-and-done stint as the Broncos' head coach.

LaFleur had his own problems. Despite a 47–19 regular-season record and two trips to the NFC Championship Game in four seasons as a head coach, he knew the deal: if the Packers lived down to expectations in 2023, he could be out of a job. After a 2–5 start, that seemed like a distinct possibility. Love, who was big, mobile, and had a great arm, still wasn't seeing the field the way LaFleur needed him to. His receivers and tight ends were all raw and inexperienced. Life without Rodgers, even after the tumultuous 2022 season, was predictably humbling. The coaches didn't know what to do; they were out of tricks.

"We changed *everything*," recalled offensive coordinator Adam Stenavich, a former offensive tackle who'd played for Shanahan (in Houston) and coached for him (as the 49ers' assistant offensive line coach in 2017 and '18). "The schedule, the way we did installs, the way we practiced. Whatever we were doing, it wasn't working. I stood up at the [offensive team] meeting and said, 'Everyone get up and switch seats. These seats are bad.' They all did it eagerly."

At the beginning of November, Green Bay was 3–6. Love had thrown 14 touchdown passes and ten interceptions and had whiffed on numerous chances to pull out close games. Then, suddenly, everything clicked. The Packers won five of seven, including wins over the Lions and Chiefs, to sneak into the playoffs, then shocked the Cowboys in the first round with a 48–32 victory in which they held a 32-point lead midway through the fourth quarter. During that stretch, Love threw 21 touchdown passes and only one interception; he looked like the player Trey Lance was *supposed* to be.

That sent the seventh-seeded Packers to Northern California for a divisional-round matchup against the 49ers—another Shanahan–LaFleur battle—and they had no intention of stopping there. The night before the game, at an old-school Menlo Park tavern called the Dutch Goose, Stenavich passed out shots of Crown Royal in plastic cups and led more than a dozen of his fellow assistants in a toast, declaring, "We're a bunch of dogs. A bunch of *dirt dogs*. That's all we are, and we are here. We're gonna burn down the Bay, we're gonna keep doing what we do, and we're gonna win the fucking Super Bowl."

IF THE PACKERS WERE AMONG THE LEAST LIKELY PLAYOFF QUALIFIERS IN 2023, the Rams were right behind them. Matthew Stafford, Cooper Kupp, and Aaron Donald were the only stars remaining from the Super Bowl team, and the roster was now the second-youngest in the league, just behind the Packers. But McVay, who'd seen a bronze statue of him unveiled at his alma mater in May and welcomed a son, Jordan John, in late October, appeared revitalized and at peace. "He's like a totally different guy," Rams defensive coordinator Raheem Morris marveled in September.

McVay had transformed his offense to feature a power running attack between the tackles, tailored to second-year back Kyren Williams's strengths. Puka Nacua, a fifth-round draft pick, emerged as an instant star, breaking a 63-year-old record for receiving yards by a rookie. Stafford, beset by elbow problems the previous summer, was slinging it at an elite level once more. Morris, with a depth chart that lacked pedigree at almost every position (aside from Donald), schemed it up adeptly enough to keep the Rams in games.

L.A. grabbed the NFC's sixth seed on the final Sunday of the season, in Santa Clara. Shanahan, with the Niners having already clinched the first-round bye, sat Purdy and removed most of his starters well before halftime. The Rams, who'd already secured a playoff berth and were playing only for seeding, made Stafford, Williams, Kupp, and Donald inactive. The Rams rallied to win, 21–20, and walked off the field firmly convinced they'd be back at Levi's in two weeks for a divisional-round rematch. The Packers would derail that plan by winning in Dallas. Later that night, McVay's former franchise quarterback would make it all moot.

Given the backstory—learning he'd been traded by the Rams while his replacement, Stafford, partied with McVay in Cabo; watching McVay and Stafford celebrate a Super Bowl victory the following February; being written off by a majority of fans and media members—Goff had a lot on the line in this first-round game that saw the third-seeded Lions host the Rams. The fans at Ford Field, who'd spent 12 seasons cheering for Stafford, certainly understood the stakes. Fifty minutes before the Lions' first home playoff game in 30 years, a "Jared Goff" chant broke out; it got even louder when Stafford, who'd failed to win a playoff game during his time in Detroit, took the field.

To Goff, it "was pretty surreal. They knew the team we were playing was the one that basically sent me off, and they're supporting me and saying I'm their guy, which obviously is awesome. I'd never experienced anything like that, and I'm not sure how many guys have."

After a brilliant performance capped by a game-sealing first-down completion just after the two-minute warning—giving the Lions a 24–23 victory, their first playoff triumph in 32 years—Goff heard the chants again, this time from his jubilant teammates as he entered the locker room. The chants would become a thing around Michigan, cropping up at Pistons, Red Wings, and Western Michigan hockey games, and even at a high school cheer competition. While obviously crushed by the outcome, McVay said of his former quarterback, "I'm really happy for him."

A week later, Goff would do it again: another standout performance saw him lead the Lions past the Tampa Bay Buccaneers and into the NFC Championship Game. McVay, meanwhile, was still taking the high road. As much as he hated the thought of losing his defensive coordinator, he was rooting hard for Morris to get a head coaching job.

IT HAD BEEN A DOZEN YEARS SINCE MORRIS HAD BEEN FIRED BY THE Bucs after a three-year stint as their head coach, and despite all his success as an assistant since then—and as the Falcons' interim coach in 2020—he wasn't sure he'd ever get another opportunity. In a league not known for its enlightened views when it comes to racial equality, he had several perceived strikes against him: he was Black, he specialized on the defensive side of the ball (though he had spent three and a half seasons as a receivers coach in Atlanta), he was a retread, and now, at 47, he was no longer considered young in his profession.

One thing Morris could boast that few, if any, other candidates could: he was a literal lifesaver. In May of 2023, he and his wife, Nicole, were poolside at the Encore Hotel in Vegas when a three-year-old boy was pulled from the water without a pulse. As a doctor was being summoned, Morris, processing information he'd learned in the wake of Buffalo Bills safety Damar Hamlin's scary cardiac arrest episode five months earlier, asked, "Where's the AED?" He then ran to retrieve the nearest automated external defibrillator, which analyzes the heart's rhythm and distributes an appropriate electrical shock designed to restore it. With Morris's help, the doctor used the device to help revive the boy, who was discharged from the hospital 24 hours later.

"You hear that story and you think, 'My goodness—I can't imagine what that was like,'" said Vikings coach Kevin O'Connell, Morris's former Rams colleague. "Then you think of Raheem being there, and it makes sense. He's the ultimate selfless human that just cares about people."

Now the question was: Would an owner conclude that Morris was the best choice to try to resuscitate an organization? It was a volatile coaching cycle, with eight openings—a quarter of the league's teams—and big names like Bill Belichick, Pete Carroll, Mike Vrabel, and Jim Harbaugh in play. Those obvious candidates were joined by the usual group of hot, young, white assistants in the "Friend of McVay" mold, a group that now included Lions offensive coordinator Ben Johnson and Slowik, the Texans' first-year coordinator. With Stroud having capped one of the best seasons ever by a rookie quarterback by guiding the Texans to a 45–14 first-round playoff victory over the Browns, Slowik was gaining traction, with at least four teams seriously pursuing him. Morris knew all about Slowik, who'd been a defensive assistant on Mike Shanahan's Washington staff from 2011 until 2013. Upon taking the 49ers' head coaching job in 2017, Kyle Shanahan hired Slowik as a defensive quality control coach before switching him to offense following the 2018 season, similar to the move he had once made with Morris in Atlanta.

As proud as Kyle Shanahan was of Slowik, the latest of his disciples to shine, he viewed Morris as the prize of the coaching cycle. Morris, he'd told me in September, "would be my first choice for a head coach if I was an owner." Though Morris was one of his best friends, Shanahan did not say such things lightly.

Morris interviewed with five teams: the Panthers, Chargers, Falcons, Seahawks, and Commanders, landing second interviews with four of them. However, the seats began filling up quickly, and it appeared as though he might be shut out again. He was scheduled to head to Seattle for a second interview when the Falcons started sending signals of serious interest. It had been presumed that Belichick, a six-time Super Bowl winner who'd just completed a 24-season run with the New England Patriots, would be Atlanta owner Arthur Blank's choice.

On January 25, 2024, the Falcons shocked the league by announcing that Morris was their man. It seemed to be a changing-of-the-guard moment. The autocratic, domineering Belichick, despite his unmatched pedigree, did not end up with a job. Nor did Vrabel, a former Patriots star linebacker with a sometimes brusque bedside manner—despite the fact that he'd been the NFL's Coach of the Year in 2021.

For their part, the Fun Bunch had never been in better positions.

A decade after Mike Shanahan's inglorious firing had compelled them to disperse, his former assistants were, collectively, a pivotal force in the football world. Kyle Shanahan, McVay, LaFleur, McDaniel, Morris, and their offshoots—a group that included Ryans, Saleh, O'Connell, and the Bengals' Zac Taylor—had taken over much of the league. Two other members of the coaching tree, Brandon Staley (Chargers) and Arthur Smith (Falcons), had been NFL head coaches at the start of 2023, and Hackett (still hanging on as the Jets' coordinator) had gotten his shot the previous season. And Slowik, Mike LaFleur, Zac Robinson (Falcons), Liam Coen (Bucs), Shane Waldron (Bears), Klint Kubiak (Saints), and Luke Getsy (Raiders) were well positioned to be future head coaches.

"They have evolved football," Vikings general manager Kwesi Adofo-Mensah said. "It used to be about plays and players; now it's about systems and players. Everybody says they have a system, but to have a system and then to be a systems thinker, those are two different things. There's an intention for why their system exists, why they do things. Then, how they tweak within that system, how they understand the interconnectedness of all those things—that's what makes them unique and separates them from everybody else. It's asking, 'Can we do it a different way?' That, to me, is what makes them special."

So far, though, only McVay, with Morris as his defensive coordinator, had hoisted a Lombardi Trophy.

————

WHEN SHANAHAN SEETHED DURING THAT UNCOMFORTABLE HALFTIME interlude against the Lions, he knew, on some level, that he was fortunate to be in that position in the first place. The 49ers—far and away the NFC's best team during the regular season—hadn't played like it in January. In the divisional-round game, the Packers came out with poise and purpose, and Love was a match for the moment. Purdy, by contrast, was uncharacteristically imprecise and hesitant, possibly a function of the rainy conditions that had also seemed to bother him during the Niners' regular-season defeat in Cleveland. His second pass should have been intercepted by Packers safety Darnell Savage, who might have returned it for a touchdown.

The quarterback later said he was late getting to his checkdowns because he was searching for big-play opportunities, among other issues. Perhaps because of Purdy's hesitancy, Shanahan was off, too. He seemed to be coaching not to lose, employing an oddly conservative strategy late in the first half. The 49ers got away with it in the end, thanks in part to Packers mistakes (including a crucial missed field goal). Purdy pulled it together to direct a 69-yard drive for a late go-ahead touchdown, and Love threw a bad interception, allowing the Niners to escape with a 24–21 victory. It represented a landmark achievement of sorts for Shanahan, whose teams had thrived when games were played on his terms but struggled in other circumstances. Until then, when entering the fourth quarter trailing by five or more points, the 49ers under Shanahan were 0–31. "That," Shanahan told me afterward as he walked through the locker room, "was as hard as it gets."

A while later, as he walked toward the Packers' team buses, LaFleur was reckoning with the result. He'd coached boldly, putting complete trust in his players. "That's how I coached all year," LaFleur told me. "And I'll never not coach that way again."

Following that abysmal first half against the Lions, who'd simply manhandled his team, Shanahan didn't have the luxury of trying to direct the flow of the game. His players would have to fight their way out of the hole, and it was quite possible they simply weren't good enough. It was time to find out.

PLAYERS OVER PLAYS. **IT WAS THE ONLY STRATEGY THAT MADE SENSE TO** Shanahan now. The 49ers opened the second half by driving for a field goal that cut Detroit's lead to 24–10, but the Lions responded by marching to the San Francisco 28. On fourth and two, Detroit coach Dan Campbell—someone who routinely coached on emotion—left his offense on the field, forgoing a field goal that could have made it a three-possession game. The 49ers made the stop. Then things got weird.

After a 17-yard completion to Deebo Samuel, Purdy dropped back and fired a deep ball over the middle toward second-team All-Pro receiver Brandon Aiyuk. The ball was overthrown, and cornerback Kindle Vildor, who'd prevented Aiyuk from getting behind him, reached out for the interception while falling backward inside the Detroit ten-yard line. The ball somehow went through Vildor's hands and bounced off his face mask. Aiyuk, who never gave up on it, dove and caught the ball at the four.

Two plays later, Purdy zipped a touchdown pass to Aiyuk. On the Lions' next offensive play, veteran safety Tashaun Gipson dislodged the football from the grip of rookie running back Jahmyr Gibbs, and defensive tackle Arik Armstead recovered at the Detroit 24. Soon, Christian McCaffrey was in the end zone, and the score was tied. It had taken just 12 minutes for the 49ers to catch up. Down by three midway through the fourth quarter, the Lions drove into range for a game-tying field goal. Again, Campbell gambled on fourth and short; again, he failed. The 49ers survived to win, 34–31.

As red, white, and gold confetti fell at Levi's and Montana joined Purdy on the victory podium, Shanahan finally exhaled. Twice in eight days, his team had been outplayed for long stretches and had managed to avoid upsets. Now, for the second time in four years, Patrick Mahomes and the Chiefs—coming off an AFC Championship Game defeat of the Ravens earlier that day—stood between Shanahan and the endpoint of his obsessive, decades-long quest.

To win Super Bowl LVIII, Shanahan would have to be at his best, and so would his players. Even that, he knew, might not be enough.

Epilogue

Peggy Shanahan had been watching football for decades, witnessing more games than just about anyone not in a jersey or employed by a team during that span. Well, that wasn't totally true. When she got nervous, which wasn't an infrequent occurrence, Peggy had developed a habit of *not* watching. She'd fallen back on that habit during much of the second half of the 49ers' divisional-round game against the Packers in January, turning her head away from the field strategically or retreating to the bathroom of the luxury suite where she and her husband were watching their only son try to move one step closer to his dream. People who didn't know her well probably thought she had an overactive bladder. In fact, she was listening for the roar of the crowd to signal that everything that would be OK. "It's a weird thing I do," Peggy conceded. "I've done it all my life. But it's worse when it's your child."

Three weeks later, as she sat on a short white bench just inside the entrance of the visitors' locker room at Allegiant Stadium, Peggy was dealing with the worst angst of all: her child was devastated, and she wasn't sure how to comfort him. After a 25–22 overtime defeat to the Chiefs in Super Bowl LVIII, Kyle Shanahan was sequestered in a private dressing room a few feet away. Peggy stared at the locker room carpet, wondering what she could possibly say when he emerged. Mothers are built for such moments, but she had nothing. She didn't know the *why* of it; she didn't know how to make the anguish go away. She spoke softly and without much conviction:

"I don't know what to say. I don't know that much about football. I just know how hard this is. We went through it a lot in the early days."

It's true that Mike Shanahan, the man seated to her right, endured three lopsided Super Bowl setbacks as a Broncos assistant before reaching the pinnacle of his profession. However, seeing a child give everything, get to the precipice, and fail hit Peggy differently, especially when that failure had taken place on the grandest stage in American sports, with hundreds of millions of strangers already dissecting it. To Peggy's left sat Kyle's three children, as quiet and helpless as their grandparents. Twice in the previous hour, they had seen two teams line up for a play that, if it had gone the 49ers' way, would have triggered the most epic celebration they could ever have imagined.

The emptiness they felt now was the opposite of that—perhaps even something worse.

The 49ers had their chances, but in the end, the greatness of Patrick Mahomes prevailed. Unlike in Shanahan's previous two Super Bowl experiences—as the Falcons' offensive coordinator seven years earlier, and as the Niners' head coach three years after that—it would be hard to frame the loss as a choke job. Yes, San Francisco had held a ten-point lead, but that was in the second quarter. It felt like a stretch for anyone to come away from this Super Sunday blaming the defeat on the losing head coach and ascribing the outcome to an inherent defect of his strategy or leadership.

That wouldn't stop some people, of course. In the coming hours, days, weeks, and months, Shanahan would be second-guessed for electing to receive the ball in overtime after winning the coin toss, and, somewhat disingenuously, for his players' apparent ignorance of the new overtime rule for the postseason that was being implemented for the first time. Comments would come from his own locker room, suggesting the 49ers weren't prepared for specific strategic wrinkles employed by Kansas City on both sides of the ball, and Shanahan's subsequent dismissal of defensive coordinator Steve Wilks would be framed as scapegoating by some critics.

All of that was annoying, but it wasn't the heart of the matter. A coach had built a team designed to meet this moment, conjured a game plan that put the 49ers in position to win, and stayed cool and clearheaded in the most charged of circumstances—and still, it wasn't enough. Sometimes the football gods cursed you—how else to explain standout linebacker Dre Greenlaw tearing his Achilles tendon while beginning to run back onto the field after a second-quarter punt? Sometimes the refs screwed you. Sometimes the ball bounced funny.

And sometimes—for Shanahan, the *third* time on a Super Sunday—an all-time great quarterback imposed his will and proved to be the difference between winning and losing. It was an excruciatingly close game, but Mahomes was the kind of player who made the result look inevitable.

However you framed it, Shanahan had once again been denied and would have to live with it. He was only 44, but he was drained. There was no guarantee he'd ever get this close again. And there was nothing his mother or anyone else could say that would make it any different.

FOR SHANAHAN, THE GOAL WAS TO COACH WITHOUT REGRET. IF HE PRE-pared as hard as he could, and, on game day, stayed true to his plan—and his instincts—he could live with the result, even if it tore him up.

If anything, the scars of past disappointments had coarsened him. He was surer of his process and his sensibilities than ever before. Before the previous season's NFC Championship Game in Philadelphia, Shanahan had been asked about those scars and he gave an expansive answer. "I just treat it as a football game, and when you lose big games, those are hard, real hard, however they happen, and you have to deal with that forever. But I feel like that's what kind of hardens you to it and makes you get back to the reality of what it really is." A little later, he said, "The only time that I ever have regrets in games is when I feel I've made decisions that I didn't want to make, or you don't feel like that was the right decision [and] you went [with it] for another reason. It's been a long time since I've done something like that. A lot of people don't like the pressure of it—players, people in general—because you put yourself out there, and it's really tough if you don't come up victorious. But like I've always said and heard growing up, there's only one team that's happy at the end of the year, and the other 31 teams aren't. And you always keep going and try to be that team, and you do that until you're done playing or you're done coaching."

With the recent dismissals of Bill Belichick and Pete Carroll, Shanahan and McVay were no longer the young geniuses of the league; they were tied at fourth on the list of the NFL's longest-tenured coaches. Unlike McVay, who had openly addressed the toll the job took and pondered how long he could withstand it, Shanahan seemed consumed with the sport, to the exclusion of even a thought otherwise. However, to his closest friends and coaching associates, it wasn't a given that Shanahan could continue at his current pace.

One Shanahan assistant believed that if Jimmy Garoppolo hadn't returned and injury hadn't intervened, and Trey Lance had been the Niners' starting quarterback for the entire 2022 season, the disaster that might have ensued would have caused Shanahan to step away. During the 2023 season, Bo Scaife, Shanahan's old Texas teammate and good friend, told me, "He's reached that level of not giving a fuck. You can't if you're a head coach. He had to learn it. People are still fucking with him about 28–3 to this day. But there's nothing he could do about that shit now, so there's no point in him giving any energy to it. His whole main thing is this fucking Super Bowl. Especially knowing how close he's been, like a few yards close. I know that's what he's going super, super hard for. Once he gets that, I think he might reevaluate his whole career."

I asked Scaife to clarify: Did he think Shanahan would quit if the 49ers won the Super Bowl? "I wouldn't be surprised," he said. "It wouldn't shock me. It's a stressful job, man. He fucking grinds."

The world very nearly found out. The 49ers, especially on defense, played much better than they had in the two previous playoff games. Purdy looked like he belonged under the glare of the sports world's brightest spotlight. In the first quarter he completed eight of ten passes for 105 yards and staked the 49ers to that 10–0 lead, one that might have been bigger if not for a Christian McCaffrey fumble in Chiefs territory. K.C.'s veteran defensive coordinator, Steve Spagnuolo, adjusted by putting his defensive backs in man-to-man coverage while continuing to blitz more than half of the time. "Brock Purdy is *really* good," Spagnuolo told *Sports Illustrated*'s Albert Breer afterward. "He knew when we were in certain things, and he found seams." The adjustments bothered Purdy, who told reporters two days later, "The Chiefs did a good job of scheming things up. And catching us off guard at some points. Them playing man, maybe it was something that we just weren't expecting a whole lot of."

Shanahan, undoubtedly, would dissect every play in the game's aftermath. Yet he wouldn't need intensive film review to understand the basics: the Chiefs made one fewer major mistake than the 49ers did. K.C. took its first lead late in the third quarter after a punt hit S.F.'s Darrell Luter's leg and return man Ray-Ray McCloud tried and failed to scoop it up, rather than attempting to fall on the fumble. The Chiefs recovered at the Niners 16 and scored on the next play. And after Purdy's ten-yard touchdown pass to Jauan Jennings put the Niners back in front, 16–13, with 11:22 remaining, Jake Moody's extra-point attempt was blocked. Shanahan, looking down at his call sheet, didn't even watch the play. "How the fuck does that happen, man?" he screamed.

Still, the 49ers had more chances. Shanahan, a master of the deliberate drive—sometimes maddeningly so, to those who wanted him to be more aggressive—had it all mapped out after a Chiefs field goal tied the game with 5:46 remaining. However, cornerback Trent McDuffie blitzed and deflected Purdy's third-and-five pass just after the two-minute warning, keeping the 49ers from extending the drive and bleeding the clock, and S.F. settled for Moody's 53-yard field goal. That left Mahomes enough time to drive the Chiefs into position for a game-tying field goal, setting up the first overtime in NFL history in which each team would be guaranteed a possession.

The Niners won the toss and elected to receive—Chiefs coach Andy Reid later said he'd have chosen to kick off in such a scenario—and after the fact, Shanahan got a ton of grief for his decision. A strong case could be made either way: If the game had remained tied after the first two possessions, sudden death would have followed, and Shanahan wanted the ball in that scenario; also, taking the ball allowed the Niners' tired defense to regroup. Conversely, getting the ball second gave the Chiefs certainty about what they'd need to do (and, accordingly, the ability to use all four downs) and, if each team were to score a touchdown, the option of going for two to make the third-possession scenario moot.

The margin for error was minuscule. The 49ers had a third and four from the Chiefs' nine, and Purdy—pressured by defensive tackle Chris Jones, who'd been freed up because of confusion caused by another Spagnuolo blitz—hastily overthrew a wide-open Jennings, leading to a Moody field goal. After the incompletion, Shanahan threw up his hands and said, "No one fucking blocked 95 again."

Then Mahomes got the ball, needing a touchdown to win, and did Mahomes things, completing all eight of his passes—including a game-winning end-zone strike to Mecole Hardman—and running twice for 27 yards. Along the way, the Niners had what amounted to a match point: the Chiefs faced fourth and one from their own 34 and needed to convert to extend the game. Said Shanahan on the sideline, "Alright, we stop 'em, we're world champs, right?" They didn't, and they weren't: Mahomes drifted right, cut inside, and gained eight yards for the first down, a truly pivotal play.

About 20 minutes after Hardman's game-ending touchdown, with the Chiefs still celebrating, Shanahan entered a tent outside the stadium and took his place at a podium. I asked him about regret—did he have any, based on the standard he'd previously enunciated? He paused to collect his thoughts. He'd called a trick play that produced the game's first touchdown—a backward pass from Purdy to Jennings, who threw back across the field to McCaffrey near the line of scrimmage, who raced forward for a 21-yard score—and had successfully gone for it on fourth and three from the K.C. 15 early in the fourth quarter to set up Purdy's go-ahead TD pass to Jennings. "Any play that doesn't work, you always think about that," he said. "But in terms of everything that we try to do, we try to prepare as hard as we can. And we try to go in there and do exactly what we think is right based off our preparation, what's going on in that game. What I can't live with is when I do stuff that I didn't plan on doing, or that I didn't do and second-guess myself. I'm proud of what we did today as a coaching staff and as players."

───

THERE WAS CONFETTI ON THE FLOOR OF THE 49ERS' LOCKER ROOM, tracked into the room by the cleats of the losers. Four years earlier, in Miami, there'd been a defiant, *we'll be back* optimism in the air after the loss; this scene was much different. Many of the team's proudest and most decorated players could barely put their thoughts into words. There was a sobering sense of finality as the players grabbed their roller bags and headed off toward the buses that would take them to a downbeat party at the Aria, on the Las Vegas Strip. (Every Super Bowl team has a party after the game, win or lose.)

Shanahan was alone with his thoughts in his private dressing room. It wasn't hard to guess what was going through his mind. Two days after the NFC Championship Game, he'd driven his Tesla to work with long-time NFL journalist Peter King as his passenger, recalling his days as his father's communications-cord holder during the Broncos' Super Bowl XXXVII upset of the Packers—one of the last people ever to serve in that role because, Kyle noted, "they went wireless the next year. But you watch the highlights of that game and you see me behind my dad, the kid with the pimples."

King asked Shanahan if he was still haunted by the Falcons' loss in Super Bowl LI. The coach gave a long, expansive answer. No, he said. "It hurts. It doesn't kill you. You understand what happened. You understand you can handle it. You can take it. 'Haunted' is just such the wrong word. It makes you stronger, really. But, you know, if you told me before that game you're going to blow a 28–3 lead and lose, I'd be like, 'Do I ever come out of my room again?' You realize, this is sports. Any one of 20 different plays would've changed that game. But I also understand that the quarterback on the other side [Tom Brady] did the most unbelievable thing I've ever seen. He performed surgery for an entire second half. The harder one was [the Super Bowl LIV to the Chiefs], personally."

Shanahan went on. "As you get older and you go through the experience, you just . . . you try to control everything. You realize you can't. You also realize you can handle it. And you realize how much you love it. When you lose, and you feel the heartbreak, you get to see how you handle it, how you react, how you handle the pressure the next time. And, oh my gosh, you realize, 'I am this. I can do this.' You get to go through something you love, something that's more important in life than almost anything. That's what I learned about football growing up, but it only gets stronger as I get older. Football teaches you who you are."

Another hard lesson had been delivered in Vegas. Many would blame the coach, writing him off as a flawed leader incapable of winning the big one. It didn't matter if it was fair, or how close he'd come, or that he'd wowed the people who knew the sport best by accomplishing so much with a quarterback no one had believed in. Shanahan knew the score.

This, too, would be part of his journey. He and his onetime understudies had collectively changed football, and their competition would become only fiercer. McVay, Matt LaFleur, and Mike McDaniel were already devising ways to give their teams an edge that might make them Super. Raheem Morris finally had a second chance to show his head coaching chops—and a chance to give the Falcons organization, still in the wilderness after 28–3, the redemption it sought.

All of those coaches, and *their* disciples, and so many others, looked up to Shanahan. So did his son, Carter, who sat there on that bench, waiting for his dad to emerge the way I'd once witnessed Mike Shanahan's son wait for him after emotionally draining games. Soon, Kyle would exit the locker room, eyes welling, wife Mandy beside him, carrying herself with pride and dignity in her husband's most difficult hour. As the family strode through the bowels of Allegiant Stadium toward a black Chevy Suburban, Kyle's youngest child, 11-year-old Lexi, wearing a red bubble jacket and sparkly boots, locked her arm around her dad's and wouldn't let go.

Mike and Peggy trailed behind, internalizing their thoughts. A few minutes earlier, I'd asked Mike the same question I'd previously posed to Peggy—"What do you plan to say to your son?"—and gotten a much blunter answer. The Mastermind, the detail-driven obsessive, had that old fire in his eyes.

"You keep fighting," he said, his voice hoarse. "That's fucking life. I don't care what job you've got. When things happen, you've got to fight through it. You want to get to the mountaintop—what, you're gonna feel sorry for yourself? Fuck that. You get back up and you keep climbing."

Acknowledgments

Taking a 19-year break between books does not typically vault an author to the top of a favored client list, especially when that list is a literary Legion of Boom. I am supremely grateful to David Black for sticking with me, helping me craft a compelling comeback project, and demanding excellence. Thanks also to Anna Zinchuk for keeping the train on the tracks and to Lucy Stille for pursuing new horizons.

Like the coaches featured in this story, Dan Gerstle has exceedingly high standards and is constantly pushing for the best possible product. His guidance and vision were immeasurably important, and you won't usually hear me voice such sentiments about a person who compels me to cut tens of thousands of words. He and the team at Norton—including Zeba Arora, Will Scarlett, Meredith McGinnis, Becky Homiski, Julia Druskin, and Don Rifkin—are truly top-notch.

The seeds of this project were planted more than three decades ago, when I was covering Mike Shanahan while his energetic teenage son, Kyle, occasionally crashed our interviews. The book would not have been possible without the openness and trust of so many of the relentlessly driven people in a sometimes-thankless profession, beginning with Mike Shanahan, Mike McDaniel, Raheem Morris, Matt LaFleur, Sean McVay, and Chris Foerster. I am greatly appreciative of Steve Young, Robert Saleh, Dan Quinn, Mike LaFleur, Adam Stenavich, Peggy Shanahan, Chandler Henley, Chris Cooley, Rich Scangarello, Kevin O'Connell, Brandon Staley, T. C. McCartney, Jedd Fisch, Nicole Morris, Ejiro Evero, Sage Rosenfels, Bo Scaife, Kwesi Adofo-Mensah, Joe Thomas, Alex Mack, Joe Barry, Kyle Juszczyk, Trent Williams, Joe Staley, Frank Smith, Greg Olson, Jared Goff, Tom Garfinkel, Anne Noland, Jimmy Garoppolo, and many others. Wink Martindale's authentic insights into football and life are a gift. Kyle Shanahan and I were not in alignment regarding this particular project, but I appreciate the access and insight he has provided during his long coaching career, and during the 2022 and 2023 seasons in particular.

Speaking of access, I'm thankful to Richmond Flowers for inviting me to numerous Quarterback Collective events, and to the *Athletic*'s Jourdan Rodrigue, for getting many of these coaches to open up and present their stories in a creative way. I'm continually inspired by the badass journalists and friends who push me to be better: Nicki Jhabvala, Albert Breer, Jarrett Bell, James Palmer, Jeff Chadiha, Sam Farmer, Steve Wyche, and so many others. And Mike Fleiss and Josh Elliott are among the former colleagues who've brightened my journey and provided help on the way.

Jeff Darlington has spent years talking me down from ledges and leading me off high dives, and, alas, his work is far from done. Dianna Russini is the relentless truth seeker I want to be, while somehow managing to keep me laughing every single day. Vic Tafur has done everything from carrying my furniture up narrow flights of stairs to indulging my farcical Rose Bowl fantasies and, despite being one of the greats of our profession, appears to be stuck with me. Peter King showed me what a great teammate is when I got to *Sports Illustrated* and has only become a more awesome confidant while establishing himself as a living legend.

Rick Telander may well be the best to ever have done this, and hanging out with him is way, way better than that. He's one of the many authors who've inspired me, including my friends Steve Kettmann, Michael Mac-Cambridge, Dennis McNally, and Seth Wickersham (who has provided me with so many good ideas, and one *muy mala* one on the eve of Super Bowl XXXVII).

Beginning in August of 2022, when I started spending more time at the 49ers' training facility, I was reminded of how many quality people frequent the joint. That includes journalists such as Matt Maiocco, Matt Barrows, Cam Inman, Nick Wagoner, Tim Kawakami, Marcus Thompson,

Jennifer Lee Chan, Jerry McDonald, Tracy Sandler, David Lombardi, Grant Cohn, Dieter Kurtenbach, Kate Rooney, Lindsey Pallares, and others. I appreciate Corry Rush and his PR lieutenants (Peter Volmut, Kristin Wojcik, Zack Teats, Caleigh Elkin) for all the help. Thanks also to Corry's counterparts at the Commanders (Sean DeBarbieri), Rams (Artis Twyman), and Packers (Jason Wahlers), and their staffs. Greg Papa, the crown jewel of play-by-play broadcasters, and Michael Zagaris, the peerless sports *and* rock 'n' roll photographer, have my deepest gratitude. And special thanks to Dr. Harry Edwards, a true American hero.

Joining forces with the *San Francisco Chronicle* has been a blessing, especially because of the great journalists I've been able to call teammates, including beat-writing beast Eric Branch and Ann Killion, my favorite columnist and postgame food-and-drink companion. Thanks to my bosses Christina Kahrl, Mike Lerseth, Jon Schultz, and Emilio Garcia-Ruiz for allowing me to do this book.

I'm truly humbled by the big-picture vision and friendship of John Marvel, Steve Mandell, and Dave Morgan. And I'm extremely stoked that my original journalistic partner-in-crime, Steve Kerr, has graciously pursued a career that aligns with my professional endeavors, giving us ample excuses to continue our adolescent dialogue at all costs.

Thanks to the many true friends I'm neglecting to single out—you know who you are—for all the love and guidance.

My parents, Steve and Susan, are beautiful and brilliant souls who set me up for a much better life than I deserve and remain my heroes. My sister, Elizabeth, is a force of nature and exceptional human. I am grateful for her awesome daughters and for my 12 other wonderful nieces and nephews from the glorious Goyette family that I'm proud to be part of—led by my exquisite mother-in-law, Barbara, and my brothers- and sisters-in-law (Paul, Janet, Mark, Anne, and Ted Goyette).

Most of all, I must thank my out-of-my-league wife, Leslie, who has empowered me to take risks and make tough choices while centering me as a human and calling B.S. on toxic forces. She would agree that our three children—Natalie, Robbie, and Greg, the centers of our existence—have all emerged from their upbringings as elite adults whose essences we revere, and who are really, really fun to be around. Our high-strung family dog, Theo, spent nearly 14 years bringing us joy before heading to the other side, and I'm grateful for the time he spent on the floor of my home office while I was grinding out many of these chapters.

Finally, I'm thankful to the public servants, journalists, and others who believe in democracy and fight to preserve its existence.

Notes on Sources

Most material in these pages is based on my on-the-record interviews with the central characters and dozens of others who know them professionally and personally. I began conducting book-specific interviews in 2018; before, during, and after that, I interviewed many of these same people, and others, in conjunction with my job as a sports journalist. I covered the 49ers for two Northern California newspapers from 1989 to 1994; I spent 13 years covering the NFL for *Sports Illustrated* (1994–2007), six for Yahoo! Sports (2007–2013), and eight as an analyst and columnist for NFL Network/NFL.com (2013–2021). Some of these conversations also took place during my subsequent time with Bally Sports, the Volume, and the *San Francisco Chronicle*, where I've been a columnist since 2022. Mike Shanahan, Sean McVay, Mike McDaniel, Raheem Morris, and Matt LaFleur were among the many, many people who spoke to me specifically for this project. Kyle Shanahan declined to do so, but has been open with me throughout the years about his thoughts, motivations, and intentions (often in on-the-record conversations) and, even after he declined, he continued to provide insight in interviews I conducted for the *Chronicle*.

While the vast majority of these interviews were on the record, some were conducted on background, meaning that I agreed not to identify subjects by name and instead used a general title (such as coach, friend, "someone who has worked with") to describe them. Some conversations, especially those detailing sensitive information, were conducted on deep background, meaning I agreed not to identify the subject at all.

I experienced some of these scenes as a firsthand witness; others were described to me directly by some or all of the participants. When dialogue is quoted, it comes from the speaker, a firsthand witness, or notes or recordings from that moment. Where dialogue is paraphrased, it reflects only a lack of certainty about precise wording. Where specific feelings or thoughts are noted, they come from the person identified, either directly to me or from public statements (in press conferences, books, podcasts, newspaper and magazine articles, and television interviews)—or from someone to whom that person has expressed those thoughts or feelings.

Additionally, I relied on hundreds of newspaper articles, magazine pieces, books, online stories, films, podcasts, and radio and television interviews from the past

30-plus years. Some of them were conducted by me, for the publications previously cited. I relied on a wealth of material from my friend Seth Wickersham, a longtime ESPN senior writer (and author of *It's Better to Be Feared*), and from my friend and fellow journalist Jourdan Rodrigue, whose 2023 podcast series for the *Athletic, The Playmakers*, featured interviews with McVay, LaFleur, Morris, McDaniel, and Kyle Shanahan, among others. I devour NFL-related content from wonderful humans and stellar journalists Peter King, Albert Breer, Jarrett Bell, Jeff Chadiha, and others on a constant basis. I process the sport with the priceless support of the exquisite Jeff Darlington and Dianna Russini and communicate with them relentlessly, including (but not limited to) this very moment. I am also indebted to the journalists who regularly cover the San Francisco 49ers—including my *Chronicle* colleagues Eric Branch, Ann Killion, Scott Ostler, Ron Kroichick, and others; along with Matt Maiocco, Jennifer Lee Chan, Tracy Sandler, Nick Wagoner, Cam Inman, Matt Barrows, David Lombardi, Tim Kawakami, Marcus Thompson, Josh Dubow, Jerry McDonald, Dieter Kurtenbach, Grant Cohn, John Dickinson, Jake Hutchinson, Kate Rooney, Lindsey Pallares, and more.

Below are additional chapter-by-chapter notes.

INTRODUCTION: THREE MANTRAS

The information in this section comes primarily from interviews with Mike McDaniel, Matt LaFleur, Dan Quinn, Mike LaFleur, Raheem Morris, Mike Shanahan, Sage Rosenfels, Chris Cooley, Jedd Fisch, Brandon Staley, Joe Thomas, Trent Williams, and other sources, and from events that I witnessed. Also:

Michael Silver, "Matt Ryan-Shanahan Bond on Display as Falcons Rip Seahawks," NFL.com, January 14, 2017.
Jason La Canfora, "Kyle Shanahan, Staff Inexperience at Core of Redskins Dysfunction," CBSSports.com, December 15, 2013.

CHAPTER 1: THE SCARS THAT BIND

The information in this chapter comes primarily from interviews with Mike Shanahan, Steve Young, and other sources. Also:

Doug Farrar, *The Genius of Desperation: The Schematic Innovations That Made the Modern NFL* (Chicago: Triumph, 2018).
Michael Silver, "Mastermind Mike Shanahan Sees All, Hears All and Seems to Know All—Which May Explain Why His Broncos Are Playing Brilliantly," *Sports Illustrated*, November 17, 1997.
Michael Silver, "The Top of His Game," *Sports Illustrated*, March 12, 2007.
Dan Pompei, "Steve Young, Girls Flag Football and Finding the Next Calling," *Athletic*, October 3, 2023.
Chris Dufresne, "Walsh: 49er Coach Is a Wall of Knowledge; Few See His Other Side," *Los Angeles Times*, January 18, 1989.
David Harris, *The Genius: How Bill Walsh Reinvented Football and Created an NFL Dynasty* (New York: Random House, 2008).

CHAPTER 2: THE MASTERMIND

The information in this chapter comes primarily from interviews with Mike Shanahan, Steve Young, Jedd Fisch, and other sources, from a conversation with Kyle Shanahan in 2010, and from events that I witnessed. Also:

Michael Silver, "Mastermind Mike Shanahan Sees All, Hears All and Seems to Know All—Which May Explain Why His Broncos Are Playing Brilliantly," *Sports Illustrated*, November 17, 1997.

Seth Wickersham, "Sean Payton Doesn't Forget Anything," ESPN.com, September 5, 2023.

Michael Silver, "Seven Up: Showing More Grit than Prowess, John Elway Executed a Brilliant Game Plan in the Broncos' Stunning Super Bowl Win over the Packers," *Sports Illustrated*, February 2, 1988.

Aric DiLalla, " 'The Career He Had Is Unbelievable': HC Sean Payton Reflects on Mike Shanahan's Influence Ahead of Pro Football Hall of Fame Vote," denverbroncos.com, August 14, 2023.

Danny Kelly, "Alex Gibbs, the Godfather of the Modern Zone Blocking Scheme," *SBNation*, July 25, 2014.

Doug Farrar, "How the Late, Great Alex Gibbs Perfected Zone Blocking in the NFL," *Touchdown Wire*, USAToday.com, July 13, 2021.

CHAPTER 3: HOLD ON TO YOUR NUTS

The information in this chapter comes primarily from interviews with Mike Shanahan, Peggy Shanahan, Steve Young, Bo Scaife, Kyle Shanahan, Raheem Morris, Robert Saleh, Sage Rosenfels, Matt LaFleur, Mike McDaniel, T. C. McCartney, and other sources. Also:

Jourdan Rodrigue, host, *The Playcallers* (podcast series), July 15, 2023.

Chris Simms, host, "49ers Coach Kyle Shanahan," *Chris Simms Unbuttoned* (podcast), July 23, 2020.

Matt Barrows, "Kyle Shanahan at 40: The 49ers Coach Reflects on the Forces That Shaped Him, Including That Damn Wrought-Iron Fence," *Athletic*, December 12, 2019.

Eric Branch, "49ers' Kyle Shanahan May Find Strength in Super Bowl 'Heartbreak,'" *San Francisco Chronicle*, March 5, 2017.

Daniel Mano, "Kyle Shanahan Explains Matching Tattoos with Chris Simms," *San Jose Mercury News*, July 20, 1017.

Mike Chiari, "Lil Wayne Sends Kyle Shanahan Gear after Learning 49ers Coach Named Son for Him," *Bleacher Report*, July 26, 2018.

Eric Branch, "What's in a Name? Kyle Shanahan Explains Influence of Lil Wayne," sfgate.com, July 27, 2018.

Ben Solak, "The Intertwined Evolutions of Kyle Shanahan and Sean McVay," *Ringer*, January 26, 2022.

Mike Tanier, "How Kyle Shanahan's Secret Weapons, Schemes Have Made 49ers a Title Contender," *Bleacher Report*, December 12, 2019.

Michael Silver, "Shanahan on Fast Track Like His Father," Yahoo! Sports, September 2, 2008.

Kaelen Jones, "Before the Super Bowl, Kyle Shanahan's Texas Teammates Remember Their Brotherhood and 'Shan-O's' Potential," *Athletic*, January 31, 2020.

CHAPTER 4: NOT THAT TYPE OF COACH

The information in this chapter comes primarily from interviews with Raheem Morris, Mike McDaniel, Dan Quinn, Nicole Morris, Greg Olson, Sean McVay, and other sources. Also:

Rick Stroud, "Bucs Assistant Arrested in Indy," *Tampa Bay Times*, March 28, 2005.
Dan Pompei, "A Dozen Years Have Taught Falcons' Raheem Morris Perception Is Everything," *Athletic*, October 13, 2020.
Ryan Dunleavy, "Raheem Morris' Rise to Rams Defensive Coordinator Took Root in Irvington, NJ," *New York Post*, February 6, 2022.
Matt Gelb, "Irvington High Alum and Tampa Bay Buccaneers Coach Raheem Morris Honored in Return to Hometown," *Newark Star-Ledger*, June 5, 2009.
Gary Shelton, "Strength Forged by Tumult," *Tampa Bay Times*, June 14, 2009.
Tara Sullivan, "Sullivan: Falcons' Raheem Morris Shaped by Jersey Roots," *Bergen Record*, February 2, 2017.
Michael Silver, "Intensity, Father's Lead Shaped Kyle Shanahan's Super Bowl Path," NFL.com, January 29, 2020.

CHAPTER 5: PSYCHOPATH BALLBOY

The information in this chapter comes primarily from interviews with Mike McDaniel, Chandler Henley, Chris Cooley, Mike Shanahan, Sage Rosenfels, Robert Saleh, Anne Noland, and other sources. Also:

Ryan O'Halloran, "The Constant for Mike McDaniel During Journey from Colorado Kid to Dolphins Head Coach: His Mom," *Denver Post*, September 11, 2022.
Matt Barrows, "Mike McDaniel Was the Walk-On Who Never Walked Away," *Athletic*, February 22, 2022.
Michael Silver, host, "Dolphins' Mike McDaniel on Decrypting Tua's Brilliance, How to Build Dolphins Around QB," *Open Mike* (podcast), March 29, 2023.
David Wilson, " 'It Sounds Crazy, But It Really Isn't': McDaniel Took Outside-the-Box Path to NFL Stardom," *Miami Herald*, February 14, 2022.

CHAPTER 6: THE INSTIGATOR

The information in this chapter comes primarily from interviews with Matt LaFleur, Robert Saleh, Mike LaFleur, Mike McDaniel, Sean McVay, Ejiro Evero, Dan Quinn, Chris Cooley, and other sources. Also:

Jourdan Rodrigue, host, *The Playcallers* (podcast series), July 15, 2023.
Jim Lahde, "All in the Family: LaFleur Family Enjoying Incredible Ride," *Mount Pleasant (MI) Morning Sun*, January 17, 2020.
Patrick Pinak, "How Matt LaFleur's Wife, BreAnne, Traded Her Career for His NFL Dream," Fanbuzz.com, January 14, 2024.
Evan Petzold, "How Central Michigan Paved Matt LaFleur and Robert Saleh's Path to NFL Stardom: 'They had no furniture,'" *Detroit Free Press*, January 19, 2020.

Eric Hansen, "QBs Coach LaFleur Ready to Step into the Bright Lights," *South Bend Tribune*, August 2, 2014.

Rob Demovsky, " 'Damn, That's a Nice Jump': How Matt LaFleur Went from Ashland to NFL," ESPN.com, January 16, 2019.

CHAPTER 7: THE MAYOR OF EARTH

The information in this chapter comes primarily from interviews with Sean McVay, Mike McDaniel, Frank Smith, Raheem Morris, Matt LaFleur, and other sources. Also:

Michael Silver, "Sean McVay Can't Stop . . . The Jaw-Dropping Youth of the Rams' Newest Sideline Savior Is Just One of the Things That Makes Him Different from Your Average Head Coach," NFL.com, January 3, 2018.

Alden Gonzalez, "Prep Football Legend: Rams Coach Sean McVay Returns to Georgia as Coach," ESPN.com, January 24, 2019.

Lindsey Thiry and Mark Schlabach, "An Inside Look at Rams Coach Sean McVay's Super Bowl Homecoming," ESPN.com, January 31, 2019.

Gary Klein, "Family, and Friendly, Ties Bind Rams' Sean McVay to Lineage of NFL Greatness," *Los Angeles Times*, September 18, 2017.

Mirin Fader, "The Mad Scientist of the NFL," *Bleacher Report*, November 10, 2017.

Zach Klein, "From Atlanta to the Super Bowl: Sean McVay's Parents Say Son Is 'Living Out Dream,' " WSBTV.com, January 30, 2019.

CHAPTER 8: THE FUN BUNCH

The information in this chapter comes primarily from interviews with Mike Shanahan, Sean McVay, Matt LaFleur, Raheem Morris, Mike McDaniel, Chris Foerster, Chris Cooley, Jedd Fisch, Trent Williams, and other sources. Also:

John Feinstein, *Next Man Up: A Year behind the Lines in Today's NFL* (New York: Little, Brown, 2005)

John Keim, "McVay, Shanahan, LaFleur on QBs, Playbooks, Learning in D.C.," ESPN .com, August 26, 2019.

Greg Bishop, "The Forgettable Years of a Coaching Staff to Remember," *Sports Illustrated*, August 26–September 2, 2019.

Greg Bishop, "The Wide-Reaching Impact of Mike Shanahan on the NFL Conference Championships," SI.com, January 17, 2020.

CHAPTER 9: FULL-BLOWN AUSTRALIAN TOILET

The information in this chapter comes primarily from interviews with Mike McDaniel, Mike Shanahan, Sean McVay, Chris Foerster, Matt LaFleur, Raheem Morris, Chris Cooley, and other sources. Also:

Michael Silver, "All Hail, King in the North," NFL.com, September 4, 2018.

Jason La Canfora, "Kyle Shanahan, Staff Inexperience at Core of Redskins Dysfunction," CBSSports.com, December 15, 2013.

Jourdan Rodrigue, host, *The Playcallers* (podcast series), July 15, 2023.

Dan Graziano, "Owner-QB Link Disillusioned Coach," ESPN.com, December 8, 2013.

Scott Allen, "Mike Shanahan Blames Daniel Snyder for RGIII's Infatuation with Being an Aaron Rodgers-Type Guy," *Washington Post*, February 18, 2015.

Brendan Vaughan, "The Second Coming of RG3," *GQ*, August 13, 2013.

Adam Schefter, "Sources: Two Teams Lose Cap Space," ESPN.com, March 12, 2012.

Mark Maske, "Bruce Allen: Salary Cap Penalty 'A Travesty of Fairness,'" *Washington Post*, March 11, 2013.

CHAPTER 10: THE FIRST LIFE RAFT

The information in this chapter comes primarily from interviews with Mike McDaniel, Dan Quinn, Raheem Morris, Nicole Morris, Matt LaFleur, Mike LaFleur, Joe Thomas, Alex Mack, Anthony Weaver, and other sources. Also:

Untold, season 3, episode 2, "Johnny Football," directed by Ryan Duffy, produced by Propogate, aired August 8, 2023, Netflix.

Chris Mortensen, "Johnny Manziel Cuts Camp Short," ESPN.com, July 14, 2013.

Nick Kostos, "2014 NFL Draft Prospects with the Biggest Red Flags," *Bleacher Report*, May 1, 2014.

Kevin Seifert, "Inside Slant: Jimmy Haslam's Homeless Fan," ESPN.com, May 9, 2014.

Vaughn McClure, "Roddy White Wants Wins, a Ring and Catches," ESPN.com, October 6, 2015.

Arthur Weinstein, "Browns Announce OC Kyle Shanahan's Resignation," *Sporting News*, January 10, 2015.

Mary Kay Cabot, "Josh Gordon Suspended by Cleveland Browns for Missing Team Walk-Through," *Cleveland Plain Dealer*, December 27, 2014.

Marc Sessler, "Ray Farmer Apologizes for Texting Scandal: It Was Me," NFL.com, February 19, 2015.

Mary Kay Cabot, "Cleveland Browns and GM Ray Farmer Facing Possible Suspension, Fine, Loss of Draft Pick for 'Textgate,'" *Cleveland Plain Dealer*, February 4, 2015.

Brian Solomon, "Billionaire Jimmy Haslam's Pilot Flying J Cuts Deal on Fraud Case," *Forbes*, July 14, 2014.

Danny Heifetz, "The Pilot Flying J Fraud Scandal Hasn't Touched Browns Owner Jimmy Haslam," *Ringer*, April 2, 2018.

CHAPTER 11: AIRING IT OUT

The information in this chapter comes primarily from interviews with Matt LaFleur, Dan Quinn, Mike McDaniel, Raheem Morris, Chandler Henley, Mike LaFleur, Alex Mack, Mike Shanahan, and other sources, and from events I witnessed firsthand. Also:

Michael Silver, "Matt Ryan-Shanahan Bond on Display as Falcons Rip Seahawks," NFL.com, January 14, 2017.

Michael Silver, "Poised Matt Ryan Seizes Moment, Lifts Falcons to Super Bowl LI," NFL.com, January 22, 2017.

Michael Silver, "49ers' Kyle Shanahan and Rams DC Raheem Morris Go from BFFs to Foes Sunday," *San Francisco Chronicle*, September 17, 2023.

Jourdan Rodrigue, host, *The Playcallers* (podcast series), July 15, 2023.

Kevin Clark, host, "Richard Sherman on What Makes Kyle Shanahan Great, His Top

DBs, and the Success of Pete Carroll and the Seahawks," *Slow News Day* (podcast), December 14, 2022.

Tim Kawakami, "Kawakami: Kyle Shanahan on His 49ers Tenure and Competing vs. Legends," *Athletic*, January 24, 2024.

Michael Silver, NFL Network segment, January 18, 2017.

Tim Kawakami, "Kawakami: Kyle Shanahan on His 49ers Tenure and Competing vs. Legends," *Athletic*, January 24, 2024.

Tom Pelissero, "Falcons' Brotherhood Helped Assistant Mike McDaniel through Alcohol Issue," *USA Today*, February 2, 2017.

CHAPTER 12: ENEMY FRIENDS

The information in this chapter comes primarily from interviews with Sean McVay, Jared Goff, Kwesi Adofo-Mensah, Mike Shanahan, Robert Saleh, Chris Foerster, Matt LaFleur, Rich Scangarello, Jedd Fisch, Joe Staley, Mike McDaniel, T. C. McCartney, Mike LaFleur, and other sources, and from events I witnessed firsthand. Also:

Michael Silver, "Sean McVay Guides Focused L.A. Rams to Cusp of Division Title," NFL.com, December 17, 2017.

Jourdan Rodrigue, host, *The Playcallers* (podcast series), July 15, 2023.

Michael Silver, "Sean McVay Can't Stop . . . The Jaw-Dropping Youth of the Rams' Newest Sideline Savior Is Just One of the Things That Makes Him Different from Your Average Head Coach," NFL.com, January 3, 2018.

Michael Silver, "Jimmy Garoppolo Making Football Fun Again for Giddy 49ers," NFL.com, December 24, 2017.

Michael Silver, "Why Shanahan vs. McDaniel in 49ers–Dolphins Could Be NFL's Ultimate Chess Match," *San Francisco Chronicle*, November 30, 2022.

Seth Wickersham, *It's Better to Be Feared* (New York: Liveright, 2021).

Michael Middlehurst-Schwartz, "Todd Gurley Calls Out Rams' 'Middle-School Offense,'" *USA Today*, December 12, 2016.

Eric Branch, "Patriots' McDaniels Bows Out; 49ers' Focus Turns to Shanahan," *San Francisco Chronicle*, January 16, 2017.

Michael Silver, NFL Network segment, January 12, 2017.

Alec Lewis, "After Years of Self-Criticism, Kirk Cousins Is Trying to Chill Out," *Athletic*, September 8, 2023.

Jay Gruden, interview with 106.7 The Fan (Washington, D.C), September 15. 2023.

Jimmy Garoppolo, press conference, February 9, 2018.

Kijuana Nige interview, "Dan Le Batard Show with Stugotz," ESPN, October 11, 2017.

Barry Jackson, "'Chris Foerster Used Me as His Cocaine Platter,' Las Vegas Model Says about Ex-Dolphins Coach," *Miami Herald*, October 11, 2017.

Rick Stroud, "Drugs and a Viral Video Wrecked Chris Foerster's NFL career. Super Bowl 54 Offers Redemption," *Tampa Bay Times*, January 31, 2020.

"NFL Coach in Apparent Cocaine Snorting Video . . . Team Investigating," TMZ.com, October 9, 2017.

Jose Lambiet, "Fallen Dolphins Coach Owes Thousands in Back Taxes," *Miami Herald*, October 9, 2017.

Omar Kelly, "Dolphins 'Shocked' by Snorting Video That Led to Chris Foerster's Resignation," *South Florida Sun Sentinel*, October 9, 2017.

Michael Silver, "Will Trey Lance Shine in 49ers' Spotlight as Jimmy G. Disappears One Last Time?" *San Francisco Chronicle*, August 11, 2022.

CHAPTER 13: DUELING SUPERPOWERS

The information in this chapter comes primarily from interviews with Mike McDaniel, Mike LaFleur, Jedd Fisch, Sean McVay, Dan Quinn, Rich Scangarello, Joe Staley, Robert Saleh, T. C. McCartney, Kwesi Adofo-Mensah, Mike Shanahan, Ejiro Evero, Matt LaFleur, and events that I witnessed firsthand. Also:

Michael Silver, "Sean McVay Can't Stop . . . The Jaw-Dropping Youth of the Rams' Newest Sideline Savior Is Just One of the Things That Makes Him Different from Your Average Head Coach," NFL.com, January 3, 2018.

Michael Silver, "Intensity, Father's Lead Shaped Kyle Shanahan's Super Bowl Path," NFL.com, January 29, 2020.

Michael Silver, "Mike Zimmer Overcomes Nerves to Lead Vikings Past 49ers," NFL.com, September 9, 2018.

Michael Silver, "Rams' Jared Goff Bests Chiefs' Patrick Mahomes in Epic Duel," NFL.com, November 19, 2018.

Michael Silver, "Bears' smothering defense grounds high-flying Rams in Chicago," NFL.com, December 9, 2018.

Michael Silver, "Jared Goff's 'Miraculous' Throw Helps Send Rams to Super Bowl," NFL.com, January 20, 2019.

Michael Silver, on *The Aftermath*, NFL Network, January 14, 2019.

Michael Silver, "California Cool: Jared Goff's Football Career Has Been a Roller-Coaster Ride, but the 24-Year-Old Rams Quarterback Offsets All Highs and Lows with an Unwavering Chill," NFL.com, January 29, 2019.

Sam Farmer, "Column: Jared Goff and Rams End Up Making the Biggest Noise in New Orleans," *Los Angeles Times*, January 20, 2019.

Kevin Clark, host, "Phil Simms, Dan Orlovsky, and Deebo Samuel: *Slow News Day*'s Super Bowl Wednesday," *Slow News Day* (podcast), February 8, 2023.

John Keim, "McVay, Shanahan, LaFleur on QBs, Playbooks, Learning in D.C.," ESPN.com, August 26, 2019.

CHAPTER 14: FRIEND OF McVAY

The information in this chapter comes primarily from interviews with Mike Shanahan, Sean McVay, Jedd Fisch, Ejiro Evero, Matt LaFleur, Robert Saleh, Kwesi Adofo-Mensah, Rich Scangarello, Mike McDaniel, and Joe Staley, from events that I witnessed firsthand, and from a videotape, viewed on Mike Shanahan's iPad, of a Kyle Shanahan 49ers team meeting from 2019. Also:

Kyle Newport, "Sean McVay 'Numb' after Super Bowl 53 Loss; Says He Did 'Poor Job' Calling Plays," *Bleacher Report*, February 3, 2019.

Nik DeCosta-Klipa, "What Sean McVay Had to Say After Getting 'Out-Coached' by Bill Belichick and the Patriots," *Boston Globe*, February 4, 2019.

Michael Silver, "Jared Goff Shoulders Blame for Rams' Offensive Ineptitude," NFL.com, February 3, 2019.

Sean McVay, Super Bowl LIII postgame press conference, February 3, 2019.

Joe Julius, "How the Patriots Shut Down the Rams Offense in Super Bowl LIII," Footballfilmroom.com, February 6, 2019.

Dan Graziano, "How the Patriots' Defense Stymied Sean McVay in Super Bowl LIII," ESPN.com, February 4, 2019.

Cameron DaSilva, "Cardinals Call Sean McVay a 'Genius' in Kliff Kingsbury Hiring Announcement," *Rams Wire*, USA Today.com, January 8, 2019.

"Cardinals Dump 'Friend of McVay' Reference from Article Announcing Kingsbury Hire," Profootballtalk.com, January 8, 2019.

Ben Weinrib, "Kliff Kingsbury Said Last Year He'd Take Kyler Murray with the First Pick in the Draft," Yahoo! Sports, January 10, 2019.

Susan Slusser, "A's Expect Top Pick Kyler Murray to Enter NFL Draft," *San Francisco Chronicle*, January 9, 2019.

Michael Silver, "19 Days: It Lasted Less than Three Weeks, but Marshawn Lynch's Surprising Late-Season Return to the Seahawks Last Year Helped Heal Broken Hearts, Mended Fences and Supplied a Sense of Closure for All Parties Involved," NFL .com, July 23, 2020.

Michael Silver, "Intensity, Father's Lead Shaped Kyle Shanahan's Super Bowl Path," NFL.com, January 29, 2020.

Jeremy Bergman, "Jimmy Garoppolo Throws 5 Consecutive INTs in Practice," NFL .com, August 14, 2019.

Michael Silver, "Niners' Defense Throttles Jared Goff, Rams to Justify Hype," NFL .com, October 13, 2019.

Michael Silver, "Sean McVay Vows to Be Better in Wake of Disappointing Season," NFL.com, December 21, 2019.

Giorgos Kassakos, "Philadelphia Eagles: Jim Washburn and the Wide-9 Formation," *Bleacher Report*, January 22, 2012.

Jonathan Tannenwald, "Ex-Eagles Assistant Jim Washburn Says He Was 'The Antichrist' in Philly," *Philadelphia Inquirer*, July 7, 2017.

Matt Barrows, " 'Like a Freight Train Running Down the Track': The Aggressive Mentality of the 'Wide 9' and How the 49ers Might Use it," *Athletic*, March 19, 2019.

Kevin Nogle, "Football 101: Understanding the Wide-Nine Technique," ThePhinsider .com, April 16, 2016.

CHAPTER 15: WE DID IT AGAIN, BUDDY

The information in this chapter comes primarily from interviews with Mike McDaniel, Matt LaFleur, Mike LaFleur, Sean McVay, Robert Saleh, Bo Scaife, Mike Shanahan, Raheem Morris, Kwesi Adofo-Mensah, and other sources, and from events that I witnessed firsthand. Also:

Jourdan Rodrigue, host, *The Playcallers* (podcast series), July 15, 2023.

Michael Silver, "Intensity, Father's Lead Shaped Kyle Shanahan's Super Bowl Path," NFL.com, January 29, 2020.

Michael Silver, "Aaron Rodgers, Matt LaFleur Navigating New Packers Partnership," NFL.com, June 17, 2019.

Michael Silver, "49ers Run Over Packers—and into Super Bowl—with Superb Plan," NFL.com, January 19, 2020.

Michael Silver, "Green Bay Packers' Defense Delivers Win in Matt LaFleur's Debut," NFL.com, September 5, 2019.

Michael Silver, "Kyle Shanahan Endures Another Devastating Super Bowl Collapse," NFL.com, February 2, 2020.

CHAPTER 16: HUNKERING DOWN

The information in this chapter comes primarily from interviews with Mike McDaniel, Sean McVay, Brandon Staley, Ejiro Evero, Kevin O'Connell, Matt LaFleur, Mike LaFleur, Robert Saleh, Chris Foerster, Raheem Morris, Greg Olson, Nathaniel Hackett, Kyle Shanahan, and other sources, and from events that I witnessed firsthand. Also:

Seth Wickersham, *It's Better to Be Feared* (New York: Liveright, 2021).

Jourdan Rodrigue, host, *The Playcallers* (podcast series), July 15, 2023.

Rick Stroud, "Drugs and a Viral Video Wrecked Chris Foerster's NFL Career. Super Bowl 54 Offers Redemption," *Tampa Bay Times*, January 31, 2020.

Michael Silver, "Jared Goff Has 'New Edge' after Disappointing Season, Unprecedented Offseason," NFL.com, September 8, 2020.

Michael Silver, "Jared Goff Replaces Injured John Wolford, Leads Rams in Wild-Card Upset of Seahawks," NFL.com, January 10, 2021.

Michael Silver, "Packers' Matt LaFleur: 'Aaron Rodgers Is the Leader' of the Team," NFL.com, April 24, 2020.

Michael Silver on The Aftermath, "Silver: Raheem Morris Held Accountability Meeting after Week 11 Loss to Saints," NFL Network, November 30, 2020.

Michael Silver, NFL Network segment, February 19, 2020.

Jason Wilde, "Aaron Rodgers Not Worried about Packers Picking a QB in NFL Draft," *Athletic*, March 6, 2020.

Joseph Zucker, "Blank: Raheem Morris Will 'Certainly' Be Falcons HC Candidate If He Goes 11–0," *Bleacher Report*, October 12, 2020.

Terry Bradshaw, segment on John Wolford, *Fox NFL Sunday*, January 9, 2020.

Lindsey Thiry, "Los Angeles Rams Coach Sean McVay Says Jared Goff 'Has Got to Take Better Care of the Football,'" ESPN.com, November 29, 2020.

Mason Bissada, "Packers Set to Sell Shares of Team Stock for Sixth Time in History," Forbes.com, November 15, 2021.

Aaron Rodgers, press conference, July 28, 2021.

Jeff Miller, "Chargers' New Leader a Family Man: 'I Am from the Bruce and Linda Staley Coaching Tree,'" *Los Angeles Times*, February 5, 2021.

Joe Reedy, "Brandon Staley's Journey: Chargers Coach's Cancer Battle Defined Him," Associated Press, October 3, 2021.

Ben Solak, "The Intertwined Evolutions of Kyle Shanahan and Sean McVay," *Ringer*, January 26, 2022.

CHAPTER 17: DEAL

The information in this chapter comes primarily from interviews with Kevin O'Connell, Brandon Staley, Sean McVay, Mike McDaniel, Raheem Morris, Nicole Morris, Matt LaFleur, Andrew Whitworth, and other sources, and from events that I witnessed firsthand. Also:

Seth Wickersham, "Welcome to the Sean McVay Moment: Inside the Pressures That Brought Him to the Pinnacle and Why Satisfaction Is Still So Hard to Come By," ESPN.com, August 9, 2022.

Sean McVay and Peter Schrager, hosts, "Kyle Shanahan on Super Bowl Regrets, Trading Up for Lance, Taking the SF Job, and Coaching With His Dad," *The Flying Coach*, July 7, 2021.

Michael Silver, "Jared Goff Excited to Be with Lions Franchise That Wants, Appreciates Him," NFL.com, January 31, 2021.

Lindsey Thiry, "Why the Sean McVay-Jared Goff Partnership Fell Apart for Los Angeles Rams," ESPN.com, March 24, 2021.

Gary Klein, "Rams General Manager Is Noncommittal about Jared Goff's Future with the Team," *Los Angeles Times*, January 26, 2021.

Ryan Dunleavy, "Aaron Rodgers' NFL Draft Shock Has Turned into a 'Beautiful Mystery,'" *New York Post*, January 21, 2021.

Michael Silver, "Aaron Rodgers' Postgame Comments a Message to Packers Brass That Organizational Mentality Must Change," NFL.com, January 24, 2021.

Aaron Rodgers, postgame press conference, January 24, 2021.

CHAPTER 18: HIDDEN HORSEPOWER

The information in this chapter comes primarily from interviews with Matt LaFleur, Mike McDaniel, Mike LaFleur, Joe Staley, Kyle Shanahan, Robert Saleh, Sean McVay, and other sources. Also:

Sam Farmer, "Finding Closure with Sean McVay Aided Jared Goff's Lions Revival," *Los Angeles Times*, November 10, 2023.

"Packers 'Not Trading' Aaron Rodgers, GM Brian Gutekunst Says," *Athletic*, April 29, 2021.

Mike Garafolo, "2021 NFL Draft: Trey Lance Won't Run 40 at Pro Day, Leaning on Tape to Show Speed," NFL.com, March 9, 2021.

Trey Lance, ESPN.com Recruiting Profile, Class of 2018.

Mike Florio, "Packers Told Aaron Rodgers They'd Trade Him, and Then Didn't," Profootballtalk.com, July 28, 2021.

Adam Schefter, "Aaron Rodgers Doesn't Want to Return to Green Bay Packers, Sources Say," ESPN.com, April 29, 2021.

Nick Shook, "49ers Reached Out to Packers This Week Regarding Trade for Aaron Rodgers," NFL.com, April 29, 2021.

CHAPTER 19: AIN'T LOSING TO THIS GUY ANYMORE

The information in this chapter comes primarily from interviews with Mike McDaniel, Matt LaFleur, Sean McVay, Kyle Juszczyk, Jimmy Garoppolo, Raheem Morris, Kevin O'Connell, Robert Saleh, Alex Mack, Joe Staley, Ejiro Evero, and other sources, and from events I witnessed firsthand. Also:

Seth Wickersham, "Welcome to the Sean McVay Moment: Inside the Pressures That Brought Him to the Pinnacle and Why Satisfaction Is Still So Hard to Come By," ESPN.com, August 9, 2022.

Michael Silver, "Jimmy Garoppolo Opens Up About His Season and Future," Bally Sports, January 30, 2022.

Michael Silver, "Loss to Cardinals Latest Setback in Rough Season for 49ers," Bally Sports, November 7, 2021.

CHAPTER 20: WHAT ELSE COULD YOU WANT?

The information in this chapter comes primarily from interviews with Sean McVay, Raheem Morris, Kevin O'Connell, Ejiro Evero, Brandon Staley, and other sources, and from events I witnessed firsthand. Also:

Jourdan Rodrigue, host, *The Playcallers* (podcast series), July 15, 2023.

Seth Wickersham, "Welcome to the Sean McVay Moment: Inside the Pressures That Brought Him to the Pinnacle and Why Satisfaction is Still So Hard to Come By," ESPN.com, August 9, 2022.

Andrew Marchand, "CBS Tried Hiring Peyton Manning before Giving Tony Romo $180 Million," *New York Post*, March 2, 2020.

Jourdan Rodrigue, "As Rams Imploded, Sean McVay Faded Away: How They Found Their Way Back to Each Other," *Athletic*, February 23, 2023.

Michael Silver, host, "Sean McVay on Stafford-Goff Trade, Rams Rivalry vs. 49ers, Skipping NFL Combine," *Open Mike* (podcast), March 29, 2023.

Nicholas Cothrel, "5 Observations from the Rams' Championship Parade and Rally," *Sports Illustrated*, February 16, 2022.

Kevin Patra, "Matthew Stafford Back Throwing as Rams Open Training Camp: 'Definitely Knocking Some Rust Off,'" NFL.com, July 25, 2022.

We Not Me: Sean McVay and the 2021 Los Angeles Rams, produced by NFL Films, aired September 7, 2021, NFL Network.

Seth Wickersham, "Kyle Shanahan Is Ready to Meet the Moment," ESPN.com, February 7, 2024.

CHAPTER 21: THE LIBERATION OF MIKE McDANIEL

The information in this chapter comes primarily from interviews with Mike McDaniel, Chandler Henley, Kwesi Adofo-Mensah, Mike LaFleur, Matt LaFleur, Joe Staley, Robert Saleh, Frank Smith, Tom Garfinkel, Anne Noland, and other sources, and from events I witnessed firsthand. Also:

Michael Silver, host, "Dolphins' Mike McDaniel on Decrypting Tua's Brilliance, How to Build Dolphins Around QB," *Open Mike* (podcast), March 29, 2023.

Mike McDaniel, interview with Josh Moser, WSVN-TV, aired February 10, 2022.

"Head Coach Mike McDaniel Calls Tua Tagovailoa," miamidolphins.com, February 8, 2022.

Armando Salguero, "NFL Hot Seat: Coach, GM, Quarterback Changes Possible with Cardinals, Dolphins, Commanders, Jets, Bucs, More," Outkick.com, January 2, 2023.

Dave Hyde, "Dave Hyde: Sean Payton Was Offered Mega-Deal by Dolphins, Tom Brady Doesn't Deny Interest—What Could Have Been," *South Florida Sun Sentinel*, June 9, 2022.

Tyreek Hill and Julius Collins, hosts, "The Trade," *It Needed to Be Said* (podcast), June 10, 2022.

Marcel Louis-Jacques, "Dolphins Coach Asked Bears QB Justin Fields to Stop Running," ESPN.com, November 7, 2022.

Alain Poupart, "How McDaniel Helped Tua Not Have to Ask Himself If He Sucks Anymore," *Sports Illustrated*, November 27, 2022.

Tua Tagovailoa, postgame interview with Aditi Kinkhabwala, CBS Sports, November 27, 2022.

Ryan Glasspiegel, "Mike McDaniel 'Quit' Vaping after Bills Playoff Game Sideline Incident," *New York Post*, June 9, 2023.

Ben Volin, "A Secret Plan, a Bombshell Lawsuit, and a Soccer Match: Inside Tom Brady's Un-Retirement," *Boston Globe*, April 8, 2022.

Alden Gonzalez, "Justin Herbert Impresses in NFL Debut, but Tyrod Taylor Still Chargers' Starter If Healthy," ESPN.com, September 20, 2020.

Brooks Kubena, "Texans GM Nick Caserio on Deshaun Watson, David Culley and No. 3 pick," *Houston Chronicle*, January 18, 2022.

Marcel Louis-Jacques, "Miami Dolphins QB Tua Tagovailoa in Concussion Protocol, No Timetable for Return," ESPN.com, September 30, 2022.

David Furones, "Tua Tagovailoa Investigation Concludes: NFL, NFLPA Say Dolphins Followed Protocol, but Add 'Gross Motor Instability' as 'No-Go' Concussion Symptom," *South Florida Sun Sentinel*, October 8, 2022.

Hal Habib, "Here's Why Dolphins Didn't Suspect Anything Was Wrong with Tua Tagovailoa during Game," *Palm Beach Post*, December 29, 2022.

Daniel Oyefusi, "How Jiu-Jitsu Can Keep Dolphins QB Tua Tagovailoa Safe after Concussions Sideline Him," *Miami Herald*, September 5, 2023.

CHAPTER 22: YOU DON'T LET HIM OUT

The information in this chapter comes primarily from interviews with Mike Shanahan, Brock Purdy, T. C. McCartney, Matt LaFleur, Mike LaFleur, Dan Quinn, Kyle Shanahan, Chris Foerster, and other sources, and from events I witnessed firsthand. Also:

Jimmy Garoppolo, press conference, February 1, 2022.

Tim Kawakami, "Kawakami: Jimmy Garoppolo on His Bizarre Offseason, Return to the 49ers and Relationship with Kyle Shanahan," *Athletic*, October 7, 2022.

Michael Silver, "Jed York Savoring this 49ers Run, and a Timely Game of Catch with His Son," *San Francisco Chronicle*, February 1, 2024.

Matt Barrows, "Worried about Trey Lance-Jimmy Garoppolo Dynamic? The 49ers Consider It a Coup," *Athletic*, August 30, 2022.

Michael Silver, "49ers Skip Convention, Embrace the Drama by Keeping Jimmy Garoppolo," *San Francisco Chronicle*, August 29, 2022.

Michael Silver, "49ers' Brock Purdy Might Be Living a Fairy Tale, but He Doesn't See It That Way," *San Francisco Chronicle*, January 13, 2023.

Eric Branch, "49ers' 'Mr. Irrelevant' Brock Purdy Sees Humor, Opportunity in Draft Status," *San Francisco Chronicle*, May 1, 2022.

Michael Silver, "How 49ers' Brock Purdy Rose from Draft Doubts to NFL's Top QB: 'I Was Real with Myself,'" *San Francisco Chronicle*, November 22, 2023.

Michael Silver, "Brock Purdy Went Home Again, and 49ers' QB Showed Hometown What It Missed," *San Francisco Chronicle*, December 17, 2023.

Albert Breer, "The 49ers Believe in Brock Purdy Even More than Most People Realize," *Sports Illustrated*, August 14, 2023.

Matt Barrows, "49ers' Brock Purdy Had Brushes with Nick Saban, Cactus on His Way to the NFL," *Athletic*, May 16, 2022.

Ken Belson, "For One Man, the N.F.L. Draft's 'Mr. Irrelevant' Meant a Lot," *New York Times*, May 1, 2022.

Michael Silver, "Pressure on 49ers' Trey Lance Heightens After 'It All Fell Apart' vs. Bears," *San Francisco Chronicle*, September 11, 2022.

Michael Silver, "Could Some Players Be Relieved 49ers' Season Is in Jimmy Garoppolo's Hands?" *San Francisco Chronicle*, September 19, 2022.

Mike Florio, "Jimmy Garoppolo on Viral Clip of Something He Said: 'I Can't Read Lips,'" Profootballtalk.com, September 30, 2022.

Jourdan Rodrigue, "As Rams Imploded, Sean McVay Faded Away: How They Found Their Way Back to Each Other," *Athletic*, February 23, 2023.

Nick Wagoner, "Los Angeles Rams Coach Sean McVay Ponders Future, Says He Wants to Prioritize Time with Family," ESPN.com, February 11, 2022.

Michael Silver, "White Lightning: With No Pomp and Precious Little Padding, the Broncos' Deceptively Fast Ed McCaffrey Has Become the NFL's Unlikeliest Star Wide Receiver," *Sports Illustrated*, November 30, 1998.

Matt Schneidman, "Aaron Rodgers, the Packers and the Long Succession: 'Just Tell the Truth, You Wanted to Move on,'" *Athletic*, May 31, 2023.

Michael Silver, "Tom Brady Struggled in Levi's, but Could He Come Back in 2023 as a 49er?" *San Francisco Chronicle*, December 11, 2022.

Eric Branch, "49ers Would Have Signed Philip Rivers If They'd Reached the Super Bowl," *San Francisco Chronicle*, August 10, 2023.

Matt Barrows, "The Night Brock Purdy Convinced the 49ers He Could Be Their 2023 Starter," *Athletic*, September 4, 2023.

Tim Kawakami, "Kawakami: Kyle Shanahan on the Moment He Knew Brock Purdy Was His QB, Searching for a 49ers Title and More," *Athletic*, July 26, 2023.

Michael Silver, "49ers' Faith in Rookie QB Brock Purdy Takes Hollywood Turn in Seattle," *San Francisco Chronicle*, December 17, 2022.

Michael Silver, "'A Savage Stat': Toll Paid by 49ers' 2022 Foes Was a Loss the Next Week," *San Francisco Chronicle*, September 5, 2023.

Michael Silver, "For an Instant, Christian McCaffrey's Improbable TD Run Made 49ers Victory Seem Possible," *San Francisco Chronicle*, January 29, 2023.

Michael Silver, "Think 49ers' QB Injuries Are Shanahan's Fault? Then You Don't Know Football," *San Francisco Chronicle*, February 4, 2023.

Michael Silver, "With Brock Purdy Possibly Out a Year, in Which Direction Will the 49ers Go?" *San Francisco Chronicle*, January 30, 2023.

Eric Branch, "49ers CEO: Shanahan Knew in 2022 Camp Purdy Was QB1, but Wasn't Sold on McCaffrey Deal," *San Francisco Chronicle*, February 1, 2024.

CHAPTER 23: TEN YEARS GONE

The information in this chapter comes primarily from interviews with Mike McDaniel, Kyle Shanahan, Mike LaFleur, Chandler Henley, Matt LaFleur, Robert Saleh, Adam

Stenavich, Raheem Morris, Jared Goff, Kevin O'Connell, Kwesi Adofo-Mensah, and from events I witnessed firsthand. Also:

Nick Wagoner, "49ers' Brock Purdy Uses Internal Motivation to Maintain Edge," ESPN.com, January 16, 2024.

Zack Rosenblatt and Dianna Russini, "Aaron Rodgers, Robert Saleh and How the Jets' Season Fell Apart: 'Something Has to Change,'" *Athletic*, January 31, 2024.

Seth Wickersham, "Kyle Shanahan Is Ready to Meet the Moment," ESPN.com, February 7, 2024.

Peter King, "FMIA Pre-Super Bowl: Kyle Shanahan on Pick 262 and Peter King's 40-Year Roster," NBCSports.com, February 5, 2024.

Henry McKenna and Eric Williams, "How Dolphins HC Mike McDaniel's Innovative 'Cheat Motion' Is Changing the NFL," foxsports.com, October 20, 2023.

Michael Silver, "How Kyle Shanahan and the 49ers Regrouped after First Quarter to Crush Eagles," *San Francisco Chronicle*, December 4, 2023.

Nick Shook, "Robert Saleh: Jets Are Among 6–8 Teams with Realistic Chance at Winning Championship in 2023," NFL.com, May 23, 2023.

Eric Branch, "49ers' Kyle Shanahan on Steve Wilks' Blitz Call: 'He Knows He Messed Up,'" *San Francisco Chronicle*, October 26, 2023.

Michael Silver, "How Brock Purdy QB'd 49ers to the Super Bowl by Shredding His 'Game Manager' Rep," *San Francisco Chronicle*, January 29, 2024.

Michael Silver, "For Kyle Shanahan, 49ers Winning Super Bowl Would Deliver on Lifetime of Expectations," *San Francisco Chronicle*, February 9, 2024.

Michael Silver, "Jared Goff's Football Journey Comes Full Circle as Lions Face 49ers," *San Francisco Chronicle*, January 23, 2024.

"'Jared Goff!' Chants Break Out at Michigan Sporting Events Ahead of Lions-49ers," foxsports.com, January 27, 2024.

Michael Silver, "49ers' Kyle Shanahan and Rams DC Raheem Morris Go From BFFs to Foes Sunday," *San Francisco Chronicle*, September 18, 2023.

Michael Silver, "49ers Survived Playing Not to Lose vs. Packers, but That Has to Change," *San Francisco Chronicle*, January 21, 2024.

Jourdan Rodrigue and Ted Nguyen, "Old, New, and Borrowed: How Sean McVay's Rams Offense Is Evolving Once Again," *Athletic*, October 5, 2023.

Eric Branch, "49ers Pull Off 24–21 Comeback Win over Packers, Advance to NFC Championship Game," *San Francisco Chronicle*, January 20, 2024.

EPILOGUE

The information in this epilogue comes primarily from interviews with Mike Shanahan, Peggy Shanahan, Bo Scaife, Kyle Shanahan, and from events I witnessed firsthand. Also:

Peter King, "FMIA Pre-Super Bowl: Kyle Shanahan on Pick 262 and Peter King's 40-Year Roster," NBCSports.com, February 5, 2024.

Albert Breer, "Inside the Chiefs' Super Bowl Win and the Travis Kelce Speech That Inspired Them to Victory," SI.com, February 12, 2024.

Michael Silver, "49ers Survived Playing Not to Lose vs. Packers, but That Has to Change," *San Francisco Chronicle*, January 21, 2024.

Michael Silver, "Why You Shouldn't Blame Kyle Shanahan for 49ers' Super Bowl LVIII Defeat," *San Francisco Chronicle*, February 12, 2024.

Eric Branch, "Forget Coin Flip and OT Rules, 49ers' Shanahan Lost to Chiefs' Spagnuolo," *San Francisco Chronicle*, February 15, 2024.

Eric Branch, "49ers' Steve Wilks under Scrutiny after Chiefs' Game-Winning Super Bowl Drive in OT," *San Francisco Chronicle*, February 13, 2024.

Kyle Shanahan, press conference, January 25, 2023.

Inside the NFL, Season 46, Episode 24, "Week 23," aired on the CW Network, February 13, 2024.

Index

Page numbers in *italic* refer to illustrations.